MW00807118

VOYAGES
IN ENGLISH
GRAMMAR AND WRITING

Patricia Healey, I.H.M.
B.A., Immaculata University
M.A., Temple University
20 years teaching; 20 years in administration

Irene Kervick, I.H.M.
B.A., Immaculata University
M.A., Villanova University
46 years teaching

Anne B. McGuire, I.H.M.
B.A., Immaculata University
M.A., Villanova University
M.A., Immaculata University
16 years teaching; 14 years as elementary principal; 10 years staff development

Adrienne Saybolt, I.H.M.
B.A., Immaculata University
Pennsylvania State Board of Education, professional certification
M.A., St. John's University
40 years teaching

LOYOLA PRESS.

Loyola Press has made every effort to locate the copyright holders for the cited works used in this publication and to make full acknowledgment for their use. In the case of any omissions, the publisher will be pleased to make suitable acknowledgments in future editions. Continued on page 548.

Cover Design: Think Book Works   Cover Artist: Pablo Bernasconi
Interior Design: Kathryn Seckman Kirsch/Will Capellaro/Loyola Press
Art Director: Judine O'Shea/Loyola Press
Editor: Jennon Bell/Loyola Press

ISBN-13: 978-0-8294-2819-3
ISBN-10: 0-8294-2819-4

© 2011 Loyola Press
All rights reserved. No part of this book may be reproduced, stored in a retrieval system, or transmitted in any form or by any means, electronic, mechanical, photocopying, recording, or otherwise, without the prior permission of the publisher.

LOYOLA PRESS.
3441 N. Ashland Avenue
Chicago, Illinois 60657
(800) 621-1008
www.loyolapress.com

Webcrafters / Madison, WI, USA / 04-10 / 1st Printing

Contents

PART 1 Grammar

Written and Oral Communication

Emergency Telephone Numbers

Mom's Cell: 555-1234   Dad's Cell: 555-2345

Dr. Levitt: 555-6363

Emergency: 911   Mrs. Hoffstedt: 555-2626

SECTION ONE
Nouns

1.1 Common and Proper Nouns

A **noun** is a word that names a person, a place, or a thing.

A **common noun** names any one of a class of people, places, or things.

PERSON	PLACE	THING
skater	rink	ice skates
citizen	country	flag
writer	library	book
governor	capital	law

A **proper noun** names a particular person, place, or thing. Proper nouns begin with capital letters.

PERSON	PLACE	THING
Shawn Johnson	Iowa	Olympics
Nelson Mandela	South Africa	Nobel Peace Prize
Columbus	Spain	*Santa Maria*
Anne Frank	Europe	Bill of Rights

EXERCISE 1 Tell whether each noun names a person, a place, or a thing. Then tell whether each is a common noun or a proper noun.

1. James Naismith
2. Massachusetts
3. inventor
4. teacher
5. basket
6. scoreboard
7. gym
8. Indiana
9. uniform
10. coach
11. LeBron James
12. Boston Garden
13. fan
14. seat
15. Yao Ming

EXERCISE 2 Tell whether each noun is a proper noun or a common noun. Then write a common noun for each proper noun and a proper noun for each common noun.

1. song
2. *Apollo*
3. city
4. Pablo Picasso
5. landmark
6. writer
7. athlete
8. Rhode Island
9. actor
10. Canada

EXERCISE 3 Identify the nouns in each sentence. Tell whether each names a person, a place, or a thing. Tell whether each is a common noun or a proper noun. The number of nouns in each sentence is shown in parentheses.

1. Michael Jordan was born in New York. (2)
2. When Michael was a baby, his family moved to North Carolina. (4)
3. Jordan played basketball in high school. (3)
4. The teen was cut from the team. (2)
5. His practice got the young man off the bench. (3)
6. The young athlete later led the University of North Carolina to a national championship. (3)
7. Jordan helped the United States win a gold medal at the Olympics. (4)
8. The now-respected player joined the Bulls, the professional team in Chicago. (4)
9. Jordan became a superstar in professional basketball. (3)
10. His incredible talent and his likable personality earned him fans around the world. (4)

EXERCISE 4 Complete each sentence with nouns.

1. I like to play _____ and _____.
2. My favorite athletes are _____ and _____.
3. Sports I like to watch are _____ and _____.
4. The _____ and the _____ are places where I play sports.

APPLY IT NOW

Write 10 nouns related to an athlete or a sport that interests you. Identify each as a common or a proper noun.

Grammar in Action. Identify all the proper nouns in the page 225 excerpt.

1.2 Singular and Plural Nouns

A **singular noun** tells about one person, place, or thing. A **plural noun** tells about more than one.

Sally Ride was an *astronaut*. (singular)
Sally Ride and Kathryn Sullivan were *astronauts*. (plural)

The plural of most nouns is formed by adding *-s* to the singular form.

SINGULAR	PLURAL	SINGULAR	PLURAL
ship	ships	airport	airports

Add *-es* to form the plural of nouns ending in *s, x, z, ch,* and *sh.*

SINGULAR	PLURAL	SINGULAR	PLURAL
box	boxes	watch	watches

For nouns ending in *y* after a consonant, change the *y* to *i* and add *-es.*

SINGULAR	PLURAL	SINGULAR	PLURAL
baby	babies	cherry	cherries

For nouns ending in *y* after a vowel, add *-s.*

SINGULAR	PLURAL	SINGULAR	PLURAL
day	days	valley	valleys

For most nouns ending in *f* or *fe,* add *-s.*

SINGULAR	PLURAL	SINGULAR	PLURAL
roof	roofs	safe	safes

For some nouns ending in *f* or *fe,* form the plural by changing the *f* or *fe* to *v* and adding *-es.*

SINGULAR	PLURAL	SINGULAR	PLURAL
leaf	leaves	shelf	shelves

EXERCISE 1 Write the plural of each noun.

1. journey
2. airplane
3. lunch
4. ray
5. machine

6. loss
7. penny
8. thief
9. chimney
10. gulf

11. fox
12. berry
13. sky
14. knife
15. family

EXERCISE 2 Find the nouns in each sentence. The number of nouns is shown in parentheses. Tell whether each noun is singular or plural.

1. Sally Ride first wanted to be a tennis player but later studied science. (3)
2. Ride heard that NASA was looking for astronauts. (3)
3. Her studies included jumps with parachutes. (3)
4. Ride was the first U.S. woman to orbit Earth. (3)
5. Ride went on two flights and worked for NASA for nine years. (4)
6. Since her trips, Ride has written books about science for students. (5)

EXERCISE 3 Complete each sentence with the plural of the nouns in parentheses.

1. Sally Ride went on two space _____ (flight), spending a total of 14 _____ (day) in space.
2. Her _____ (duty) included helping during _____ (launch) and conducting _____ (experiment).
3. On one mission the _____ (astronaut) took peanut butter, _____ (loaf) of bread, and _____ (candy).
4. Sally is one of the _____ (advocate) of science education.
5. Young women had fewer _____ (opportunity) in science when Ride was growing up.
6. One of her current _____ (project) lets middle-school _____ (class) shoot photos of Earth from space.
7. Her _____ (hope) are for _____ (astronaut) to go to even more _____ (place) in space and to have more _____ (responsibility).

Sally Ride

APPLY IT NOW

Choose one paragraph from a newspaper article. List each noun. Write *S* if the noun is singular or *P* if it is plural.

Grammar in Action

Identify the plural nouns in the last paragraph of page 214 excerpt.

5

1.3 More Singular and Plural Nouns

For a noun ending in *o* after a vowel, form the plural by adding *-s* to the singular.

SINGULAR	PLURAL		SINGULAR	PLURAL
radio	radios		rodeo	rodeos

For a noun ending in *o* after a consonant, form the plural by adding *-es* to the singular.

SINGULAR	PLURAL		SINGULAR	PLURAL
potato	potatoes		hero	heroes

For some nouns ending in *o* after a consonant, however, the plural is formed by adding *-s*.

SINGULAR	PLURAL		SINGULAR	PLURAL
piano	pianos		solo	solos

Some singular nouns use a different word to show the plural.

SINGULAR	PLURAL		SINGULAR	PLURAL
goose	geese		man	men
woman	women		ox	oxen
child	children		mouse	mice
tooth	teeth		person	people

Some nouns use the same word for both singular and plural.

SINGULAR	PLURAL		SINGULAR	PLURAL
deer	deer		fish	fish
sheep	sheep		series	series
Iroquois	Iroquois		species	species

Use a dictionary to check plural forms.

Sheep

EXERCISE 1 Write the plural of each noun.

1. tomato
2. studio
3. shrimp
4. silo
5. foot
6. moose
7. echo
8. trio
9. alto
10. mosquito
11. salmon
12. corps

EXERCISE 2 Complete each sentence with the plural of the noun or nouns in parentheses.

1. In colonial days _____ (person) did different tasks.
2. The _____ (woman) often gathered to make quilts.
3. The _____ (man) worked together to build houses.
4. The _____ (child) did work in the home.
5. The girls would cook the meals and do the _____ (dish).
6. The boys would feed the farm _____ (animal): _____ (turkey), _____ (chicken), _____ (goose), and _____ (calf).
7. Instead of horses, farmers sometimes used _____ (ox).
8. The _____ (sheep) provided wool to make clothing.
9. Warm _____ (scarf) and _____ (shawl) were made from this animal fiber.
10. Crops grown in the _____ (colony) included _____ (tomato), _____ (bean), and _____ (pumpkin).
11. Cotton from the South was used to make _____ (shirt) and _____ (dress).
12. In New England _____ (fish) became important in the colonists' diet.
13. Colonists ate _____ (cod), _____ (turtle), and _____ (lobster).
14. New England colonists sometimes hunted wild game such as _____ (deer) and _____ (rabbit).
15. At night _____ (family) did chores, played board _____ (game), or danced.
16. The _____ (life) of colonial _____ (person) on farms was difficult.

APPLY IT NOW

Write the plural form of these nouns. Use each in a sentence.

1. tomato
2. photo
3. statue
4. deer
5. chimpanzee
6. country

Sheep

1.4 Possessive Nouns

The **possessive form** of a noun expresses possession, or ownership. The apostrophe (') is the sign of a possessive noun.

> ***Kevin's* tuba is in its case.**

The tuba belongs to Kevin. The word *Kevin's* is a possessive noun.

To form the singular possessive, add an apostrophe and *-s* to the singular form of the noun.

> **The *singer's* voice was powerful.**

To form the possessive of plural nouns ending in *s*, add an apostrophe only.

> **The *singers'* voices were loud.**

To form the possessive of plural nouns that do not end in *s*, add *-'s*.

> **The *women's* voices were beautiful.**

The possessive of a singular proper noun ending in *s* is formed by adding *-'s*.

> ***Iris's* favorite song is "America the Beautiful."**
> ***James's* song in the recital was in Spanish.**

The plural possessive of a proper noun is formed just as the plural possessive of a common noun is formed.

> **The *Phillipses'* home was the site of many concerts.**
> **The *Whites'* donations to the orchestra helped buy many instruments.**

EXERCISE 1 Write the singular possessive and the plural possessive form of each noun.

> EXAMPLE **baby** **baby's** **babies'**

1. sister
2. child
3. puppy
4. goose
5. teacher
6. player
7. bear
8. dinosaur
9. athlete
10. mother
11. deer
12. man
13. hero
14. astronaut
15. mayor

EXERCISE 2 Identify the possessive noun in each sentence. Tell whether it is singular or plural in form.

1. Andres Segovia's work elevated the place of the guitar in classical music.

2. Before Segovia many people's view was that the guitar was neither a serious nor an important instrument.

3. Composers' works for orchestras did not include guitar.

4. Segovia played classical musicians' works on his guitar.

5. The Spanish guitarist's concerts became celebrated.

6. The translation of Bach's work to the guitar resulted in amazing pieces.

7. Other guitarists' debt to Segovia is recognized, and he is called the father of classical guitar.

EXERCISE 3 Rewrite each of the following, using singular possessive nouns.

> EXAMPLE **the performance of the guitarist**
> **the guitarist's performance**

1. the guitar of the musician
2. the efforts of this man
3. the music of Bach
4. the lessons of the teacher
5. the applause of the audience
6. the sound of the orchestra

EXERCISE 4 Rewrite each of the following, using plural possessive nouns.

> EXAMPLE **the performances of the guitarists**
> **the guitarists' performances**

1. the legacy of the musicians
2. the voices of the sopranos
3. the cases of the violinists
4. the sound of the drums
5. the works of classical composers
6. the lessons of my teachers

APPLY IT NOW

Write four sentences about a famous musician or singer. Include at least three possessive nouns in your writing.

Tech Tip   In an online article, identify all the possessive nouns.

1.5 Collective Nouns

A **collective noun** names a group of people, animals, places, or things that are considered a unit. A collective noun usually acts as a singular noun.

> The *public* likes stories of impossible victories.

> An international *committee* organizes the Olympics.

Here is a list of some common collective nouns.

army	committee	group
audience	council	herd
bunch	crowd	jury
chorus	faculty	orchestra
cast	family	staff
class	flock	swarm
club	government	team

A singular collective noun usually uses a singular verb. When the group is viewed as acting as a unit, the verb form is singular. Note that singular verbs in the present tense end in *s*.

> A *crew* cleans the ice at the hockey rink at halftime.
> The *team* spends hours practicing together on the ice.

EXERCISE 1 Write a collective noun for each word. Use it in a sentence.

> EXAMPLE   players   team   I am on the soccer team.

1. students
2. grapes
3. sheep
4. soldiers

5. teachers
6. spectators
7. relatives
8. actors

9. musicians
10. cows
11. bees
12. singers

EXERCISE 2 Identify the collective noun in each sentence.

1. The 1980 U.S. Olympic hockey team won a gold medal.
2. This bunch of players obviously was skilled.
3. However, this hockey club lacked experience.
4. The team was not expected to win by most sports experts.
5. The audience filled the arena at Lake Placid, New York, for the final game against the Soviet Union.
6. The home crowd was excited and boisterous.
7. The group of young players beat the favored Europeans.
8. A swarm of players celebrated on the ice.
9. A committee voted them into the Hockey Hall of Fame.
10. Our class watched a movie about this famous game.

EXERCISE 3 Complete each sentence with a collective noun. Use words from the list on page 10. More than one answer may be correct.

1. Our school _____ usually sings at assemblies.
2. The U.S. _____ has its center in Washington, D.C.
3. A _____ of sheep once lived on the White House grounds.
4. The city _____ governs our town, together with the mayor.
5. The drama _____ puts on a school play every year.
6. The _____ is totally made up of student actors.
7. My still-life painting shows a _____ of grapes.

EXERCISE 4 Complete each sentence with the correct form of the verb in parentheses.

1. A hockey team _____ (play) on an ice rink.
2. The Olympic Committee _____ (choose) the sports for the winter and summer games.
3. A jury _____ (decide) on the winners in some sports, such as figure skating.
4. The crowd _____ (applaud) winners as they receive their medals.

APPLY IT NOW

Choose three collective nouns that relate to after-school activities. Write five sentences about yourself, using the collective nouns.

1.6 Nouns as Subjects and Subject Complements

A noun can be the **subject** of a verb. The subject tells what a sentence is about.

Martin Luther King Jr. **was born on January 15, 1929.**

Martin Luther King Jr.

The subject of this sentence is *Martin Luther King Jr.* To find the subject, ask *who* or *what* before the verb. Who was born? The answer is *Martin Luther King Jr.*

A noun can be a **subject complement**. A subject complement follows a linking verb, such as *am, is, are, was,* or *were.* It renames the subject.

Martin Luther King Jr. was a *minister.*

(Martin Luther King Jr. = minister)

The subject complement in this sentence is *minister.* Can you find the subject and subject complement in this sentence?

Nelson Mandela was a leader in South Africa.

You are correct if you said the subject is *Nelson Mandela.* The subject complement is *leader.* It renames the subject (Nelson Mandela = leader).

EXERCISE 1 Complete each sentence with a subject noun from the list.

country	hometown	King	laws
marches	monument	people	speech

1. King's childhood _____ was Atlanta, Georgia.

2. His _____ helped Americans understand the existence of inequality in the country.

3. _____ used words, not violence, to win fights.

4. _____ crowded his church for his powerful sermons.

5. New _____ in the 1960s helped African Americans gain their rights.

Nelson Mandela won the Nobel Peace Prize in 1993.

6. The _____ changed because of King's work.

7. King's most famous _____ had the words "I Have a Dream."

8. A _____ in Alabama honors him and others who died for civil rights.

EXERCISE 2 Identify the subject in each sentence.

1. Martin Luther King Jr. skipped ninth and twelfth grades.

2. Morehouse College admitted him at the age of 15.

3. His ordination as a minister occurred in 1948.

4. A church in Montgomery, Alabama, offered him the position of pastor.

5. The young minister became an important figure in the civil rights movement, a crusade for equal rights for African Americans.

6. People admire King for his courage.

7. His message was one of nonviolent protest.

8. African Americans sought the equal right to use public facilities and schools.

9. King's vital personality attracted many followers.

10. A march brought together 200,000 people in Washington, D.C.

11. A national holiday in January marks his birthday.

Mahatma Gandhi was known for being a peaceful protester.

EXERCISE 3 Identify the subject in each sentence. Then identify the subject complement.

1. Gandhi was an inspiration to Martin Luther King Jr.

2. Gandhi was a supporter of nonviolent protest in India.

3. King was a determined leader.

4. An early protest was a bus boycott.

5. Birmingham was the place of the protest.

6. King was a powerful speaker.

7. His speech was an invitation to action.

8. King was the youngest winner of the Nobel Peace Prize.

9. King was the victim of an assassination in 1968.

10. Coretta Scott King was King's widow.

11. Mrs. King was a supporter of her husband's work.

APPLY IT NOW

Write three sentences about a historical figure. Use at least two nouns as subject complements. Underline the subjects and the subject complements in your sentences.

1.7 Nouns as Objects

A noun can be used as a **direct object** of a verb. The direct object answers the question *whom* or *what* after an action verb.

In this sentence the direct object is *cartoons*. It answers the question *What did Charles Schulz draw?*

Charles Schulz drew *cartoons*.

In this sentence the direct object is *Charles Schulz*. It answers the question *Whom did the readers of the* Peanuts *comic strip appreciate?*

Readers of the *Peanuts* comic strip appreciated *Charles Schulz*.

A noun can be the **object of a preposition.** Prepositions show place, time, direction, and relationship. Some prepositions are *about, at, by, for, from, in, into, of, on, throughout, to, with,* and *without.* A prepositional phrase consists of a preposition and a noun or a pronoun, which is the object of the preposition.

The *Peanuts* comic strip featured a group <u>of</u> *children*.
The comic strip appeared <u>in</u> many *newspapers*.

In the first sentence, *of* is the preposition and *children* is the object of the preposition. In the second sentence, *in* is the preposition and *newspapers* is the object of the preposition.

EXERCISE 1 Identify the direct object in each sentence.

1. Charles Schulz created famous characters.
2. One character, Linus, always carries a blanket.
3. The character Lucy has superior knowledge about everything.
4. Schulz created Charlie Brown.
5. Readers loved the ordinary boy.
6. Charlie had problems.
7. For example, he didn't often win his baseball games.
8. Schulz had a smart dog with the name of Spike.
9. Spike inspired the creation of the dog Snoopy.
10. We read Snoopy's thoughts in cartoon bubbles.

Charles Schulz drew inspiration from his own life in creating *Peanuts*.

EXERCISE 2 Complete each sentence with a direct object.

1. I really enjoy _____.
2. I read _____.
3. I watch _____.
4. I play _____.
5. I study _____.
6. I am learning _____.
7. I might get _____.
8. I often eat _____.

EXERCISE 3 Identify the preposition or prepositions in each sentence. Then identify the object of each preposition.

1. Charles Schulz wrote about everyday problems.
2. Newspapers throughout the world published his comics.
3. *Peanuts* reached millions of readers in 75 countries.
4. Fans of the cartoonist read his comic strips eagerly.
5. People identified with Schulz's characters.
6. Experiences with failure are part of everyone's life.
7. Schulz worked primarily in his studio in California.
8. He wrote and drew *Peanuts* for 50 years.
9. Charles Schulz left his imprint on people's lives.
10. The work of Schulz still makes us think—and smile.

Snoopy at a parade

EXERCISE 4 Identify the direct object in each sentence. Then identify each object of a preposition.

1. Charles Schulz's comic strip got the name of *Peanuts*.
2. Schulz had a friend with the name of Charlie Brown.
3. The famous character in the strip got his name from that person.
4. Newspapers around the country printed Schulz's strip.
5. People read Schulz's work in the newspapers.
6. People around the world now recognize Snoopy.
7. Someone even wrote a play with the characters.
8. Actors play the *Peanuts* characters on the stage.
9. Many people watched cartoons with the *Peanuts* characters.
10. Have you seen these films on TV?

APPLY IT NOW

Write six sentences about a character from a cartoon or a fiction book. Underline each direct object and each object of a preposition. You might start this way:

I like _____*name of the character*_____.

I like _____ about _____.

I first read _____ in _____.

Tech Tip Type and underline your sentences, using a computer.

1.8 Nouns as Indirect Objects

A noun can be the indirect object of a verb. The **indirect object** tells *to whom, to what, for whom,* or *for what* the action was done.

	VERB	INDIRECT OBJECT	DIRECT OBJECT
Mother Teresa	showed	*people*	*compassion.*

In this sentence the direct object is *compassion.* The indirect object is *people.* It answers the question *to whom* after the verb: *To whom did Mother Teresa show compassion?* Here is a list of verbs that can take indirect objects.

assign	donate	grant	pay	serve
award	earn	hand	promise	show
bring	forgive	lend	read	teach
buy	get	offer	sell	tell
deny	give	owe	send	write

A sentence can have an indirect object only if it has a direct object. The indirect object always comes after the verb and before the direct object. Can you find the verb, the direct object, and the indirect object in this sentence?

Mother Teresa offered poor people help.

You're correct if you said the verb is *offered.* What did Mother Teresa offer? The answer is *help,* the direct object. To whom did she offer help? The answer is *people,* the indirect object.

EXERCISE 1 Identify the indirect object in each sentence. The direct object is italicized.

1. As a nun in India, Agnes Gonxha Bojahiu taught young girls *religion.*

2. Sister Teresa gave many sick people her *time and devotion.*

3. In 1948 the Church granted Sister Teresa *permission* for a different kind of work.

4. She offered the very poorest people *service.*

5. Many women gave Mother Teresa their *help.*

Mother Teresa of Calcutta

EXERCISE 2 Identify the direct object and indirect object in each sentence.

1. The club assigns students community-service projects.
2. My neighbor Randy assigns the new members their duties.
3. Randy and his friends offer senior citizens company.
4. They serve homeless people food.
5. They read blind people the latest best sellers.
6. Our work earned the club citywide attention.
7. People gave our causes money.
8. The principal awarded Randy the Good Citizen prize for his service to the community.
9. Randy owed his parents all his success in the service of others.
10. Randy teaches us character-building.

EXERCISE 3 Rewrite the sentences, adding indirect objects. Use the nouns in parentheses.

1. The schoolwide committee told its plans for the fund-raising project—a secondhand-item sale. (classes)
2. Many students promised their help. (the committee)
3. People gave old clothes and other items. (the students)
4. The students gave fliers on the street. (people)
5. Students sent invitations to the sale. (relatives)
6. Other students offered help on the day of the sale. (the organizers)
7. The students sold these items at low prices. (customers)
8. The students gave the money to help poor people in India. (a charity)
9. The committee also donated classroom supplies. (Indian schools)
10. The schoolchildren in India wrote a card to express their thanks. (us)

APPLY IT NOW

Choose five verbs from the list on page 16. Use the verbs to write five sentences containing indirect objects about a community project you know.

Grammar in Action. Identify the noun used as an indirect object in the fourth paragraph of the model on page 215.

Nouns • 17

1.9 Nouns in Direct Address

A noun in **direct address** names the person spoken to. A noun used in direct address is set off from the rest of the sentence by a comma or commas.

> *Class*, here are the scripts for our play on the American Revolution.
> Do you know your lines, *Alicia*?
> Be sure, *Ryan*, that you bring your costume.

In the first sentence, *class* names a group of people being spoken to and is, therefore, a noun used in direct address. *Alicia* and *Ryan* name individuals being spoken to and so are nouns in direct address. Because *Ryan* appears in the middle of the sentence, it is set off by two commas, one before and one after the noun.

EXERCISE 1 Identify the noun in direct address in each sentence.

1. Do you want to help make the costumes, Louise?
2. George, are you making the scenery?
3. Students, help me make signs for the colonists to carry.
4. Do you have the "No Taxation Without Representation" sign, boys?
5. Girls, what are your roles in the play?
6. Here is your Betsy Ross costume, Mei Ling.
7. I lost my tricorn, Ms. Bryne.
8. Go to your place, fifth graders, with the rest of those in the Boston Tea Party.
9. Please hand me my wig, Rosalie.
10. Ben is sick today, so, Kevin, you'll play John Adams.

EXERCISE 2 Rewrite the sentences. Use commas to set off the nouns in direct address in these sentences.

1. Say your lines louder Elaine.
2. Michael where is the script for the narrator?
3. Lillian put your hat on straight.
4. Students it's time for the play to start.
5. Congratulations fifth graders on a great job.

EXERCISE 3 Identify whether the nouns in each sentence are used in direct address.

1. Malik, please collect the props from storage.
2. Anna lent Mr. Hoffmann her wig collection for the play.
3. Read clearly and loudly, Marta, so the back row can hear you.
4. Mrs. Tuttle explains Benjamin Franklin's role in securing independence.
5. Mr. Franklin captured the spirit of the struggle for independence.
6. As my assistant, Javier, you are responsible for making sure all the signers are onstage.
7. John Hancock of Massachusetts was the first signer of the Declaration of Independence.
8. The women of the Revolutionary period, though less famous, were equally as important, Timothy.

EXERCISE 4 Tell whether the italicized noun in each sentence is a subject, a subject complement, a direct object, an object of a preposition, an indirect object, or a noun in direct address.

1. The 13 colonies wanted *independence* from Britain.
2. The colonies paid *England* taxes.
3. The *colonies* had no voice in the decisions of the British government.
4. *Students*, do you know about the Boston Tea Party?
5. On December 16, 1773, colonists threw *tea* into the harbor.
6. They were protesting against unfair *taxes*.
7. Paul Revere was a *leader* of the protest.
8. His *actions* were perhaps the start of the American Revolution.
9. John Adams was a *lawyer* from Massachusetts.
10. He supported *independence* for the colonies.
11. Leaders of the 13 *colonies* met in Philadelphia.
12. Who was the first signer of the declaration, *Mr. Daniels*?
13. Benjamin Franklin was not only a *statesman* but also an inventor and author.

Paul Revere

APPLY IT NOW

Imagine you are cleaning out the garage or attic with your family. Write five sentences about things you find and give directions about what to do with the items, using nouns in direct address.

1.10 Words Used as Nouns or as Verbs

A noun is a naming word. A verb expresses action or being. Many words can be used as either nouns or verbs, depending on their roles in a sentence.

In this sentence *practice* is a noun because it names a thing.

> **Our *practice* lasted for about an hour.**

In this sentence *practice* is a verb because it tells about an action.

> **We *practice* soccer every day.**

Tell whether each word in italics is a noun or a verb.

> **A Leg *stretches* are really important.**
> **B Each team member *stretches* before practice.**

You are correct if you said *stretches* is a noun in the first sentence. It is the subject of the verb *are.* In the second sentence, *stretches* is a verb. It describes an action performed by the subject.

EXERCISE 1 Tell whether each italicized word is a noun or a verb.

1. If I stretch before a game, I usually *play* better.
2. The coach always goes over each *play* before a game.
3. In practice we always work on our *passes*.
4. Our coach always *passes* the ball to each player.
5. Last night I missed my first *pass*.
6. This was really a *surprise* to me.
7. It *surprised* the coach too.
8. The next thing we worked on was *kicks*.
9. My first *kick* missed the goal.
10. I didn't *kick* the ball hard enough.
11. My second kick didn't *miss*.
12. I got several balls into the net without a *miss*.
13. My hard *work* had paid off.
14. I will *work* even more on my kicks.

EXERCISE 2 Complete each sentence with a word from the list. Tell whether it is used as a noun or a verb.

commands	control	drills
exercise	need	offer
play	starts	volunteer

1. Soccer is good _____.

2. Many schools _____ soccer programs to their students.

3. At our school the soccer season _____ in September.

4. We _____ on Tuesdays and Thursdays.

5. We _____ mouth guards for protection when we play.

6. We follow the coaches' _____.

7. Parents and teachers _____ as coaches.

8. Some _____ focus on speed.

9. Some practice sessions focus on _____ of the ball.

EXERCISE 3 Tell whether each italicized word is a noun or a verb. If the word in italics is a verb, write a new sentence using it as a noun. If the word in italics is a noun, write a new sentence using it as a verb.

1. During each soccer *practice,* our coach instructs us on technique.

2. These drills greatly *help* our playing skills.

3. We worked on push *passes* last night.

4. According to our coach, we will *try* this movement several times each day.

5. The coach said a player should *approach* the ball with his or her foot aligned with the ball.

6. My first *attempt* was not very successful.

7. We will *study* passes again during our next session.

EXERCISE 4 Write sentences using each word as a noun and as a verb. Tell how you use each.

1. dance	5. work	9. copy
2. photograph	6. dream	10. blossom
3. pilot	7. stay	11. plant
4. camp	8. shop	12. drop

APPLY IT NOW

Write a short paragraph about an experience you had trying to learn something new. Include some of these words: *study, try, experiment, surprise, play, step, cause, start, result, hope, end, plan.* Then tell whether they are used as nouns or verbs.

1.11 Words Used as Nouns or as Adjectives

A noun names a person, place, or thing. An adjective describes a noun. Many words can be used as either nouns or adjectives.

In this sentence the word *baseball* is a noun because it names a thing. It acts as the direct object of the verb *enjoy*.

> **We really enjoy** *baseball*.

In this sentence the word *baseball* is an adjective because it describes the noun *team*.

> **I play on the** *baseball* **team at school.**

Tell whether each italicized word is a noun or an adjective.

> **A It is important to be a** *team* **player.**
> **B Our** *team* **got ready for the game by stretching.**

You are correct if you said that the word *team* is an adjective in sentence A. It describes the noun *player*. The word *team* is a noun in sentence B. It is the subject of the sentence.

EXERCISE 1 Tell whether each underlined word is a noun or an adjective.

1. <u>Women</u> once played professional baseball in a league.
2. <u>Women</u> players helped keep baseball alive during World War II.
3. Philip K. Wrigley was the owner of a chewing gum company and of a baseball <u>team</u> called the Chicago Cubs.
4. Women made up all the <u>team</u> members in a league he started called the All-American Girls Professional Baseball League.
5. The teams played <u>professional</u> baseball and had more than a million fans.
6. Each player earned a good salary as a true <u>professional</u>.
7. A popular <u>film</u> about the league was titled *A League of Their Own.*
8. <u>Film</u> star Tom Hanks played a team manager in the fictional movie about the league.

EXERCISE 2 Complete each sentence with a words from the list. Tell whether it is used as a noun or an adjective.

baseball   women   league   public   spring

1. Baseball played by _____ players was somewhat different.
2. During the early years of the league, the _____ used a large ball and pitched it underhand.
3. Later the _____ was smaller, and they threw overhand.
4. The women included some outstanding _____ players.
5. _____ interest in the league was high.
6. The _____ enjoyed seeing these professional players.
7. In the _____ the women would train.
8. _____ training began in May.
9. The _____ once had 10 teams, all in the Midwest.
10. The _____ championship was decided by play-off games.

Dottie Schroeder was a member of the AAGPBL.

EXERCISE 3 Tell whether each italicized word is a noun or an adjective. If the word in italics is an adjective, write a new sentence using it as a noun. If the word in italics is a noun, write a new sentence using it as an adjective.

1. Some young baseball players participate in *summer* camps.
2. Some camps are for the *day,* while others last a week.
3. Participants can improve their *baseball* skills.
4. *Staff* members help students play better.
5. Players can show their *talent* at hitting, pitching, and running.
6. At some camps major league players make *guest* appearances.

EXERCISE 4 Write two sentences with each word, using it once as a noun and once as an adjective. Tell how you use the word in each sentence.

1. ocean
2. newspaper
3. school
4. kitchen
5. rain
6. street
7. forest
8. farm

APPLY IT NOW

Use your imagination. Write a story that uses eight of the words below. Tell whether you use the words as nouns or adjectives.

prize	garden
family	city
computer	house
soccer	television
zoo	surprise
silver	holiday

Noun Review

1.1 **Identify the nouns in each sentence. Tell whether each is a common noun or a proper noun.**

1. Denver is the capital of the state of Colorado.

2. The Rocky Mountains divide the state.

3. Colorado is the only state entirely above 3,281 feet.

4. The Rockies in Colorado are covered with snow all winter.

5. Pike's Peak is a mountain in Colorado.

1.2 **Identify the nouns in each sentence. Tell whether each noun is singular or plural.**

6. The Pony Express riders rode horses to carry mail from Missouri to California.

7. Messages could get across the country in only 10 days.

8. The riders rode over mountains and prairies.

9. Letters used to travel by ship, and delivery could take weeks.

10. The Pony Express ended after the telegraph connected cities in the West.

1.3 **Complete each sentence with the plural of the noun in parentheses.**

11. Talented _____ (person) play musical instruments.

12. The band room at school has two _____ (piano).

13. Many _____ (child) signed up for choir.

14. The choir sang a song about _____ (hero).

1.4 **Identify the possessive noun in each sentence. Tell whether it is singular or plural in form.**

15. The students' favorite game to play on rainy days is charades.

16. Toby's team acts out first.

17. The boys' clues were difficult to figure out.

18. Even the teacher's hints did not help at first.

19. Finally, the children's guesses were correct.

1.5 **Identify the collective noun in each sentence.**

20. The squad of firefighters showed great bravery.

21. They saved a group of people from a burning building.

22. The city council gave the firefighters an award for courage.

23. As the firefighters accepted their medals, the audience cheered.

24. A couple who was rescued thanked the firefighters.

1.6 Identify the subject and the subject complement in each sentence.

25. Robert Louis Stevenson was a writer.

26. Stevenson was a native of Scotland.

27. His most famous book is *Treasure Island*.

28. My sister is a fan of his writing.

1.7 Identify the underlined word in each sentence as a direct object or an object of a preposition.

29. Brad enjoys skateboarding after <u>school</u>.

30. He often practices <u>tricks</u>.

31. Responsible skateboarders always wear <u>helmets</u>.

32. A group of friends built a ramp on the <u>weekend</u>.

33. They will get better with <u>practice</u>.

1.8 Identify the indirect object in each sentence.

34. Nina gave her sister a cold.

35. Mom gave the children cough syrup.

36. The teacher sent sick students their homework.

37. Nina taught Kelly the missed lesson.

38. Kelly read Nina the answers.

1.9 Identify the noun in direct address in each sentence.

39. Class, please stand next to your science projects.

40. Why is chlorophyll necessary, Jing Mae, for most plants?

41. Todd, please explain the results of your experiment.

42. Tell the class what you learned, Amy.

1.10 Tell whether each underlined word is a noun or a verb.

43. Do you know how to do that <u>dance</u>?

44. My first <u>attempt</u> to dance was not very successful.

45. I often <u>step</u> on my dance partner's feet.

46. Please just <u>copy</u> my movements.

47. Let's take a <u>photograph</u> together at the dance.

1.11 Tell whether each underlined word is a noun or an adjective.

48. Did you sign up for the <u>newspaper</u>?

49. Every <u>newspaper</u> article is written by a student.

50. Our <u>computer</u> club meets before school.

51. Unfortunately, that <u>computer</u> has a virus.

 Tech Tip Go to www.voyagesinenglish.com for more activities.

Noun Challenge

Read the selection and answer the questions.

1. Did you know, class, that some plants live on insects? 2. For example, the butterwort plant catches its prey on its sticky leaves. 3. The plant's leaf rolls up on the trapped insect. 4. Juices from the leaf dissolve the insect's body. 5. Like the leaves of a butterwort, the sticky leaves of a sundew plant are a trap for a careless intruder. 6. Another plant, the Venus flytrap, captures its dinner in its "fingers." 7. Slowly, the liquid from the leaf digests the victim. 8. Nature's insect-eating plants have given writers ideas for many horror books and movies.

1. In sentence 1 name a noun in direct address.
2. In sentence 2 how would you write the singular form for the word *leaves*?
3. In sentence 3 name the subject of the sentence.
4. In sentence 4 name the direct object of the verb *dissolve*.
5. In sentence 5 name a subject complement.
6. In sentence 6 name a prepositional phrase. What is the object of the preposition?
7. In sentence 6 is the word *plant* a verb or a noun?
8. In sentence 7 name the direct object.
9. In sentence 7 is the word *liquid* a noun or an adjective?
10. In sentence 8 name the possessive noun.
11. In sentence 8 what is the indirect object?
12. In sentence 2, is the word *prey* a noun or a verb?
13. In sentence 8, is the word *horror* a noun or an adjective?
14. List at least four singular nouns and four plural nouns from this paragraph.

Pronouns

2.1 Singular and Plural Pronouns

Homer is the author of the epic poems *The Iliad* and *The Odyssey*.

A **pronoun** takes the place of a noun. A **personal pronoun** changes form depending on who or what is referred to and on the role it plays in a sentence.

> Homer was a famous Greek writer. *Homer* lived many hundreds of years ago.
>
> Homer was a famous Greek writer. *He* lived many hundreds of years ago.

Pronouns help avoid repetition of the same word. In the second set of sentences above, the pronoun *he* is used instead of the noun *Homer*. In this way *Homer* does not need to be repeated.

A personal pronoun is **singular** when it refers to one person, place, or thing. The pronoun *he* is singular.

> *He* is famous for writing poems of adventure.

A personal pronoun is **plural** when it refers to more than one person, place, or thing. The pronoun *we* is plural.

> *We* are going to read about the adventures of Odysseus.

Here is a list of the personal pronouns.

SINGULAR	PLURAL
I, me, mine	we, us, ours
you, yours	you, yours
he, him, his, she, her, hers, it, its	they, them, theirs

EXERCISE 1 Identify the personal pronoun in each sentence.

1. We still read stories from ancient Greece.
2. They frequently tell about gods and goddesses.
3. Some, however, tell us about the deeds of human heroes.
4. Do you know much about Mount Olympus?
5. It was the home of the gods.
6. Aphrodite was a Greek goddess, and she was beautiful.

Aphrodite, a Greek goddess

7. Have you heard of Odysseus?

8. His was an epic tale that included many adventures.

9. They were written about in two long poems by Homer.

10. One of them is called *The Odyssey*.

EXERCISE 2 Tell whether each underlined pronoun is singular or plural.

1. The teacher told <u>us</u> about the poet Homer.

2. With great oratory skills, <u>he</u> recited his poetry.

3. He didn't write <u>it</u> down because that was not the custom at the time.

4. After his death, people continued to recite his stories and eventually wrote <u>them</u> down.

5. His stories were told long ago, yet <u>they</u> are still popular in modern times.

6. The teacher said <u>she</u> would test us on his stories.

7. To <u>me</u>, they are interesting stories, so the test was easy.

8. If <u>you</u> study, the test on Homer's stories will be a breeze.

EXERCISE 3 Identify the personal pronoun in each sentence. Tell whether it is singular or plural.

1. We read about the Trojan War.

2. It was won by the crafty Greeks.

3. Tricks are often used in wartime, and theirs helped conquer the Trojans.

4. The Greeks fooled them with a wooden horse filled with soldiers.

5. Odysseus was clever, and he thought of the trick.

6. Homer gave us the story of the war in *The Iliad.*

APPLY IT NOW

Paint a picture of someone with words. Choose one person—a friend, a family member, or a neighbor. Write five sentences telling about things you and this person do together. Use the personal pronouns you studied in this lesson.

Grammar in Action. Identify all the singular pronouns in the first paragraph of the model on page 253.

2.2 Personal Pronouns

A personal pronoun names the speaker, the person spoken to, or the person, place, or thing spoken about.

The personal pronouns that name the speaker are *I, me, mine, we, us,* and *ours.* These are **first person** pronouns.

> **I** read the stories from *The Odyssey* in class last year.
> The teacher told **us** about Homer.

The personal pronouns that name the person spoken to are *you* and *yours.* These are **second person** pronouns. *You* and *yours* can be singular or plural.

> **What do *you* know about Odysseus?**

The personal pronouns that name the person, place, or thing that is spoken about are **third person** pronouns. These are *he, him, his, she, her, hers, it, its, they, them,* and *theirs.*

> **She** offered to lend me a copy of *The Odyssey.*
> **They** wanted to read more myths.
> I lent my copy of the book to *him*.

EXERCISE 1 Identify the first person pronoun in each sentence.

1. We studied ancient Greece.
2. Our teacher assigned us a project.
3. She said that ours could be on mythology.
4. I chose the adventures of Odysseus as my topic.
5. A partner joined me to work on the project.

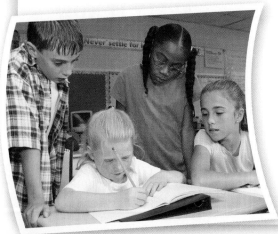

EXERCISE 2 Identify the second person pronoun in each sentence.

1. Have you ever read *The Odyssey?*
2. I told you about this wonderful story, didn't I?
3. When can you help me with this project on *The Odyssey?*
4. Is this project yours?

EXERCISE 3 Identify the third person pronoun or pronouns in each sentence.

1. Odysseus wanted to go home after the Trojan War, but he and the crew encountered many problems along the way.
2. At one point they arrived at the island of Lotus Eaters.
3. The people there gave them a magical flower to eat.
4. It made the crew forget about their homes and wives.
5. Odysseus had to force the crew to return to the ships, and thus he saved them from the flower's spell.

EXERCISE 4 Identify the personal pronouns in the sentences. Tell whether each is a first, second, or third person pronoun.

1. Can you add any details to the story of the Lotus Eaters?
2. We read more details about the story in a book.
3. Odysseus forced them back onto the ship.
4. He tied the sailors on to the boat so they wouldn't go back to the island.
5. You recall that gradually the memories of home and family returned to them.
6. I saw illustrations in a book of the sailors tied to the ship.

EXERCISE 5 Complete each sentence with a personal pronoun. Use the directions in parentheses.

1. _____ read about the Lotus Eaters. (first person, plural)
2. Do _____ know the story? (second person)
3. The flower hypnotized the men, and _____ didn't want to leave. (third person, plural)
4. Odysseus's wife was waiting for him; _____ was named Penelope. (third person, singular)

APPLY IT NOW

Write a paragraph with at least four sentences to tell a friend about a book you have read. Explain why it would be enjoyable to read. Use four personal pronouns in your sentences.

2.3 Subject Pronouns

A personal pronoun may be used as the subject of a sentence. A **subject pronoun** tells who or what the sentence is about. Here is a list of the subject pronouns.

SINGULAR	PLURAL
I	we
you	you
he, she, it	they

To find the subject of a sentence, ask *who* or *what* before the predicate.

> **They came upon an island.**

Who came upon an island? The answer is *They.* The pronoun *They* is the subject of the sentence.

A subject pronoun can also take the place of a noun used as a subject complement. A subject complement follows a linking verb and refers to the same person, place, or thing as the subject of the sentence.

> **The captain of the ship was *he*.**

The pronoun *he* is a subject complement in this sentence. *He* renames the subject, *captain.*

EXERCISE 1 Identify the pronoun used as a subject in each sentence.

1. He landed on Circe's island with his crew.
2. It was a beautiful island.
3. She was a bewitching enchantress.
4. They became friends.
5. I wondered about the dangers ahead on the trip.
6. Do you know the story of any of these dangers?
7. She encouraged him to stay on her island.
8. We can continue reading Odysseus's stories.
9. If you like these stories, there are more in the library.
10. Usually, I find the moral of the stories relevant to my life.

EXERCISE 2 Replace the italicized noun or phrase used as a subject in each sentence with the correct pronoun.

1. *The goddess Circe* warned Odysseus to beware of the singing Sirens.
2. *Their music* was both sweet and bewitching.
3. *Ships* tried to draw near the music but hit sharp rocks.
4. *Odysseus* didn't put wax in his ears as his men did.
5. *The song* enticed him to join the Sirens.
6. *Ropes,* however, held him tightly to the mast.
7. *Odysseus's* efforts to escape were in vain.
8. *Circe's* advice was good, but Odysseus did not listen.

EXERCISE 3 Identify the pronoun used as a subject complement in each sentence.

1. The person who faced many dangers was he.
2. The creatures who enticed Odysseus were they.
3. The sailors who bound Odysseus to the mast were they.
4. The person Odysseus wanted to see again was she.
5. It was I who drew an illustration of the episode for the report.

EXERCISE 4 Identify the subject pronouns in the sentences. Tell whether each is used as a subject or as a subject complement.

1. The voyagers from Ithaca were he and his crew.
2. They were the creatures whose songs were deadly.
3. In Odysseus's story, after years of war, he was returning home with his crew.
4. The person tied to the mast was he.
5. The sailors most lured by the Sirens were they.
6. Like Odysseus, they were eager to get to Ithaca.
7. The students who like the story the best are we.

Odysseus fights against the deadly power of the Sirens.

APPLY IT NOW

Imagine you are introducing your family to the class. Write a short paragraph using personal pronouns as subjects and subject complements to describe hobbies and activities that you all enjoy.

Grammar in Action. Identify the subject pronouns in the second paragraph of the excerpt on page 252.

2.4 Object Pronouns

A personal pronoun may be used as the object of a verb. This is called an **object pronoun**. Here is a list of the object pronouns.

SINGULAR	PLURAL
me	us
you	you
him, her, it	them

Use object pronouns for direct objects. A **direct object** names the receiver of the action of the verb. To find a direct object, ask *whom* or *what* after the predicate.

> **Odysseus heard** *them*.

Odysseus heard what? The answer is *them,* the direct object.

An object pronoun may be used as the object of a preposition. A preposition shows a relationship between two words in a sentence. An **object of a preposition** follows a preposition, such as *about, at, between, by, for, from, in, into, of, on, to, under, next to,* and *with.*

> **The crew sailed** *with him*.

In this sentence the preposition is *with.* The object of the preposition is *him.*

EXERCISE 1 Identify the pronoun used as a direct object in each sentence.

1. Odysseus visited the underworld, and an oracle told him about a danger.
2. He thanked her for the warnings.
3. According to the oracle, the monsters Scylla and Charybdis wait for sailors to pass by and then destroy them.
4. Odysseus and his men saw them in the distance.
5. The swirling waters of the whirlpool Charybdis, on the left, identified it.
6. Scylla's cave, on the right, hid her.
7. An area of water separated them.
8. Odysseus's solution to avoid the dual dangers interested us.

EXERCISE 2 Replace the italicized noun or phrase used as a direct object in each sentence with the correct pronoun.

1. The whirlpool Charybdis might pull *the ship* down.
2. The six-headed monster Scylla ate *sailors*.
3. How could the ship pass *Scylla and Charybdis* safely?
4. The problem intrigued *my friend and me*.

EXERCISE 3 Identify the pronoun used as an object of a preposition in each sentence.

1. Circe gave warnings, and Odysseus listened to her.
2. Odysseus saw two cliffs and had to sail between them.
3. On the left was Charybdis, and the ship could easily be swallowed by it.
4. On the right Scylla's arms and heads were a danger to him.

EXERCISE 4 Identify the object pronoun in each sentence. Tell if the pronoun is used as a direct object or as the object of a preposition.

1. Poseidon was the sea god, and Odysseus had angered him.
2. The goddess Athena supported Odysseus, and he was helped by her.
3. Poseidon set the oceans against him.
4. The waves swelled, but Odysseus escaped them.
5. The seas took control of Odysseus's ship with its crew and destroyed them.
6. Athena had an idea to help Odysseus, and discussed it with her father, Zeus.
7. Zeus listened to her and granted Odysseus safe passage home.

APPLY IT NOW

You and a friend have been chosen to take a flying-carpet ride to an exotic place. You see unusual things and meet many interesting people. Write a paragraph about your trip. Use at least four object pronouns, two as direct objects, and two as objects of prepositions.

2.5 Indirect Objects

Some sentences contain two objects: a direct object and an indirect object. The direct object is the receiver of the action. The **indirect object** tells *to whom, for whom, to what,* or *for what* the action is done.

Circe gave *him* advice.

The direct object answers *whom* or *what* after the verb. *Circe gave what?* The answer is *advice,* the direct object. *To whom did Circe give advice?* The answer is *him. Him* is the indirect object. *Him* tells *to whom* the advice was given.

A noun used as an indirect object can be replaced by an object pronoun.

Odysseus gave *the sailors* their orders.
Odysseus gave *them* their orders.

Object pronouns are used as indirect objects: *me, us, you, him, her, it,* and *them.*

Here are some verbs that may take indirect objects: *assign, bring, buy, deny, do, forbid, give, grant, hand, lend, offer, pay, promise, read, refuse, sell, send, show, sing, teach, tell, wish,* and *write.*

Can you identify the indirect object in this sentence? What pronoun can replace the indirect object?

Odysseus told Circe his story.

The indirect object *is Circe.* The pronoun *her* can replace *Circe.*

Odysseus told *her* his story.

EXERCISE 1 Identify the personal pronoun used as an indirect object in each sentence. The direct object is italicized.

1. Many books tell us the *actions* of the Greek gods and goddesses.
2. The ancient Greeks gave them human *qualities.*
3. Homer brought us the *stories* of Odysseus.
4. The gods and goddess sometimes sent him *help* in his journeys.
5. The librarian gave me *a book* of Greek and Roman myths to read for class.
6. I agreed to show her the mythology *section* in the library.

EXERCISE 2 Identify the personal pronoun used as an indirect object in each sentence.

1. Prometheus stole fire from Olympus for humans and gave them this gift.

2. Zeus had denied them fire and was angry at Prometheus for disobeying.

3. Zeus sent him a cruel punishment.

4. Calling an eagle, he assigned it a task: to gnaw at Prometheus's body.

5. To punish humans, Zeus sent them a magical woman named Pandora.

6. He gave her a beautifully decorated box with a heavy latch.

7. He told her the dangers of opening the box, but Zeus knew she would not listen.

8. Pandora's opening of the box brought them many evils, such as greed and envy.

EXERCISE 3 Identify the object pronouns in the sentences. Tell how each is used: as a direct object, an indirect object, or an object of a preposition.

1. Minotaur, a half-bull, half-man monster, terrorized humans and ate them.

2. People in Crete eventually locked him in a labyrinth so confusing that no one could find the way out.

3. Theseus was a strong, young hero, and the task of slaying the monster was given to him.

4. Ariadne, the daughter of the king, gave him a magic ball of thread to help find his way out.

5. It rolled ahead of him and guided him through the labyrinth to the Minotaur.

6. Thesus killed him and followed the thread out of the labyrinth back to her.

APPLY IT NOW

Write three sentences about gifts that you have given friends and family members for holidays or birthdays. Explain who each person is. Use personal pronouns as indirect objects to describe the gifts.

Example: Sarah is my best friend. I gave her a CD by her favorite singer.

 Identify the indirect objects in an online article.

2.6 Uses of Pronouns

Pronouns are used in different ways in sentences. The **subject pronouns** are *I, you, he, she, it, we,* and *they.* Each can be used as the subject of a sentence or as a subject complement.

> *I* **would like to read the adventures of Odysseus.** (subject)
>
> **The owner of the book is** *she.* (subject complement)

The **object pronouns** are *me, you, him, her, it, us,* and *them.* Each can be used as the direct object or the indirect object of a sentence, or as the object of a preposition.

> **I told** *them* **about Odysseus's adventures.** (direct object)
>
> **I loaned** *her* **my copy of** *The Odyssey.* (indirect object)
>
> **The stories about** *him* **are fascinating.** (object of a preposition)

Can you choose the correct pronoun to complete the sentence?

> **My friend and (I me) are doing a report on** *The Iliad.*

You are correct if you said *I.* It is part of the compound subject of the sentence. Don't be confused if a pronoun is part of a compound. Look for how the pronoun acts in the sentence.

EXERCISE 1 Complete each sentence with the pronoun *I* or *me.*

1. Will you lend _____ your copy of *The Iliad?*
2. _____ need to go to the library for a copy.
3. My friend and _____ enjoyed the story of the Sirens.
4. Tell _____ the story of the Sirens.
5. That copy of *The Odyssey* belongs to _____.

EXERCISE 2 Complete each sentence with the pronoun *he* or *him.*

1. _____ arrived back in his country after 20 years.
2. A goddess warned _____ of dangers.
3. _____ and his son plotted to destroy his wife's suitors.
4. The beggar in Penelope's home was _____.
5. No one recognized _____.

EXERCISE 3 Complete each sentence with the pronoun *she* or *her.*

1. Odysseus's wife was Penelope; he had left _____ many years before to fight in the Trojan War.

2. _____ and her son did not know whether Odysseus was alive.

3. Many suitors wanted to marry _____.

4. _____ began to weave a tapestry.

5. _____ promised to marry when it was finished.

EXERCISE 4 Complete each sentence with the pronoun *they* or *them.*

1. _____ believed Penelope's promise.

2. Penelope didn't tell _____ her secret.

3. She would weave the threads during the day and then rip _____ out each evening.

4. She was waiting for her husband's return and wasn't interested in _____.

5. _____ fled or were killed by Odysseus and his son.

EXERCISE 5 Choose the pronoun that correctly completes each sentence. Tell how each is used: as a subject, a subject complement, a direct object, an object of a preposition, or an indirect object.

1. Odysseus was united with his son, and he fought with (he him) against the suitors.

2. Odysseus and (he him) defeated Penelope's suitors.

3. Odysseus and (she her) were now reunited.

4. The conflict between the god Poseidon and (he him) was ended.

5. The gods finally allowed (they them) a life together.

6. His son and (they them) lived a peaceful life in Ithaca.

The Trojan War was mainly centered in the area once known as Troy.

APPLY IT NOW

Write five sentences about an activity that you have participated in, such as baking bread or going to a ball game. Use personal pronouns in your sentences. When you have finished, circle each pronoun and note whether it is a subject pronoun or an object pronoun.

2.7 Possessive Pronouns and Adjectives

A **possessive pronoun** shows possession or ownership. A possessive pronoun takes the place of a possessive noun.

> **This report on the Sirens is** *Lola's.* (possessive noun)
> **This report on the Sirens is** *hers.* (possessive pronoun)

Here is a chart of the possessive pronouns.

	SINGULAR	PLURAL
FIRST PERSON	mine	ours
SECOND PERSON	yours	yours
THIRD PERSON	his, hers, its	theirs

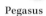

Pegasus

Note the spelling of the forms. Unlike possessive nouns, possessive pronouns do not contain apostrophes. A possessive pronoun stands alone and is not followed by a noun.

A **possessive adjective** also shows possession. A possessive adjective always comes before a noun. In this example the possessive adjective comes before the noun *report*.

> **This is** *her* **report.**

Remember that a possessive pronoun stands alone, and a possessive adjective always precedes a noun.

> **The book is** *mine.* (possessive pronoun)
> **This is** *my* **book.** (possessive adjective)

Here is a chart of the possessive adjectives.

	SINGULAR	PLURAL
FIRST PERSON	my	our
SECOND PERSON	your	your
THIRD PERSON	his, hers, its	their

EXERCISE 1 Identify the possessive pronoun in each item.

1. Helen was a beautiful woman. According to tradition, the fault for the Trojan War was hers.

2. Hercules was superhuman. An extraordinary strength was his.

3. The gods ruled from Mount Olympus. Theirs were special golden thrones on the mountain.

4. The Muses were each associated with one of the arts, and theirs was the gift to make magnificent music together.

5. Atlas was a powerful creature finally defeated by Zeus; his was the job of holding up the world.

EXERCISE 2 Identify the possessive adjective in each item.

1. Bellerophon was a hero in Greek mythology. The ability to tame horses was one of his special gifts.

2. Pegasus was a winged flying horse. Its job was to carry Zeus's thunderbolts.

3. My favorite story is about Bellerophon and Pegasus defeating the Chimera.

4. The Chimera was a hideous monster. Her body had parts of a lion, a goat, and a snake.

5. Bellerophon and Pegasus are the main topics of your presentation.

Atlas carries the weight of the world.

EXERCISE 3 Tell whether the possessives in the following sentences are adjectives or pronouns.

1. The students displayed their projects on ancient Greece.

2. His was made of balsa and tissue paper.

3. Ours was devoted to Pegasus, the winged horse.

4. Your model of Mount Olympus was the best.

5. Medusa's head with its many serpents was spectacular.

APPLY IT NOW

Imagine that you went to a science fair or an art show at school. Write four sentences telling about the projects you saw. Use possessive pronouns and possessive adjectives in your writing.

2.8 Intensive and Reflexive Pronouns

Intensive and reflexive pronouns end in *self* or *selves*.

	SINGULAR	PLURAL
FIRST PERSON	myself	ourselves
SECOND PERSON	yourself	yourselves
THIRD PERSON	himself, herself, itself	themselves

An **intensive pronoun** is used to emphasize a noun that comes before it. In this sentence *himself* emphasizes *Odysseus,* the noun that comes before it.

Odysseus *himself* devised a plan to win the Trojan War.

A **reflexive pronoun** is used as the direct or indirect object of a verb or as the object of a preposition. It generally refers to the subject of the sentence. In this sentence *himself* is an indirect object. It refers to the subject of the sentence, *Odysseus.*

Odysseus earned *himself* a reputation as a smart leader.

Can you find the reflexive pronoun in the following sentence? What role does it play in the sentence? What word does it refer to?

Some Greeks hid themselves inside a large horse to get into Troy.

You are correct if you said that the reflexive pronoun is *themselves.* It is the direct object of the verb *hid,* and it refers to the third person plural noun *Greeks.* The words *hisself* and *theirselves* are not acceptable terms and should never be used in speaking or writing.

EXERCISE 1 Identify the intensive or reflexive pronoun in each sentence. Tell what word each pronoun refers to.

1. Zeus himself, the chief god, was the father of Hephaestus.
2. Hera herself, the chief goddess, was his mother.
3. The gods often bickered among themselves.
4. Once Hephaestus tried to break up a quarrel between his parents and was thrown to earth by the angry Zeus himself.

Hera, a Greek goddess

5. Hephaestus injured himself badly when he fell from Mount Olympus.

6. From then on, Hephaestus couldn't walk by himself.

7. He built himself two special robots of gold and silver who were able to think for themselves.

8. The powerful Hephaestus himself was actually most famous as the blacksmith for the gods.

EXERCISE 2 **Complete the sentences with intensive or reflexive pronouns. Each should refer to the italicized word in the sentence.**

1. *We* decided on our project for the unit among _____.

2. *I* made a chart of the gods by _____.

3. *Amy* _____ could name 20 gods and goddesses.

4. *Mr. Peterson* _____ praised our work.

5. Dave, *you* can see our project _____ in the library.

6. The *projects* _____ show a lot of hard work.

7. The model *robot* can move by _____.

8. Those *students* are very proud of _____.

EXERCISE 3 **Identify the intensive or reflexive pronoun in each sentence. Tell whether each pronoun is singular or plural and whether it is first, second, or third person.**

1. Athena sometimes transformed herself into a bird.

2. Apollo turned himself into a dolphin when he wanted to get on a ship.

3. The gods themselves acted a lot like humans, and they sometimes took human or animal shapes.

4. I made myself a chart with the names of the ancient Greek and Roman gods.

5. Do you find yourself amazed by these Greek and Roman stories?

APPLY IT NOW

Imagine that you are giving a surprise party for your friend. What do you need to do by yourself? What do your other friends need to do by themselves? Write five sentences detailing the planning procedure. Use two intensive and two reflexive pronouns in your writing.

2.9 Antecedents

The word to which a pronoun refers is its **antecedent**. The antecedent is the word that the pronoun replaces.

> **Did *Odysseus* return home? Yes, *he* did, but only after many difficulties.**

The pronoun *he* refers to the noun *Odysseus* in the question. *Odysseus* is the antecedent of *he.*

> **The *Iliad* is an epic poem. *It* was written by Homer.**

The pronoun *it* refers to *The Iliad* in the previous sentence. The antecedent of *it* is *The Iliad.*

The pronoun must agree with its antecedent in person and number and in whether it refers to a male, a female, or a thing. In the first example, *he* is the third person singular male to agree with *Odysseus.* In the second example, *it* agrees with a third person singular thing, *The Iliad.*

What is the antecedent of the italicized pronoun in this set?

> **Donna worked on a project on Odysseus. *She* looked for information about him on the Internet.**

You are correct if you said the antecedent is the noun *Donna. She* is third person singular female; it agrees with *Donna.*

EXERCISE 1 Identify the pronoun for each italicized antecedent.

1. *Orpheus* was a figure in Greek myth, and he had an interesting story.
2. Orpheus had a special *ability*. It was to make beautiful music.
3. His mother was one of the *Muses*. They were patron goddesses of such arts as painting, dance, and music.
4. When *Orpheus* was grown, he brought music to the earth.
5. His *music* was so lovely that even the trees moved to listen to it.
6. Orpheus met a lovely *woman*, and he fell in love with her.
7. Her name was *Eurydice*, and she loved him in return.
8. *Orpheus and Eurydice* married, and they were happy.

EXERCISE 2 Identify the antecedent for each italicized pronoun.

1. One day a snake bit Eurydice; *it* had a deadly poison.
2. Eurydice fell to the ground, where *she* died.
3. Hermes, the messenger god, came for Eurydice, and *he* gently carried her to the underworld.
4. Orpheus was sad, and *he* lost all joy in life.
5. He searched for the underworld's entrance and found *it*.
6. As *he* walked, Orpheus played sad music.
7. He wanted to meet Hades and ask *him* to free Eurydice.
8. Hades and his queen were crying; the music moved *them*.
9. The queen was heartbroken, and *she* begged for Eurydice's release.
10. Hades consented, but *he* set a condition.

EXERCISE 3 Complete each sentence with a pronoun. The antecedent for the pronoun is italicized.

1. If Orpheus looked at his *wife* on the way, _____ would have to return to the underworld forever.
2. *Orpheus* started out eagerly, but then _____ began to doubt.
3. He heard *footsteps* behind him, but were _____ Eurydice's?
4. Orpheus turned and got just a brief glimpse of *Eurydice* before _____ was banished to the underworld forever.
5. *Orpheus* had lost Eurydice, and _____ became distraught.
6. The *music* he played changed, and now _____ was sad and depressing.
7. *Orpheus and Eurydice* were reunited in the underworld, and people still tell stories about _____ .

Orpheus and Eurydice

APPLY IT NOW

Write five sentences using personal pronouns about a Greek myth you know. Remember to match pronouns with antecedents.

2.10 Pronouns and Contractions

Personal pronouns can be joined with some verbs to form **contractions.** An apostrophe (') replaces the missing letter or letters in contractions.

Here is a list of common contractions that contain pronouns.

I'm = I am	I've = I have
you're = you are	you've = you have
we're = we are	we've = we have
they're = they are	they've = they have
he's = he is *or* he has	she's = she is *or* she has
it's = it is *or* it has	

Will can also be joined with pronouns to form contractions: *I'll, you'll, we'll, she'll, he'll,* and *they'll.*

> *I've* read about Gaia. = *I have* read about Gaia.
> *She's* been called Mother Earth. = *She has* been called Mother Earth.

Possessive adjectives are often confused with contractions. Possessive adjectives express possession but do not contain apostrophes.

PRONOUN + VERB	POSSESSIVE ADJECTIVE
You're (= You are) late.	Your report is late.
It's (= It is) long.	Its title is "Greek Gods."
They're (= They are) old.	Their story is long.

EXERCISE 1 Complete the chart by writing the correct contraction or the words that form the contraction.

CONTRACTION	WORDS THAT FORM THE CONTRACTION
	we will
	you have
they're	
	he is
you're	
	it has
I'll	
	I have

EXERCISE 2 Identify the contraction in each sentence. Write the words that make up the contraction.

1. I've read an interesting Greek myth.

2. It's about two strong brothers, Otus and Ephiatles.

3. "I'm worried about Otus and Ephiatles," said Zeus.

4. "They're more than 60 feet tall and still growing."

5. We're going to write a play based on our favorite Greek myths.

6. If you're going to be in the play, please sign up here.

7. We drew straws to see which parts we'll each play.

8. He's playing Otus, and Jay is playing Ephiatles.

Zeus, the king of the Greek gods

EXERCISE 3 Write the contraction for the italicized words in each sentence.

1. Mother Earth, an enemy of Zeus, said to the brothers, "*You will* be able to overthrow Zeus."

2. The brothers said, "*We are* going to build a mountain as big as Mount Olympus."

3. From its top they called, "Zeus, *you have* ruled too long."

4. Zeus grew angry at their disobedience and said, "*I am* sending thunderbolts against you."

5. Apollo said to Zeus, "*I have* got a plan."

6. Apollo told Artemis, "*You are* going to change yourself into a deer and dart between the brothers."

7. "Instead of shooting the deer, *they are* going to shoot each other, and the victory will be ours."

8. *It is* exactly what happened.

APPLY IT NOW

Write five clues to the identification of a historical character. Use contractions with pronouns in them. Exchange your clues with classmates. How many characters can you name?

2.11 Demonstrative and Interrogative Pronouns

Demonstrative pronouns are used to point out people, places, and things.

SINGULAR	PLURAL
this	these
that	those

Use *this* and *these* to point out things that are near.

These are books of myths.

Use *that* and *those* to point out things that are farther away.

That was my favorite book.

Because *this* and *that* are pronouns, they stand alone.

An **interrogative pronoun** is used to ask a question. The interrogative pronouns are *who, whom, what,* and *whose.*

What happened after Pandora opened the box?

The interrogative pronoun *who* is used when the person is the subject of a sentence.

Who opened the box that released evils into the world?

Who is the subject of *opened.*

The interrogative pronoun *whom* is used when the person is the object of a verb or a preposition.

Whom did Prometheus help?

Whom is the direct object of the verb *help.*

The interrogative pronoun *whose* is used to ask about ownership.

Whose was the punishment that resulted in being gnawed by an eagle?

EXERCISE 1 Identify the demonstrative pronoun in each sentence. Tell whether it is singular or plural.

1. Those are nonfiction books.
2. This is the section with fiction books.
3. These are all books of myths.
4. Is that a good book to read?
5. The librarian suggested this to me.
6. Students are allowed to research on those.

EXERCISE 2 Complete each sentence with a demonstrative pronoun. Follow the directions in parentheses.

1. I found _____ in the library. (singular, far)
2. _____ are all books from the library. (plural, near)
3. _____ are all myths. (plural, far)
4. Have you read _____? (singular, near)
5. No, but I've read _____ and liked it very much. (singular, far)
6. I want to read _____ over the summer break. (plural, far)

EXERCISE 3 Complete each sentence with the correct interrogative pronoun.

1. (Who Whom) was Zeus?
2. To (whom who) did Prometheus give fire?
3. (What Whose) was Prometheus's punishment?
4. (Whose Whom) was the job of bringing life to earth?
5. (Whose Who) was the box that released evils into the world?
6. (Who Whom) gave Pandora the box?
7. (Who Whom) did Zeus send to the world with a box?

APPLY IT NOW

Write five questions to ask your parent, teacher, or grandparent. Use interrogative pronouns. Ask about places and things that you want to know more about.

Print digital images of figures in Greek mythology.

Pronoun Review

2.1 Identify the personal pronoun in each sentence. Tell whether it is singular or plural.

1. We are learning about minerals in science class.

2. I like the way granite sparkles.

3. Please pass the limestone rock to him.

4. Mrs. Barnes told us to rub one of the stones on paper.

5. It left a streak

2.2 Identify the personal pronoun in each sentence. Tell whether each is a first person, second person, or third person pronoun.

6. What do you know about dams?

7. They hold back rivers to create water reservoirs.

8. We visited Hoover Dam recently.

9. It is the country's most famous dam.

10. My family enjoyed the visit, and I took a lot of photos.

2.3 Identify each subject pronoun. Tell whether it is used as a subject or as a subject complement.

11. We celebrated Chinese New Year.

12. The best lion dancer was he.

13. Do you want a fortune cookie?

14. The person who gave out "lucky money" was she.

2.4 Identify each object pronoun. Tell whether it is used as a direct object or as an object of a preposition.

15. Steve told us about scary things in the woods.

16. The dark path frightened them.

17. Amy had a flashlight with her.

18. Amy walked behind me, holding the flashlight.

2.5 Identify the pronoun used as an indirect object in each sentence.

19. Mom brought them soup.

20. We passed him the pepper.

21. He gave us a choice of vegetables for the soup.

22. She handed me a napkin to wipe my hands.

23. Avery showed her the way to slurp a bowl of soup.

2.6 Choose the pronoun that correctly completes each sentence.

24. (They Them) preserve fruit and vegetables at the end of summer.

25. (She Her) and her friends pick the best peaches.

26. Emily and (he him) washed and peeled the peaches.

27. Mom gave Emily and (I me) the clean jars.

28. Dad helped Luke and (she her) with the canning.

2.7 Identify the possessive in each sentence. Tell whether it is a pronoun or an adjective.

29. The Murphys were worried because their dog was lost.

30. Theirs is a Labrador.

31. His name is Max.

32. The signs around the neighborhood were theirs.

33. The bark we heard was his.

34. Max had found his way home.

2.8 Choose the pronoun that correctly completes each sentence.

35. The girls decided to make bread for (themselves ourselves).

36. Sue invented the recipe by (herself myself).

37. Sam (itself himself) could eat an entire loaf of bread.

38. Mom, taste the bread for (herself yourself).

2.9 Identify the pronoun in each sentence and tell its antecedent.

39. Lucille Ball was an actress, and she starred in a TV show.

40. Desi Arnaz played her husband on the show, and he was her husband in real life.

41. Fred and Ethel were the other characters on the show, in which they played neighbors.

42. The weekly comedy show was funny, and it made audiences laugh.

2.10 Identify the contraction in each sentence. Write the words that make up the contraction.

43. They're worried that frost will damage the flowers.

44. We're going to the nursery to buy ground cover.

45. She's been covering the flower beds with hay.

46. It's necessary, or the flowers will not bloom next summer.

47. They've got a good layer of insulation on them now.

2.11 Identify the pronoun in each sentence. Tell whether it is demonstrative or interrogative.

48. To whom was the letter addressed?

49. That is Bill's letter.

50. This is the wrong-sized envelope.

51. What is the zip code for Julie's town?

52. These arrived in today's mail.

 Tech Tip Go to www.voyagesinenglish.com for more activities.

Pronoun Challenge

Read the paragraph and answer the questions.

1. In 1804 Meriwether Lewis and William Clark set out on their famous expedition. 2. They wanted to explore the western United States and find a water route connecting the Mississippi River and the Pacific Ocean. 3. At this time only Native Americans lived there. 4. One Shoshone woman, Sacagawea, guided them on their journey. 5. In addition she obtained food and ponies for them by trading with the Native American peoples. 6. Without her help, the trip could not have continued. 7. In their diaries Lewis and Clark praised her. 8. What would they have done without her help? 9. This is a question historians often ask. 10. She herself is one of the reasons for their success. 11. We Americans should thank her because a good deal of the credit for the success of the expedition is hers.

1. Name the personal pronoun in sentence 2.
2. Tell whether the pronoun in sentence 2 is singular or plural.
3. In sentence 3 substitute a personal pronoun for *Native Americans*.
4. In sentence 4 is the personal pronoun a subject or an object pronoun?
5. Name the pronoun used as the subject of sentence 5.
6. In sentence 5 the pronoun *she* takes the place of what noun?
7. Name the pronoun used as an object in sentence 7.
8. Name the interrogative pronoun in sentence 8.
9. Name the demonstrative pronoun in sentence 9. Is it singular or plural?
10. Find the intensive pronoun in sentence 10.
11. Name the possessive pronoun in sentence 11.
12. In sentence 11 find the pronoun naming the speaker.

Adjectives

3.1 Descriptive Adjectives

An **adjective** describes a noun. Adjectives that tell about the size, shape, color, or weight of the things they describe are called **descriptive adjectives.** They can tell how something looks, sounds, tastes, smells, or feels.

> **Mark made a model of a dinosaur with claws.**
> **Mark made a model of a *gigantic brown* dinosaur with *long, sharp* claws.**

The words *gigantic, brown, long,* and *sharp* were added to the second sentence. These words are adjectives. *Gigantic* and *brown* tell about the noun *dinosaur. Long* and *sharp* tell about the noun *claws.*

A descriptive adjective generally comes before a noun. Can you find the descriptive adjectives in these sentences? Which noun does each describe?

> **Dinosaurs are large animals.**
> **Dinosaurs could be fierce hunters.**

In the first sentence, the adjective *large* describes the noun *animals.* In the second sentence, the adjective *fierce* describes the noun *hunters.*

EXERCISE 1 Find the descriptive adjectives in these sentences. The number of adjectives in each sentence is in parentheses.

1. *Dinosaur* means "terrible lizard." (1)
2. Dinosaurs were the dominant species on earth for millions of years. (1)
3. Like modern reptiles, dinosaurs probably had green or brown skin. (3)
4. Small dinosaurs that ate meat were usually speedy animals so that they could escape large predators. (3)
5. Dinosaurs that ate plants were often huge animals. (1)
6. Tracks show that big dinosaurs walked in long, easy steps. (3)
7. These dinosaurs often had long necks and heavy, massive tails. (3)
8. Their lengthy necks helped them reach food on tall plants. (2)
9. Small, fast dinosaurs could outrun predators. (2)
10. Swift dinosaurs called raptors had large claws on their hands and feet. (2)

EXERCISE 2 **Find the descriptive adjectives in these sentences. Tell which noun each describes.**

1. Paleontologists have difficult jobs.
2. They spend long hours looking for fossils of dinosaurs.
3. They do slow, painstaking work.
4. New dinosaurs are always being discovered.
5. Fossils form as the hard, bony parts of an animal turn to stone.
6. The soft parts just dissolve and disappear.
7. Brittle fossils can easily break up as they are being removed, and so they need to be handled with special care.
8. Fossils are generally found in dry, rocky areas.
9. The dry climate helps in the long process of forming fossils.
10. Fossils give paleontologists important information about dinosaurs.

DIG NAME: High Salt Plain
ARTIFACT ID: 41B
DATE FOUND: Aug 23
ITEM FOUND: Dinosaur Claw
LOCATION: Lodgepole Bluff, 18G

EXERCISE 3 **Add a descriptive adjective before each noun.**

1. _____ dinosaurs
2. _____ snakes
3. _____ skyscraper
4. _____ artist
5. _____ sandwich
6. _____ movie
7. _____ jacket
8. _____ story
9. _____ radio
10. _____ lighthouse

EXERCISE 4 **Add a noun after each descriptive adjective.**

1. loud _____
2. delicious _____
3. muddy _____
4. smooth _____
5. polite _____
6. swift _____
7. green _____
8. funny _____
9. crunchy _____
10. smelly _____

APPLY IT NOW

Choose three objects or people. Write three descriptive adjectives to describe each.

Grammar in Action. Identify two adjectives in the excerpt on page 296.

3.2 Proper Adjectives

A proper noun names a particular person, place, or thing. Some descriptive adjectives come from proper nouns and are called **proper adjectives.** Like proper nouns, proper adjectives begin with capital letters.

PROPER NOUN	PROPER ADJECTIVE
Africa	African
America	American
Brazil	Brazilian
Cambodia	Cambodian
France	French
Greece	Greek
Hungary	Hungarian
Iceland	Icelander
Italy	Italian
Japan	Japanese
Jefferson	Jeffersonian
Mexico	Mexican
Poland	Polish
Rome	Roman
Shakespeare	Shakespearean
Sweden	Swedish
Switzerland	Swiss

EXERCISE 1 Write a proper adjective for each proper noun. Use a dictionary to check your spelling.

1. Russia _____
2. Turkey _____
3. Spain _____
4. Australia _____
5. Pakistan _____
6. Cuba _____
7. Peru _____
8. Ireland _____
9. Amazon _____
10. Egypt _____
11. Israel _____
12. Vietnam _____
13. India _____
14. Alaska _____
15. Germany _____
16. Hawaii _____

EXERCISE 2 Choose five proper adjectives that you wrote in Exercise 1. Write five sentences, each using one of the proper adjectives.

EXERCISE 3 Complete each sentence with a proper adjective formed from the proper noun in parentheses. Use a dictionary if you need help.

1. Fossils of one of the largest plant-eating dinosaurs, *Argentinosaurus,* are found only on the _____ continent. (South America)

2. A complete skeleton of *Tyrannosaurus rex* is in a _____ museum. (Midwest)

3. Mary Anning, a _____ fossil hunter of the 19th century, found many important fossils. (Britain)

4. _____ scientists began discovering and studying other fossils at about the same time. (Europe)

5. A large armored dinosaur, *Minmi,* was named after an _____ town. (Australia)

6. *Huayangosaurus* is named after a _____ province. (China)

7. *Triceratops* was as big as a present-day _____ elephant. (Africa)

8. The *Leaellynasaura* lived in the cold climate of the _____ Circle. (Antarctica)

9. One amazing fossil, now in an _____ museum, shows a *Velociraptor* attacking another dinosaur. (Asia)

10. _____ dinosaur fossils include many footprints and eggshells. (Canada)

11. In 1896 a _____ scientist found evidence that some plant-eating sauropods had armor to protect them. (France)

12. in 1952 a sauropod fossil was found in a _____ quarry. (Wales)

Mary Anning, fossil hunter

APPLY IT NOW

Imagine you have just returned from a trip around the world. Use proper adjectives in sentences that tell about five things you brought back with you as souvenirs.

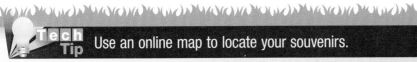

Tech Tip Use an online map to locate your souvenirs.

3.3 Articles

A, an, and *the* are **articles.**

A and *an* are **indefinite articles.** An indefinite article refers to any one of a class of things.

> **A fossilized cockroach that lived in North America many years ago was discovered by geologists.**
> **An estimate of its age is 300 million years.**

A is used before words beginning with a consonant sound. *An* is used before words beginning with a vowel sound.

VOWEL SOUNDS	CONSONANT SOUNDS
an iceberg	a stone
an egg	a nest
an hour	a unit

If the article precedes a descriptive adjective, the article agrees with the vowel sound of the adjective: a *large* microscope, an *old* microscope.

The is the **definite article.** It refers to one or more specific people, places, or things.

> **The fossil of this cockroach was discovered by geologists from Ohio State University.**
> **The roach lived 55 million years before *the* dinosaurs.**
> **The scientist told us that crocodiles, crabs, and some roaches lived at *the* same time as *the* early dinosaurs.**

EXERCISE 1 Write the correct indefinite article, *a* or *an*, before each item.

1. _____ ocean
2. _____ pebble
3. _____ insect
4. _____ bug
5. _____ web

6. _____ archaeologist
7. _____ eagle
8. _____ geologist
9. _____ fossil
10. _____ ancient fossil

A fossilized cockroach

EXERCISE 2 Identify the articles in each sentence. Tell whether each is a definite article or an indefinite article.

1. A fossil of a cockroach was found by geologists, and the ancient insect was about three inches long.

2. The insect was twice as large as the typical modern roach.

3. The fossil was a rare find.

4. It was discovered in a coal mine in Ohio.

5. The color pattern of the ancient cockroach was still visible.

6. Geologists discovered a fossil of another insect.

7. Can you imagine a creature like that?

8. The well-preserved cockroach was a welcome find, but a roach remains an unwelcome guest in most places.

9. The prehistoric creature was five feet long and one foot wide!

EXERCISE 3 Complete the sentences by adding an indefinite article (*a* or *an*) or the definite article (*the*). More than one choice may be correct.

1. There is _____ unusual cockroach in Madagascar.

2. Its name is _____ Madagascar hissing cockroach.

3. _____ Madagascar hissing cockroach is often called _____ living fossil.

4. It uses _____ air sac on its abdomen to make _____ hissing sound.

5. _____ hiss is useful to scare predators.

6. Other insects can make _____ hissing sound, but they do so by rubbing body parts together.

7. _____ average hissing cockroach lives about two to five years.

8. It is two to three inches long and is one of _____ largest cockroaches.

Madagascar hissing cockroach

APPLY IT NOW

Write five sentences about a strange animal. Underline each article you use in your sentences.

Grammar in Action Identify two articles in the excerpt on page 291. Tell whether each is definite or indefinite.

3.4 Repetition of Articles

When two or more nouns joined by *and* refer to different people, places, or things, use an article before each noun.

The paleontologist and the geologist worked together to find the fossils.

In the above example, two different people are mentioned. The repetition of the article before the two nouns shows this.

When two or more nouns joined by *and* refer to the same person, place, or thing, use an article before the first noun only.

The paleontologist and professor organized a dig.

In the above example, one person is mentioned. The article *the* is used only before the first noun.

Which of the following refers to more than one person?

A a student and aspiring paleontologist
B the photographer and the biochemist
C the professor and leader of the dig crew

The correct answer is B because the photographer and the biochemist are two different people.

EXERCISE 1 Tell whether each italicized phrase refers to one person, place, or thing or to more than one. Check for repetition of the article.

1. *A writer and an illustrator* worked together on the book about dinosaurs that I used for my report.

2. *A writer and editor* wrote an interesting book about dinosaurs.

3. *A young rancher and rodeo cowboy* discovered a dinosaur skeleton in 1998.

4. *The museum guide and the volunteer* gave us a lecture about dinosaurs.

5. *The scientist and professor* Paul Sereno has made some amazing discoveries of early dinosaurs in Argentina.

6. I learned the most about dinosaurs from *the professor and the paleontologist.*

EXERCISE 2 Add an article where an article is needed. Put an X if none is needed. Look at the description of the number of people.

1. *There was one judge:* _____ science teacher and _____ fair director picked the best project.

2. *There were two presenters:* _____ principal and _____ district superintendent presented the prize.

3. *One student did the project:* _____ writer and _____ illustrator of the project on dinosaurs was a fifth grader.

4. *Two students worked on the project together, doing different tasks:* _____ writer and _____ illustrator of the winning project on dinosaurs were fifth-grade students.

5. *There were two officers:* _____ fifth-grade class president and _____ head of the student council invited a writer to speak at our school.

EXERCISE 3 Add articles to complete the paragraph. Put an X if no article is needed. More than one article may be correct.

My class and I went to visit (1) _____ museum with many exhibits on dinosaurs. There was even (2) _____ dig site where visitors to (3) _____ museum could actually look for fossils. I used (4) _____ chisel and (5) _____ brush to uncover my fossil. In another area I touched (6) _____ tooth from (7) _____ *T. rex* and (8) _____ horn from (9) _____ *Triceratops.* Bold visitors put their hands between (10) _____ sharp teeth of a dinosaur skull. (11) _____ museum also featured (12) _____ skeleton of (13) _____ *Gigantosaurus.* Some say that it was (14) _____ largest meat eater ever to walk the earth. (15) _____ volunteer guide and (16) _____ former teacher was preparing fossils in a lab. We were able to see her work and ask questions.

APPLY IT NOW

Have you ever seen a dinosaur exhibit in a museum? Have you ever watched a film about dinosaurs? Write a note to a friend about what you saw. Underline the articles in your sentences.

3.5 Demonstrative Adjectives

A **demonstrative adjective** points out a specific person, place, or thing and is more specific than an *a, an,* or *the.* The demonstrative adjectives are *this, that, these,* and *those.* They come before nouns and point out *which one* or *which ones.*

This and *that* point out one person, place, or thing. *These* and *those* point out more than one person, place, or thing.

This and *these* point out items that are near. *That* and *those* point out items that are farther away.

> **This fossil belonged to a raptor.** (singular, near)
> **That tool is used by paleontologists.** (singular, far)

> **These teeth are from a *T. rex*.** (plural, near)
> **Those horns are from a *Triceratops*.** (plural, far)

Which nouns do the demonstrative adjectives point out?

> **I think these skeletons are amazing.**
> **That dinosaur is a *Velociraptor*.**

In the first sentence, *these* points out the plural noun *skeletons.* In the second sentence, *That* goes with the singular noun *dinosaur.*

Actual size of a *T. rex* tooth

EXERCISE 1 Add the correct demonstrative adjective before each noun to describe an object or objects that are near.

1. _____ skeleton
2. _____ guide
3. _____ eggs
4. _____ pictures
5. _____ fossils
6. _____ tool

EXERCISE 2 Add the correct demonstrative adjective before each noun to describe an object or objects that are far.

1. _____ plants
2. _____ skull
3. _____ trees
4. _____ nest
5. _____ behavior
6. _____ displays

EXERCISE 3 Identify the demonstrative adjective in each sentence. Tell whether each demonstrative adjective is singular or plural and tell the noun it goes with.

1. This skull is from a *Herrerasaurus*, a dinosaur from the Triassic period.

2. That period is often called "the age of reptiles."

3. Dinosaurs first appeared in the Triassic period, when these animals flourished.

4. Those drawings show the plants that grew during the Jurassic period.

5. During this period dinosaurs were dominant.

6. Look at those two huge skeletons of *Tyrannosaurus rex*.

7. They're attacking that *Triceratops*.

8. Those animals lived during the Cretaceous period.

9. At the end of that period, dinosaurs became extinct.

10. Scientists dispute the reason for that abrupt disappearance.

EXERCISE 4 Write the correct demonstrative adjective to complete each sentence. Follow the directions in parentheses.

1. _____ exhibit at the museum is amazing. (near)

2. _____ workers are actually preparing and cleaning fossils. (far)

3. _____ museum has a large dinosaur section. (near)

4. _____ brushes are used to remove dirt from fossils. (near)

5. Let's ask _____ woman about her work. (far)

6. _____ are real dinosaur eggs—or at least fossils. (near)

7. _____ tool looks like a dentist's drill, and it removes dirt from the fossils. (far)

8. The volunteer guide explained _____ dinosaur fossils to us. (far)

9. _____ fossil is a backbone of a dinosaur. (far)

10. We can take _____ brochures about dinosaurs with us. (near)

APPLY IT NOW

Imagine you are giving a tour of your classroom to a visitor. Write five sentences about items you would point out to the visitor. Use demonstrative adjectives as you point out the objects. Underline the adjectives in your sentences.

3.6 Adjectives That Tell How Many

Some descriptive adjectives tell how many or about how many. Each of these adjectives comes before a noun. A number can be used as an adjective that tells how many.

one photograph   **50** bones   **three** tour guides

A word that tells number order can be an adjective that tells how many.

the *first* visit   the *fifth* trip   the *100th* visitor

The following words can be used as adjectives that tell about how many.

all	each	few	much	some
any	either	many	neither	
both	every	most	several	

All dinosaurs died out millions of years ago.
Every student in my class is interested in dinosaurs.

What is the adjective that tells how many in this sentence?

The huge *Brachiosaurus* ate many plants in order to survive.

You're correct if you said *many*. It tells about the noun *plants*.

EXERCISE 1 Add an adjective that tells how many or about how many. The adjective should go with the noun.

1. _____ dinosaurs
2. _____ bones
3. _____ feet
4. _____ miles per hour
5. _____ teeth
6. _____ years
7. _____ scientists
8. _____ fossil
9. _____ students
10. _____ museums

Paleontologists study fossil remains to learn about the past.

EXERCISE 2 Write a sentence using each phrase you wrote in Exercise 1.

EXERCISE 3 Identify the adjective or adjectives that tell how many or about how many in each sentence.

1. The *Brachiosaurus* weighed about 80 tons.
2. It had two front legs that were longer than its back legs.
3. It was a plant-eating dinosaur that walked on four legs.
4. A few scientists believe that it never stopped growing.
5. This could be the reason that a *Brachiosaurus* could reach up to 50 feet when it stretched its long neck.
6. Every *Brachiosaurus* had two nostrils on top of its head.
7. Many believe that this permitted it to eat constantly.
8. Two almost-complete *Brachiosaurus* skeletons have been discovered.
9. One skeleton is in Germany, and the second fossil is in Chicago.
10. Some *Tyrannosaurus* rex grew to be 40 feet tall.
11. After many years of evolution, they became the perfect killing machine.
12. Each *T. rex* had two large feet and two short arms.
13. One *T. rex* tooth that was found was 14 inches long.
14. Many scientists believe that the *T. rex* could run as fast as 35 miles per hour.

EXERCISE 4 Choose the correct adjective to complete each sentence.

1. _____ student has a fossil kit on the field trip to the museum.
2. I found _____ of the dinosaur bones in the practice dig.
3. We measured _____ of the *Velociraptor's* front claws.
4. Scientists can learn much from _____ dinosaur.
5. _____ dinosaur can offer valuable information about the past.

APPLY IT NOW

Write five sentences describing a place that interests you, such as the ocean or a museum. Give facts about the place, using adjectives that tell how many or about how many. Underline the adjectives you use.

Use a PowerPoint presentation to describe your place.

3.7 Adjectives as Subject Complements

An adjective that follows a linking verb and completes the sentence is called a **subject complement.** The subject complement describes the subject of the sentence.

The *T. rex* was *powerful*.

The adjective *powerful* is a subject complement. It follows the linking verb *was,* and it describes the subject *T. rex.* Common linking verbs are forms of the verb *be* and words such as *become, feel, grow, look, remain, seem, smell, sound,* and *taste.*

Can you identify the adjective subject complements in these sentences?

A The *T. rex's* teeth were sharp with cutting edges.
B *T. rex* was not necessarily green, as some myths claim.

You're right if you said that in sentence A *sharp* describes *teeth,* and in sentence B *green* describes *T. rex.*

An adjective usually comes before a noun. A subject complement, however, follows a linking verb and comes after the noun it describes.

The *fierce T. rex* preyed on animals. (before a noun)
The animal was *frightening*. (subject complement)

EXERCISE 1 Identify the subject complement in each sentence. Tell the noun the subject complement describes.

1. The *Triceratops* was huge.
2. Its three horns were gigantic.
3. The horn on its nose was smallest.
4. The creature's body seems bulky.
5. The dinosaur looks clumsy to me.
6. Its skull was unusually large—even for dinosaurs.
7. Its tails and legs were short, though.
8. If threatened, the *Triceratops* became aggressive.
9. The modern-day rhinoceros looks as intimidating as the *Triceratops.*
10. The similarities between the rhinoceros and the *Triceratops* remain close.

A rhinoceros is built similar to the *Triceratops.*

EXERCISE 2 Identify the position of each italicized adjective. Tell whether it appears before a noun or as a subject complement.

1. The *Triceratops* is *famous* for its horns.
2. *Triceratops* traveled in *large* groups.
3. This *massive* dinosaur was a herd animal.
4. *Triceratops* usually ate *low* plants.
5. Each one ate an *enormous* amount of food.
6. Their skulls were *remarkable* for their size and strength.
7. A *Triceratops* was fairly *tall*—the height of a basketball hoop.
8. Its head was *long*—about the length of a human adult.
9. The animals engaged in *fierce* fights among themselves.
10. A *Triceratops* probably charged its enemies, and its horns were an *effective* defense.

EXERCISE 3 Add an adjective to complete each sentence. Tell whether the adjective comes before a noun or whether it is a subject complement.

1. The work of a paleontologist seems _____ to me.
2. To me, dinosaurs are _____.
3. Dinosaurs were _____ animals.
4. I saw _____ skeletons at a museum.
5. The _____ *T. rex* fascinates many people.
6. Micah thinks that the skin of the dinosaur feels _____, like a lizard's.
7. Do you see how the _____ claws and toes of a *T. rex* are deadly weapons?
8. The tails of full-grown dinosaurs are _____.
9. A museum guide showed us _____ skeletons of different kinds of dinosaurs.
10. The museum's display of *T. rex* seems _____, even though it's just a skeleton.

APPLY IT NOW

Write two sentences for each of the following adjectives. Use the adjective before a noun in one sentence and as a subject complement in the other.

1. unusual   3. green
2. adventurous   4. colorful

3.8 Adjectives That Compare

Giganotosaurus

Most adjectives have three degrees of comparison: positive, comparative, and superlative. The **positive degree** of an adjective shows a quality of a noun. The **comparative degree** is used to compare two items or two sets of items. It is often used with *than*. The **superlative degree** is used to compare three or more items.

> The *T. rex* was a *large* predatory dinosaur. (positive)
> The *Carcharodontosaurus* may have been *larger* than the *T. rex*. (comparative)
> The *Giganotosaurus* may have been *largest* of all predatory dinosaurs. (superlative)

For adjectives of one syllable and some adjectives of two syllables (generally those ending in *y*), the comparative is formed by adding *-er* to the positive. The superlative is formed by adding *-est* to the positive.

POSITIVE	COMPARATIVE	SUPERLATIVE
smart	smarter	smartest
narrow	narrower	narrowest

To form the comparative and superlative degrees, follow these rules.

- If an adjective ends in *e,* add *-r* or *-st.*

tame	tamer	tamest

- If an adjective ends in *y* preceded by a consonant, change the *y* to *i* before adding *-er* or *-est.*

clumsy	clumsier	clumsiest

- If a single-syllable adjective ends in a consonant preceded by a vowel, double the consonant before adding *-er* or *-est.*

hot	hotter	hottest

Some adjectives have irregular forms of comparison.

POSITIVE	COMPARATIVE	SUPERLATIVE
good	better	best
well	better	best
bad	worse	worst

EXERCISE 1 Write the comparative and the superlative forms of these adjectives.

1. tiny
2. sad
3. brave
4. pretty
5. good
6. thin
7. light
8. happy
9. early
10. wise
11. easy
12. bad

EXERCISE 2 Identify the adjective in the comparative or superlative degree in each sentence. Tell the degree of each adjective.

1. The earliest dinosaurs lived during the Triassic period.

2. The Jurassic period was later than the Triassic.

3. During the Jurassic period, the climate was warmer than before, and dinosaurs flourished.

4. The longest dinosaur was probably *Seismosaurus*, a sauropod that was 120 to 150 feet long.

5. The latest period in which dinosaurs lived was the Cretaceous period.

Model of *Seismosaurus*

EXERCISE 3 Choose the correct word to complete each sentence.

1. The (bigger biggest) dinosaurs of all were the long-necked plant eaters called sauropods.

2. Meat-eating dinosaurs had (stronger strongest) legs and jaws than plant-eating dinosaurs.

3. Plant-eating dinosaurs had (larger largest) stomachs than meat eaters because plants are (harder hardest) to digest.

4. The (smaller smallest) dinosaur was probably *Compsognathus*, a meat-eating dinosaur that was three feet long.

5. Scientists think that the (faster fastest) dinosaurs ran 40 miles per hour.

6. The (heavier heaviest) dinosaur was probably *Argentinosaurus*, which weighed 100 tons.

APPLY IT NOW

Use each of these adjectives in a sentence.

1. scarier
2. hardest
3. softest
4. smarter
5. crunchier
6. longer

3.9 *More, Most* and *Less, Least*

Most adjectives of three or more syllables and some adjectives of two syllables do not add *-er* or *-est* to form the comparative and superlative degrees.

Instead, the comparative is formed by adding *more* or *less* before the positive form of the adjective. Form the superlative by adding *most* or *least* before the positive form of the adjective.

POSITIVE	COMPARATIVE	SUPERLATIVE
mysterious	more mysterious less mysterious	most mysterious least mysterious
famous	more famous less famous	most famous least famous

Dinosaurs can be *more mysterious* than suspense novels. (comparative)

I think the really huge dinosaurs are *most mysterious* of all. (superlative)

Insects are *less interesting* than *T. rex*. (comparative)

What is the *least interesting* dinosaur? (superlative)

You can check a dictionary for the proper forms of adjectives.

It is incorrect to use *more* or *less* and *-er* together, or *most* or *least* and *-est* together. Do not say "the more smarter dinosaur" or "the most smartest dinosaur."

EXERCISE 1 Write the comparative and superlative degrees for the positive form of each adjective. Use *more* and *most*.

1. powerful
2. difficult
3. generous
4. important
5. intelligent
6. courteous
7. frightful
8. fortunate
9. courageous

EXERCISE 2 Write the comparative and superlative degrees for each positive-degree adjective. Use *less* and *least*.

1. careful
2. delicious
3. astonishing
4. confusing
5. delicate
6. bizarre
7. dangerous
8. graceful
9. nervous

EXERCISE 3 Choose the correct adjective to complete each sentence.

1. Many people think that dinosaurs were the (more fascinating most fascinating) animals that ever lived.

2. The earth's climate was (more moderate most moderate) during the age of the reptiles than it is today.

3. (More intelligent Most intelligent) of all the dinosaurs was *Troodon*, a small meat eater.

4. It had to make quick decisions as it went after its prey, so it needed a (more efficient most efficient) brain.

5. The large, plant-eating sauropods were probably (less intelligent least intelligent) of all the dinosaurs.

6. *T. rex* was (more successful most successful) than other hunters because of its size and its sharp teeth and claws.

7. (More enormous Most enormous) of all dinosaur eggs was one about the size of a soccer ball.

8. The (more widespread most widespread) dinosaur was probably *Iguanodon*.

9. Were horns (more effective most effective) weapons for dinosaurs than clubs at the end of tails?

10. I think that paleontologists need to be (more patient most patient) than people in many other jobs.

11. Dinosaurs may have been (more agile most agile) than early researchers thought.

12. Blue whales are actually (more massive most massive) than any of the dinosaurs were.

The earth's climate during the dinosaur era was warmer than today's climate.

APPLY IT NOW

Compare and contrast two of your favorite books, movies, or TV shows. Write six sentences using these adjectives in the comparative or superlative form: *interesting, boring, humorous, exciting, suspenseful.*

3.10 *Fewer, Fewest and Less, Least*

Less, least, fewer, and *fewest* are used in comparing things. Use *less* and *least* with abstract nouns. Use *fewer* and *fewest* with concrete nouns.

Concrete nouns name things that you can see, touch, and count: *birds, trees, children.* They have plural forms. **Abstract nouns** name things that generally cannot be seen, touched, or counted: *sleep, sadness, patience.* They do not have plural forms.

Less and *fewer* are comparative forms and are used to compare two things or two sets of things.

Least and *fewest* are superlative forms and are used to compare more than two things.

COMPARATIVE

There were *fewer* types of plants during the Jurassic period than during the Cretaceous. (with a concrete noun)

There was *less* rain during the Triassic period. (with an abstract noun)

SUPERLATIVE

The *fewest* plants existed during the Triassic period. (with a concrete noun)

The *least* moisture was present during the Triassic period. (with an abstract noun)

Tell whether *less* or *fewer* should be used with each of these nouns.

    A dinosaurs   **B food**   **C footprints**

You are correct if you said the following:

    A fewer dinosaurs **B less food** **C fewer footprints**

Tell whether *least* or *fewest* should be used with these nouns.

    A forests   **B rain**   **C sunlight**

You are correct if you said the following:

    A fewest forests **B least rain** **C least sunlight**

EXERCISE 1 Write phrases with each noun and *less* or *fewer*. Tell whether each noun is a concrete noun or an abstract noun.

　　　EXAMPLE　**creatures**　　**fewer creatures, concrete**

1. mammals
2. knowledge
3. interest
4. heat
5. time
6. teeth
7. fossils
8. plants

EXERCISE 2 Write phrases with each noun and *least* or *fewest*. Tell whether each noun is a concrete noun or an abstract noun.

1. love
2. eggs
3. evidence
4. bones
5. intelligence
6. babies
7. nests
8. courage

EXERCISE 3 Choose the correct word to complete each sentence.

1. The (fewest fewer) animals are at the top of a food chain.
2. (Less Fewer) food for animals at the bottom of the food chain can mean starvation for animals at the top.
3. The animals who find the (fewest least) grass will die, which can affect the entire food chain.
4. (Fewer Less) trees can also have a negative effect.
5. There were (fewer less) carnivores than herbivores because the carnivores were at the top of the food chain.
6. The (fewest least) fossils in the museum are in the east wing because it is under construction.
7. Scientists have (fewer less) evidence about individual dinosaurs than a person might expect.
8. Of all the dinosaurs, scientists have the (fewest least) amount of information about the smaller dinosaurs.
9. The reason is that scientists have found (fewer less) skeletons of small dinosaurs than large ones.
10. Smaller dinosaurs were more likely to be eaten, so they have left (fewer less) fossils.

APPLY IT NOW

Imagine you are on a class trip to a museum. Write five sentences using phrases from those you wrote in Exercises 1 and 2.

3.11 Interrogative Adjectives

An **interrogative adjective** is used in asking a question. The interrogative adjectives are *what, which,* and *whose.* An interrogative adjective comes before a noun.

> **What** prey did *T. rex* eat?
> **Which** dinosaurs had spoon-shaped teeth?
> **Whose** dinosaur sketches are on the table?

What is used for asking about people or things.

> **What** animals should we have in our classroom?

Which is usually used to ask about one of two or more people or things.

> **Which** dinosaur was bigger—*Argentinosaurus* or *Seismosaurus*?

Whose asks about possession.

> **Whose** model of a *T. rex* is this?

Can you identify the interrogative adjective in this question and the noun it goes with?

> **What** plants did *Brachiosaurus* eat?

You are correct if you said that *what* is the interrogative adjective and that *plants* is the noun it goes with.

EXERCISE 1 Identify the interrogative adjective in each sentence.

1. Can you identify which dinosaur had long, sharp, curved claws?
2. What discoveries did the scientist Paul Sereno make?
3. Which dinosaur was a meat eater—*Brachiosaurus* or *Giganotosaurus*?
4. Which dinosaur ate fish primarily—*Baryonyx* or *Velociraptor*?
5. What kinds of fossils did you see at the museum?
6. Whose presentation on the *Allosaurus* was best?
7. What question would you like to ask about *T. rex*?
8. Do you know what kind of food *Argentinosaurus* ate?
9. Whose favorite dinosaur is the *Spinosaurus*?
10. In what period did *Triceratops* appear?

EXERCISE 2 Identify the interrogative adjective in each sentence. Then tell the noun it goes with.

1. Whose job is it to study fossils?
2. Which continents have the most fossils?
3. In what era did that dinosaur appear?
4. Which museum has the most kinds of dinosaur fossils?
5. The dinosaurs on display at the American Museum of Natural History are which?
6. Whose task is it to find dinosaur fossils?
7. What dinosaur would you like to know more about?
8. The facts about dinosaurs you find the most surprising are what?
9. What theories do scientists have about whether dinosaurs were hot-blooded or cold-blooded?
10. The books that give clear, interesting information about dinosaurs are whose?

EXERCISE 3 Complete each sentence with the correct interrogative adjective. More than one adjective may be correct.

1. _____ large group of animals did dinosaurs belong to?
2. John, please tell me _____ group of dinosaurs had clubs on their tails—*Ankylosaurs* or *Ceratopsians*?
3. _____ event might have ended the era of the dinosaurs?
4. Do you know _____ theory it is that a meteorite caused the extinction of the dinosaurs?
5. _____ kinds of tools do paleontologists use?
6. _____ turn is it to make the next presentation on dinosaurs?
7. Class, _____ interesting fact did you learn about dinosaurs?
8. _____ presentation was most interesting?

APPLY IT NOW

Work with a partner to choose a topic you are studying. Write 10 questions with interrogative adjectives to ask about the topic. Use books and the Internet to help find the answers.

Adjective Review

3.1 Find the descriptive adjectives in these sentences.

1. Mount St. Helens is now an active volcano.

2. The previously quiet volcano erupted in 1980.

3. Gray smoke billowed out of its cone.

4. A huge landslide swept down the steep sides of the mountain.

3.2 Complete each sentence with a proper adjective formed from the proper noun in parentheses.

5. _____ wool is famous around the world. (Ireland)

6. _____ chocolates are delicious. (Switzerland)

7. Authentic _____ goulash contains paprika. (Hungary)

8. Seaweed is used in _____ sushi. (Japan)

3.3 Identify the articles in these sentences. Tell whether each is a definite article or an indefinite article.

9. Did you know an invertebrate has no backbone?

10. The longhorn beetle is an invertebrate.

11. A sea star does not have a backbone.

12. The life cycle of an ant is interesting.

3.4 Tell whether each italic phrase tells about the same person, place, or thing or about different people, places, or things.

13. Examples of invertebrates include *a millipede and a worm.*

14. A shrimp is *an arthropod and invertebrate.*

15. The list of anthropods includes *a crab and a lobster.*

16. My aunt was *an author and illustrator* of a book on shellfish.

3.5 Write the correct demonstrative adjective to complete each sentence. Follow the directions in parentheses.

17. _____ odd-looking plant is a Venus flytrap. (far)

18. _____ leaves look like teeth. (near)

19. _____ leaves are actually sensitive hairs. (far)

20. The plant ate _____ fly. (far)

21. People are interested in _____ unusual plant. (near)

3.6 Identify the adjective that tells how many or about how many in each sentence.

22. Beaver dams can be several feet tall.

23. Beavers will pile many sticks together to build a dam.

24. Each dam is inhabited by a beaver family.

25. A beaver can stay under water for 15 minutes.

3.7 Identify the subject complement in each sentence. Tell the noun the subject complement describes.

26. The coral reef was quite beautiful.

27. The tropical fish near the reef were bright with color.

28. Coral feels rough.

29. However, the substance itself is really delicate.

3.8 Identify the adjective in the comparative or superlative degree in each sentence. Tell the degree of each adjective.

30. The largest organ in the world was displayed in 1904.

31. The organ was made to be louder than others.

32. The biggest pipe on the organ was 32 feet tall.

33. It was later broken down into smaller pieces and sent to Philadelphia.

3.9 Choose the correct word to complete each sentence.

34. Becky is the (more most) courteous person in class.

35. She is (less least) talkative than Donovan.

36. Abigail is the (more most) generous girl I know.

37. She always donates toys and books to those with the (less least) amount of things.

38. It is hard to tell if Joe or Sandra is (most more) excited about the ball game.

3.10 Choose the correct word to complete each sentence.

39. Years ago people had (fewer less) interest in endangered birds.

40. Today there are many (fewer less) whooping cranes than there were 150 years ago.

41. (Less Fewer) area for a habitat caused the decline in numbers.

3.11 Identify the interrogative adjective in each sentence.

42. What facts should we include in our report?

43. Whose note cards are these?

44. Which diagram is clearer— this one or that one?

45. Which student will talk about the brain—Tom or Michelle?

Go to www.voyagesinenglish.com for more activities.

Adjective Challenge

Read the paragraph and answer the questions.

1. Which state is the youngest state in the United States?
2. Hawaii became a state in 1959, and it consists entirely of islands.
3. Hawaii is beautiful at any time of year. 4. On the islands you are surrounded by sparkling blue seas, clear waterfalls, beautiful palms, and colorful flowers. 5. Polynesian wanderers first settled Hawaii, and most Hawaiians of today are descended from them. 6. These settlers also started many of Hawaii's most delightful customs. 7. The first and last word the visitor to Hawaii hears is *aloha.* 8. *Aloha* means "love" and is used for both *hello* and *good-bye.* 9. According to Hawaiians, however, this word has a deeper meaning than hello or good-bye.

1. In sentence 1 is the adjective *youngest* in the positive, comparative, or superlative degree?

2. In sentence 1 what kind of adjective is *which*?

3. What is the article in sentence 2? Is it definite or indefinite?

4. In sentence 3 find an adjective used as a subject complement.

5. In sentence 4 find five descriptive adjectives.

6. In sentence 5 what kind of adjective is *Polynesian*?

7. In sentence 5 what kind of adjective is *most*?

8. In sentence 6 find the demonstrative adjective. Is it singular or plural?

9. In sentence 6 find a descriptive adjective. What degree is it in?

10. In sentence 9 is the article definite or indefinite?

11. In sentence 9 find two adjectives. Tell what degree each adjective is.

Verbs

4.1 Action Verbs and Being Verbs

A **verb** is a word used to express action or being.

> **The ice cream *melts* in the sun.** (action verb)
> **The ice cream *is* delicious.** (being verb)

In each sentence the subject is *ice cream*. In the first sentence, *melts* expresses action. In the second sentence, *is* expresses being. Both words are verbs.

An **action verb** expresses action. Here are a few action verbs: *dance, run, dream, write, sing, study, ring, chime, clang, toll,* and *jingle.*

A **being verb** expresses a state of being. The verb *be* and its various forms are the most common being verbs: *is, are, was, were, am, be, been,* and *being.*

Can you find the verb in each of these sentences? Is it an action verb or a being verb?

> **There are many fascinating stories about ice cream.**
> **Marco Polo possibly tasted ice cream in Asia in about 1254.**

You are correct if you said *are* is the verb in the first sentence. It expresses being. You are correct if you said *tasted* is the verb in the second sentence. It expresses action—the act of tasting.

EXERCISE 1 Identify the action verb or verbs in each sentence.

1. Americans eat a lot of ice cream.
2. I read a fascinating article about the history of ice cream.
3. The Chinese discovered an ice-preservation method—the use of ice houses.
4. They used this technique 3,000 years ago.
5. Over time, people added syrups and flavorings to the ice.
6. At first chefs kept the addition of cream to the ice a secret.
7. Only royalty served ice cream at meals in the 1600s.
8. By the 1700s, however, many people made and sold ice cream.
9. The first ice cream parlor in the United States opened in 1776.
10. Presidents Washington and Jefferson gave ice cream to guests.

EXERCISE 2 Identify the being verb in each sentence.

1. Crushed ice with syrup or fruit was probably the original iced dessert.

2. The Emperor Nero's favorite dessert was snow mixed with honey and fresh fruit.

3. Fruit, ice, and milk are the typical ingredients for sherbet.

4. The major ingredient of ice cream is cream.

5. Various sweet syrups are still popular additions to ice cream.

6. Frozen yogurt was first a dessert in the United States in the 1970s.

7. At first frozen yogurt was more tart than ice cream.

8. Now there are sweet varieties too.

9. The ingredients for a smoothie are frozen yogurt and fresh fruit.

10. A popular flavor combination is strawberry and banana.

EXERCISE 3 Identify the verb in each sentence. Tell whether it is an action verb or a being verb.

1. What is the history of the ice-cream sundae?

2. In the late 1800s, people enjoyed ice-cream sodas.

3. Their ingredients were ice cream, syrup, and soda water.

4. In Evanston, Illinois, a law prohibited the sale of soda water on Sunday.

5. So ice-cream parlors eliminated the soda water.

6. The result was the ice-cream sundae.

EXERCISE 4 Add a verb to each sentence. Tell whether each is an action verb or a being verb.

1. The most popular ice-cream flavor _____ vanilla.

2. Many people also _____ chocolate.

3. Many people _____ sprinkles on their ice cream.

4. Fruit _____ a healthful addition to many snacks.

5. People _____ ice cream in cones.

APPLY IT NOW

Supply at least two action verbs for each of the following nouns. Write two sentences with each noun as a subject.

chefs   volcanoes acrobats
musicians boats   horses

4.2 Verb Phrases

Cacao pods

A **verb phrase** is a group of words that does the work of a single verb. A verb phrase contains a main verb and one or more **helping verbs** such as *is, are, has, have, can,* and *do.*

ONE-WORD VERB	VERB PHRASE
Manufacturers *use* cacao beans for chocolate.	Manufacturers *have used* cacao beans for chocolate for hundreds of years.
Rain forests in the Americas *have* cacao trees.	The cacao tree *can be found* in the rain forests of the Americas.

In each sentence in the left column, the verb is only one word. In the right column, the verbs are verb phrases of two or more words. Groups of words such as *have used* and *can be found* are verb phrases. Each phrase does the work of a single verb.

In questions and some statements, the parts of the verb phrase may be separated.

> *Did* chocolate *originate* in the Americas?
> Chocolate bars *were* not *invented* until 1876.

Here are some common helping verbs.

> am, is, are, was, were, be, being, been
> has, have, had
> do, does, did
> may, can, might, could, must, should, would, will

Can you identify the verb phrase in each sentence?

> Cacao beans were used as money by early Americans.
> You can see cacao trees at most botanical gardens.

You are correct if you said *were used* is the verb phrase in the first sentence and *can see* is the verb phrase in the second sentence.

EXERCISE 1 Identify the verb phrase in each sentence.

1. The seeds from a cacao tree are processed for chocolate.
2. The ancestors of people in Mexico and Central America have been credited with the discovery of chocolate.
3. The Maya and the Aztec peoples did process chocolate centuries ago.
4. Did they mix the ground seeds with spices and water?
5. Such a mixture could have been the first chocolate drink.
6. By the 1600s hot chocolate had become popular in Europe.
7. Its taste and texture have changed over the years.
8. Its many varieties are enjoyed by people the world over.
9. My mom was boiling hot chocolate for us after school.
10. She has added peppermint sticks and orange peels to her recipe in the past.

Traditional Mexican chocolate

EXERCISE 2 Identify the main verb and the helping verb in each sentence.

1. Have you ever read anything about the cacao tree?
2. It can grow only in tropical climates.
3. Cacao trees are usually planted in shady areas.
4. After a few years, they are transplanted to sunny areas.
5. A full-grown cacao tree can be 25 feet tall.
6. Some trees, though, have grown to 60 feet or more.
7. As many as 50 cacao beans can be found in a pod.
8. The cacao beans are dried for chocolate.
9. How many beans does it take for a pound of chocolate?
10. It may take about 400 beans.

APPLY IT NOW

Write six sentences using these verb phrases: *can eat, will finish, have been, have seen, had traveled, might try.*

4.3 Principal Parts of Verbs

A verb has **four principal parts:** the **present,** the **present participle,** the **past,** and the **past participle.**

PRESENT	PRESENT PARTICIPLE	PAST	PAST PARTICIPLE
talk	talking	talked	talked
name	naming	named	named
stop	stopping	stopped	stopped

The present participle is formed by adding *-ing* to the present. The present participle is often used with a form of the helping verb *be* (*am, is, are, was, were,* and *been*).

> **My friend** *prepares* **delicious salads.** (present)
> **He** *is preparing* **a chicken salad for lunch.** (present participle)

The past and the past participle of regular verbs are formed by adding *-d* or *-ed* to the present. The past participle is often used with the helping verb *has, have,* or *had.*

> **My friend** *prepared* **a shrimp salad yesterday.** (past)
> **He** *has prepared* **a different salad each day.** (past participle)

To form the present participle of verbs ending in *e,* drop the final *e* and add *-ing: prepare + ing = preparing.*

> **My friend is** *preparing* **a shrimp salad.** (present participle)

To form the present participle of a verb ending in a consonant following a vowel, double the consonant before adding *-ing: chop + ing = chopping.* To form the past participle, also double the consonant before adding *-ed: chop + ed = chopped.*

> **I am** *chopping* **the vegetables for a salad.** (present participle)
> **I** *chopped* **the vegetables for a salad.** (past participle)

When the subject is a singular noun or *he, she,* or *it,* add *-s* to the present part of the verb.

> **My friend** *prepares* **delicious salads.** (present)
> **He often** *serves* **his salads to friends.** (present)

EXERCISE 1 Write the present participle, the past, and the past participle of each verb.

1. call
2. skate
3. visit
4. serve
5. explore
6. skip
7. look
8. carry
9. cry
10. walk
11. type
12. bake

EXERCISE 2 Tell whether the verb in italics is present, present participle, past, or past participle. For verbs ending in *-ed*, look for a helping verb to see if the form is a past participle.

1. People are *consuming* more and more yogurt nowadays.
2. People *obtain* it in small cartons in supermarkets.
3. Yogurt has *existed* for thousands of years.
4. Yogurt is *produced* by special bacteria in milk.
5. The Bulgar people are *credited* with the discovery of yogurt.
6. Yogurt *remained* a European food until the early 1900s.

EXERCISE 3 Complete each sentence with the form of the verb in parentheses.

1. Fruit is often _____ to yogurt. (add—past participle)
2. People _____ its flavor in the yogurt. (like—present)
3. I'm _____ berries into mine. (stir—present participle)
4. Have you ever _____ strawberry yogurt? (taste—past participle)
5. I _____ yogurt at home for a smoothie. (prepare—past)
6. My dad _____ a variety of healthful snacks for us. (buy—present)
7. I am _____ out the granola pieces because I don't like them. (pick—present participle)
8. My sister _____ our dad would buy our favorite cereal. (hope—past)
9. She has _____ it into her yogurt before and liked it. (mix—past participle)

APPLY IT NOW

Think about activities you do during the winter. Write a sentence using each verb in the principal part in parentheses.
1. describe (present)
2. try (past participle)
3. study (present participle)
4. provide (past)

Grammar in Action. Identify the past principal parts in the first paragraph of the excerpt on page 328.

4.4 Irregular Verbs

The simple past and the past participle of irregular verbs do not end in *-ed*. These parts of irregular verbs take a variety of forms.

PRESENT	PAST	PAST PARTICIPLE
bring	brought	brought
come	came	come
have	had	had
know	knew	known
teach	taught	taught

I sometimes *buy* lunch in the cafeteria. (present)
I *bought* lunch there yesterday. (past)
I have *bought* macaroni and cheese for lunch on occasion. (past participle)

Which word correctly completes the sentence?

We (knowed knew) what was for lunch.

You are correct if you said *knew*. The simple past part of *know* is *knew*.

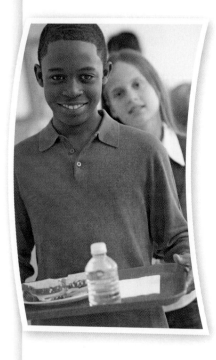

EXERCISE 1 Write the present, the past, and the past participle of each verb. Check a dictionary if you need help.

1. give
2. leave
3. fall
4. do
5. stand
6. swim
7. write
8. sink

9. grow
10. make
11. hurt
12. see
13. begin
14. bite
15. dig
16. build

EXERCISE 2 Complete each sentence with the past or the past participle of the irregular verb in parentheses. Remember to use the past participle if the sentence has a helping verb.

1. The Spanish explorers _____ (find) many foods new to Europe in South America.

2. Potatoes were _____ (grow) in the Andes mountains.

3. Fried potatoes _____ (become) popular in the 1800s.

4. Joseph Malines, a British restaurant owner, _____ (put) a dish of fried fish and fried potatoes on his menu.

5. This _____ (become) Britain's national dish, under the name of "fish and chips."

6. The French also _____ (make) fried potatoes.

7. In World War I, American soldiers _____ (eat) them there.

8. These soldiers _____ (give) the fried potato a new name.

9. They _____ (say) it should be called the "French fry."

10. Billions of French fries are _____ (eat) each year.

11. My father _____ (teach) me how to make mashed potatoes.

12. I hadn't _____ (know) the potato had such an interesting history.

EXERCISE 3 Complete the paragraph by using either the past or the past participle of the word in parentheses. Some verbs are regular.

People all over the world have _____ (1. put) ketchup on their French fries for years. Did you know that people _____ (2. have) ketchup in the 1600s? It _____ (3. begin) in China as a fish sauce and was _____ (4. call) *kechiap*. Travelers _____ (5. bring) it to the United States, but they _____ (6. use) somewhat different ingredients in their ketchup. I have _____ (7. hear) that some ketchup originally _____ (8. have) nuts in it. Enjoying ketchup (without the nuts) on fries has _____ (9. become) an American tradition.

APPLY IT NOW

Write five sentences about the origin of your family or ancestors. Underline the irregular verbs and tell whether each is simple past or past participle.

Tech Tip With an adult, research your family origin online.

4.5 More Irregular Verbs

Here are the principal parts of some other irregular verbs.

PRESENT	PRESENT PARTICIPLE	PAST	PAST PARTICIPLE
break	breaking	broke	broken
choose	choosing	chose	chosen
go	going	went	gone
see	seeing	saw	seen
take	taking	took	taken

Which verb form completes the sentence correctly?

Have you (went gone) to the new pizzeria already?

You are correct if you chose *gone.* The helping verb *Have* comes before it, so the past participle is correct.

EXERCISE 1 Complete each sentence with the correct form of *break.*

1. We _____ the bread and dipped it into the olive oil.

2. I almost _____ the glass when I reached for the salt.

3. I seldom _____ things by being careless.

4. After my mom had _____ the fortune cookie, she read the fortune.

5. Don't _____ your curfew or Dad will be angry.

EXERCISE 2 Complete each sentence with the correct form of *see.*

1. I _____ Hannah at the pizzeria last night.

2. We _____ the chef making pizza.

3. Earlier Hannah had _____ the pizza go into the large brick oven.

4. We usually _____ kids from school at the pizzeria down the street.

5. _____ if you can eat just one slice.

EXERCISE 3 Complete each sentence with the correct form of *go*.

1. Our family always _____ to the skating rink on Friday.

2. We _____ there two weeks ago for Family Night.

3. Friends and I had _____ to Skate-O-Rama before bowling on my last birthday.

4. Are you _____ with the group or will you meet us there?

5. Hank _____ to the wrong rink last year.

6. My mom and I are _____ there right now.

EXERCISE 4 Complete each sentence with the correct form of *choose*.

1. Bob _____ bacon bits as a topping for his salad.

2. He usually _____ mushrooms though.

3. Greg and I are _____ our dressing now.

4. I have _____ blue cheese before.

5. What toppings have you _____ for your salad?

6. Malcolm is _____ different vegetables because they help him stay healthy.

EXERCISE 5 Complete each sentence with the correct form of *take*.

1. We are _____ our new puppy home today.

2. We have _____ the puppy with the white spot on his head.

3. Mia had _____ her puppy home a week ago.

4. She _____ it to the park and to the dog beach.

5. We are _____ obedience class together with our puppies next month.

6. Last night, George and Sandie _____ many photographs of the new puppy to show Grandma.

APPLY IT NOW

Imagine that you and a friend spent the summer working on a special tree house. Use the irregular verbs on page 86 and 88 to answer these questions.

1. How did you get ready to build?
2. What problems did you have?
3. What did you choose to include in the tree house?

Tech Tip Copy five irregular verbs from an online article.

Verbs • 89

4.6 Simple Tenses

The **tense of a verb** shows the time of its action. There are three simple tenses: the present, the past, and the future.

The **simple present tense** tells about something that is always true or about an action that happens again and again. Use the present part of the verb to form the present tense. If the subject is a third person singular noun or *he, she,* or *it,* add *-s* to the end of the verb.

The **simple past tense** tells about an action that happened in the past. Use the past part of the verb to express the past tense. The past tense of regular verbs ends in *ed.*

The **future tense** tells about an action that will happen in the future. Use *will* or a form of *be* with *going to* and the present part of the verb to express future tense.

Simple present:	We *eat* Greek salad for lunch every Tuesday.
	She *eats* shrimp salad every Friday.
Simple past:	We *ate* tossed salad last night.
Future:	We *will eat* Caesar salad tomorrow.
	We *are going* to have fruit salad for dessert.

What is the verb in each sentence? What is its tense?

A We always make our dinner salad in a wooden bowl.
B Last night we put tomatoes and olives on our salad.
C I will order a taco salad for lunch tomorrow.

You are correct if you said the following:

A. The verb is *make;* the tense is simple present.
B. The verb is *put;* the tense is simple past.
C. The verb phrase is *will order;* the tense is future.

EXERCISE 1 Find the verb or verb phrase in each sentence. Tell whether the tense of each is simple present, simple past, or future.

1. Many cultures make a food similar to pizza.

2. The ancient Greeks baked a similar flat, round bread.

3. Tomatoes possess a fairly recent history in Europe.

4. Explorers took tomatoes to Europe from the Americas in the 1500s.

5. When will the tomatoes and the bread finally come together as pizza?

6. According to tradition, the combination of the two into pizza occurred in Naples in the 1800s.

7. Raffaele Esposito created a special pizza for Queen Margherita of Italy in 1899.

8. People still eat a "margherita" pizza today.

9. You are going to taste it also.

10. Later, Marcy will tell us her favorite pizza toppings.

Queen Margherita

EXERCISE 2 Complete each sentence with the form of the verb in parentheses.

1. The Italians _____ pizza to the United States in the late 1800s. (introduce—simple past)

2. During the late 1950s, a company _____ the first frozen pizza into what we know today. (develop—simple past)

3. I often _____ frozen pizza in the microwave. (cook—simple present)

4. I usually _____ pizza with mushrooms. (eat—simple present)

5. I _____ a different pizza tomorrow. (try—future)

6. Next Tuesday is Colin's birthday, and we _____ him at the Marliotti's Pizza Parlor. (surprise—future)

7. John _____ to keep it a secret because Colin loves surprises. (decide—past)

8. He _____ Colin's birthday in a new way every year. (celebrate—present)

9. Megan _____ Colin to the party blindfolded later in the afternoon. (bring—future)

10. Colin _____ off the blindfold as we shout "Happy Birthday!" (take—future)

APPLY IT NOW

Write six sentences about things you do every day. Change the time and tense, but keep the same verb for all. Go back a hundred years. Then go forward a hundred years.

Example: I watch television every day. I watched the first airplane flight by Orville Wright. I will watch people ride bicycles that can fly.

4.7 Progressive Tenses

The **progressive tenses** consist of a form of the verb *be* (*is, am, are, was, were*) and the present participle.

The **present progressive tense** tells what is happening now. It is used for ongoing actions. The present progressive tense uses a present form of the verb *be* (*am, is, are*) and the present participle.

> My mother *is cooking* a pot roast for dinner.

The **past progressive tense** tells what was happening in the past. The past progressive tense uses a past form of the verb *be* (*was, were*) and the present participle.

> We *were eating* our roast when the doorbell rang.

The **future progressive tense** tells about something that will be happening in the future. The future progressive uses *will, is going to,* or *are going to* with *be* and the present participle.

> Mom *will be serving* leftover pot roast tomorrow.
> She *is going to be preparing* several vegetables also.

What is the verb phrase in each sentence? What is its tense?

> A I was looking for new pot-roast recipes.
> B I am making a spicy side dish tonight.
> C My sister will be reading the recipe as I mix the ingredients.

You are correct if you said the following:

A. The verb phrase is *was looking;* it is past progressive. It has *was,* a past form of the verb *be,* and the present participle.

B. The verb phrase is *am making;* it is present progressive. It has *am,* a present form of the verb *be,* and the present participle.

C. The verb phrase is *will be reading;* it is future progressive. It has *will* with *be* and the present participle.

EXERCISE 1 Identify the verb phrase in the progressive tenses in each sentence. Tell whether each phrase is in the present progressive, the past progressive, or the future progressive tense.

1. We were planning our meals for the week yesterday.
2. We are going to be making pasta primavera for dinner.
3. I am cutting the onions now.
4. My eyes are tearing a little.
5. Ron is cutting the zucchini and the carrots.
6. Harry is putting garlic and oil in the pan.
7. My sister will be helping us if she gets home in time.
8. We were measuring the olive oil when the phone rang.
9. The pasta was boiling while we were cleaning up.

EXERCISE 2 Complete each sentence with the form of the verb in parentheses.

1. We _____ Dad cook last night. (help—past progressive)
2. I _____ the flour in a bowl when the phone rang. (put—past progressive)
3. The bowl slipped from my hands and broke as I _____ for the phone. (reach—past progressive)
4. We _____ curry for dinner. (have—future progressive)
5. The telephone _____ now. (ring—present progressive)
6. I _____ the sauce, and I don't plan to answer the telephone. (stir—present progressive)
7. We _____ these leftovers tomorrow. (enjoy—future progressive)
8. Dad _____ the table when the doorbell rang. (set—past progressive)
9. Now, Mom _____ for ordering take-out as a backup for Dad's dinner. (apologize—present progressive)

APPLY IT NOW

Write a short letter to someone you haven't talked to in more than a year. Make two comparisons between then and now. Use the present progressive and past progressive tenses.

Grammar in Action.
Identify the verbs in progressive tenses in the last paragraph of the excerpt on page 328.

4.8 Present Perfect Tense

The **present perfect tense** uses the past participle and a form of *have* (*have* or *has*).

The present perfect tense tells about an action that happened at some indefinite time or an action that started in the past and continues into the present time.

> **The students *have learned* about ethnic foods.**
> **He *has helped* in the kitchen since he was seven.**

What are the verb phrases in the present perfect tense in these sentences?

> **I have chosen some recipes from that cookbook.**
> **Louis has never tasted squid.**

You are correct if you said that in the first sentence, *have chosen* is in the present perfect tense, and in the second sentence, *has tasted* is in the present perfect tense.

EXERCISE 1 Identify the present perfect tense verb phrase in each sentence.

1. Our class has organized an international food day.
2. The students have decided to bring dishes characteristic of various countries.
3. Some students have already chosen what dishes to bring.
4. We have decorated the cafeteria for the event.
5. Sergio has come with an Italian eggplant dish.
6. His grandmother has used the recipe for many years.
7. Nguyen has brought the ingredients for Vietnamese spring rolls.
8. I have used my mother's instructions to make German potato salad.

EXERCISE 2 Identify the verb phrases in the present perfect tense in the sentences below. Not all sentences are in the present perfect tense.

1. Richard has a recipe for peanut butter soup from Ghana.
2. He has put peanut butter, yams, and chicken into the soup.
3. I have not tasted it yet, but I like peanut butter, so I think I'll like it.
4. Pedro's dad has prepared his specialty, a paella.
5. The Spanish dish contains rice, tomatoes, and shellfish.
6. Bina has prepared a chicken curry from India.
7. Around it she has placed small dishes of condiments.
8. Elaine and I have placed some coconut and raisins on top of our curry.
9. Michael has never eaten curry before tonight.

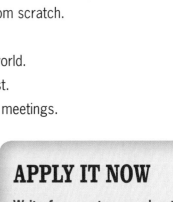

EXERCISE 3 Complete each sentence with the present perfect tense of the verb in parentheses.

1. Arun _____ (mix) watermelon, ice, and honey for a Thai dessert.
2. We _____ (put) it into the refrigerator to stay cool.
3. Marta _____ (bring) some tortillas.
4. She _____ (get) some cheese, lettuce, and beans as filling for tacos.
5. Jane's parents _____ (make) their own scones from scratch.
6. We _____ (spread) a special cream on ours.
7. We _____ (try) so many meals from around the world.
8. Our food club _____ (grow) into such a tasty feast.
9. Jamal and Cindy _____ (open) their home for our meetings.
10. I _____ (want) to eat my way around the world.
11. Chris _____ (sample) Padma's spicy curry.
12. The organizers _____ (pack) the leftovers for everyone to take home.

APPLY IT NOW

Write four sentences about interesting foods that you have tried and four sentences about foods that you haven't tried but would like to try. Use the present perfect tense.

4.9 Past Perfect Tense

The **past perfect tense** tells about a past action that was completed before another past action started.

The past perfect tense is formed by using *had* and the past participle of the verb.

> After Italians *had introduced* pizza to the United States, it became a popular food here.
> Before I tasted pizza with pineapple topping, I *had* not *thought* of it as an appealing ingredient.
> By the 1950s the Chicago deep-dish pizza *had become* popular.

In the first sentence, the action of the verb phrase in the past perfect (*had introduced*) occurred before the action of the other verb (*became*). In the second sentence, the action of the verb phrase in the past perfect (*had thought*) occurred before the action of the verb *tasted*. In the third sentence, the action of the verb in the past perfect (*had become*) occurred before the time given (*the 1950s*).

Can you identify the verb in the past perfect in this sentence? Can you tell what action the verb preceded?

> I had cooked supper before mom arrived home.

You are correct if you said the verb *had cooked* is in the past perfect. Its action occurred before the action of the verb *arrived*.

EXERCISE 1 Identify the verb phrase in the past perfect tense in each sentence.

1. I wrote my report on food history after I had gathered a lot of information from books and Web sites.

2. Before 10,000 BC people had developed bread making.

3. By 2400 BC people in China had discovered the pleasures of tea.

4. According to legend, after a Chinese emperor had ordered the boiling of water for health reasons, some tea leaves fell into the hot water.

5. By 100 AD the Chinese had formed rice and wheat into long noodles for ease in eating.

6. Before the Spanish came to the Americas, people in Europe had not known about tomatoes, potatoes, squash, or corn.

7. Before 1870 bananas had been rare in the United States; now they are the world's most popular fruit.

8. Peanut butter had not joined jelly in sandwiches until the 1900s.

EXERCISE 2 Complete each sentence with the past perfect tense of the verb in parentheses.

1. I decided to try a simple recipe for frozen yogurt treats after I _____ (find) it while doing research on my food project.

2. After I _____ (got) a cup of yogurt, a cup of fruit juice, and a teaspoon of vanilla, I mixed them together.

3. After I _____ (pour) the mixture into paper cups, I put a stick into each one and put the cups into the freezer.

4. Before I ate one of the frozen treats, I _____ (run) hot water it.

5. After we _____ (eat) all the treats, we decided to make another batch.

EXERCISE 3 Write sentences with the past perfect tense. Use the verbs in Column A in the past perfect tense. Use the verbs in Column B in the past tense.

EXAMPLE   **taste the bread   want the recipe**
After I had tasted the bread, I wanted the recipe.

Column A	Column B
1. get the recipe	read it carefully
2. gather the ingredients	follow the directions
3. put the bread in the oven	clean the kitchen
4. take the bread out of the oven	taste a slice
5. let the bread cool	offer it to my family

APPLY IT NOW

Write a paragraph about the steps required in making one of your favorite foods. Use the past perfect tense in your writing. When you are finished, circle each verb phrase in the past perfect tense.

4.10 Future Perfect Tense

The **future perfect tense** is used to talk about a future event that will be started and completed before another future event begins. It is formed by using *will have* and the past participle.

> **Jan and Ben *will have made* supper by the time you arrive home.**

The verb in the future perfect tense is *will have made.* It indicates something that will start in the future but that will be finished before the action described by the other verb, *arrive,* begins.

> **We *will have eaten* supper by seven o'clock tonight, and then I'll watch the game on TV.**

The verb in the future perfect tense is *will have eaten.* It tells about an action that will begin in the future but will be completed before the time mentioned, seven o'clock.

Can you identify the verb in the future perfect tense in this sentence? Can you tell the action the verb will precede?

> **Our group will have decided on the topic for our project by next Monday, after which we will assign roles.**

You are correct if you said that the verb in the future perfect tense is *will have decided.* It describes an action that will start and end before next Monday, the time given. It will also be completed before the group assigns roles.

EXERCISE 1 Identify the verb phrase in the future perfect tense in each sentence.

1. By Friday night we will have finished the preparations for the big family picnic on Saturday.
2. By then Uncle Joe will have raised the tent in our yard.
3. Aunt Sally will have made eight apple pies.
4. Dad will have bought lots of juice and water.
5. I will have carried many chairs into the tent.
6. My brothers will have arranged tables in the tent.
7. We will have borrowed many dishes from our neighbors.
8. My mom will have phoned everyone to confirm arrivals.

EXERCISE 2 Complete each sentence with the future perfect tense of the verb in parentheses.

1. By Saturday morning I _____ all the platters. (wash)
2. Susan _____ the decorations on the table. (place)
3. Uncle Peter _____ lots of tomatoes and carrots from his garden for the salads. (pick)
4. Our cousins from out of town _____. (arrive)
5. We _____ chairs from our neighbors. (borrow)
6. By then I _____ my cousin Al and his daughter Danielle for the first time. (meet)
7. By late Sunday afternoon, the guests _____ most of the food. (eat)
8. My uncle _____ the children with his magic tricks. (entertain)

EXERCISE 3 Complete each sentence with the verb *attend* in the tense in parentheses.

1. Susan _____ many family reunions. (present perfect)
2. In fact, she _____ a family reunion before she was one year old. (past perfect)
3. She _____ every reunion for the last 10 years. (present perfect)
4. By next month she _____ 12 reunions in all. (future perfect)

EXERCISE 4 Complete each sentence with the form of the verb in parentheses.

1. I wish I _____ to a family reunion before this year. (be—past perfect)
2. I _____ many emails to my cousin Zach. (write—present perfect)
3. We just _____ in person for the first time. (meet—present perfect)
4. By tonight I _____ for the first time to several relatives. (speak—future perfect)
5. I _____ e-mail addresses with a lot of family members. (exchange—future perfect)

APPLY IT NOW

You are having a party. Write five sentences about what you will do in the meantime to prepare for it. Use the future perfect tense.
Example: By two weeks before the party, I will have sent invitations.

4.11 Linking Verbs

A **linking verb** links, or joins, a subject with a subject complement that identifies or describes the subject. The subject complement may be a noun, a pronoun, or an adjective.

The verb *be* and its various forms are the most common linking verbs: *am, is, are, was, were, have been, has been, had been,* and *will be.* Some other common linking verbs are *become, feel, grow, look, remain, seem, smell, sound,* and *taste.*

Broccoli *is* an extremely healthful vegetable.

In this sentence the linking verb is *is.* The subject complement is the noun *vegetable*; it renames the subject *broccoli.*

These bananas *seem* ripe.

In this sentence the linking verb is *seem.* The subject complement is the adjective *ripe;* it describes the subject *bananas.*

The health teacher *will be* she.

In the sentence the linking verb is *will be.* The subject complement is the pronoun *she.* It renames the subject *teacher.*

Can you find the linking verb in the following sentence? Can you name both the subject complement and its part of speech?

These peaches look rotten with their darkened skin.

The linking verb is *look.* The subject complement is *rotten,* which is an adjective.

EXERCISE 1 Complete each sentence with a linking verb.

1. Vegetables and fruits _____ healthful foods.
2. Spinach _____ rich in many nutrients, such as iron and fiber.
3. Broccoli _____ good, especially the way Mom makes it.
4. Some pears in the fruit bowl _____ ripe.
5. The bananas in the bowl _____ green.
6. This peach _____ sweet.
7. Mandy's pomegranate tea _____ fragrant.

EXERCISE 2 Identify the linking verb in each sentence. Tell whether the italicized subject complement is a noun, a pronoun, or an adjective.

1. A food pyramid is a *picture* of a recommended diet.
2. The designer of the American food pyramid is the U.S. *government.*
3. Whole grains are *essential* to a healthy diet.
4. Fruits and vegetables are important *foods* in the pyramid.
5. Bread, pasta, and grain are *rich* in carbohydrates.
6. In the correct amounts, carbohydrates are important *nutrients* for the body.
7. Some foods are *high* in calories.
8. Such foods, however, may be *low* in nutritional value and negatively affect your health.
9. Sweets, for example, taste *good.*
10. Sweets, however, are not very healthful *foods.*
11. Daily exercise remains a necessary *component* of a person's health.
12. The nutritionist who explained the pyramid was *he.*

The USDA Food Chart shows what a healthy, balanced diet looks like.

EXERCISE 3 Identify the linking verb and the subject complement in each sentence.

1. Diets in different places have become quite different.
2. In the Asian diet, rice is the basic grain.
3. Italy, Spain, Greece, and Tunisia are several Mediterranean countries.
4. Bread and couscous are other grain products in that diet.
5. Tea is a common beverage in several regions.
6. Olive oil is essential in the Mediterranean diet.
7. Pasta is basic in that diet.
8. In several diets fresh fruit remains the typical dessert.

APPLY IT NOW

Write four sentences about your favorite foods and explain why you like them. Include linking verbs. When you have finished, circle the linking verbs and underline the subject complements.
Example: Blueberries (are) my favorite summer snack.

Verb Review

4.1 Identify the verb in each sentence. Tell whether it is an action verb or a being verb.

1. A winter storm dumped snow on the town.
2. Each snowflake was different.
3. I shovel snow whenever it blocks the stairs.
4. The children built a snow fort.
5. Winter is my favorite season.

4.2 Identify the verb phrase in each sentence.

6. The cats were abandoned by their owners.
7. The cats have lived outside for a while.
8. They do not make good house pets anymore.
9. Jeff will build a permanent shelter for the cats.
10. The cats can sleep inside.

4.3 Tell whether the underlined verb is present, present participle, past, or past participle.

11. The squirrel is <u>arranging</u> leaves into a nest.
12. Bad weather often <u>damages</u> fragile nests.
13. Those squirrels <u>placed</u> their nest in a tree.
14. The young squirrels have <u>climbed</u> the tree.

4.4 Complete each sentence with the past or past participle of the verb in parentheses.

15. Jacinta _____ my knitting teacher. (become)
16. She has _____ me some basic stitches. (teach)
17. I _____ work on a scarf. (begin)
18. Jacinta _____ that my scarf was a good first try. (say)

4.5 Complete each sentence with the past or past participle of the verb in parentheses.

19. My friend _____ her arm. (break)
20. She had _____ to the hospital right away. (go)
21. In the emergency room, she _____ a doctor. (see)
22. She had _____ a blue cast. (choose)
23. Her dad _____ her to have the cast removed. (take)

4.6 Find the verb or verb phrase in each sentence. Tell whether the tense of the verb is simple present, simple past, or future.

24. We pick blueberries in Maine every summer.
25. Michelle put her berries into a wicker basket.
26. Plump, ripe blueberries taste sweet.

27. I mixed blueberries into my cereal some mornings.

28. Mom will freeze our extra blueberries.

4.7 Identify the verb phrase in each sentence. Tell whether each is in the present progressive, past progressive, or future progressive tense.

29. Felicity and Riley are wrapping a gift.

30. Riley was cutting the paper with scissors.

31. They will be tying the ribbon into a big bow.

32. I am opening the beautifully wrapped gift.

4.8 Complete each sentence with the present perfect tense of the verb in parentheses.

33. The archaeologist _____ a dig. (organize)

34. She _____ a group of workers. (gather)

35. The team members _____ numerous pieces of pottery and tools. (find)

36. The sponsor _____ any discoveries to the natural history museum. (promise)

4.9 Identify the verb phrase in the past perfect tense in each sentence.

37. My mother had given me a recipe for banana bread.

38. It had been my great grandmother's recipe.

39. As my great grandmother had instructed, I mashed three ripe bananas in a bowl.

40. I used a mixer, but my great grandmother always had mixed everything by hand.

4.10 Complete each sentence with the future perfect tense of the verb in parentheses.

41. Michael _____ his report by Monday. (finish)

42. By then the teacher _____ the next lesson. (begin)

43. His classmates _____ their reports by the deadline. (complete)

44. The class _____ their reports before spring break. (share)

4.11 Identify the linking verb and the subject complement in each sentence.

45. The mango is a tropical fruit.

46. The skin of the mango feels leathery.

47. Mangoes taste delicious in fruit salad and in salsa.

48. India was the original home of the mango.

Tech Tip Go to www.voyagesinenglish.com for more activities.

Verb Challenge

Read the selection and answer the questions.

1. We are studying about Egypt and the Nile River in school. 2. I had known that Egypt is in Africa. 3. I didn't know, however, that the Nile River passed through Egypt. 4. It is the longest river in the world. 5. It flows northward, providing water to more than one million square miles of African land.

6. Every year the Nile overflows its banks, leaving behind rich, fertile soil. 7. Because of this, the river has supported farming along its banks for thousands of years. 8. The Nile had flooded its banks annually since 5,000 BC—until the building of the Aswan Dam.

9. The Nile River makes it possible for Egypt to be one of the major producers of cotton in the world. 10. Egypt is a fascinating country. 11. We will have learned many interesting facts about Egypt and the Nile by the end of the year.

1. Name the verb phrase in sentence 1. Is it present progressive or past progressive?

2. Name the verb phrase in sentence 2. What is its tense?

3. What is the helping verb in sentence 2?

4. Name the verb in sentence 4. Does it express action or being?

5. Name the subject complement in sentence 4. Is it a noun, a pronoun, or an adjective?

6. Name the verb phrase in sentence 7. What is its tense?

7. Name the verb in sentence 8. Is it regular or irregular?

8. Name the verb in sentence 9. Name its principal parts.

9. Find a sentence with a verb that is in the future perfect tense.

10. Find any regular verb in this paragraph. Name the principal parts of the regular verb you chose.

Adverbs

5.1 Adverbs of Time, Place, and Manner

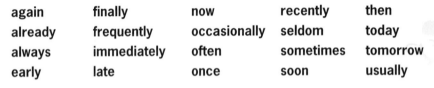

An **adverb** describes a verb. Adverbs tell when, how often, where, or how an action happens.

> John Chapman worked *tirelessly* on his special mission.

The word *tirelessly* tells how. It is an adverb that describes the action of the verb *worked*.

An **adverb of time** answers the question *when* or *how often*.

> John Chapman *always* carried a bag of apple seeds.

Here is a list of common adverbs of time.

again	finally	now	recently	then
already	frequently	occasionally	seldom	today
always	immediately	often	sometimes	tomorrow
early	late	once	soon	usually

An **adverb of place** answers the question *where*.

> Johnny Appleseed walked *far* each day.

Here is a list of common adverbs of place.

above	below	forward	on	there
ahead	down	here	out	up
away	everywhere	inside	outside	upstairs
back	far	off	overhead	within

An **adverb of manner** answers the question *how*.

> He *carefully* planted each apple seed.

Here is a list of some common adverbs of manner.

angrily	correctly	happily	smoothly	truthfully
calmly	courageously	hard	steadily	uncomfortably
carefully	fast	kindly	swiftly	well
confidently	gracefully	quickly	thoroughly	wisely

EXERCISE 1 Tell whether the adverb in italics indicates time, place, or manner.

1. Americans *sometimes* told stories about Johnny Appleseed.
2. John Chapman grew up in Massachusetts in the 1700s, but he didn't stay *there*.
3. He walked *far* on foot, through the country to the western frontier.
4. He started a farm and worked *hard*.
5. *Carefully* he tended his apple orchard.
6. *Soon* he realized that his mission was to encourage planting trees throughout the country.
7. *Generously* he gave seeds and seedlings to all settlers.
8. He had few possessions himself, and *often* he had no shoes and wore a soup pot on his head for a hat.

EXERCISE 2 Find the adverb or adverbs in each sentence. Tell whether the adverb is an adverb of time, place, or manner.

1. Johnny Appleseed treated people and animals kindly.
2. Once he was walking on a cold, snowy winter evening.
3. Then he saw a hollow log and quickly crawled into it for warmth.
4. To Johnny's surprise, a family of bears was sleeping there!
5. Slowly he backed out of the log.
6. Because he refused to chase the bears away, he slept outside in the cold.
7. The legends of Johnny Appleseed continue to delight people today.
8. Jasmine read a book about Johnny Appleseed once.
9. She said I could buy a copy at the store near her home.
10. I want to live adventurously like Johnny Appleseed.

APPLY IT NOW

Write eight sentences. Use one of the verbs and one of the adverbs below in each sentence.

Verbs	Adverbs
finish	quickly
sing	often
dance	completely
shop	happily
	cheerfully

Grammar in Action ✎ Find an adverb of manner in the book report on page 366.

5.2 Adverbs That Compare

Like adjectives, some adverbs can be compared. These adverbs have three degrees of comparison: positive, comparative, and superlative.

The **positive degree** of an adverb is the base form. It describes one action. The **comparative degree** is used to compare two actions. It is often used with *than*. The **superlative degree** is used to compare three or more actions.

> **My father reads the newspaper** *quickly*. (positive)
> **My brother reads** *more quickly* **than I do.** (comparative)
> **My sister reads** *most quickly* **of anyone in my family.** (superlative)

The comparative degree of most adverbs that end in *ly* is formed by adding *more* or *less* before the positive form. The superlative degree is formed by adding *most* or *least* before the positive form.

POSITIVE	COMPARATIVE	SUPERLATIVE
quickly	more (less) quickly	most (least) quickly
carefully	more (less) carefully	most (least) carefully
politely	more (less) politely	most (least) politely

> **My sister goes to the library** *more frequently* **than I do.**
> **My sister listened to the storyteller** *least attentively* **of all.**

The comparative of many adverbs that do not end in *ly* is formed by adding *-er*. The superlative is formed by adding *-est*.

POSITIVE	COMPARATIVE	SUPERLATIVE
fast	faster	fastest
near	nearer	nearest
late	later	latest

> **We got to the library** *sooner* **than our friends.**
> **Jackson arrived** *latest* **and missed the start of the presentation.**

Paul Bunyan

EXERCISE 1 Write the comparative and superlative degrees of each adverb.

1. swiftly
2. carefully
3. hard

4. brilliantly
5. smoothly
6. long

7. noisily
8. diligently
9. faithfully

EXERCISE 2 Identify the adverb in the comparative or the superlative degree in each sentence. Tell the degree of each adverb.

1. Of all folk heroes, those in American tall tales seem to act most amazingly.
2. Figures such as Paul Bunyan worked more powerfully than any real human could.
3. Jonathan and Emily were less obviously intrigued than Raj with this story.
4. Characters like Pecos Bill act more daringly than most folk heroes—even riding a tornado.
5. The one who listens least attentively to the storyteller is Keisha.
6. John Henry acted most nobly of all the folk heroes.

EXERCISE 3 Choose the correct form of the adverb to complete each sentence.

John Henry

1. John Henry could drive steel (fastest faster) of all the workers cutting tunnels for the railroads.
2. He worked (harder hardest) than any ordinary human.
3. Legend says that of all the workers, John Henry was (less likely least likely) to quit before the job was done.
4. In a contest he drove steel (more rapidly most rapidly) than a machine, but he died as a result of the effort.
5. He showed (more impressively most impressively) of all the folk heroes the power of the human spirit.
6. John Henry might be (least widely less widely) known than Paul Bunyan, but John Henry is still a great American folk hero.

APPLY IT NOW

Choose four comparative and superlative adverbs from Exercise 1. Use each adverb in a sentence.

Grammar in Action.

Identify the superlative adverb in the book report on page 367.

5.3 Troublesome and Negative Words

Good and *Well*

Good is an adjective that answers the question *what kind* about a noun. *Well* is generally an adverb that answers the question *how* about a verb. Be careful not to use *good* when the adverb *well* is needed.

> **Pecos Bill was a good cowboy.** (*What kind of cowboy?* A *good* cowboy. *Good* tells what kind about the noun *cowboy*.)

> **He could twirl a lasso well.** (*How could he twirl a lasso?* He could twirl it *well*. *Well* tells how about the verb *twirl*.)

Well can be used as an adjective but only in reference to a person's health.

> **I'll bet Pecos Bill felt *well* every day—never sick for a minute.**

Real and *Very*

Real is an adjective that means "genuine" or "true." *Very* is an adverb that describes an adjective or another adverb. *Very* means "extremely" or "to a high degree." Be careful not to use *real* when the adverb *very* is needed.

> **Pecos Bill was not a real person.** (*What kind of person? Real* tells about the noun *person*.)

> **Pecos Bill was very clever.** (*How clever was he? Very* clever. *Very* tells more about the adjective *clever*.)

No, Not, and *Never*

A negative idea is expressed by using one negative word. This negative word may be *no, not, none, never,* or *nothing*. If a sentence already has a negative adverb, avoid using another negative word. Use a word such as *any* or *ever* instead.

> **There is no cowboy more famous than Pecos Bill.** (one negative word, *no*)

> **There isn't any cowboy more famous than Pecos Bill.** (one negative word, *n't* [*not*], used with *any*)

EXERCISE 1 Complete each sentence with *good* or *well.*

1. Swamp Angel did _____ deeds for the people of Tennessee.

2. The settlers spoke _____ of her.

3. She was _____ at such pioneer skills as building cabins.

4. She could rope _____ too—once even roping a tornado.

5. She was even _____ at fighting bears.

6. There are several _____ stories about Swamp Angel.

EXERCISE 2 Complete each sentence with *real* or *very.*

1. Swamp Angel's _____ name was Angelica Longrider.

2. Actually, Swamp Angel is not a _____ character from the past.

3. According to her creator, Swamp Angel grew _____ big and tall.

4. She was _____ strong—once lifting a wagon train out of a bog.

5. I think the stories about her are _____ entertaining.

6. The funny story about her and the wagon train was not _____ , of course, but it's _____ fun to pretend.

EXERCISE 3 Choose the correct word to complete each sentence.

1. I haven't read (any   no) stories more enjoyable than tall tales.

2. There wasn't (any   no) person in Tennessee more appreciated than Swamp Angel.

3. (Any   No) creature did more harm than the hungry bear.

4. There wasn't (anyone   no one) who could defeat it.

5. There was (no   any) battle more fierce than the one between that bear and Swamp Angel.

6. (Nothing   Anything) was thrown as far as Swamp Angel threw that bear—right up into the sky.

APPLY IT NOW

Write one sentence for each word: *good, well, real, very, no, not, never.*

 Tech Tip   Find examples of troublesome words in an online article.

Adverbs • 111

5.4 *There Is and There Are*

When a sentence begins with *there* followed by a form of the verb *be,* the subject of the sentence comes after the verb.

> **There is a famous *spider* in many folk tales.**
> **There are, in fact, many *stories* about the trickster spider.**

In the sentences above, the subjects are in red and the verbs are underlined. The subject follows the verb in each sentence.

There is or *there was* is used with a singular subject. *There are* or *there were* is used with a plural subject.

	VERB		SINGULAR SUBJECT	
There	is	a	tale	about Anansi in this book.

	VERB	PLURAL SUBJECT		
There	are	several animal	characters	in this tale.

What verb correctly completes the sentence?

> **There (is are) tales from Africa and from the Caribbean.**

You are correct if you chose *are.* This verb form goes with the plural subject *tales.*

EXERCISE 1 Identify the subject in each sentence. Tell whether it is singular or plural.

1. There is one major contribution of spiders.
2. There are fewer harmful insects because of them.
3. There are some poisonous spiders.
4. So there is a good reason to avoid some spiders.
5. There is a major difference between a spider and an insect.
6. There are eight legs on a spider's body—not six.
7. There is oil on the tips of spiders' legs—so the spiders won't get caught in their own webs.
8. There is no fiber in nature stronger than spider's silk.

EXERCISE 2 **Choose the correct form to complete each sentence.**

(1. There is There are) a well-known story about Anansi, the trickster spider. (2. There is There are) two other characters in the tale—Firefly and Tiger.

Anansi said to Firefly, "Let's go egg hunting tonight." (3. There was There were) fields nearby, and the pair started to look for eggs in them. (4. "There is "There are) no light," said Anansi. "Firefly, please light your light." Every time Firefly did this, Anansi picked up any eggs that could be seen. Soon (5. there was there were) many eggs in Anansi's basket, but (6. there wasn't there weren't) even one egg in Firefly's basket. Firefly, seeing that it was being tricked, flew away. Now (7. there was there were) a big problem for Anansi—he couldn't see in the dark.

Suddenly (8. there was there were) a big tiger in front of him. Tiger said, (9. "There is "There are) many eggs in your basket. Let's go to my home and eat them." Anansi was too afraid to say no. Soon Tiger was hungrily eating all the eggs. (11. There was There were) only eggshells in the bottom of the pot for Anansi! And worse, (12. there was there were) no way for Anansi to find the field with the eggs. It was Firefly's secret.

EXERCISE 3 **Complete each sentence with *there is* or *there are*.**
Tell whether the subject is singular or plural.

1. _____ orb weaver spiders that trap insects in their webs.

2. For spiders, _____ hairs on their bodies, which stick to the web.

3. _____ a circle at the center of an orb web.

4. _____ tubes on a spider's stomach to make silk.

5. _____ a spider that lives under water in a dome-shaped web.

6. _____ spiders on every continent except Antarctica—it's too cold there!

7. In an African legend, _____ a story of a spider who helped create the moon.

APPLY IT NOW

Write four clues about a well-known book or story you have read. Use *there is* and *there are* in the clues. Trade your clues with a partner. Guess the title of book or story.
Example: There is an old shoe. There are several children.

Tech Tip Find an online article that uses *there is.*

5.5 Adverb Clauses

A **clause** is a group of words with a subject and a predicate. A **dependent clause** does not express a complete thought. In a sentence it is used together with an **independent clause**, which does express a complete thought.

An **adverb clause** is a dependent clause that is used as an adverb. An adverb clause often answers the question *when.*

> **My mother often read me fables** *when I was little.*

In this sentence *My mother often read me fables* is the independent clause. *When I was little* is a dependent clause. It has a subject and a verb, but it cannot stand alone as a sentence. The dependent clause is an adverb clause because it begins with the conjunction *when* and answers the question *When did mother read me fables? When I was little.*

Common conjunctions used to introduce adverb clauses include *after, as, as soon as, before, once, since, until, when, whenever,* and *while.*

Can you find the adverb clause in this sentence?

> **After the hungry billy goat had searched for food all day, it found a patch of chili peppers.**

You are correct if you said *After the hungry billy goat had searched for food all day.* It is introduced by *After* and tells when.

An adverb clause generally comes at the beginning or at the end of a sentence.

> **The hungry billy goat found a patch of chili peppers** *after it had searched for food all day.*

EXERCISE 1 Identify the adverb clause in each sentence. Look for the conjunctions for help.

1. The farmer yelled when the hungry billy goat started eating peppers in her field.

2. After a dog heard the farmer's cries, it came to help her.

3. The farmer was talking to the dog while the goat kept crunching the peppers.

4. When the dog barked loudly and asked the goat to leave the pepper patch, the goat simply said, "No!"

5. Other animals offered their help too once they became aware of the problem.

6. Whenever an animal talked to the goat, it just laughed and ate more peppers.

7. When an ant offered to help, the farmer almost refused the small and powerless creature.

8. The ant crept up silently until it reached the goat.

9. Once it climbed up to the goat's ear, the ant took a big bite out of the ear.

10. The goat ran out of the pepper field as soon as he felt the ant's bite.

EXERCISE 2 Complete the adverb clause in each sentence with a conjunction.

1. _____ I go to the library, I use the computer catalog.

2. I looked for a book of fables _____ I got to the library.

3. _____ I had the information on where to find the books, I found several on the shelves.

4. _____ I looked through the books, Zara browsed the periodical section.

5. I won't be able to read the book _____ I get home.

6. _____ I finished the book, I wrote my reaction to each fable and shared it with my parents.

EXERCISE 3 Complete each sentence with an adverb clause.

1. I read books _____.

2. I saw many interesting books _____.

3. I usually go to the library _____.

4. I haven't been to the bookstore _____.

5. I will read that book _____.

APPLY IT NOW

Write five sentences about the plot of a story that you remember. Use adverb clauses and underline them in your sentences.

Adverb Review

5.1 Find the adverb in each sentence. Tell whether the adverb is an adverb of time, place, or manner.

1. The artist firmly patted the clay into a ball.
2. He immediately began to spin the potter's wheel.
3. The wheel turned quickly, and a pot took shape.
4. His hands moved inside to shape the pot.
5. The artist worked often to keep up with demand.
6. The artist worked carefully.
7. He then baked the pot so that it would harden.
8. He put a glaze on to give it some color.
9. He baked the pot again.
10. The potter successfully sells his pots at art shows.
11. He places fragile items above the display so they don't break.

5.2 Identify the adverbs in the positive, comparative, or superlative degree in each sentence. Tell the degree of each adverb.

12. Of all the volunteers, Maria worked most diligently washing cars.
13. Paul washed cars more quickly than Charles did.

14. My aunt eagerly helped us with our fund-raiser.
15. One group of volunteers worked the fastest of all.
16. Michael polished more carefully than I did.
17. The volunteers worked harder after a break.
18. I hummed quietly while I did my work.
19. We finished earliest of all the teams and helped them for the rest of the afternoon.
20. Bob was the wettest because he was using the hose.
21. We worked faster than we thought.
22. The customers responded more enthusiastically than we expected.
23. Of all our fund-raising efforts, the car wash worked out most successfully for us.
24. The charity gratefully accepted our donations.

5.3 Choose the correct word to complete each sentence.

25. *The Polar Express* is a (good well) book.
26. Reading this book around the holidays is a (real very) treat.
27. Chris Van Allsburg is a (well good) writer and illustrator.

28. Shel Silverstein also writes (good well).

29. His poems are (real very) clever and fun to read.

30. There is (none no) other poet I like more than W. B. Yeats.

31. There wasn't (anyone no one) in class who wasn't interested in his poem.

32. Beverly Cleary writes (real very) funny books.

33. There are (no any) characters as funny as hers.

34. Roald Dahl created a (very real) fascinating character in his book *Matilda*.

35. We haven't found (any no) copies of the movie *Matilda* in the library.

5.4 Choose the correct verb to complete each sentence.

36. There (is was) a splinter in my finger yesterday.

37. There (were are) tools in the cabinet last week.

38. When I apply first aid, there (are is) several steps to follow.

39. There (were is) the tip of the splinter!

40. In medieval days, there (was were) medical practices we would consider strange today.

41. There (were was) theories that leeches help heal patients.

42. Today there (is are) more advanced methods of practicing medicine.

43. There (is were) one easy way to help prevent illness, which is by washing your hands.

5.5 Identify the adverb clause in each sentence.

44. You need to find a sunny place before you start a vegetable garden.

45. You need to decide on your plants once you have a place.

46. Before you plant tomatoes, you should put fertilizer on the ground.

47. After you place the fertilizer, you need to dig holes for the tomato plants.

48. Once you have placed the plants in the holes, you can add wire cages for support.

49. It is important to break up the soil before you plant lettuce.

50. After you till the soil, you plant the lettuce seeds in clearly marked rows.

51. You should water the seeds as soon as they are planted.

52. While the plants are growing, you should water them regularly.

53. You need to check for bugs as the plants are growing.

Tech Tip Go to www.voyagesinenglish.com for more activities.

Adverb Challenge

Read the paragraph and answer the questions.

1. "Swish, step, crack." 2. You might not immediately recognize these noises as the sounds of a dance. 3. The sounds are part of doing the tinikling, a traditional dance of the Philippines. 4. The dance gets its name from the long-legged tikling birds. 5. These birds hop swiftly between tall reeds and the branches that hang overhead. 6. Dancers imitate the bird's hop as they jump gracefully up and down between two sticks. 7. Two other people hold the sticks and move them rhythmically to the music. 8. As the dance continues, the sticks begin to move back and forth more rapidly. 9. People dancing the tinikling wear loose, bright clothes. 10. They usually dance barefoot. 11. They themselves look a little like the birds. 12. The dance is traditionally performed with Filipino martial arts demonstrations.

1. In sentence 2 is the adverb *immediately* an adverb of time, place, or manner?
2. In sentence 5 find an adverb of manner. In what degree is the adverb?
3. In sentence 5 find an adverb of place.
4. In sentence 6 find the adverbs of place.
5. In sentence 7 find the adverb. What kind of adverb is it?
6. In sentence 8 find an adverb in the comparative degree. What are its positive and superlative degrees?
7. What is the adverb clause in sentence 8?
8. What is the adverb of time in sentence 10?
9. What is the adverb of manner in sentence 12?

Prepositions, Conjunctions, and Interjections

6.1 Prepositions and Their Objects

A **preposition** is a word that shows the relationship between a noun or a pronoun and another word in the sentence. The noun or pronoun that follows the preposition is called the **object of the preposition.**

	PREPOSITION	OBJECT
My mother read me a story	by	Aesop.

	PREPOSITION	OBJECT
Aesop lived	in	ancient times.

In the first sentence, the preposition is *by.* The object of the preposition is the noun *Aesop.* In the second sentence, the preposition is *in.* The object of the preposition is *times.*

Common prepositions include the following:

about	around	by	in	through
above	at	down	into	to
across	before	during	of	toward
after	behind	for	off	with
against	beside	from	on	without

What are the prepositions and objects in these sentences?

Aesop's fables become famous during his lifetime.
Some fables are retellings of older stories.

In the first sentence, *during* is the preposition and *lifetime* is the object. In the second sentence, *of* is the preposition and *stories* is the object.

Samos

EXERCISE 1 Identify the preposition or prepositions in each sentence.

1. Aesop was born on Samos.
2. Samos is an island in the Aegean Sea near Greece.
3. Aesop began his life in slavery.
4. He was eventually freed by his master
5. One of his most famous fables about his experiences is *The Miser.*

120

EXERCISE 2 Identify the preposition and its object in each sentence.

1. A miser sold all of his possessions.

2. With the money, he bought gold coins.

3. He had the coins made into a gold bar.

4. He buried the big bar in a field.

5. Every day he went to the field.

6. Someone spotted the miser, guessed his secret, and took the gold from its hiding place.

7. The next day the miser found a hole without any gold.

8. He was weeping bitterly about his loss.

9. A passerby talked to him and heard his story.

10. The passerby suggested that the miser put a stone into the earth.

11. The passerby said, "The stone will serve the same purpose for you—you didn't use the gold, and you won't use the stone."

EXERCISE 3 Complete each sentence with a preposition. Then identify the object of the preposition.

1. A farmer _____ three sons had a problem.

2. The farmer decided to teach a lesson _____ his sons.

3. He gave a bundle of three sticks to each _____ his sons.

4. Each son was unable to break the bundle despite a lot _____ effort.

5. The father untied the bundle and placed one stick _____ each son.

6. Each son broke his stick _____ ease.

7. "If you don't stay together, your enemies will triumph _____ you."

APPLY IT NOW

Imagine that you are exploring the attic of an old house. What interesting discoveries might you make? Write sentences using six of the following prepositions to describe your discoveries:

along	into	upon
below	near	under
beneath	off	without

Grammar in Action

Identify two prepositions in the second paragraph of the excerpt on page 366.

6.2 Prepositional Phrases as Adjectives

A preposition and its object, along with any words that describe the object, form a **prepositional phrase.** A prepositional phrase acts as an adjective or an adverb.

A prepositional phrase used as an adjective is called an **adjective phrase.** It describes a noun or a pronoun. An adjective phrase tells what kind, which ones, how many, or how much about the word it describes.

Have you ever heard the story *about Rip Van Winkle*?

The prepositional phrase is *about Rip Van Winkle.* The preposition is *about.* The phrase describes the noun *story.* It tells which story—the story *about Rip Van Winkle.* Therefore this prepositional phrase is an adjective phrase.

Notice how the descriptive adjectives in sentences A and C become adjective phrases when they are rewritten using prepositions and noun objects, as in sentences B and D.

A The setting is the *colonial* period.
B The setting is the time *of the colonies*.

C There are similar *European* stories.
D There are similar stories *from Europe*.

Washington Irving

EXERCISE 1 Complete each sentence with a prepositional phrase from the list.

of popular short stories   across the globe   of an early American story
from Irving's memories   by Irving

1. Washington Irving was a writer _____.
2. One famous story _____ is "Rip Van Winkle."
3. Many stories came _____ of upstate New York.
4. Americans and people _____ enjoyed his stories.
5. Irving's scary "The Legend of Sleepy Hollow" is an example _____ that is still read today.

EXERCISE 2 Identify the prepositional phrase used as an adjective in each sentence. Tell the noun the prepositional phrase describes.

1. Rip Van Winkle from the Hudson River Valley had a messy farm.

2. Lazy Rip never completed the chores on his farm.

3. One day he was resting when he heard the voice of an unfamiliar little man.

4. The stranger and his companions asked directions to a certain mountain.

5. Together they reached a huge cave in the mountain.

6. Rip, the man, and the man's friends spent a long night of merrymaking before Rip fell asleep.

7. When he woke, all the other people in the cave had gone.

8. Back home, Rip found that things in the village seemed odd.

9. Many houses in the village had been replaced.

10. He saw a young woman with strange clothing.

11. He asked her questions about the changes.

12. When he told her his name, she exclaimed, "Rip Van Winkle! Why, you've had a nap of one hundred years!"

EXERCISE 3 Rewrite each sentence. Change the word in italics to an adjective phrase.

EXAMPLE   I bought a *wooden* carving.
I bought a carving of wood.

1. We were in the Catskills, the home of Rip Van Winkle, for a *summer* festival.

2. The *tour* guide described the history of the mountains.

3. She pointed out the *stone* statue of Rip Van Winkle.

4. The *Canadian* tourist asked many questions.

5. The *shop* owner showed us colorful souvenirs.

6. One souvenir was a tiny *feather* pillow.

APPLY IT NOW

Use the following groups of words as adjective phrases in sentences.

1. from the museum
2. with bright lights
3. across the field
4. at the circus

6.3 Prepositional Phrases as Adverbs

Prepositional phrases used as adverbs are called adverb phrases. An **adverb phrase** generally describes or tells more about a verb. An adverb phrase answers the question *where, when,* or *how.*

> **The teacher discussed Native American tales** *during class.*

During class is the prepositional phrase. It acts as an adverb describing the verb *discussed* and answers the question *when.* Study these sentences.

> **We went** *to the library.* (describes *went,* tells where)
> **We arrived** *at noon.* (describes *arrived,* tells when)
> **The storyteller read the tale** *in a dramatic voice.* (describes *read,* tells how)

Adverbs can be changed into prepositional phrases that act as adverbs.

> **A Otter swam** *skillfully.*
> **B Otter swam** *with skill.*
>
> **C Otter swam** *northward.*
> **D Otter swam** *to the north.*

Find the prepositional phrases used as adverbs in these sentences.

> **We arrived at the lake early.**
> **By noon we had caught eight fish.**

In the first sentence, *at the lake* is a prepositional phrase that describes the verb *arrived.* It tells where. In the second sentence, *by noon* is a prepositional phrase that describes the verb *had caught.* It tells when. Both are adverb phrases.

EXERCISE 1 Identify the adverb phrase in each sentence.

1. One day Rabbit was sitting near a lake.
2. Otter was swimming in the water.
3. Otter caught an eel with her mouth.
4. She invited Rabbit to dinner.
5. Otter cooked the eel at her house.
6. She shared the delicious meal with Rabbit.
7. In the morning Rabbit went to fish too.
8. Rabbit jumped into the icy water.
9. Rabbit couldn't swim and soon was sinking in the water.

10. Otter swam to Rabbit.
11. Otter pulled Rabbit from the water.
12. Otter asked, "Why did you jump into the lake?"
13. Rabbit said in a loud voice, "I was fishing."
14. Otter replied, "But you can't swim, so you shouldn't be jumping into deep water."
15. Then Otter caught a fish, and the pair ate dinner on the shore.

EXERCISE 2 **Complete each sentence with a prepositional phrase from the list.**

> by a clever rabbit   by Native Americans   in the end
> in the tales   like people

1. Many tales with animals were told _____.
2. Animals such as rabbits and otters often appear _____.
3. The animals act _____.
4. In some fables other animals are tricked _____.
5. Sometimes the rabbit's trickery backfires _____.

EXERCISE 3 **Rewrite each sentence. Change each italicized adverb to an adverb phrase.**

> EXAMPLE   **Rabbit shouted *fearfully*.**
>   **Rabbit shouted in fear.**

1. Otter *hastily* jumped into the water to save Rabbit.
2. Otter moved *gracefully* through the water.
3. Rabbit can't move *skillfully* in the water.
4. Rabbit didn't act *cautiously*.
5. Otter *thoughtfully* invited Rabbit over for dinner.
6. Otter cooked the dinner *efficiently*.

APPLY IT NOW

Use each of the following as an adverb phrase in a sentence.
1. into a backpack
2. onto the boat
3. down the pier
4. under the water
5. out of the lake
6. above the mountains

Tech Tip Type your sentences and highlight the adverb phrase.

6.4 Coordinating Conjunctions

A **conjunction** is a word that connects words or groups of words. A **coordinating conjunction** connects words or groups of words that are of equal importance in a sentence. The coordinating conjunctions are *and, or,* and *but.*

A coordinating conjunction may connect compound subjects, compound predicates, compound direct objects, or compound subject complements.

> **Animals _and_ people** are characters in some Native American myths. (compound subject)
>
> **Different Indian tribes collected _and_ retold** these stories over many generations. (compound predicate)
>
> **Some people enjoy the antics _and_ actions** of a character like Nanabozho. (compound direct object)
>
> **Nanabozho was smart _and_ creative.** (compound subject complement)

Sentences can be connected by a coordinating conjunction. The resulting sentence is called a compound sentence. The conjunction *and* in this example connects two complete sentences.

> **Native Americans made up stories about their world, _and_ these story characters often change into different forms.**

EXERCISE 1 Identify the conjunction in each sentence. Tell the words the conjunction connects.

1. An Inuit myth explains and describes how sunshine came to their cold, dark part of the world.

2. The main characters in the story are Crow, the Inuit people of the north, and a family from the south.

3. The Inuit beg and plead for Crow to bring them light from the south.

4. The daylight will give them more time to hunt or fish.

5. Crow flies far south to find a family and a box of glowing sunshine.

6. Crow becomes a speck of dust, which tricks and convinces the family to take the box outside.

7. Then Crow borrows or steals the sunshine from the box to take to the happy Inuit people.

8. Crow is tricky but caring.

EXERCISE 2 Identify the conjunction in each sentence. Tell whether each connects subjects, predicates, direct objects, subject complements, or sentences.

1. The boring beige colors in the field got the attention and interest of Nanabozho.

2. The flowers and leaves were all the same off-white color.

3. Nanabozho painted or decorated the flowers, using many different colors.

4. Two bluebirds played or flew across the sky.

5. The birds swooped but dipped into his paint pots with their feathers.

6. Stripes and colors appeared in the sky.

7. Nanabozho was surprised, but he was also pleased.

8. The sunlight and mist above the waterfall would always form a rainbow.

9. Nanabozho's rainbow was accidental but beautiful nonetheless.

EXERCISE 3 Complete each sentence with the correct conjunction. Tell whether each connects subjects, predicates, direct objects, subject complements, or sentences.

1. Myths _____ legends are used by many Native American storytellers to explain how the world began.

2. Animals often imitate _____ help humans.

3. Characters like Crow and Nanabozho are tricky _____ helpful.

4. They want to help the people _____ animals around them.

5. Sometimes these characters become other creatures, _____ the characters become spirits to accomplish their goals.

APPLY IT NOW

Write four sentences about what you did last weekend. Use at least three coordinating conjunctions to connect subjects, predicates, direct objects, subject complements, or sentences.

Grammar in Action. Identify the coordinating conjunctions in the last paragraph of the literature excerpt on page 366.

6.5 Subordinate Conjunctions

A **subordinate conjunction** connects a dependent clause to an independent clause in a sentence. An independent clause—also referred to as the main clause—has a subject and a predicate. An independent clause can stand alone as a sentence. A dependent clause has a subject and a predicate, but it cannot stand alone as a sentence.

Subordinate conjunctions introduce dependent clauses, such as adverb clauses. An adverb clause can answer the question *when.*

Laura Ingalls Wilder grew up *when* pioneer life still existed in the Midwest.

In this sentence the subordinate conjunction is *when.* The independent clause is *Laura Ingalls Wilder grew up.* The dependent clause is *when pioneer life still existed in the Midwest.*

Common subordinate conjunctions include *after, as, before, once, since, when, whenever, while,* and *until.*

Can you identify the subordinate conjunction and the dependent clause it introduces in this sentence? Can you identify the independent clause?

Laura's family moved from Wisconsin after free land was offered to homesteaders.

You are correct if you said that the subordinate conjunction is *after* and that it introduces the dependent clause *after free land was offered to homesteaders.* The independent clause is *Laura's family moved from Wisconsin.*

Laura Ingalls Wilder's girlhood home

EXERCISE 1 Identify the subordinate conjunction in each sentence.

1. Laura Ingalls Wilder didn't write a book about her pioneer experiences until she was in her 60s.

2. She wrote *Little House on the Prairie* after she wrote *Little House in the Big Woods.*

3. *Little House on the Prairie* tells about her experiences when she was about six years old, in the 1870s.

4. When her family experienced financial problems, they decided to move to Kansas and start a farm.

5. They had many adventures as they were traveling.

6. While they were crossing a big creek, the wagon wheels stopped turning, and the wagon was actually floating.

7. Once they arrived in Kansas, Laura's father built a cabin.

8. While the cabin was still unfinished, a pack of wolves circled it and spent the night howling.

9. Before winter began, her father added a roof, a chimney, a fireplace, and a door to the cabin.

10. Laura and her sister were happy their first Christmas in the cabin when they each received a tin cup, a penny, and some sweets.

EXERCISE 2 Identify the subordinate conjunction in each sentence. Then identify the independent clause and the dependent clause.

1. Life was hard for Laura as she was growing up.

2. She was only 15 years old when she became a teacher.

3. Whenever the weather was bad, a farmer named Almanzo James Wilder would drive her home from school.

4. After they had dated for two years, they married in 1885 and remained so for 64 years.

5. People have loved her simple but touching stories since they were first published.

Laura Ingalls Wilder

EXERCISE 3 Add an independent clause to complete each sentence. Then identify the subordinate conjunction.

1. When I visit the library, _____.

2. _____ after Margaret read *Little House on the Prairie*.

3. Before my brother read *Farmer Boy*, _____.

4. Now whenever I think of covered wagons, _____.

5. _____ until I researched that period in American history.

6. As interesting as the pioneers are, _____.

APPLY IT NOW

Write five sentences describing an author of a book you like. Use subordinate conjunctions in each sentence and underline them.

With an adult, search online for your favorite authors.

6.6 Interjections

An **interjection** is a word that expresses a strong or sudden emotion. Interjections are frequently used in greetings and to get the attention of others.

An interjection is usually set off from the rest of the sentence by an exclamation point.

> *Wow!* I didn't know Paul Bunyan was so big.
> I finished my report. *Great!*

Here are some common interjections used to express emotions.

EMOTION	INTERJECTION
joy	Oh! Hooray! Bravo! Yes! Wonderful!
sorrow	Oh! Ah! Alas!
caution	Shh! Uh-oh!
pain	Oh! Ouch!
wonder	Oh! Ah! My!
disgust	Ick! Yuck! Ugh! Ha! Yikes! Rats! Good grief!
surprise	Oh! Well! Aha! Hurrah!
greeting	Hello! Hi! Good-bye! Aloha!

EXERCISE 1 Identify the interjection in each sentence.

1. Well! Paul Bunyan was the biggest baby ever born in the state of Maine.

2. He weighed 200 pounds when he was two weeks old. Wow!

3. Oh! He had a beard as a baby.

4. Great! He saved a big baby ox from a snowdrift and had a helper for life.

5. He became the greatest lumberjack in the entire United States. Bravo!

6. Oh! He once used bees to scare away the mosquitoes that were bothering his loggers.

7. The mosquitoes mated with the bees and produced bee-squitoes, with stingers at both ends. Ugh!

8. Hooray! Bunyan got rid of the bee-squitoes by luring them to a sugar ship, which took them to a circus.

9. Ah! No one knows for sure where Paul is now—maybe logging near the Arctic Circle.

10. Wonderful! We may hear more tall tales about Paul Bunyan.

EXERCISE 2 Identify the interjection in each sentence. Tell what emotion you think each interjection expresses.

1. Wow! Pecos Bill was an amazing cowboy in tall tales.
2. My! He rode a horse as soon as he was able to sit up.
3. No! He fell out of his family wagon when he was just a baby.
4. Hurray! He taught himself how to swim right away.
5. A coyote found him. Uh-oh!
6. Wonderful! The coyote took him and raised him with her cubs.
7. A long, ornery snake tried to fight Pecos Bill. Yikes!
8. Bravo! Pecos Bill fought the snake and won.
9. He now uses the snake as a lasso. Yuck!

EXERCISE 3 Write an appropriate interjection for each sentence. Remember to include an exclamation point for each interjection.

1. _____ Our class is having a storytelling festival.
2. _____ Luke designed a great flyer for our festival—with illustrations of Pecos Bill and Slewfoot Sue.
3. I really like Sarah's retelling of a tale about Flatboat Annie. _____
4. _____ I forgot to bring my prop to school—a lasso to use in telling about Pecos Bill.
5. Brian brought to class a giant cardboard blue ox as a prop for his presentation on Paul Bunyan. _____
6. _____ The audience still liked my presentation.
7. _____ Kendra acted out different scenes while she retold the story of Flatboat Annie.
8. Mandy dressed up like Slewfoot Sue. _____
9. _____ We all had a lot of fun.
10. _____ I'll see everyone at next year's festival.

APPLY IT NOW

Write five sentences about a tall-tale character, one that you know about or one that you create. Use an interjection in each sentence.

Section 6 Review

6.1 Identify the preposition and its object in each sentence.

1. Redwood trees grow from very small seeds.

2. The trees are among the oldest living things.

3. A redwood can grow 379 feet during its lifespan.

4. Under the bark the wood is a bright brown-red color.

5. Giant redwoods are found only in California.

6. The trees grow along the Pacific Coast.

7. A ranger gave helpful information to us.

8. She talked about the trees.

9. A redwood forest includes other types of trees.

10. In some parts tourists can drive through the redwood trunk.

6.2 Identify the prepositional phrase used as an adjective in each sentence. Tell the noun the prepositional phrase describes.

11. Our class did an art project for a language arts unit.

12. The topic of the unit was Hawaiian folktales.

13. We read folktales from Hawaii.

14. We studied the illustrations in the books.

15. The students examined the style of the illustrations.

16. Each student then drew an illustration for a folktale.

17. They drew a design for a wood block print.

18. Adults at the school cut out the designs.

19. The students inked the wood blocks and printed pictures of their designs.

6.3 Identify the adverb phrase in each sentence.

20. The teacher talked about the Lewis and Clark's expedition.

21. The explorers Lewis and Clark went to the West.

22. Their expedition started in August 1803.

23. The expedition was ordered by President Thomas Jefferson.

24. Lewis and Clark's long journey began at the Mississippi River.

25. They walked through the wilderness.

26. They went across many rivers and streams.

6.4 Identify the conjunction in each sentence. Tell whether each connects subjects, subject complements, predicates, direct objects, subject complements, or sentences.

27. Matter has mass and volume.

28. Two forms of matter are solids and gases.

29. Orange juice and water are examples of liquids.

30. A liquid's particles constantly move and change shape.

31. Gas has no exact shape or volume.

32. A gas changes shape, but a solid does not change shape.

33. Examples of gases are oxygen and hydrogen.

34. Solids have a definite shape and volume.

35. Water is commonly a liquid, but in cold temperatures it turns into solid ice.

36. Solid water particles are close together and become tightly bonded.

6.5 Identify the subordinate conjunction in each sentence.

37. My family will go out to eat after my dad gets home.

38. I decided on tacos as soon as I read the menu.

39. I could always change my mind before the server took my order.

40. I couldn't change my mind after I ordered.

41. We talked about our day until the food arrived.

42. Once the food arrived, I started eating right away.

43. While we were eating, we kept talking.

44. Since we have been eating, I've been thinking about dessert.

6.6 Identify the interjection in each sentence.

45. Hooray! We're going to watch fireworks at the lake.

46. Shh! I want to hear the band play "The Stars and Stripes Forever."

47. Wow! That last skyrocket made a loud noise.

48. Look at the beautiful colors. Oh my!

49. Oh! The applause is really loud.

50. No! I missed that last display.

51. You just stepped on my foot. Ouch!

52. That fireworks looked like a huge spider. Ugh!

53. Ah! The show is over.

54. This was the best fireworks display ever. Bravo!

 Tech Tip Go to www.voyagesinenglish.com for more activities.

Section 6 Challenge

Read the paragraph and answer the questions.

1. Computers may run the farms of the future. 2. Tractors or robots run by computers will do much of the actual farm work. 3. They will plant and harvest all by themselves! 4. Wheat and corn will also be "grown" by computers. 5. Computers will determine the best time to plant and will control the watering of crops. 6. Farmers will know where all their animals are—without leaving the farmhouse. 7. A tiny computer will be placed on each animal. 8. While they remain sitting in their houses, farmers will check computer screens and see the locations of all the animals. 9. Oh! If the farmers of 100 years ago could see the farms of the future, they might recognize only the cows and the chickens.

1. In sentence 1 find the prepositional phrase.
2. Is the prepositional phrase in sentence 1 used as an adjective or an adverb?
3. In sentence 2 find the conjunction.
4. In sentence 3 does the conjunction join subjects, predicates, or direct objects?
5. In sentence 4 find the words connected by the conjunction and tell how they are used in the sentence.
6. In sentence 5 find the coordinating conjunction. Tell if it connects two subjects, two predicates, or two sentences.
7. In sentence 7 find the prepositional phrase.
8. Tell whether the prepositional phrase in sentence 7 is used as an adjective or an adverb.
9. In sentence 8 find the prepositions.
10. In sentence 8 find the subordinate conjunction. Identify the independent clause and the dependent clause.
11. Find the interjection in the paragraph.

#13   #109   #65   #112

Sentences

7.1 Kinds of Sentences

There are four kinds of sentences: declarative, interrogative, imperative, and exclamatory.

A **declarative sentence** makes a statement. It ends with a period.

> **The ancient Olympics were part of a festival honoring both Zeus and Pelops.**

An **interrogative sentence** asks a question. It ends with a question mark.

> **Whom did ancient Greek Olympic games honor?**

An **imperative sentence** gives a command or makes a request. It ends with a period.

> **Lend me your book on the Olympics.**

An **exclamatory sentence** expresses strong emotion. It ends with an exclamation point.

> **Wow, the Olympic games date back to 776 BC!**

What kind of sentence is each of the following?

> **A It is amazing how old the Olympics are!**
> **B Tell me more about the ancient Olympic games.**
> **C Where did the ancient Olympics take place?**
> **D The ancient Olympics took place for almost 12 centuries.**

Sentence A is an exclamatory sentence. It shows emotion. Sentence B is an imperative sentence. It makes a request. Sentence C is an interrogative sentence. It asks a question. Sentence D is a declarative sentence. It makes a statement.

EXERCISE 1 Tell whether each sentence is declarative or interrogative. Add the correct end punctuation.

1. The first ancient Olympic games were held in Greece
2. What were the events in the first Olympics
3. A foot race was probably the first Olympic event
4. There was no Olympic flame at the ancient Olympics

5. When and where did the Olympic flame originate

6. It was first used in 1928, at the games in Amsterdam

7. Were prizes awarded in the ancient Olympics

8. The prizes included wreaths, not medals

EXERCISE 2 Tell whether each sentence is exclamatory or imperative. Add the correct end punctuation.

1. Tell me the distance of the modern marathon

2. Wow, I didn't know it was 26 miles

3. What a long distance that is

4. Name some winners of Olympic marathons

5. What great athletes they were

6. Find out what the marathon commemorates

7. Hand me that book about the Olympics

8. How remarkable the old photos of events are

EXERCISE 3 Tell whether each sentence is declarative, interrogative, imperative, or exclamatory. Add the correct end punctuation.

1. In 1896 where were the first modern Olympics held

2. Winning athletes in the ancient Olympic games received free food and didn't have to pay taxes

3. When did chariot racing become part of the Olympics

4. What surprising facts this book reveals about the Olympics

5. Tell me the most interesting fact that you learned

6. Give me a brief overview of Olympic history

7. Which athlete won the most medals

8. Larissa Latynina, a Russian gymnast, won 18 medals

9. What an amazing record that is

APPLY IT NOW

Write a four-sentence paragraph on the Olympics: one declarative, one interrogative, one imperative, and one exclamatory.

Grammar in Action. What kinds of sentences are in the last paragraph of the excerpt on page 404?

7.2 Simple Subjects and Predicates

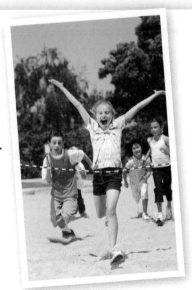

The **simple subject** of a sentence is the noun or pronoun that names who or what a sentence is about. To determine the subject, ask *who* or *what* before the verb.

> The *Olympics* **occurred every four years for almost 12 centuries.**

What occurred? The answer is the noun *Olympics.*

The **simple predicate** is the verb or verb phrase that describes the action or the state of being of the subject.

> **Ancient Greeks** *participated* **in many athletic events.**

The subject is *Greeks.* What did the Greeks do? They *participated.* The simple predicate is *participated.*

A simple predicate includes the helping verbs as well as the main verb.

> **The Pan-Hellenic Festival at Delphi** *has been called* **the most prestigious of all the ancient Greek competitions.**

The simple predicate is the verb phrase *has been called.*

Identify the simple predicate and the simple subject in each of these sentences.

> **A Victors received a wreath made from leaves.**
> **B In Olympia the wreath was made from olive leaves.**

You are correct if you said the following:

> **A.** The simple predicate is *received.* The simple subject is *Victors.*
> **B.** The simple predicate is *was made.* The simple subject is *wreath.*

EXERCISE 1 Identify the simple subject in each sentence.

1. Women participated in an athletic competition in ancient Greece.
2. This competition was in honor of Hera, Zeus's wife.
3. Unmarried girls participated in foot races.
4. This women's festival might be as old as the men's.
5. The celebration took place every four years.

EXERCISE 2 Identify the simple predicate in each sentence.

1. Runners raced at the first Olympics.
2. Later other sports were added.
3. The discus and javelin first appeared in 708 BC.
4. A violent form of boxing permitted kicking and strangleholds.
5. The rules of the sport excluded biting, however.
6. Some sports in the modern Olympics were included in the ancient games.
7. Chariot races began the ancient games in the arena.
8. Major crashes sometimes occurred between the racers.
9. Jockeys rode without saddles in horse races.
10. Horses could win a race even without their jockeys.

A discus

EXERCISE 3 Identify the simple subject and the simple predicate in each sentence.

1. A truce during the Olympic games prohibited fighting in the area of Olympia.
2. Messengers announced the Olympic truce throughout Greece every four years before the start of the next Olympics.
3. The truce protected the athletes and the spectators.
4. The final day of the games featured foot races.
5. Runners sped along one or two lengths of the stadium.
6. The last contest was a special race for soldiers.
7. Heavy armor was worn by runners in that race.
8. The modern Olympics arose from the desire for international cooperation.
9. Athletes from all over the world gather today.
10. This spirit of cooperation has remained important over the years.

The Olympic Stadium in Munich, Germany

APPLY IT NOW

Write five sentences about your favorite sport. Circle the simple subjects and underline the simple predicates in your sentences.

Tech Tip With an adult, research your favorite sport online.

7.3 Complete Subjects and Predicates

The simple subject with all the words that describe it is called the **complete subject.**

> *New sports* **are added to the Olympics every four years.**

In this sentence the complete subject is *New sports.* It includes the simple subject *sports* and the adjective *New.*

The simple predicate with all its objects, complements, and describing words is called the **complete predicate.**

> **The pentathlon event** *started in ancient Greece.*

In this sentence the complete predicate is *started in ancient Greece.* The simple predicate is *started.* The prepositional phrase *in ancient Greece* acts as an adverb.

Identify the complete subject and the complete predicate in each sentence.

> A **Sports at the 1896 Olympics included track and field, gymnastics, tennis, and swimming.**
> B **Sailing was inaugurated at the 1900 Olympics.**

You are correct if you said the following:

> A. The complete subject is *Sports at the 1896 Olympics.* The complete predicate is *included track and field, gymnastics, tennis, and swimming.* The simple subject is *Sports,* and the simple predicate is *included.*
> B. The complete subject is *Sailing.* The complete predicate is *was inaugurated at the 1900 Olympics.* The simple subject is *Sailing,* and the simple predicate is *was inaugurated.*

EXERCISE 1 Identify the complete subject in each sentence.

1. Pierre de Coubertin is considered the father of the modern Olympics.
2. Sportsmanship is the cornerstone of the modern Olympics.
3. The pentathlon was introduced at the 1912 Olympics.
4. Five events make up the pentathlon.
5. Contestants in the 1912 Olympics participated in the long jump, the javelin, the discus, and two races.

EXERCISE 2 Identify the complete predicate in each sentence.

1. Jim Thorpe won the first Olympic pentathlon in 1912.

2. Many people have described Thorpe as the greatest all-around athlete.

3. His athletic talent was recognized at Carlisle Industrial Indian School in Pennsylvania.

4. Thorpe's extraordinary skills helped him excel at football, track, and many other sports.

5. The American team for the Olympics in 1912 included many who won gold medals.

Jim Thorpe

EXERCISE 3 Identify the complete subject and the simple subject in each sentence.

1. The amazing athlete won both the pentathlon and decathlon.

2. His records at these events lasted many years.

3. His later career as a professional baseball and football player was very successful.

4. Jim Thorpe's Olympic medals were contested afterwards.

5. This athlete had once received money to play sports.

6. This action made Thorpe a professional in the Olympic committee's eyes.

7. All Olympic athletes were amateurs at that time.

EXERCISE 4 Identify the complete subject and the complete predicate in each sentence. Then identify the simple subject and the simple predicate.

1. Olympic management stripped Jim Thorpe of his medals in 1913.

2. The Olympic Committee pardoned Thorpe in 1982.

3. He had died 29 years earlier.

4. Thorpe's medals were returned to his children.

5. The reputation of a great athlete was restored.

APPLY IT NOW

Add words to the simple subject and the simple predicate in each sentence. Then name the complete subject and the complete predicate of each sentence.

1. Runners raced.
2. Spectators clapped.
3. Winners waved.
4. Flags flew.

7.4 Direct and Indirect Objects

The **direct object** is a noun or a pronoun that answers the question *whom* or *what* after an action verb.

> **Some Olympic athletes earned long-lasting *fame*.**

In this sentence *fame* is the direct object. *Fame* answers the question *what* after the verb *earned*. What did some Olympic athletes earn? The answer is *fame*, the direct object.

> **The book describes Olympic *heroes*.**

In this sentence *heroes* is the direct object. *Heroes* answers the question *whom* after the verb *describes*. Whom does the book describe? The answer is *heroes*, the direct object.

Some sentences contain a direct object and an indirect object. The **indirect object** tells to whom, for whom, to what, or for what an action is done. The indirect object comes before the direct object and after the action verb in a sentence.

> **The press gives Olympic *athletes* much attention.**

In this sentence *attention* is the direct object. It answers the question *what* after the verb *gives*. What does the press give? It gives *attention*, the direct object. *Athletes* is the indirect object. It answers the question *to whom* the action was done. To whom is much attention given? The indirect object, *athletes*, receives the attention.

Here is a list of some verbs that can take indirect objects.

assign	owe
bring	pay
buy	promise
deny	read
forgive	sell
get	send
give	show
hand	teach
lend	tell
offer	write

Nadia Comaneci after her gold-medal win

EXERCISE 1 Identify the direct object in each sentence.

1. Fourteen-year-old Nadia Comaneci earned three gold medals in gymnastics at the 1976 Summer Olympics.
2. She established a special record.
3. She earned a score of 10.
4. A 10 represents a perfect mark.
5. Her coach, Bela Karolyi, discovered the young athlete during a visit to a school in Romania.
6. The six-year-old was doing cartwheels.
7. The coach invited Nadia to his gymnastics school.
8. According to her coach, Nadia possessed courage.
9. She tried difficult gymnastic moves without fear.
10. She had mental and physical discipline.
11. Nadia inspired young athletes with her determination.

EXERCISE 2 Identify the direct object and the indirect object in each sentence.

1. Bela Karolyi taught young gymnasts moves.
2. He awarded his pupils trophies.
3. He offered Nadia good training.
4. At the Montreal Olympics, Nadia showed the world her amazing skills.
5. The judges first gave Nadia a perfect score on the uneven bars for her amazing movements and somersault off the bar.
6. Her three gold medals earned her worldwide fame.
7. Judges awarded Nadia two other medals, a silver and a bronze.
8. In 1996 the International Gymnastics Hall of Fame gave the gymnast a place in its hall.
9. Nadia Comaneci now teaches young athletes competitive gymnastics.

Nadia Comaneci

APPLY IT NOW

Use five of the verbs listed on page 142 in sentences. Be sure to include a direct object and an indirect object in each sentence. Circle each direct object and underline each indirect object.

7.5 Subject Complements

A **subject complement** completes the meaning of a linking verb in a sentence. It is part of the predicate. If the subject complement is a noun or a pronoun, it renames the subject. If the subject complement is an adjective, it describes the subject.

> **Wilma Rudolph was an Olympic *medalist*.**

Medalist is a noun subject complement. It renames the subject *Wilma Rudolph*.

> **Wilma Rudolph was *courageous* in the face of difficulties.**

Courageous is an adjective subject complement. It describes the subject *Wilma Rudolph*.

The most common linking verb is the verb *be* in its various forms: *am, is, are, was, were, have been, had been,* and *will have been*.

Identify the complement in each sentence. Tell if it is a noun subject complement or an adjective subject complement.

> **A Wilma Rudolph was an inspiration to many people.**
> **B Wilma Rudolph was competitive despite her physical challenges.**

A. The subject complement is *inspiration*. It is a noun, and it renames the subject *Wilma Rudolph*.
B. The subject complement is *competitive*. It is an adjective, and it describes the subject *Wilma Rudolph*.

EXERCISE 1 Complete each sentence with a subject complement from the list. Then tell whether the subject complement is a noun or an adjective.

athlete   trouble   famous   numerous   poor

1. Wilma Rudolph was an amazing _____.
2. The obstacles she faced were _____.
3. She had _____ with her health.
4. Her family was very _____.
5. Her athletic achievements are still _____.

EXERCISE 2 Identify the subject complement in each sentence. Tell whether the subject complement is a noun or an adjective.

1. Wilma Rudolph's family was large.
2. Wilma was the 20th child in a family of 22 children.
3. Her parents were industrious.
4. Wilma was often sick as a child.
5. She was a victim of polio.
6. Her family was diligent in helping with physical therapy.
7. Everyone in the family was supportive of Wilma and her dreams.
8. Wilma was a hard worker.
9. She was successful in reaching her goal—to walk again.
10. Soon she was a fast runner.
11. She was a member of the U.S. Olympic team in 1956 and again in 1960.
12. She was the winner of three gold medals in 1960.
13. Her family and all Americans were proud of her.
14. She was a famous athlete of her time.
15. Her accomplishments were truly wonderful.

Wilma Rudolph

EXERCISE 3 Complete each sentence with a noun or an adjective used as a subject complement.

1. A famous athlete of today is _____.
2. My favorite athlete is _____.
3. My favorite sport is _____.
4. I am _____ at running fast.
5. I was so _____ when we won our first game!
6. My coach is _____.
7. The goalie on our team is _____.

APPLY IT NOW

Use each of the following as a subject complement in a sentence.
1. referee
2. diligent
3. enthusiastic
4. coach
5. winter
6. team

7.6 Sentence Order

A sentence is in **natural order** when the verb follows the subject.

	SUBJECT	VERB	
Rhythmic	*gymnasts*	*twirl*	long ribbons.

A sentence is in **inverted order** when the main verb or a helping verb comes before the subject.

	VERB		SUBJECT
Around the floor gracefully	*dance*	the	*gymnasts.*

In the above sentence, the verb *dance* comes before the subject *gymnasts*. A prepositional phrase comes at the start of the sentence, before the verb and subject. Many questions are in inverted order.

VERB		SUBJECT	VERB
What	*do*	rhythmic	*gymnasts*	*twirl?*

In the above sentence, the helping verb *do* comes before the subject *gymnasts*. Even though the main verb *twirl* follows the subject, the sentence is still in inverted order.

Tell whether each sentence is in natural order or inverted order.

A **Across the finish line ran the lead runner.**
B **Runners dashed around the track.**
C **Do runners wear special tracksuits?**
D **After the race the winner seemed jubilant.**

You are correct if you said the following:

A. The sentence is in inverted order. The subject *runner* comes after the verb *ran.*
B. The sentence is in natural order. The subject *runners* comes before the verb *dashed.*
C. The sentence is in inverted order. The helping verb *do* comes before the subject *runners.*
D. The sentence is in natural order. The subject *winner* comes before the verb *seemed.*

EXERCISE 1 Tell whether each sentence is in natural order or inverted order.

1. Onto the diving board stepped the diver.
2. She jumped up and down.
3. At the edge of the board she paused.
4. Off the diving board she leapt with a smooth motion.
5. Gracefully through the air turned her body.
6. Into the water went the diver almost without a splash.
7. Up above the water bobbed her head.
8. Her score flashed on the board.

EXERCISE 2 Rewrite each sentence, putting it in natural order.

1. Around the track sped the cyclists.
2. Faster and faster moved the bikes.
3. Up the hill pedaled the road racer.
4. Across the finish line sped the cyclist.
5. From the stands came a roar.
6. On the podium stood the winner.

EXERCISE 3 Rewrite each sentence in inverted order. Write questions where indicated.

1. The horse jumped over the hurdle.
2. The word *equestrian* comes from the Latin word for *horse*. (question)
3. The top bar of the hurdle fell down.
4. Points were taken off the rider's score for stumbling. (question)
5. Dressage is the name of an Olympic event. (question)

APPLY IT NOW

Make two sentences from each set of scrambled words. One sentence should be in natural order, and the other should be in inverted order.

1. the cave echoed through our voices
2. waddled to the lake the ducks
3. the paint down red the wall dripped

7.7 Compound Subjects and Predicates

A sentence with two or more subjects is said to have a **compound subject.** The connecting word for a compound subject is generally the coordinating conjunction *and* or *or*.

> Gymnastics **and** *ice-skating* attract large TV audiences.

In this sentence the compound subject is *Gymnastics* and *ice-skating*. They are the subjects of the verb *attract*.

When *or* is the coordinating conjunction, the verb agrees with the subject closer to the verb.

> The *swimmers* or the *coach is* featured on the TV show.

Coach is singular; therefore, the verb agrees with a singular subject.

Two or more predicates joined by a coordinating conjunction form a **compound predicate.**

> Athletes *develop skill* and *build strength to compete*.

In this sentence the compound predicate is *develop skill* and *build strength to compete*. *Develop* and *build* tell two things that athletes do.

EXERCISE 1 Identify the compound simple subjects and the compound simple predicates in these sentences.

1. Sydney and Athens were sites of recent Olympics.
2. Golf and tug-of-war were once Olympic sports.
3. The bobsled and the luge involve sleds on icy tracks.
4. Olive leaves or pine twigs were used to make crowns for winning athletes at the ancient Olympics.
5. Poems were written and presented at the ancient Olympics.
6. You should research and explain chariot racing.
7. Physical ability and hard work combine to produce an Olympic champion.
8. Spectators cheered or applauded the athletes.
9. The modern Olympics continue the same traditions and add new improvements to the Games.

EXERCISE 2 Complete each sentence with a compound subject or a compound predicate.

1. _____ and _____ are exciting sports I'd like to try.

2. Is _____ or _____ your favorite sport?

3. _____ and _____ are my favorite activities.

4. _____ and _____ are team sports at my school.

5. Olympic traditions _____ and _____ the world for decades.

EXERCISE 3 Choose the correct verb to complete each sentence.

1. Olympic swimming or basketball (is are) going to be on TV this evening.

2. A swimmer or a runner (is are) carrying our country's flag.

3. Jody and Shawna (like likes) to watch gymnastics with their teammates.

4. The boats from Canada (is are) going to win the race or (fight fought) hard to come close.

5. Physical ability and hard work (make makes) an Olympic winner.

EXERCISE 4 Combine each pair of sentences into one sentence with a compound subject or a compound predicate.

1. The Winter Olympic Games are exciting to watch.
   The Summer Olympic Games are exciting to watch.

2. Jim Thorpe earned an Olympic gold medal.
   Jim Thorpe lost the medal because he had played professional baseball.

3. Athletes take an oath at the games.
   Officials take an oath at the games.

4. Machines determine winners.
   Judges determine winners.

5. Coaches train athletes in the skills of their sports.
   Coaches motivate athletes to do their best.

6. Ice hockey is an Olympic sport.
   Field hockey is an Olympic sport.

APPLY IT NOW

Write five sentences about an activity or a sport you do with a friend. Include compound subjects and compound predicates in your sentences.

Grammar in Action. Identify the compound simple predicate in the excerpt on page 415.

7.8 Compound Direct Objects

A verb that has two or more direct objects is said to have a **compound direct object**.

> **Football players wear** *helmets* **and** *pads*.

To find the direct object, ask *who* or *what* after the verb. In the above sentence, the verb is *wear*. Football players wear what? They wear *helmets* and *pads*. The compound direct object is *helmets* and *pads*.

Compound direct objects are usually connected by the coordinating conjunction *and* or *or*.

EXERCISE 1 Identify the compound direct object in each sentence.

1. Should I bring an umbrella or a rain slicker to the football game?
2. We took scarves and sweaters because of the cold.
3. Bring sandwiches and thermoses of hot chocolate.
4. My dad drove my cousin, her friend, and me to the game.
5. Some people had coolers and grills in the parking lots.
6. They were grilling hot dogs, hamburgers, and kebabs.
7. My dad enjoys soccer, hockey, and football.
8. We found an old program and some stale popcorn in the back of Dad's car.
9. Many spectators wore team hats and jackets.
10. The vendor handed us programs and pencils.
11. My dad told us the players' names and the basic rules of the game.
12. My dad bought us popcorn, peanuts, and nachos at halftime.
13. We watched the bands and cheerleaders stir up the crowd.
14. The concession stand sold T-shirts and pennants.
15. We bought souvenirs and photographs of our favorite players.
16. We told our family, friends, and classmates about our good time at the game.

EXERCISE 2 Complete each sentence with a compound direct object. Use additional words to complete each direct object if necessary.

1. My friend invited _____, _____, and _____ to a game.

2. Mom gave us _____ and _____ for snacks.

3. We put _____ and _____ into thermoses.

4. We wore _____, _____, and _____.

5. I would like _____ and _____ from the food stand.

6. Spectators see _____, _____, and _____ at a game.

7. Do you like _____ or _____?

8. Do you play _____ or _____ after school?

EXERCISE 3 Combine each pair of sentences into one sentence with a compound direct object.

1. We saw some good passes from the quarterback.
   We saw some good runs from the quarterback.

2. Greg packed sandwiches for the trip.
   Greg packed snacks for the trip.

3. I bought a team jersey.
   I bought a team photograph.

4. The audience applauded the players.
   The audience applauded the halftime entertainment.

5. We enjoyed the bands.
   We enjoyed the cheerleaders.

6. We brought some autographs home.
   We brought a pennant home.

7. I met the coach after the game.
   I met some players after the game.

8. The band members played trumpets.
   The band members played drums.

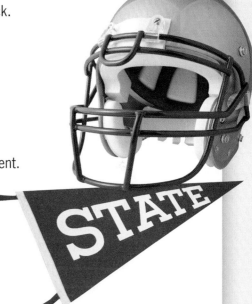

APPLY IT NOW

Write five sentences about things you enjoy doing or imagine you would enjoy doing at the ocean, a lake, a river, or a pool. Use a compound direct object in each sentence.

7.9 Compound Subject Complements

A verb with two or more subject complements is said to have a **compound subject complement**.

> **The skater Peggy Fleming was a world** *champion* **and an Olympic** *medalist*.
> **Peggy Fleming was** *graceful* **and** *athletic*.

In the first sentence, *champion* and *medalist* are noun subject complements. They make up a compound subject complement.

In the second sentence, *graceful* and *athletic* are adjective subject complements. They form a compound subject complement.

Compound subject complements are usually connected by the coordinating conjunction *and* or *or*.

Identify the subject complements in each sentence. Tell whether they are nouns or adjectives.

> **A** **I am anxious and nervous about skating in my first competition.**
> **B** **After the Olympics, Peggy Fleming became a professional skater and a businesswoman.**

You are correct if you said the following:

> **A.** The compound complement is *anxious* and *nervous*. The connecting word is *and*. This compound complement is an adjective complement. It describes the subject *I*.
> **B.** The compound complement is *skater* and *businesswoman*. The connecting word is *and*. This compound complement is a noun complement. It renames the subject *Peggy Fleming*.

EXERCISE 1 Identify the compound subject complement in each sentence. Tell whether the complements are nouns or adjectives.

1. Peggy Fleming is an ice-skater and a sports announcer.
2. She has always been stylish and smooth on the ice.
3. Her spins are lovely, graceful, and amazing.
4. Peggy's childhood loves were baseball and climbing.

5. From the beginning her movements on ice skates were effortless and sure.

6. Becoming a good skater was always her dream and goal.

7. In 1968 she was the Olympic champion, gold medal winner in women's figure skating, and a role model for young girls everywhere.

8. She was the star of many TV ice specials and the winner of two Emmy awards.

9. She has been famous, successful, and respected for decades.

10. She is currently a spokesperson for and supporter of many charitable causes.

11. She is a member of the U.S. Olympic Hall of Fame and the recipient of a *Sports Illustrated* award for special athletes who changed their sport.

EXERCISE 2 Combine each pair of sentences into one sentence with a compound subject complement. Make certain that the subjects and verbs agree. You may need to use plural subjects.

1. Figure skating is athletic.
   Figure skating is artistic.

2. An important feature of competitive figure skating is jumping.
   An important feature of competitive figure skating is spins.

3. An Olympic figure skating competition is pair skating.
   An Olympic figure skating competition is ice dancing.

4. A famous Olympic figure skater is Peggy Fleming.
   A famous Olympic figure skater is Michelle Kwan.

5. The winning figure skater was excited.
   The winning figure skater was jubilant.

EXERCISE 3 Complete each sentence with a compound subject complement.

1. My favorite female athletes are _____, _____, and _____.

2. Are you _____ or _____?

3. My favorite winter sports are _____, _____, and _____.

4. We were _____ and _____ when we went to our first skating event.

5. These teams are _____ and _____.

Michelle Kwan

APPLY IT NOW

Write a sentence for each pair of adjectives and nouns. Use them as compound subject complements.

1. hockey player, soccer player
2. contestant, winner
3. scared, excited
4. fast, energetic

7.10 Compound Sentences

A **compound sentence** contains two or more independent clauses. An independent clause has a subject and a predicate and can stand alone as a sentence. A compound sentence is formed when two or more independent clauses are connected by the coordinating conjunction *and, but,* or *or.*

> **The Summer Olympics and the Winter Olympics originally took place during the same year, but now they are held two years apart.**

Use a comma before the conjunction when two independent clauses are combined. A semicolon (;) may be used between independent clauses instead of the comma and the coordinating conjunction.

> **The Olympic flag has a white background. It has five rings on it.**
> (two separate sentences)
>
> **The Olympic flag has a white background, and it has five rings on it.**
> (compound sentence with a comma and *and*)
>
> **The Olympic flag has a white background; it has five rings on it.**
> (compound sentence with a semicolon)

Because a compound sentence has more than one clause, it must have at least two subjects and two predicates.

EXERCISE 1 Identify the complete subject and the complete predicate in each independent clause in these compound sentences.

1. The five rings on the Olympic flag are in different colors, and each ring represents an inhabited continent.

2. Athletes from all over the world compete in the games, and the interlocking rings represent international cooperation.

3. The original Olympic flag was presented at the 1914 Olympic Congress, but it was not used until 1920.

4. The flag is lowered at the closing ceremony, and it is presented to the mayor of the next host city.

5. The motto of the Olympic Games is *citius, altius, fortius;* this Latin phrase translates as "faster, higher, stronger."

6. Athletes should strive for their best; the achievement of one's best is every athlete's goal.

7. The country hosting the Olympics plans years in advance, or it risks not being prepared for the event.

EXERCISE 2 Combine each pair of sentences to form a compound sentence. Use a comma before the coordinating conjunction *and, but,* or *or.*

1. The original Olympic flag was retired after the 1984 Games. A new flag was flown in 1988 in Seoul, South Korea.

2. The Olympic flag is used at ceremonies. It is stored in the host city's town hall until the next games.

3. Ancient Greeks held torch relays. They were not part of the Olympics.

4. The flame of the modern torch is lit at Olympia, Greece. It is then transported by various means to its destination.

5. The Olympic anthem was composed in 1896 for the first modern Olympics. It is now the official Olympics anthem.

6. The head of state of the host country declares the Games open. The Olympic flag is raised.

EXERCISE 3 Combine each pair of sentences to form a compound sentence. Use a semicolon.

1. In the opening ceremony, the procession is always led by the Greek team. The other teams follow in alphabetical order of country name.

2. China was the host country for the 2008 Summer Olympics. It won the most medals in the Games that year.

3. There were over 200 countries in the 2008 Summer Olympics. More than 10,000 athletes participated.

4. Women could not compete in the first modern Olympics in 1896. They did compete in the 1900 Olympics.

5. The Olympic flame burns during the Games. It is put out at the end of the Games.

6. The ancient Olympics lasted five days. The modern Olympics last about 16 days.

APPLY IT NOW

Write four sentences about an event at which you were a spectator. Describe what happened and what you saw. Use at least two compound sentences in your writing. Underline the independent clauses.

Tech Tip Find a compound sentence in an online article.

7.11 Complex Sentences

A **complex sentence** contains one independent clause and one dependent clause. An independent clause has a subject and a predicate and can stand on its own as a sentence. A dependent clause has a subject and a predicate, but it cannot stand alone as a sentence. A dependent clause is always used with an independent clause.

Dependent clauses that act as adverbs are called **adverb clauses.** An adverb clause can tell when something occurred.

> **After he had won two world titles in 1988, Dan Jansen was the favorite for a gold medal in speed skating.**

The independent clause is *Dan Jansen was the favorite for a gold medal in speed skating.* The dependent clause is *after he had won two world titles in 1988.* It is an adverb clause that begins with the subordinate conjunction *after* and answers the question *when.* The dependent clause doesn't make sense by itself. It cannot stand alone as a sentence.

A complex sentence has a subject and a predicate in each of its clauses. In the sentence above, the subject of the dependent clause is *he,* and the verb is *had won.* In the independent clause, the subject is *Dan Jansen,* and the verb is *was.*

Some of the subordinate conjunctions used to introduce adverb clauses that indicate time are *after, as, before, since, until, when,* and *while.*

Can you identify the dependent clause, the independent clause, and the subordinate conjunction in this sentence?

> **Dan Jansen had won world titles before he raced in the Olympics.**

The dependent clause is *before he raced in the Olympics,* and the independent clause is *Dan Jansen had won world titles.* The subordinate conjunction is *before.*

EXERCISE 1 Tell whether each clause is dependent or independent.

1. Dan Jansen was born in 1965 in Wisconsin
2. Until he began speed skating
3. Since he was a child
4. He had many disappointments
5. After he won sprint championships in 1988
6. When he tried for the eighth time for an Olympic medal

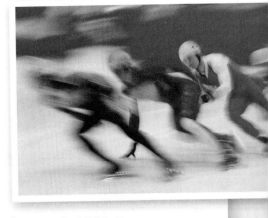

EXERCISE 2 Identify the adverb clause in each of these complex sentences.

1. Before he competed in the 500-meter speed-skating race in 1988, Dan Jansen learned about the death of his sister from leukemia.
2. While he was rounding a turn, he fell and lost.
3. In 1992 at Albertville, Jansen was again the favorite in the 500 after he had won the World Cup championship in that event.
4. He fell again in the race as he was skating.
5. After he failed at a medal for the seventh time, his last chance was in the 1,000–meter race.
6. When he tried this time, many fans were rooting for him.
7. While he was skating at a world-record pace, he slipped again but still won the race—in world-record time.
8. After he received the gold medal, he dedicated it to his sister.

EXERCISE 3 Identify whether each sentence is complex or not complex. Then identify the adverb clause in each complex sentence.

1. After he won his gold medal, he established the Dan Jansen Foundation.
2. The foundation raises money for the fight against leukemia, as well as for youth programs.
3. He often acts as a TV sports commentator when the Olympics occur.
4. He also has acted as a skating coach.

APPLY IT NOW

Write four sentences about your favorite athlete. Use at least three adverb clauses indicating time in your sentences. Underline the dependent clauses.

Research your favorite athlete online.

Sentence Review

7.1 Tell whether each sentence is declarative, interrogative, imperative, or exclamatory. Add the correct end punctuation.

1. Pennies are made from copper and zinc

2. What president is featured on the penny

3. Collecting coins is such fun

4. Do you have any old coins

5. Show me the most valuable coin in your collection

7.2 Identify the simple subject and the simple predicate in each sentence.

6. The bald eagle serves as a symbol of the United States.

7. The early colonists wanted an official seal.

8. Benjamin Franklin argued strongly for the turkey as a national bird.

9. The back of some quarters displays the bald eagle.

7.3 Identify the complete subject and the complete predicate in each sentence.

10. Muscle tissue forms the human heart.

11. A healthy heart beats more than 100,000 times a day.

12. The right ventricle pumps blood to the lungs.

13. The left ventricle sends oxygenated blood through the body.

7.4 Identify the direct object and indirect object in each sentence.

14. Walt Disney taught himself art skills.

15. As a boy Walt Disney sold his neighbors his artistic pieces.

16. He gave the world Mickey Mouse in the 1920s.

17. His animated films and theme parks earned Disney a place in entertainment history.

7.5 Identify the subject complement in each sentence. Tell whether the subject complement is a noun or an adjective.

18. My uncle is a fan of Lou Gehrig.

19. Gehrig was a baseball player from 1925 to 1939.

20. He had been very successful in his career.

21. He was humble in his retirement speech from baseball.

7.6 Tell whether each sentence is in natural order or inverted order.

22. What do pastry chefs make?

23. Pastry chefs create all types of desserts.

24. The chef kneaded more butter into the dough.

25. Into the oven go their creations.

26. Is that decorative bow edible?

7.7 **Identify the compound subject or the compound predicate in each sentence.**

27. Kangaroos and koalas carry their young in pouches.

28. Young kangaroos live and drink milk in their mothers' pouches.

29. We researched and reported on marsupials.

30. Possums and wallabies are also marsupials.

7.8 **Identify the compound direct object in each sentence.**

31. Swimmers wear goggles and caps in the pool.

32. Caleb packed a towel and sandals in his bag.

33. My mom drove my friend and me to swim practice.

34. Mia swims freestyle and butterfly during the swim meets.

7.9 **Identify the compound subject complement in each sentence. Tell whether the complements are nouns or adjectives.**

35. Michael Jordan was a basketball star and role model.

36. He was an Olympic gold medal winner and an NBA champion.

37. His shots were effortless and impressive.

38. Jordan's baseball career was brief and unimpressive.

7.10 **Identify the simple subject and simple predicate in each independent clause.**

39. Lance Armstrong has won many Tour de France races, and he is considered the world's greatest cyclist.

40. The athlete became ill in 1996, and doctors diagnosed cancer.

41. Many people admire Lance Armstrong; he triumphed over difficult odds.

7.11 **Identify the adverb clause in each sentence.**

42. Before telephones, people communicated by letters and telegraph.

43. After Alexander Graham Bell invented the telephone in 1876, the first system was installed in Connecticut.

44. Boston and New York City had a telephone link once another system was built in 1883.

45. As the use of telephones grew, many telephone companies and rural cooperative companies started.

Tech Tip Go to www.voyagesinenglish.com for more activities.

Sentence Challenge

Frédéric Bartholdi

Read the selection and answer the questions.

1. Have you ever been to the Statue of Liberty? 2. It stands on Liberty Island in New York Harbor; it is a beautiful historic monument. 3. Two spiral staircases lead from the base to the crown. 4. A separate, shorter staircase is then used to reach the torch, which is 305 feet above the base of the statue. 5. The view of New York City from there is magnificent and unique!

6. "Statue of Liberty" is actually a nickname for the huge monument. 7. Its actual name is *Liberty Enlightening the World.* 8. It arrived as a giant birthday present to the United States from France on July 4, 1884. 9. After a French historian had suggested a monument to freedom, the French sculptor Frédéric Bartholdi designed and built the statue. 10. The citizens of France offered the Americans the statue as a gift.

11. In Paris stands a small version of the Statue of Liberty. 12. The large statue in New York Harbor and the small one in Paris are reminders of the longtime friendship of the two countries.

1. What kind of sentence is sentence 1? Is it in natural order or inverted order?

2. Is sentence 2 a simple sentence or a compound sentence?

3. In sentence 3 find the simple subject and the simple predicate.

4. In sentence 3 find the complete subject and the complete predicate.

5. What kind of sentence is sentence 5?

6. In sentence 6 what is the subject complement? Is it a noun or an adjective?

7. In sentence 10 what is the direct object and indirect object?

8. Find a sentence that has a compound subject.

9. Find a sentence with a compound subject complement.

10. Find the complex sentence with an adverb clause indicating time.

11. Is sentence 11 in natural order or inverted order? Rewrite it to reverse the order.

Punctuation and Capitalization

8.1 End Punctuation

Punctuation marks show how various parts of a sentence relate to each other. They also signal what type a sentence is. Understanding the proper use of punctuation helps in both writing and reading. The end punctuation marks of sentences are periods, question marks, and exclamation points.

Use a period at the end of a declarative sentence or an imperative sentence.

- A declarative sentence makes a statement.

  Scientists believe that water once flowed on Mars.

- An imperative sentence gives a command.

  Lend me your book about the planets, please.

Use a question mark at the end of an interrogative sentence.

- An interrogative sentence asks a question.

  Was there ever life on Mars?

Use an exclamation point at the end of an exclamatory sentence.

- An exclamatory sentence expresses strong emotion.

  What a fascinating question that is!

EXERCISE 1 Look at the end punctuation of each sentence. Tell what type of sentence it is and give the rule for end punctuation that applies.

1. Find Olympus Mons, the largest known volcano in our solar system, on the map of Mars.
2. It is three times higher than Mount Everest.
3. That's really huge!
4. The North and South Poles of Mars are covered with ice caps.
5. What are these ice caps made of?
6. Look for the answer on this page.
7. They consist of frozen carbon dioxide and water.
8. What a fascinating planet Mars is!

EXERCISE 2 Rewrite the sentences, adding correct end punctuation.

1. Come here and look at this model of Mars
2. According to some findings, water must have existed on Mars at some time
3. Will scientists find evidence of past life there
4. Are there fossils of microorganisms to be found in Mars rock
5. What an interesting discovery that would be
6. Read more about current research on Mars
7. What did the rovers on Mars discover
8. How interesting the rovers' photos are
9. Why has Mars been referred to as the red planet
10. Its reddish soil has rusted iron in it

EXERCISE 3 Rewrite each sentence, changing each sentence into the type in parentheses.

> EXAMPLE **Is Mars near Earth?** (declarative)
> **Mars is near Earth.**

1. Mars is cooler than Earth. (interrogative)
2. Did you read the book about Mars? (imperative)
3. Mars has two moons. (interrogative)
4. Mars is an interesting planet. (exclamatory)
5. Is Mars smaller than Earth? (declarative)
6. Did you find information about possible life on Mars? (imperative)
7. I find the solar system fascinating. (exclamatory)
8. How vast the universe is! (declarative)

APPLY IT NOW

Write four sentences about a planet. Write one declarative, one interrogative, one imperative, and one exclamatory sentence. Be sure to use the correct end punctuation.

8.2 Commas in a Series

Commas are used to separate three or more words in a series. A comma comes before the coordinating conjunction.

> **Mercury, Earth, Venus, *and* Mars are solid planets—or terrestrial planets—in the solar system.**

In the sentence above, the coordinating conjunction is *and*. A comma precedes *and*. A comma goes after each word in the series before *and*.

Words in a series should be similar in nature and serve the same purpose in the sentence. A series may consist of all nouns, all verbs, all adverbs, or all adjectives.

> **Jupiter, Saturn, Uranus, *and* Neptune are gaseous planets.**

In the sentence above, commas separate a series of nouns. The series of nouns acts as the subject of the sentence. The nouns form a compound subject.

In this sentence commas are used to separate verbs used as simple predicates—*observe, study,* and *chart.* They form a compound predicate.

> **Scientists observe, study, *and* chart the Red Spot, a gigantic whirlwind on Jupiter.**

In each sentence below, commas separate a series of nouns that functions as an object.

> **The atmosphere of Jupiter includes hydrogen, helium, *and* ammonia.**
> **The teacher assigned Carl, Fred, *and* Missy different planets for their reports.**
> **Several students wrote stories about imaginary trips to Saturn, Venus, Pluto, *and* Neptune.**

In each sentence above, the series functions as an object. In the first sentence, the series is the direct object of *includes.* In the second sentence, the series is the indirect object of *assigned,* and in the third sentence, the series is the object of the preposition *to.*

> **Jupiter is gigantic, gaseous, *and* stormy.**

In the sentence above, commas separate adjectives in a series that functions as a subject complement.

EXERCISE 1 Rewrite the sentences. Add commas to these sentences to separate words or phrases in a series.

1. The inner planets are small rocky and solid.

2. Jupiter is large gaseous and liquid.

3. Storms constantly form swirl and rage on Jupiter.

4. Like Earth, Jupiter tilts spins and orbits the sun.

5. Europa has a shiny icy and cracked surface.

6. Jupiter was studied by the three early scientists Simon Marius Galileo Galilei and Robert Hooke.

7. Scientists have used telescopes satellites and space probes to view Jupiter.

8. The spots ovals and streaks on Jupiter's cloud tops are weather flare-ups.

9. Io Europa Ganymede and Callisto are the four biggest moons of Jupiter.

10. Astronomers view Jupiter's features photograph the exterior from space and use the information to analyze the planet.

EXERCISE 2 Use the following series of words to write sentences of your own, using the function in parentheses.

EXAMPLE   **museum, theater, zoo** (object of a preposition)
We like to go on field trips to the museum, the theater, and the zoo.

1. crowded, bustling, noisy (adjective)

2. planetariums, aquariums, oceanariums (subject)

3. question, theorize, experiment (predicate)

4. model, report, diagram (direct object)

5. learn, study, teach (predicate)

6. students, scientists, researchers (indirect object)

7. vast, dark, deep (adjective)

APPLY IT NOW

Think about a visit to a park, a mall, or some other place in your neighborhood. What would you see? Write five sentences, each of which contains words in a series. Use commas correctly to punctuate the sentences.

8.3 Commas with Conjunctions

A comma is used before the coordinating conjunction *and, but,* or *or* when two independent clauses are joined to form a compound sentence.

> **Astronomy is the study of the universe,** *and* **it has existed since ancient times.**
>
> **Astronomers use large telescopes,** *but* **you can study the sky with simple binoculars.**
>
> **You can first study the moon,** *or* **you can look for constellations.**

Commas are used in compound sentences but not in compound sentence parts.

> **A** **Asteroids** *and* **comets are flying rocks.**
>
> **B** **A comet is a solar body of ice** *and* **dust.**
>
> **C** **Asteroids may contain carbon** *or* **other materials.**
>
> **D** **Comets** *and* **asteroids fascinate me, and I will eventually research** *and* **submit a report on them.**

- In sentence A no comma is needed to separate the two parts of the compound subject *Asteroids* and *comets*.
- In sentence B *ice* and *dust,* objects of the preposition *of,* are not separated by a comma.
- In sentence C a comma does not separate the direct objects *carbon* and *materials*.
- In sentence D a comma is used to separate the independent clauses. Commas are not used, however, in the compound subject *Comets and asteroids* in the first clause or in the compound predicate *will research and submit* in the second clause.

Can you explain why a comma is not needed in the following sentence?

> **Astronomers observe and map the stars.**

The sentence has a compound predicate, *observe and map,* and compound sentence parts are not separated by commas.

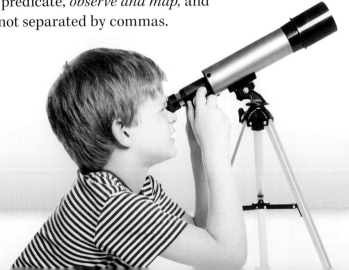

EXERCISE 1 Rewrite the sentences, adding commas where needed.

1. You must use your eyes carefully and you will see many new things in the sky.

2. Some people buy telescopes but even binoculars are a good tool for star viewing.

3. Many books show the locations of planets and stars at different times of the year and these books are useful tools.

4. You can view the constellation Orion in the evening in winter or you can look for it during the morning in summer.

5. The stars really are different colors and the star on Orion's shoulder looks red at certain times of the year.

EXERCISE 2 Rewrite the sentences, adding commas where needed. Not all the sentences need commas.

1. Most cities have a lot of pollution and star watching is difficult in them.

2. Both air pollution and city lights make star viewing hard in cities.

3. People in cities can usually see only the brighter objects and many stars are faint or hidden.

4. City dwellers should go far from the city and sit in an isolated area under the sky for a good night of star watching.

5. There is less pollution in isolated areas and a whole new sky will appear before your eyes.

EXERCISE 3 Rewrite the following paragraph. Combine the underlined sentences, using a conjunction and commas where needed.

It was a cold night. We were getting ready to go outside. We wanted to watch the meteor shower that was supposed to begin at midnight. I brought a big thermos of hot chocolate. My dad brought some blankets. We didn't have to wait long. The meteor show was spectacular. We watched meteors shooting across the sky. You can make a wish for every one you see. I must have made a hundred wishes that night.

APPLY IT NOW

Imagine you just returned from a great adventure. Write five sentences about your experience by combining independent clauses. Circle the coordinating conjunction in each sentence.

Find photos online to go with your adventure.

8.4 Direct Address and Yes and *No*

Commas are used to separate words used in direct address. A noun in direct address names the person spoken to.

When the name of a person addressed is the first word of a sentence, it is followed by a comma.

> **Greg, did you know that Mercury is the planet closest to the sun?**

When the noun in direct address is the last word of a sentence, a comma is placed before the name.

> **Mercury has practically no atmosphere, *Alex*.**

If the name of the person is used within a sentence, one comma is placed before the name and one after the name.

> **The planet Mercury, *Bob*, is quite rocky.**

Commas are used after the words *yes* and *no* when either introduces a sentence.

> **Yes, the temperature varies greatly on Mercury.**
> **No, Mercury is not far away from the sun.**

Can you explain the use of commas in this sentence?

> **No, Mercury is not a gaseous planet, Lisa.**

The first comma separates *No* from the rest of the sentence. The second comma separates the noun in direct address, *Lisa*, from the rest of the sentence.

EXERCISE 1 Rewrite the sentences. Add commas for nouns in direct address.

1. A day on Mercury is equal to 58.65 days on Earth Janet.
2. Class Mercury turns slowly on its axis.
3. Luis a year on Mercury lasts only 88 Earth days.
4. Mercury orbits the sun Ling faster than any other planet.
5. During the day Kim Mercury's temperature is hotter than an oven.
6. Students the core of Mercury is iron.
7. The atmosphere of the planet is very thin Tony.

EXERCISE 2 Rewrite the sentences. Add a comma after *yes* or *no* when either begins a sentence.

1. Yes Mercury is named after the Roman god.
2. Yes the nights on Mercury are colder than a freezer.
3. No there aren't any seasons on Mercury.
4. No Mercury's axis is not tilted.
5. Yes Mercury has craters.
6. Yes Mercury is the closest planet to the sun.
7. No Mercury is not a large planet.

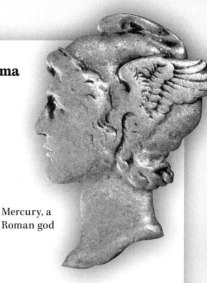

Mercury, a
Roman god

EXERCISE 3 Rewrite the sentences. Add commas where needed. Apply all the rules you learned.

1. Yes Mercury is the planet closest to the sun.
2. Craters on Mercury have names such as Bach Beethoven and Shakespeare.
3. It is the smallest planet Ellie in our solar system.
4. Yes some scientists George compare Mercury's surface to that of our moon.
5. Mercury shrank over time and its surface wrinkled.
6. No I didn't know Kevin that Mercury is only a little larger than Earth's moon.
7. Yes Joseph Mercury is difficult to see sometimes because of its proximity to the sun.

EXERCISE 4 Complete each sentence with a noun in direct address. Add commas where needed.

1. Yes I would like to go stargazing with you tonight _____.
2. No I don't have a telescope _____.
3. Yes it would be great _____ if I could share your telescope.
4. No I can't meet you _____ until about 9:30.
5. Yes I checked with my mom this morning _____.
6. Yes she said I could go _____.

APPLY IT NOW

Imagine three of your friends offered to help you with your chores while you are on vacation. Write brief instructions for each friend to take care of your pet fish, cut the grass, and water the houseplants. Use nouns in direct address to clarify who is to do what.

8.5 Apostrophes

An **apostrophe** (') is used to show ownership or possession.

To show that one person or thing owns or possesses something, place an apostrophe and an *s* (*'s*) after the singular noun.

> This *scientist's* research is about the surface of Mars.
> *Janis's* report will explain the research project.

To show that more than one person or thing owns or possesses something, place an apostrophe after the *s* at the end of a regular plural noun.

> The *scientists'* new telescope is big and powerful.
> The *students'* report was on astronomy.

If a plural noun does not end in *s*, place an apostrophe and *s* (*'s*) after the noun.

> The *children's* telescope is at a window in the attic.

An **apostrophe** is used in a contraction to show where a letter or letters have been omitted.

> I *didn't* know that Earth is the third planet from the sun.

In the above sentence, *didn't* stands for *did not*. The apostrophe stands for the missing *o* in *not*.

Here is a list of some common contractions.

aren't = are not	I've = I have
can't = cannot	she's = she is, she has
didn't = did not	there's = there is, there has
doesn't = does not	they're = they are
don't = do not	they've = they have
hasn't = has not	wasn't = was not
haven't = have not	we'll = we will
he's = he is, he has	we're = we are
I'll = I will	we've = we have
I'm = I am	won't = will not
isn't = is not	you're = you are
it's = it is, it has	you've = you have

EXERCISE 1 Add an apostrophe to show possession where needed in these sentences.

1. Sarahs report had many interesting facts about the moon.
2. The classs interest in the subject goes back to an earlier visit by a NASA scientist.
3. The early Romans name for the moon was *luna*.
4. Explorers trips into space have given us a great deal of information about the moon.
5. Almost a half ton of rock samples from the moon was included in the astronauts cargoes back to Earth.
6. Scientists work on these samples is still going on today.
7. Neil Armstrongs first words on the moon are still quoted.
8. Several astronauts have landed on the moon, and the mens courage has always impressed me.

EXERCISE 2 Rewrite the following, using one contraction in each sentence.

1. There is no atmosphere on the moon.
2. I have read that the moon may have been part of Earth.
3. Scientists do not know whether a huge object once collided with Earth.
4. We will probably never know whether a piece of Earth broke off and formed the present moon.
5. There is one important effect of the moon on Earth—it causes tides.
6. The moon does not have any light of its own.
7. It is simply reflecting the light of the sun.
8. I am learning more about the moon from this book.
9. One side of the moon cannot be seen from Earth.
10. We have received images of that side from space probes.
11. The moon does not have life of any kind.
12. There is a possibility of more missions to the moon in the future.

APPLY IT NOW

Draw a floor plan of your home or school, showing the location of the things in it. Label your floor plan to tell what belongs to whom; for example, Bob's desk, Alan's bedroom. Write a paragraph about your floor plan. Include at least four contractions.

Grammar in Action. Identify two examples of apostrophes in the letter on page 443. How are they used?

8.6 Capitalization

The first word of every sentence begins with a capital letter.

Not all planets in the solar system have moons.

A proper noun begins with a capital letter. A proper noun names a particular person, a particular place, or a particular thing.

People:	Sally Ride, Copernicus, Aristotle
Places:	Mercury, China, New Jersey, Pittsburgh, Lake Erie, Columbia River, Smithsonian Air and Space Museum, Mars
Organizations:	United Nations, Red Cross
Streets and avenues:	Main Street, Elm Avenue
Holidays:	New Year's Day, Labor Day, Memorial Day
Schools:	Lakin School, Harvard University
Religious denominations:	Catholicism, Methodism, Catholics, Methodists
Members of a political party:	Democrats, Republicans
Days of the week:	Monday, Tuesday, Sunday
Months of the year:	November, May, September

EXERCISE 1 Rewrite the phrases, adding capital letters where needed.

1. independence day on july 4
2. the letter to the johnson space center written by the students of forest park school
3. national aeronautics and space administration located on e street in washington, d.c.
4. the first person on the moon on july 20, 1969
5. langley research center in hampton, virginia
6. future exploration of mars
7. a field trip in may or june to houston, texas
8. a landing at edwards air force base in california
9. the kennedy space center at cape canaveral in florida
10. neil armstrong and buzz aldrin, the first astronauts on the moon

Buzz Aldrin

EXERCISE 2 Rewrite the sentences, adding capital letters where needed. Not all the sentences need capital letters.

1. The students of Forest school visited a special exhibit at the Johnson Space center in Houston, texas.

2. Our teacher, Mrs. Portman, organized the trip.

3. We went on a tuesday morning in October.

4. we experienced what it is like to be in a weightless environment in a special space capsule.

5. A film showed photos of the first flight into space by an american, which was taken by alan Shepard in may 1961.

6. My class is going to make a return visit in January or February.

EXERCISE 3 Rewrite each sentence, adding capital letters where needed.

1. astronomers have been studying the definition of planets.

2. the international astronomical union set requirements for planets in august 2006.

3. scientists once classified the body pluto as a planet.

4. now pluto is considered a dwarf planet.

5. other dwarf planets are ceres, makemake, and eris.

6. the astronomer julio angel fernandez from uruguay contributed to the idea for the new class of dwarf planets.

7. scientists are still studying bodies in space to determine if they are planets or not.

8. mike brown of the california institute of technology has been studying bodies far out in space.

9. he discovered the dwarf planet of eris.

10. scientists are still discovering large bodies farther in space than the planet neptune, which may be dwarf planets.

Apollo rocket engine at Kennedy Space Center, Florida

APPLY IT NOW

Write six sentences about a historic event or person. Trade papers with a partner. Proofread each other's work.

8.7 Titles of Works

A capital letter is used for the first letter of each important word in the titles of works. Articles, conjunctions, and short prepositions usually are not capitalized. These include words such as *a, an, the, and, to, in, of,* and *from.* The first word after a colon also is capitalized. The first and last words of a title always begin with capital letters.

Book title:	*The War of the Worlds* by H. G. Wells
Play title:	*Peter Pan* by J. M. Barrie
Poem title:	"Letter to the Moon" by Jane Yolen
Magazine title:	*National Geographic*
Song title:	"Celebration" by Kool and the Gang
Movie title:	*The Wizard of Oz*
Artwork title:	*Evening Star* by Georgia O'Keeffe
Sacred book title:	Bible, Koran, Torah
Article, short story, or essay title:	"Is There Life on Mars?"

The first word of every line of most poetry and songs:

A flea and a fly
Flew up in a flue.
Said the flea, "Let us fly!"
Said the fly, "Let us flee!"

Titles of books (except sacred books), plays, magazines, movies, and artworks are italicized when typed and underlined when handwritten. Titles of poems, stories, and magazine articles have quotation marks around them.

EXERCISE 1 Rewrite the phrases, adding capital letters where needed. Use underlining for italicized titles.

1. Christina Rossetti's poem "Who Has Seen the wind?"

2. and the rockets red glare, the bombs bursting in air, gave proof through the night that our flag was still there —"the Star-Spangled banner"

3. H. A. Rey's book *The Stars: a new way to see them*

4. the song "I want to hold your hand" by the Beatles

5. Vincent van Gogh's painting *starry night*

6. ancient copies of the torah, the bible, and koran

7. Eleanor Estes's book *the hundred dresses*

EXERCISE 2 Rewrite the sentences, adding capital letters where needed. Use underlining for italicized titles.

1. Jules Verne's *from the earth to the moon* is an early science-fiction book, with a spaceship shot from a cannon.

2. Janet and Isaac Asimov's *norby chronicles* features robots, people, and travel through time and space.

3. *home on the moon* by Marianne J. Dyson traces humans' interest in the moon.

4. Maura Gouck's book *the solar system* tells readers what they would actually see on a journey among the planets.

5. Ray Bradbury's story "all summer in a day" is about a place where the sun shines for one hour every seven years.

6. Franklyn Branley's *the moon hoax* tells about a newspaper that published made-up stories about life on the moon.

7. *how the stars fell into the sky* is a book by Jerrie Oughton that retells an ancient Navajo legend.

8. *harnessing power from the sun* is a book by Niki Walker that describes the possible uses of solar power in our everyday lives.

9. Robert Louis Stevenson's poem "the moon" is a favorite of mine.

10. I read an article titled "the century's longest solar eclipse" in *time for kids* magazine.

EXERCISE 3 Rewrite the sentences, adding capital letters and italics where needed. Use underlining for italicized titles.

1. I like fairy tales, so Nikki recommended I read the story the little mermaid.

2. Jorge said that the book called grimm's fairy tales by the Brothers Grimm was his favorite.

3. Maria found an article about fairy tales in a magazine called cricket.

4. Lewis Carroll wrote the poem jabberwocky, which we read in class.

5. He also wrote a book called through the looking glass about Alice and her adventures.

APPLY IT NOW

Write five sentences about books, poems, or magazine articles you've read recently, or about movies you've seen. Tell what you liked or disliked about each.

Tech Tip Using a computer, italicize the titles in your sentences.

8.8 Other Uses of Capitalization

In addition to uses with proper nouns and in titles, capital letters are used for

- the first word in a direct quotation

  NASA officials reported, "The second Mars rover, *Opportunity*, has safely touched down."

- the directions *North, South, East,* and *West,* when they refer to specific regions of a country

  On our trip to the South, we watched the launch of the space shuttle from Cape Canaveral.

  The rover *Opportunity*

- the pronoun *I*

  My family and I visited the Kennedy Space Center.

- titles that precede a person's name

  When he was elected in 2008, President Barack Obama became the country's 44th president.

- initials in a person's name

  H. G. Wells = Herbert George Wells

EXERCISE 1 Rewrite the phrases, using the correct capitalization.

1. the space centers in the south
2. colonel Buzz Aldrin
3. general Omar Bradley
4. a novel by Arthur c. Clarke
5. a U.S. space shuttle landing site in the west

EXERCISE 2 Write each of the following names, using an initial instead of the middle name.

1. Sally Kristen Ride
2. Captain Neil Alden Armstrong
3. George Walker Bush
4. Franklyn Mansfield Branley
5. Alan Barlett Shepard

Sally Ride

EXERCISE 3 Rewrite the sentences, adding capital letters where needed. Use underlining for italicized words.

1. mr. jackson began, "it was in 2004 when the first rovers landed on mars."

2. he continued, "these rovers have taken thousands of full-color photos of the surface of mars."

3. dev asked, "doesn't the west have the best views of the sky?"

4. serena said, "you know, i've seen amazing photos of mars online."

5. paolo added, "the surface of mars is rocky and eerie."

6. mr. jackson then asked, "why are these missions to mars important?"

7. "i think space exploration could unlock secrets of our planet," answered mike.

8. keisha said, "the names of the two rovers on mars are *spirit* and *opportunity*."

9. *postcards from mars* is a book of photos taken by the rovers.

10. another space device, called *phoenix*, landed on mars in may 2008.

11. this device, sent by NASA, discovered existing ice on mars.

12. a canadian instrument on the phoenix even noticed snow falling from a cloud.

13. i wondered, "why does mars look red in all the photos?"

14. mr. jackson answered, "mars owes its color to the minerals in its soil."

15. "does any life exist on mars?" riley asked.

16. "these probes may help us find the answer," said our teacher, ms. kelly.

APPLY IT NOW

Select a paragraph in a newspaper article. Rewrite it, removing all the capital letters. Trade your rewritten article with a partner. Rewrite your partner's article, putting back the capital letters. Compare the paragraph to the original.

8.9 Abbreviations

A period is used after many abbreviations. An **abbreviation** is a shortened form of a word.

Capital letters are used for abbreviations when capital letters would be used if the words were written in full.

Titles are capitalized when they appear before proper names.

TITLES

Sr. = Senior	Jr. = Junior	Dr. = Doctor
Rev. = Reverend	Gov. = Governor	Mr. = Mister
Mrs. = Missus	Prof. = Professor	Capt. = Captain

CALENDAR

Jan. = January	Sept. = September	Apr. = April
Sun. = Sunday	Fri. = Friday	Thurs. = Thursday

May, June, and *July* are not abbreviated.

TIME

sec. = second	min. = minute	hr. = hour
a.m. = before noon	p.m. = after noon	

UNITS OF MEASURE

in. = inch	ft. = foot	yd. = yard	oz. = ounce
qt. = quart	lb. = pound	gal. = gallon	

m = meter	cm = centimeter	km = kilometer	l = liter
g = gram	mg = milligram	mm = millimeter	

The abbreviations used in the metric system do not begin with capital letters and are not followed by periods.

POSTAL ABBREVIATIONS

St. = Street	Ave. = Avenue	Rd. = Road
NJ = New Jersey	ID = Idaho	PA = Pennsylvania

The postal abbreviations for the states have two capital letters and are not followed by periods.

EXERCISE 1 Write the abbreviations for the following words. Look in a reference book for the state postal abbreviations.

1. February
2. Doctor
3. Vermont
4. liter
5. gram
6. Mister
7. pound
8. California
9. Street
10. Avenue
11. Boulevard
12. August
13. after noon
14. New York
15. December
16. Senior
17. kilogram
18. Maine
19. Governor
20. Sunday

EXERCISE 2 Rewrite the phrases. Use abbreviations for the italicized words.

1. 2 *kilograms* of hamburger
2. *Wednesday, September* 8
3. 10 *ounces* of milk
4. *Reverend* Martin Luther King *Junior*
5. Seattle, *Washington*
6. 27 Pershing *Road*
7. 1 *quart* of apple juice
8. *Saturday, November* 11

Seattle

EXERCISE 3 Rewrite the sentences to correct any mistakes in the use of capital letters, abbreviations, and punctuation.

1. I started a diary for my sky watching, and I wrote "mar 5" at the top of the first page
2. The heading for the day that I first saw a meteor shower was "nov 8"
3. Our neighbor, mr Peterson, has let me use his telescope
4. The instructions with the telescope give these dimensions for the eyepiece: 2 in diameter, 40 mm focal length
5. According to the ad, the diameter of the reflector is 8 in
6. I saw the meteor shower at 11:15 pm

APPLY IT NOW

Write an identification card for yourself. Include your name, address, city, state, hair and eye color, and date of birth. Use abbreviations where possible.

Grammar in Action. Identify three items that can be abbreviated in the second paragraph of the letter on page 443.

8.10 Direct Quotations

A **direct quotation** is the exact words a person has spoken. A direct quotation is enclosed in quotation marks and is separated from the rest of the sentence by one or more commas. Use a capital letter for the first word of every direct quotation.

When a direct quotation comes at the beginning of a sentence, a comma is placed after the quotation.

> **"The planet Saturn is the sixth planet from the sun," explained our teacher.**

When a direct quotation comes at the end of the sentence, a comma is placed before it.

> **Mr. Stephens explained, "Its beautiful rings are made mostly of rocks and ice chunks."**

When the exact words of a speaker are divided, more than one comma is used to separate the quotation from the rest of the sentence. Use a capital letter for the first word of a direct quotation, but do not use a capital letter where the quotation continues.

> **"The planet," said Gregory, "is visible without the use of a telescope."**

When a question mark or an exclamation point ends a quotation at the beginning of a sentence, a comma is not needed.

> **"Is it the second largest planet in our solar system?" asked Debbie.**
> **"Saturn has such beautiful rings!" my sister exclaimed.**
> **"Eureka!" cried the scientist, "I think we've got it!"**

When a question mark or an exclamation point is part of the direct quotation, as above, it is placed inside the end quotation marks. When the question mark or exclamation point is not part of the quotation, it is placed outside the quotation marks.

> **Did the teacher say, "Choose just one planet to study"?**
> **I was stunned when I heard Jim say, "I finished my report yesterday"!**

EXERCISE 1 Rewrite the sentences, adding quotation marks, commas, and end punctuation where needed.

1. The planet Saturn is made up almost entirely of liquid gases explained Mr. Valentine

2. Saturn's rings continued Mr. Valentine can only be seen with a telescope

3. Can you see the rings of Saturn without a telescope asked Kevin

4. Seen through a telescope said Jessica Saturn has a yellowy color

5. What are Saturn's rings made of asked Orlando

6. They are made of ice-covered pieces of rock answered Mr. Valentine

7. I think she continued it looks very beautiful

8. It is the second biggest planet in the solar system added Luke after Jupiter

9. If Saturn were hollowed out, 764 Earths could fit inside exclaimed May

10. Did Mr. James say You know you can take a pretend flight around Saturn on the NASA Web site

EXERCISE 2 Rewrite the sentences, adding quotation marks, commas, end punctuation, and capital letters where needed.

1. a day on Saturn equals 11.5 Earth hours explained our teacher

2. how many moons does Saturn have asked Marcia

3. Saturn has 18 moons answered Mick and Titan is the largest of them

4. Mr. James asked did you know that a space probe has entered Saturn's orbit to study it more closely

5. everyone in our class answered at once no, we didn't

6. we will have more information Mr. Valentine explained as the probes relay it

APPLY IT NOW

Imagine you meet a creature from another planet. Write what you said to each other to learn about the creature's planet and what the creature said to you to learn about Earth. Remember to punctuate direct quotations correctly.

8.11 Addresses and Letters

All letters have these parts: (1) heading, (2) salutation, (3) body or the message, (4) closing, and (5) signature.

When writing a personal letter, you need to include only the date in the heading. For business letters include your address.

The inside address of a business letter includes the name and address of the person to whom the letter is being sent.

The salutation is a greeting used at the beginning of a letter. The first word and the name of the person being addressed in the salutation start with capital letters. A comma is used after the salutation in a personal letter. A colon is used in business letters.

Dear Aunt Jane,   Dear Mr. Wade:

The closing ends a letter. The first word in the closing begins with a capital letter. Use a comma after the closing.

Sincerely,   Your friend,   Very truly yours,

In the inside address and the address on the envelope, capitalize

- the name of the person addressed
- the name of the street and the city or town
- both letters of a state's postal abbreviation
- abbreviations such as *N.* for *North, S.* for *South, E.* for *East,* and *W.* for *West*

Use a comma after the name of the city or town.

Antonia Markham
1200 N. Bank Street
Oakland, IL 60025

EXERCISE 1 Rewrite the following, adding capital letters and punctuation where needed. Use abbreviations where possible.

1. dear aunt Beatrice
2. very truly yours
3. warmest regards
4. dear mister Andrews
5. sincerely yours
6. dear professor Robins
7. your niece
8. all the best

EXERCISE 2 Rewrite the following addresses to correct capitalization and punctuation mistakes. Use abbreviations where possible.

1. beatrice taylor
   1759 niles avenue
   mayfield, ohio 44124

2. Christopher philips
   2203 country lane
   mcHenry, Illinois 62579

3. Roberto Martinez
   955 spruce street
   new haven, Connecticut 06510

4. Marian mahoney
   9626 south millard avenue
   estes park, colorado 80511

5. doctor emily ruth
   412 sheridan drive
   Lincoln, nebraska 68503

6. erich Mueller
   11281 caso street
   orlando, florida 32801

EXERCISE 3 Rewrite the letter. Add capital letters and punctuation where needed. Use abbreviations where possible.

742 jackson avenue
elizabeth new jersey 07201
january 7, 20—

richard vernon
Telescopes to the Universe
173 palm lane drive
oceanside california 92054

dear mr vernon

I am very interested in ordering the telescope you advertised in *Astronomer* magazine.

Can you tell me the dimensions of the telescope? I am interested in a telescope that is easy to pack and move. I plan to use it outdoors, away from the city.

You can respond to the above address or e-mail at alexthomas@city.com.net. You can also call me at home. My phone number is (201) 555-1212.

sincerely yours
Alexander Thomas

APPLY IT NOW

Write a letter to a video game company to share your idea for a new game. Also address an envelope to the company. Be sure to use all the parts needed for a business letter and to use capital letters and punctuation correctly.

Punctuation and Capitalization Review

8.1 Rewrite the sentences, adding the correct end punctuation. Tell whether each sentence is a declarative, interrogative, imperative, or exclamatory sentence.

1. Do you like pancakes
2. Blueberry pancakes are truly wonderful
3. What kind of pancake is your favorite
4. Pancakes are made from flour, eggs, and milk
5. Flip the pancake when bubbles start to form

8.2 Rewrite the sentences, adding commas to separate the words in each series. Tell whether each series functions as nouns, verbs, adjectives, or direct objects.

6. January February and March are dreary months in many parts of the country.
7. Sometimes it rains sleets and snows on the same day.
8. This sweater is wooly itchy and warm.
9. Mom asked Megan Jamal and Anthony to shovel a path.
10. People sled ice-skate and ski in the cold weather.

8.3 Rewrite the sentences, adding commas to separate the parts of compound sentences. Not all the sentences need commas.

11. The farmer planted corn but rains threatened its growth.
12. The farmer wakes up early and works long days.
13. Farming can be tough but it can also be rewarding.
14. My parents were farmers and my uncle ran the store.

8.4 Rewrite the sentences, adding commas where needed.

15. Molly have you seen Old Faithful in Yellowstone National Park?
16. Yes I saw it during my visit last summer.
17. Old Faithful Amelia is a world-famous geyser.
18. The geyser shoots up more than 100 feet in the air Joe.

8.5 Rewrite the sentences, adding apostrophes where they are needed.

19. Snakes arent Tammys favorite animal.
20. The garter snake we saw in the backyard isnt poisonous.
21. Theres a long list of snakes that are harmless.
22. Weve read the groups report on poisonous snakes.

8.6 Rewrite the sentences, adding capital letters where they are needed.

23. the students visited the adler planetarium in chicago.

24. the field trip was scheduled for friday morning.

25. the planetarium is at 1300 s. lake shore drive.

26. was copernicus from poland or germany?

8.7 Rewrite the sentences, correcting the titles as needed.

27. My family attended the Broadway show the lion king.

28. I subscribe to the magazine ranger rick.

29. Sonia titled her report "why i like cats."

30. Let's watch the sound of music on TV tonight.

31. We read a magazine article titled "animals in danger."

8.8 Rewrite the sentences, adding capital letters where they are needed.

32. matt said, "what a beautiful photo, tanya!"

33. tanya and i worked in the darkroom.

34. matthew b. brady was one of the first important photographers.

35. ansel adams took magnificent photos of nature in the west.

8.9 Write an abbreviation for each underlined word.

36. New Year's Day is <u>January</u> 1.

37. <u>Doctor</u> Briggs invited my family to a party.

38. She lives at 2121 Forest <u>Avenue</u>.

39. <u>Mister</u> Cookson brought a tin of crackers for the guests.

8.10 Rewrite the sentences, adding quotation marks, commas, and end punctuation where needed.

40. Mr. Lock is here to talk to us about snow said Mrs. Bell

41. Snowflakes said Mr. Lock are made up of many crystals

42. Hannah asked Is every snowflake really different

43. My brother likes to eat snow said Brian

8.11 Rewrite the items, adding punctuation, capitalization, and abbreviations where needed.

44. sincerely yours

45. dear aunt maria

46. lucy Murphy

47. 59 peachtree lane Atlanta Georgia 30308

48. dear doctor rosenberg

Tech Tip
Go to www.voyagesinenglish.com for more activities.

Punctuation and Capitalization Challenge

Read this story carefully and answer the questions. Paragraphs 1 and 2 have the correct punctuation. Paragraphs 3, 4, 5, 6, and 7 are missing some punctuation marks and capital letters.

1. Paul woke up on Saturday morning. "Hooray!" he announced to his family. "Today is the day I go ballooning with my friend Nick."

2. Paul dressed, ate, and rode out to Washington State Park with Nick and his family. A pilot, Mr. Jacques A. Charles, met them at the field with a huge orange and red hot-air balloon. A large brown basket was attached to the bottom. Paul's heart beat faster when the pilot called to them, "Hurry and get in!"

3. how does this work asked nick.

4. the air inside the balloon is heated to make it become lighter than the air outside the balloon, mr charles explained. that is what makes the balloon rise he said.

5. to come down, well have to burn less fuel. Then ill open the rip panel with this cord to deflate the balloon, Mr Charles explained.

6. lets get started cried nick.

7. everyone had a wonderful time that day. when Paul got home, he wrote a letter to Nick. he began, "dear nick." in his letter he thanked Nick for inviting him for the ride. that day Paul decided that hot-air ballooning was an exciting hobby

1. In paragraph 1 why are there quotation marks around "Hooray!" and "Today is the day I go ballooning with my friend Nick"?

2. In paragraph 2 why are there commas after *dressed* and *ate*?

3. In paragraph 2 why is Washington State Park capitalized?

4. In paragraph 2 why are periods used after *Mr* and *A*?

5. In paragraph 2 why does *Paul's* have an apostrophe?

6. Rewrite paragraphs 3, 4, 5, 6, and 7 with the correct punctuation. Add periods, commas, exclamation points, question marks, apostrophes, and quotation marks where needed. Also add capital letters where needed.

Diagramming

9.1 Subjects, Predicates, Direct Objects, Modifiers

A **diagram** shows how all the words in a sentence fit together. It highlights the most important words in a sentence, and it shows how the other words relate to these important words.

The most important words in a sentence are the subject and the verb. The subject names the person, place, or thing the sentence is about. The verb is the main word in the predicate. It tells what the subject is or does.

- Start the diagram by drawing a horizontal line.
- Find the verb in the sentence. Write it on the right side of the line.
- Find the subject. Write it in front of the verb.
- Draw a vertical line between the subject and the verb. The vertical line cuts through the horizontal line.

SENTENCE **Volcanoes erupt.**

Volcanoes	erupt

In this sentence the subject is *volcanoes,* and the verb is *erupt.* Another important word in some sentences is the direct object. The direct object answers the question *whom* or *what* after the verb.

- To diagram a direct object, first write the subject and the verb on the horizontal line of the diagram.
- Write the direct object on the horizontal line to the right of the verb.
- Draw a vertical line between the verb and the direct object. This line touches the horizontal line but does not cut through it.

SENTENCE **Volcanoes spout lava.**

Volcanoes	spout	lava

Words that describe the subject, verb, or direct object are written on slanting lines under those words. Adjectives modify, or describe, nouns, and adverbs modify verbs.

SENTENCE **The hot lava was flowing slowly.**

The article *the* and the adjective *hot* go under the noun *lava*.
The adverb *slowly* goes under the verb *was flowing*.

EXERCISE 1 Complete the sentence with a direct object of your choice. Add adjectives to describe it if you want. Complete the diagram.

I saw _____.

I	saw

EXERCISE 2 Diagram the sentences.

1. Dolphins play.
2. Susie gathered shells.
3. The door squeaks noisily.
4. Koalas eat leaves.
5. Timmy opened the mysterious trunk cautiously.
6. The ancient Greeks built the first theaters.
7. Moira climbed the tall ladder carefully.
8. Christopher Columbus explored Puerto Rico.
9. Sundials tell time.
10. The rain stopped suddenly.
11. Egyptians speak Arabic.
12. Beth was picking colorful flowers.
13. My mother writes a daily blog.
14. Oxen plowed the land.
15. Pilots fly large airplanes.

APPLY IT NOW

Look at one of the photos in this book. Write four short sentences about it. Diagram the sentences.

Grammar in Action. Diagram the third sentence of the excerpt on page 503. Identify the compound direct object.

9.2 Indirect Objects

An indirect object tells to whom, for whom, to what, or for what the action of a verb is done.

Some verbs that can have indirect objects are the following:

assign	hand	promise	teach
bring	lend	read	tell
buy	offer	sell	write
get	owe	send	
give	pay	show	

In a diagram an indirect object is written on a horizontal line beneath the verb. The indirect object is connected to the verb by a slanting line.

SENTENCE **Dad bought Lila an orange balloon.**

In this sentence *Dad* is the subject, *bought* is the verb, and *balloon* is the direct object. The indirect object is *Lila*. It tells for whom the balloon was bought.

Words that describe the indirect object go on a slanting line under the indirect object.

SENTENCE **Franco sent his grandmother a card.**

In this sentence *grandmother* is the indirect object. The possessive adjective *his* describes *grandmother* and is written on a slanting line under *grandmother*.

EXERCISE 1 Add an indirect object of your choice to this sentence. Complete the diagram.

1. Kristy gave _____ a present.

2. Grandpa Tom told _____ funny jokes.

3. Jonathan writes _____ a long letter.

EXERCISE 2 Diagram the sentences.

1. The waiter handed Mom the bill.
2. The visitors brought the patient roses.
3. The magician showed the audience many tricks.
4. My sister lent me her bicycle.
5. A friend wrote Ruben a long e-mail.
6. Our grandmother baked us cookies.
7. The principal handed the students diplomas.
8. Food gives people energy.
9. The shop sells customers old records.
10. His sister slowly read Jeff the difficult directions.
11. The ancient Romans gave the months their names.
12. The stand sells fans programs.
13. Our class sent the newspaper a letter.
14. Martha wrote Chase a secret message.
15. The teacher assigned the students a big project.

APPLY IT NOW

Write four sentences with indirect objects, each with a different verb from the list on page 190. Diagram the sentences.

 Diagram the topic sentence in an online article.

9.3 Subject Complements

A subject complement follows a linking verb and renames or describes the subject. The most common linking verbs are *be* and its various forms, such as *am, is, are, was, were, have been,* and *has been.* Other common linking verbs are *appear, become, feel, grow, look, remain, seem, sound, stay,* and *taste.* A subject complement can be a noun, a pronoun, or an adjective.

In a diagram a subject complement is written on the horizontal line after the verb. A line that slants to the left separates the subject complement from the verb. The slanting line touches the horizontal line but does not cut through it.

SENTENCE **A turtle is a reptile.**

The subject complement *reptile* is a noun that renames the subject *turtle.*

SENTENCE: **Reptiles' skin can be scaly.**

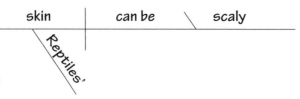

In this sentence the subject complement is the adjective *scaly.* It describes the subject *skin.*

Can you identify the subject complement in this sentence? What part of speech is it?

SENTENCE **Dinosaurs are extinct reptiles.**

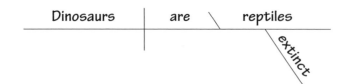

The subject complement *reptiles* is a noun, which renames the subject *dinosaurs.* The adjective *extinct* describes the subject complement.

EXERCISE 1 Add a subject complement of your choice to this sentence. Complete the diagram.

1. A snake is _____.

2. Alligators are _____.

Alligators	are

EXERCISE 2 Diagram the sentences. Tell if each subject complement is a noun, a pronoun, or an adjective.

1. Breakfast is ready.
2. The gift was a camera.
3. LaToya is a good guitarist.
4. Tundra is frozen land.
5. The pickles are sour.
6. Dogs are my favorite pets.
7. Is chess difficult?
8. The sunflowers are tall.
9. Asia is vast.
10. The cheese looks moldy.
11. *Apatosaurus* was a large dinosaur.
12. Jason was a Greek hero.
13. The winner was she.
14. Penguins are nonflying birds.
15. My new backpack is purple.

APPLY IT NOW

Write and diagram two sentences with subject complements about animals. Use a noun subject complement in one sentence and an adjective subject complement in the other sentence.

9.4 Prepositional Phrases

A preposition and its object form a prepositional phrase. The object can be a noun or a pronoun. A prepositional phrase acts as an adjective when it describes a noun or a pronoun. A prepositional phrase acts as an adverb when it describes a verb. A prepositional phrase used as an adverb tells how, when, or where.

In a diagram a prepositional phrase goes beneath the word it describes.

- The preposition is written on a slanting line.
- The object of the preposition is written on a horizontal line connected to the slanting line with the preposition.
- Any word that describes the object is written on a slanting line beneath the object.

SENTENCE **We lost a piece of the puzzle.**

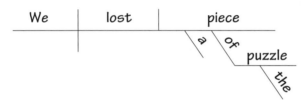

The prepositional phrase *of the puzzle* describes the noun *piece*, so it is an adjective phrase.

SENTENCE **Susan skated on the thin ice.**

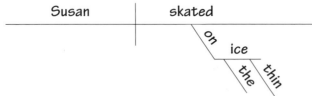

The prepositional phrase *on the thin ice* describes the verb *skated*. It tells where Susan skated. The phrase goes under the verb. The adjectives *the* and *thin* describe the object of the preposition, *ice*, and they are written on slanting lines beneath that object.

EXERCISE 1 Diagram the sentences. Underline the prepositional phrases.

1. The cow jumped over the moon.
2. Native Americans hunted on the prairies.
3. The smell of hot bread filled the kitchen.
4. The hippopotamus is a relative of the pig.
5. The cave is a home for bats.
6. A hammock swung in the breeze.
7. H_2O is the chemical formula for water.
8. The path through the woods is a shortcut.
9. My best friend lives across the street.
10. *Gracias* is the Spanish word for *thank you*.

EXERCISE 2 Diagram these sentences. Each sentence has more than one prepositional phrase.

1. The trunk in the attic belongs to my grandmother.
2. Motorists in England drive on the left side of the street.
3. The tail of a comet reflects the light of the sun.
4. In the afternoon my sister planted flowers in the garden.
5. The trumpets in an orchestra are located near the trombones.

APPLY IT NOW

Think about your last birthday. Write and diagram four sentences with prepositional phrases, two with adjective phrases and two with adverb phrases. Then write a sentence that has both an adjective phrase and an adverb phrase and diagram it.

Grammar in Action. Identify the prepositional phrases in the fourth paragraph of the research report on page 481.

9.5 Interjections

An interjection is a word that expresses strong or sudden emotion. Interjections may express emotions such as happiness, disgust, pain, agreement, impatience, surprise, and sadness. They include words such as *Ah, Oh, Well, Sh, Hey, Good, Ouch, Oops, Yikes,* and *Wow.* These words or the sentences in which they appear are usually followed by exclamation points.

In a diagram an interjection is written on a line that is separate from the rest of the sentence. The line is above, at the left of, and parallel to the main horizontal line.

SENTENCE **Oh! The water is cold.**

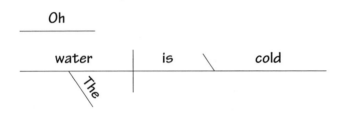

The placement of the interjection remains the same whether the interjection is separated from the rest of the sentence by an exclamation point or by a comma.

SENTENCE **Wow, that acrobat did an incredible somersault!**

SENTENCE **Ugh! The lemonade is tart.**

EXERCISE 1 Diagram the sentences.

1. Yuck! You put ketchup on your pizza.
2. Ouch! The sand is hot.
3. Wow! That was an exciting ride.
4. Oh! A brown bear is near that tree.
5. Sh! You should be quiet during the movie.
6. Your song was wonderful. Bravo!
7. Great! I will bring my new sled.
8. No! You are sick on your birthday.
9. Yikes, we have another test on Monday!
10. Hooray! Our team scored a goal.
11. This huge box came for me. Great!
12. Ah! The dog has a sore paw.
13. Ouch! I hit my toe against the refrigerator.
14. Ah, that peacock has lovely feathers!
15. What! You are wearing my sweater.
16. Gee, that is a funny costume!
17. Uh-oh! Do you have the tickets?
18. Sh! Can you hear that strange noise?
19. Ick! A piece of seaweed stuck to my ankle.
20. Ah, this is a peaceful spot for a picnic!

APPLY IT NOW

Imagine you are at the circus. Write and diagram two sentences containing interjections.

9.6 Compound Subjects and Predicates

The subject and the verb in a sentence may be compound. The subject and the predicate may each have two or more words connected by a coordinating conjunction, usually *and, but,* or *or.* Although a sentence may have more than one subject or predicate, it may still be a simple sentence.

- Each part of a compound subject or of a compound verb is written on a separate line. The lines with the compound parts are parallel.
- The coordinating conjunction is written on a dashed line between the parallel lines.
- The parallel lines are connected to the main horizontal line in the usual position of a subject or a verb.

In this sentence the subject is compound.

SENTENCE **Todd and Janet went to camp in July.**

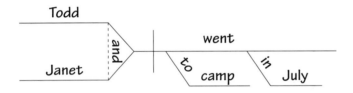

In this sentence the verb is compound.

SENTENCE **The performers sang and danced.**

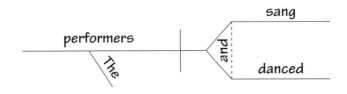

The direct object in this sentence is the object of both verbs.

SENTENCE **Don mowed and raked the lawn.**

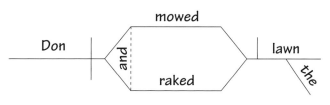

EXERCISE 1 Diagram the sentences.

1. A giraffe and a zebra approached the camp.
2. Scales or plates cover the bodies of reptiles.
3. The gelatin dessert on the plate wiggled and shimmered.
4. We washed and waxed the cars.
5. The violin and the viola are instruments with strings.
6. I researched butterflies and then wrote my report.
7. Jasmine and Alexis always walk to school.
8. I held and fed the tiny pig.
9. Peter and Petra are twins.
10. Moos and oinks came from the barnyard.
11. Keesha or Ron speaks Swahili.
12. Paula designed and made her costume.
13. Dictionaries and encyclopedias are good sources of information.
14. That automatic door opens quickly and closes slowly.
15. Chocolate and coffee come from beans.
16. Raisins and carrots are healthful snacks.
17. I sat under the tree and read.
18. California and Florida produce oranges.

APPLY IT NOW

What is your after-school routine like? Write two sentences with compound subjects and two sentences with compound predicates. Then diagram the sentences.

9.7 Compound Direct Objects and Indirect Objects

A sentence may have more than one direct object, each of which answers the question *who* or *what* after the verb. Compound direct objects are usually connected by the conjunction *and* or *or*.

- The parts of a compound direct object are written on separate parallel lines after the verb.
- The coordinating conjunction is written on a vertical dashed line between the two parts.
- The compound parts are connected to the main horizontal line in the usual position of a direct object with a vertical line separating the verb and the direct object.

SENTENCE **The performer wore a silk hat and shiny shoes.**

A sentence may have a compound indirect object. An indirect object tells to whom, for whom, to what, or for what the action of a verb is done.

- The parts of a compound indirect object are written on separate horizontal lines under the verb.
- The coordinating conjunction is written on a dashed vertical line between the two parts.
- A slanting line connects the indirect objects to the verb.

SENTENCE **We sent Helen and Marie invitations to the Halloween party.**

EXERCISE 1 Diagram the sentences.

1. Paulette studies Spanish and French.

2. The waves tossed seaweed and foam onto the rocks.

3. Skateboarders wear helmets and pads for safety.

4. The Incas made dishes and combs from gold.

5. Some dinosaurs ate fruit and insects.

6. We can choose soup or salad with our meal.

7. Mom bought dishes and skis at the garage sale.

8. Students can take ballet or modern dance at this school.

9. Do moose have horns or antlers?

EXERCISE 2 Underline the indirect objects. Diagram the sentences.

1. I offered Sam and Carrie popcorn.

2. The visitors from Brazil taught Katy and Lee Portuguese words.

3. The committee awarded my mother and my father the top prize.

4. The sun gives Earth and other planets light.

5. My mother gave my brother and my sister spaghetti for supper.

6. Our class sent our senator and our representative letters.

7. Jefferson gave Lewis and Clark a difficult mission.

8. Martin wrote Jackson and Milos a message in code.

9. The teacher assigned Uma and Leland the job of cleanup.

APPLY IT NOW

Complete the sentences with compound direct objects or indirect objects. Then diagram the sentences.

I eat _____ and _____ for breakfast.

I offered _____ and _____ suggestions.

Tech Tip Diagram the sentences, using a computer program.

9.8 Compound Subject Complements

A sentence may have more than one subject complement. The parts of a compound subject complement are usually connected by the conjunction *and* or *or*. A subject complement comes after a linking verb and renames or describes the subject.

- The parts of a compound subject complement are written on separate parallel lines after the verb.
- The coordinating conjunction is written on a dashed vertical line between the parts.
- The parallel lines are connected to the main horizontal line and separated from the verb by a line that slants toward the subject.

This sentence has nouns as a compound subject complement.

SENTENCE **The best pitchers on the team are Rosalyn and Lillian.**

This sentence has adjectives as a compound subject complement.

SENTENCE **Our dog is friendly and smart.**

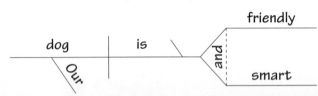

Can you tell whether this compound subject complement consists of nouns or adjectives?

SENTENCE **The steps to the attic are steep and narrow.**

EXERCISE 1 Underline the subject complements.
Tell if they are nouns or adjectives. Diagram the sentences.

1. The bread was hard and moldy.
2. Two forms of water are steam and ice.
3. The violin is old and priceless.
4. The words from the parrot were loud and shrill.
5. Two young fictional detectives are Encyclopedia Brown and Nancy Drew.
6. These young detectives are clever and inquisitive.
7. The name of my new turtle will be Swifty or Shelly.
8. Big Ben is a famous clock and a symbol of Great Britain.
9. The stars of the play are Bianca and Brody.
10. Shakespeare was an actor and a playwright.
11. Homegrown tomatoes are tasty and juicy.
12. Rain forests are warm and humid.
13. My breakfast was cereal and a banana.
14. The piglets are tiny and cute.
15. Tea can be green or black.
16. Mercury is a metal but a liquid.

Big Ben

APPLY IT NOW

Complete the following sentences with compound subject complements. Then diagram the sentences. Tell whether each subject complement consists of nouns or adjectives.

The weather in spring is _____ and _____.

My favorite sports are _____ and _____.

My favorite characters from TV are _____ and _____.

9.9 Compound Sentences

A compound sentence contains two or more independent clauses connected by the coordinating conjunction *and, but,* or *or.* An independent clause has a subject and a predicate and expresses a complete thought.

- The clauses are written on parallel horizontal lines.
- Each independent clause is diagrammed as a separate sentence, on its own horizontal line—with its own subject, verb, and complements or objects.
- The coordinating conjunction is written on a dashed vertical line that connects the left edge of the horizontal lines.

SENTENCE **My skateboard is yellow, and Gwen's skateboard is blue.**

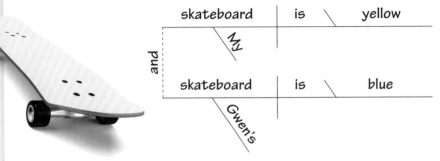

In each clause the subject is *skateboard,* and the verb is *is.* The coordinating conjunction *and* connects the left edge of the horizontal lines.

SENTENCE **I studied my lines for the play, but I forgot them during rehearsal.**

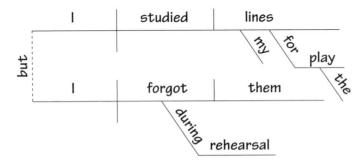

In the first clause, the subject is *I,* and the verb is *studied.* In the second clause, the subject is *I,* and the verb is *forgot.* The coordinating conjunction *but* connects the left edge of the horizontal lines.

EXERCISE 1 Diagram the sentences.

1. Iran is a country with a rich history, and its former name was Persia.

2. The store opened its doors for the sale, and the crowds rushed inside.

3. The circus of P. T. Barnum began its tours in the 1800s, and traveling circuses are still popular.

4. You should read the recipe carefully, or you might forget an ingredient.

5. The project on solar power won first prize at school, and the school entered it in the statewide competition.

6. My little brother will be a pumpkin in the Thanksgiving play, and I will be a Pilgrim.

7. In Greek mythology, Helios rode a fiery chariot across the sky, and this ride warmed the earth with sunlight.

8. George Washington Carver studied peanuts and soybeans, and he found many new uses for them.

9. The moon determines the months of the Chinese calendar, and the first day of each month is the darkest day.

10. My sister got the ingredients, and we made s'mores over the campfire.

11. We often water the orchid, but we rarely water the cactus.

12. I did well in the spelling contest, but I missed *spelunker*.

13. People sometimes take wild animals into their homes, but wild animals are usually poor choices for pets.

14. Iguanas live in trees, but they lay eggs in the ground.

15. Dad raked the soil, and I planted the seeds.

Helios

APPLY IT NOW

Add an independent clause to each of the following. Then diagram each compound sentence.

The parade started _____.

The glass fell _____.

The park was empty _____.

We searched the Web _____.

9.10 Adverb Clauses

A dependent clause has a subject and a verb, but it does not express a complete thought and it cannot stand alone. In a sentence a dependent clause always accompanies an independent clause.

An adverb clause is a dependent clause that describes a verb in the independent clause. A subordinate conjunction connects an adverb clause to an independent clause. Some common subordinate conjunctions that tell when are *after, as, before, once, since, when, whenever, while,* and *until.*

- The adverb clause—with its subject, verb, and any complements or objects—is written on a horizontal line under the line for the independent clause and parallel to it.
- The subordinate conjunction is written on a slanting dashed line that connects the verb in the adverb clause to the word in the independent clause that the adverb clause describes. The dashed line usually goes to the verb.

SENTENCE **Whenever I have a chance, I eat bananas.**

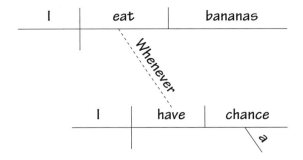

The subject of the independent clause is *I,* and the verb is *eat.* The subject of the dependent clause is *I,* and the verb is *have.* The clauses are connected by the subordinate conjunction *Whenever.*

SENTENCE **I always break a granola bar into pieces before I eat it.**

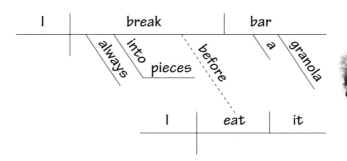

In the independent clause, the subject is *I,* and the verb is *break.* In the dependent clause, the subject is *I,* and the verb is *eat.* The subordinate conjunction *before* connects the two clauses.

EXERCISE 1 Underline the subordinate conjunctions. Diagram the sentences.

1. We go to the planetarium whenever Grandma Sophia visits.
2. When I returned the lost cat, the owner gave me a reward.
3. The ground shook violently when the earthquake struck.
4. Gold ore is dull when it is in the ground.
5. The performance artist was motionless for a long time as a large crowd gathered around her.
6. After Kyle opened the door, the dog ran outside.
7. Sherry's experiment was going well until she dropped the beaker.
8. Catherine and Susan take a volleyball whenever they go to the park.
9. When Atalanta stopped for the golden apples, she lost the race.
10. Rodney took the message after he answered the phone.
11. My dog barks and jumps when I arrive at the door.
12. You can taste the muffins after they cool.
13. Sadie worked hard until she solved the puzzle.
14. I carefully prepared before I gave the presentation.
15. Our team goes for pizza after we play soccer.

APPLY IT NOW

Add independent clauses to these adverb clauses to form sentences. Then diagram the sentences.

When the bell rang, _____.
After we went on the field trip, _____.

9.11 Diagramming Practice

Can you identify the main parts of these sentences?

SENTENCE **Oranges contain vitamin C.**

| Oranges | contain | vitamin C |

SENTENCE **The tongues of anteaters are long.**

Both sentences have subjects and verbs. The first sentence has a direct object (*vitamin C*), and the second sentence has a subject complement (*long*).

Can you identify all the adjectives, adverbs, adjective phrases, and adverb phrases in this sentence?

SENTENCE **Colorful animals and useful plants survive together in the damp, dense tropical forests of South America.**

Can you identify the compound part in this sentence? How does it function in the sentence?

SENTENCE **Alaska produces lumber and oil.**

A compound sentence and a sentence with an adverb clause have separate horizontal lines. Which kind of sentence is this?

SENTENCE **When the curtain rose, I was alone on stage.**

EXERCISE 1 Write out the sentences.

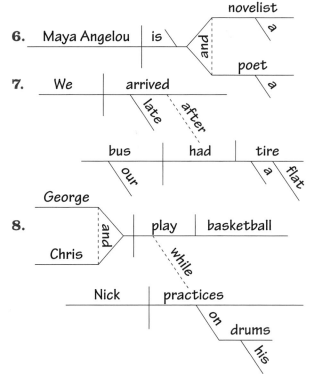

APPLY IT NOW

Write five sentences about your family, incorporating as many sentence parts as possible. Exchange sentences with a partner. Diagram each other's sentences.

Diagramming • 209

Diagramming Review

Diagram the sentences.

9.1

1. Jason bought gigantic balloons.
2. Alexis carefully wrote notes.
3. Jane slowly sipped the hot drink.

9.2

4. My friend lent me her sweater.
5. I sent Grandma a letter.
6. The students handed Mrs. Wheatley their homework.

9.3

7. Carambola is a tropical fruit.
8. Light blue is my favorite color.
9. Porcupines' quills are prickly.

9.4

10. The sun set over the lake.
11. Madison left her lunch on the bus.
12. The boy in the red shirt won.

9.5

13. Ah! The cat broke the vase.
14. Sh! I am reading.
15. Yuck! Mom made liver for dinner.

9.6

16. The flute and the clarinet are musical instruments.
17. Kate and Jenny washed and dried the dishes.
18. Oil and gas are natural resources.

19. Alice likes hats and belts.

20. He offered Sunny and Leo help with homework.

21. We had chicken and peas for dinner.

22. Our parrot is smart and sassy.

23. The chair is old but valuable.

24. New York is a center of finance and a home for millions.

25. Sheila studied for the spelling test, and she earned a perfect score.

26. Tommy bought supplies, and we made a fort.

27. We went to the movie, but we missed the beginning.

28. Seth washed the walls before he painted the room.

29. Peter ate a fruit cup after he finished the casserole.

30. When Nicole was thirsty, she drank some juice.

9.11 **Write out the sentences.**

31.

| brother | collects | stamps |

My / for fun

32.

| tusks | are \ ivory |

The / of elephants

33.

| Lincoln Memorial | is |

The / in Washington, D. C.

and

| I | visited | it |

once

The Lincoln
Memorial

Tech Tip — Go to www.voyagesinenglish.com for more activities.

Diagramming Challenge

Study the diagram and answer the questions.

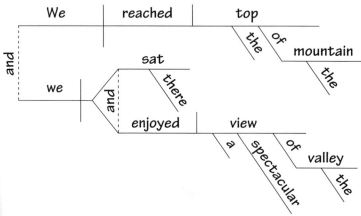

1. Is the sentence simple or compound?
2. What is the coordinating conjunction connecting the clauses?
3. Identify the subject and the verb in each clause in the sentence.
4. What is the compound sentence part? What is the coordinating conjunction?
5. Identify the adjectives and the adverb in the sentence.
6. Identify the prepositional phrases. Do the prepositional phrases act as adjectives or adverbs?
7. Write out the sentence.

Written and Oral Communication

Chapters

Personal Narratives

LiNK

Anne Frank:
The Diary of a Young Girl
Sunday, 14 June, 1942

On Friday, June 12th, I woke up and no wonder; it was my birthday. But of course I was not allowed to get up at that hour, so I had to control my curiosity until a quarter to seven. Then I could bear it no longer, and went to the dining room, where I received a warm welcome from Moortje (the cat).

Soon after seven I went to Mummy and Daddy and then to the sitting room to undo my presents. The first to greet me was you, possibly the nicest of all. Then on the table there were a bunch of roses, a plant, and some peonies, and more arrived during the day.

I got masses of things from Mummy and Daddy, and was thoroughly spoiled by various friends. Among other things I was given *Camera Obscura,* a party game, lots of sweets, chocolates, a puzzle, a brooch, *Tales and Legends of the Netherlands* by Joseph Cohen, *Daisy's Mountain Holiday* (a terrific book), and some money.

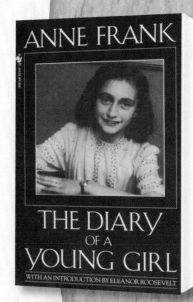

> A personal narrative tells a story about something that happened to the writer. Young Anne Frank wrote about her life when she and her family hid from the Nazis during World War II.

CHAPTER 1

Alicia Brueggemann
Room 105

Knight of the Road

Last year my family took a trip to the Grand Canyon, but we never reached it. What we saw instead was a lot of water. And while our van didn't survive the trip, we did make a new friend along the way.

The trip started smoothly. It wasn't until we reached the Mississippi River that we ran into trouble. I could see thunderheads gathering over the horizon and heard the low rumbling of thunder in the distance. Rain began to fall. At first the drops hit the van unevenly, then all at once we were in a raging storm. It was like driving through Niagara Falls.

Suddenly, we came to a place in the highway where water had gathered in a pool. Dad couldn't see how deep it was, but it quickly became very deep. The van fishtailed and spun around. I grabbed the handle above the side door. My sister Jenny saw something outside her window, and her eyes grew as big as saucers. I looked in her direction and saw it too. It was an 18-wheel truck, and it looked like it was bearing down on us. Luckily, the truck had stopped at the edge of the pool of water. I could see the driver climb out of the cab.

He ran to our van, carrying a flashlight. When he reached us, he offered us help. Dad told us to pick up our stuff, and we quickly got out. Just as we cleared the van, it started moving. We stood in the rain and watched it float away. The driver said he was sorry about our van. Then he offered to let us sit in the cab of his trailer while we waited for the state police to arrive.

Mom and Dad looked sad because we lost our van, but when they saw how much fun Jenny and I were having talking to other truckers on the driver's CB radio, broad smiles broke out on their faces. That's when I learned that real vacations are not about where you go, but how you get there and who you have along for the ride.

What Makes a Good Personal Narrative?

A personal narrative tells a story about something that happened to the writer. You can see personal narratives in many kinds of writing. It can be an e-mail from a friend or a personal letter to a relative.

Here are some ideas to remember when you write a personal narrative.

Point of View

Personal narratives are told from the writer's point of view. This is the first-person point of view. When you write a personal narrative, use words such as *I, me, my, our,* and *we* to tell the story.

Topic

The topic of a personal narrative is an experience that actually happened to you. When you select a topic, choose something that has some special meaning for you. Think of times that you have learned something important. Good personal narratives use the experience to show something that readers can think about.

Details

A good personal narrative has many details that paint in the reader's mind a clear picture of what happened. Descriptive details make events in personal narratives more real to the reader. However, not all details are needed. Unnecessary details can slow down a reader and become distracting.

ACTIVITY A **Which idea in each pair is a good idea for a personal narrative? Explain why you chose each one.**

1. **a.** how scuba equipment works
   b. how I learned to swim

2. **a.** when I found a turtle in my garden
   b. the life cycle of the giant sea turtle

3. **a.** the history of airplanes
   b. the first time I sailed

4. **a.** why I always wear a hat
   b. hats from around the world

5. **a.** the rules of baseball
   b. my trip to the Baseball Hall of Fame

6. **a.** how to get a ticket to an air show
   b. the day I took a helicopter ride over the city

ACTIVITY B **The personal narratives below each contain two sentences that are not necessary. Which sentences do not belong?**

1. My clown act was funnier than I had planned. I had practiced for days until I could balance a red ball on my nose. I borrowed the ball from my cousin Jake. But when I began to perform, I sneezed and dropped the ball. I often catch colds in the summer. I picked it up quickly and balanced it. Afterward, my family said I was so good that I was almost ready to join the circus.

2. Everybody talks about the peace and quiet of the country. My cousin in the country invited me for a weekend. I live on the first floor of an apartment building in the city. The first night at my cousin's cabin I was sleeping peacefully. Then in the middle of the night, I was awoken by a noise—a rattling of metal. I didn't want to wake up my cousin. I tried to go back to sleep, but the noise continued. Finally, I woke up my cousin. He told me that it was just the raccoons that came around at night. Raccoons have black fur under their eyes that looks like a mask. By the end of the weekend, I was happy to go back home to the city to get a good night's sleep.

WRITER'S CORNER

Brainstorm a list of five possible topics for a personal narrative. Some topics could be the time you first met a friend, an adventure while traveling, or an embarrassing moment. Save your list.

Grammar in Action Identify the collective noun in the page 214 excerpt.

Diary of Anne Frank

Saturday, 11 July, 1942

I expect you'd be interested to hear what it feels like to "disappear"; well, all I can say is that I don't know myself yet. I don't think I shall ever feel really at home in this house, but that does not mean I loathe it here, it is more like being on vacation in a very peculiar boardinghouse. The "Secret Annexe" is an ideal hiding place.

Anne Frank's first journal from 1942 to 1944

Audience

The kind of information and language you include in your writing will depend on your audience. For example, if you are writing a personal narrative about your family to be read by your teacher, you might tell who your brothers or sisters are.

The writer of the personal narrative on page 215 tells the reader in the third paragraph that her sister's name is Jenny. When Jenny's name is mentioned in the last paragraph, the reader knows who Jenny is.

Some details could be unnecessary if the reader knows the people in the personal narrative. For example, if the reader was the writer's grandmother, do you think the writer would need to tell that Jenny is her sister?

Voice

The voice of a personal narrative tells the reader how the writer feels about what happened. The voice of a personal narrative also tells a little about the writer's personality. Just as when listening to a person speak, readers can often "hear" the writer's voice. A writer makes the voice clear by choosing certain adjectives and adverbs.

ACTIVITY C The following sentence pairs are from personal narratives about a science fair. Each sentence in a pair is written for a different audience—a teacher or a friend. Tell which sentence was written for each audience.

1. **a.** You know how I am always trying to invent stuff.

   b. Because you encouraged my interest in science, I wanted to tell you what I invented.

2. **a.** I invented a machine that a dog can use to knock on a door.

   b. I figured out how to make a cool doggy door knocker.

3. **a.** I entered it in the Palos Park science fair, and I won first prize.

   b. Your buddy's invention won first prize in our science fair.

4. **a.** You can buy me a magazine when I see you next weekend.

   b. Thanks again for all you taught me.

ACTIVITY D Each example below describes the same event, but each uses a different voice. Read each example. Then answer the questions.

Example 1

Last night I saw the world's most popular rock band, Jelly, perform at the Horse Castle. Fans jammed the entrances and the aisles, but I managed to get a seat. For the first two hours, the performers delighted us with their classic songs. After intermission the high-spirited Jelly pulled out all the stops. Under the flashing lights, the performers stunned us with hits from their recent album. We lingered long afterwards just to recover from hours of thrills and excitement.

Example 2

Last night's concert by Jelly was fantastic. There were thousands of people there. In fact there were so many that there were not enough seats for everyone. I could see people jammed in the aisles. I couldn't figure out why anybody needed a seat anyway. Jelly had everybody hopping along from the moment they started playing. For the first two hours of the concert, there was a light show that was beyond belief. Red and green laser lights waved over the crowd and pulsed in time with the beat. That concert was one of the coolest times I've ever had.

1. Which example uses a serious voice?
2. Which example uses an excited voice?
3. What words from the serious example lead you to think the voice is serious?
4. What words from the excited piece lead you to think the writer was excited about the concert?

WRITER'S CORNER

Freewrite about what happened when you woke up this morning. Write the events from the first-person point of view and include necessary details.

Introduction, Body, and Conclusion

Like most writing, personal narratives have parts that can be easily identified. The introduction, body, and conclusion are the parts of a personal narrative.

Introduction

The introduction of a personal narrative should grab the reader's attention. It should make the reader want more. The introduction should tell the reader the topic of the personal narrative. It should also lead the reader into the body of the narrative.

Body

The body is the main part of a personal narrative. It has details that let the reader see, smell, hear, feel, and taste what the writer experienced. It includes all the details that are important to the story. It does not include unnecessary details.

Every sentence in the body should keep the story going in time order from one event to the next.

Conclusion

The conclusion of a personal narrative is where the writer closes the story. The writer can use the conclusion to sum up ideas, comment on what the story means, or share what he or she may have learned.

ACTIVITY A Which sentence in each pair makes a better introduction for a personal narrative? Explain why you think so.

1. **a.** My older sister painted my face.
   b. Having your face painted can turn your day around.

2. **a.** I'll never forget what happened at the Metropolitan Museum.
   b. One day my family went to the Metropolitan Museum.

3. **a.** I like to play computer games.
   b. Once, for a whole week, I was computer-game champion of my neighborhood.

4. **a.** My father and I often go fishing together.
   b. My father is usually a calm guy, but on one recent fishing trip I saw him get really excited.

5. **a.** The house next door burned down last night.
   b. I was almost asleep last night when the fire engines screamed around the corner.

ACTIVITY B Write a conclusion for each personal narrative.

1. **What a Fish Story!**

   I usually hate fishing because I never catch anything, but last Saturday was different.

   I rowed out to the middle of the lake with my cousin, who loves fishing and who always catches a lot of fish. I baited my hook and cast it into the water. Almost immediately, I felt a tug on the line. I reeled in the biggest fish I'd ever seen. Ten minutes later, I landed another huge fish. By the end of the day, I'd caught 17 beauties. And my cousin? Well, she didn't catch a thing.

2. **Stage Fright**

   I thought I was prepared for my first speaking role in a school play.

   I was playing one of Tom Sawyer's friends. I had memorized my lines thoroughly. I recited them to myself in the mirror, I practiced with my mom, and I rehearsed with the class. I knew the lines backward and forward. But when I walked onstage in front of the audience, I froze. I couldn't remember a word.

WRITER'S CORNER

Choose a topic from the list you brainstormed for the Writer's Corner on page 217. Write a seven sentence introduction for it. Be sure to write each sentence so that your audience wants to read more about your topic.

Grammar in Action Identify three proper nouns in the model on page 215 and tell if they are people, places, or things.

LiNK

Diary of Anne Frank

Friday, 25 September, 1942

Yesterday evening I went upstairs and "visited" the Van Daans. I do so occasionally to have a chat. Sometimes it can be quite fun. Then we have some moth biscuits (the biscuit tin is kept in the wardrobe which is full of moth balls) and drink lemonade.

Time Order

In a personal narrative, events should be in the order that they happened. When you remember an experience for a personal narrative, take time to think about everything that happened. Writing about an experience in time order can help the reader understand what happened and why things happened.

Sometimes it's helpful to freewrite about an experience so that you can remember all the details about it. When you freewrite about something, write everything you can remember. Later you can put the events together in the order that they happened.

Writers use transition words, such as *then, yesterday, first, last,* and *next,* to show how events are connected. Read the paragraph below, then study the time line. The transition words help create a story of the events.

This has been such a busy week. *First,* I had Maggie's birthday party. *Then* we all slept over to celebrate. *Next,* my dad and I practiced batting for the upcoming game. We met Mom and George *later* for dinner at the pizza parlor. *Yesterday* I hit a double, and our team won the game. What a tiring week!

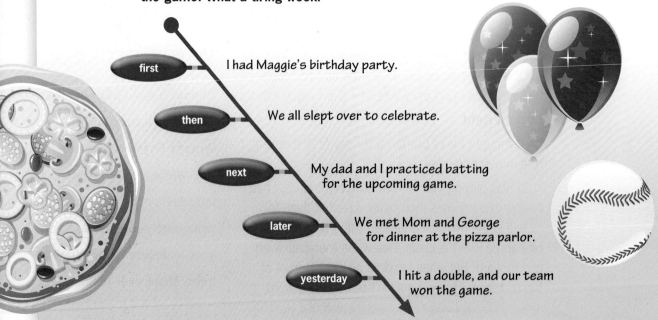

first — I had Maggie's birthday party.

then — We all slept over to celebrate.

next — My dad and I practiced batting for the upcoming game.

later — We met Mom and George for dinner at the pizza parlor.

yesterday — I hit a double, and our team won the game.

ACTIVITY C Read the personal narrative below. Find the transition words. Then choose the best introduction from the list that follows the personal narrative. Explain your choice.

_____ I had never ice-skated before last weekend, but my sister insisted that I try. I put on a pair of her old skates and hobbled over to the rink. At first, I held my sister's hand. Then I took a small step on my own. My ankles wobbled, my feet slid, and I fell flat on the cold, hard ice. I spent most of the afternoon "practicing" how to fall. But I finally made it all the way around the rink in an upright position. Next week I may try doing a spin!

    a. It was a very cold day.

    b. Learning a new skill often has its ups and downs.

    c. I love ice-skating.

ACTIVITY D Molly wrote these notes about her first time babysitting her sister Rayna. Write the notes as a personal narrative, using transition words. Add an introduction and a conclusion to the story.

- Rayna started crying when Mom left.
- It took forever to get her into her high chair.
- I had to fight to put her bib on.
- She spilled her food on the floor.
- I gave up trying to feed her and decided to let her play.
- She started grabbing the cat's tail.
- She tried to eat the TV remote.
- She looked up at me and said, "I'm hungry."

WRITER'S CORNER

Think about what you did last weekend. Write five sentences describing what happened. Use time order. Save your work.

Tech Tip Use a computer program to create a time line graph.

Sentence Variety

Writing different kinds of sentences will make your writing more interesting. When all the sentences are the same kind, readers might become bored. To add variety to your writing, you can do these things:

- Change a sentence to a question.
- Change a sentence to an exclamation.
- Change the order of the words in a sentence.

Read each set of sentences below. Think about how sentence A has been changed to make sentence B.

SET 1
A I always wanted to go white-water rafting.
B Have you ever wanted to go white-water rafting?

In Set 1 sentence A was changed to a question. Questions invite readers to think about what they're reading. By asking a question, writers can get readers to start thinking.

SET 2
A Gliding swiftly down the river was exciting.
B How exciting it was to glide swiftly down the river!

In Set 2 sentence A is changed to an exclamatory sentence. An occasional exclamation helps readers share the enthusiasm and excitement of the writer. But be careful with exclamations and questions. Too many exclamations and questions can lose their effect and make your writing repetitive.

SET 3
A We hit some rapids suddenly, and the raft spun around.
B Suddenly, we hit some rapids, and the raft spun around.
A I didn't know whether to be excited or scared as the raft spun wildly.
B As the raft spun wildly, I didn't know whether to be excited or scared.

In the first pair in Set 3, the word order of the sentence was changed. The word *suddenly* was moved to the beginning of the sentence to add variety. Changing the order of words in a sentence can shift the emphasis of a sentence. The change makes the event seem more urgent.

In the second pair in Set 3, the words *as the raft spun wildly* was moved to the beginning of the sentence. Changing the word order gives the background information about the raft first.

ACTIVITY A Rewrite each sentence, first as a question and then as an exclamatory sentence. You may change or add any words to make the sentences more interesting.

1. I was surprised to see a sandwich with corn flakes on it.
2. On Saturday I saw my first rodeo.
3. Visiting the Statue of Liberty was very cool.
4. Everything seemed to go wrong this morning.
5. It took me many tries to jump that distance.
6. It's a long drive to Emma's house.
7. Eric didn't believe me when I told him about my beanbag collection.
8. Training a dog can be very difficult.
9. The first time I babysat was a disaster.
10. I'd always wanted to learn to ride a horse.
11. Life on a farm can be fun.
12. My penalty kick was going toward the goal.

LiNK

Diary of Anne Frank

Monday, 21 September, 1942

. . . I had just written something about Mrs. Van Daan when in she came. Slap! I closed the book.

"Hey, Anne, can't I just have a look?"

Naturally it gave me a frightful shock, because there was an unflattering description of her on this particular page.

WRITER'S CORNER

Rewrite the sentences you wrote for the Writer's Corner on page 223 into a paragraph. Add variety by using questions or exclamations. You might also change the order of the words in some sentences. Do your revisions improve your paragraph?

ACTIVITY B Rewrite each sentence by moving the words in italics to a new position in the sentence. You may change or add any words to make the sentences more interesting.

1. I awoke *as the cuckoo clock began to strike.*
2. Black smoke poured out *when I opened the oven door.*
3. Everyone looked up *when I walked into the library with my squeaky shoes.*
4. We met Charlie and Doug *on the way to the costume party.*
5. Our backyard looked like an ice palace *after the winter storm.*
6. It was getting dark *when I realized I had taken the wrong road.*
7. I finally succeeded *after many attempts at twirling spaghetti on a fork.*
8. The telephone rang *just as we were going out the door.*
9. A big yellow snowplow rumbled down the street *just in time.*
10. We went to the Brooklyn Children's Museum *while we were in New York.*

ACTIVITY C Rewrite each sentence using the word or words in parentheses. Write two different sentences for each item.

1. The sandbags gave way. (unexpectedly)
2. The water flowed over the banks of the river. (swiftly)
3. We ran onto higher ground. (quickly)
4. The water stopped rising. (in a little while)
5. The water went down. (gradually)
6. We started cleaning up. (immediately)

ACTIVITY D This is the first paragraph of a personal narrative. Rewrite the paragraph by following the directions.

Taking Off

My first plane trip was very exciting. The engines roared and the plane vibrated as it prepared for takeoff. The ground seemed to rush by as the plane sped down the runway. It was a thrilling moment when the plane rose from the ground.

1. Add a question to the beginning of the narrative.
2. Change the word order in two of the sentences.
3. End the paragraph with an exclamation.
4. You may change or add words to make the sentences more interesting.

ACTIVITY E Change the sentences to make the paragraphs more interesting. Try not to change the meanings of the paragraphs.

1. Jogging is not my idea of fun exercise. Running for the sake of running bores me to tears. Playing tennis is more exciting to me. Chasing after that fuzzy, little ball wears me out, but at least I'm enjoying myself. Learning to play, however, was not as easy as I first thought it would be.

2. I was happily on my way to the movie. Suddenly, it started to rain very hard! How kind this stranger is, I thought, to share her umbrella with me! If only I had known what she had in mind! I couldn't refuse her request. Collecting signatures for a petition is no fun. What a wasted afternoon! I would rather have gotten drenched! Imagine how you would feel if you spent your holiday the way I spent mine!

3. Have you ever flown down a snowy hillside on a toboggan? Can you imagine screaming with three friends on a narrow wooden board as it skims downward at nearly 40 miles per hour? Can you feel your heart race as the wind lashes against your face? Would you like to know how I first got involved in this thrilling sport?

4. I was making cinnamon bread for the first time. I was using a recipe from a classmate. I really wanted to make the recipe after I had tasted my classmate's scrumptious bread. I went to the store, and I got all the ingredients. I made the batter. I went to look for the bread pan. I couldn't find it. I looked high and low. Finally, I asked my mom. I found out that she had taken the bread pan to work and had forgotten to bring it home. I was upset. I couldn't make the bread.

5. Can you believe it? My roller skates are here. I wanted to earn enough money. I babysat my brothers. I walked my neighbor's dogs. I raked my grandmother's lawn. I washed Mrs. Waverly's windows. Enough money to buy my roller skates is what I have. Buying the skates tomorrow will be the first thing I do.

WRITER'S CORNER

Choose an article from a newspaper. Change five sentences in the article to add variety. How do your revisions affect the article?

Thesaurus

A dictionary can help you check that you use words correctly. But where do you turn if you think of a word, but it isn't the exact word you want? What tool can help you replace a word that you have used too often? A thesaurus is the answer to these problems.

A thesaurus lists synonyms, or words with similar meanings. A thesaurus can help you find words that say exactly what you mean.

Jenna wrote a personal narrative about playing a game with her baby sister. She wanted to change *jumped* because she had already used that word three times in one paragraph. This was her original sentence.

Magda clapped her hands and jumped over a garden hose.

Her baby sister's jump over the garden hose was tiny. Look at these pages from a thesaurus. Which word would best describe Magda's jump as tiny?

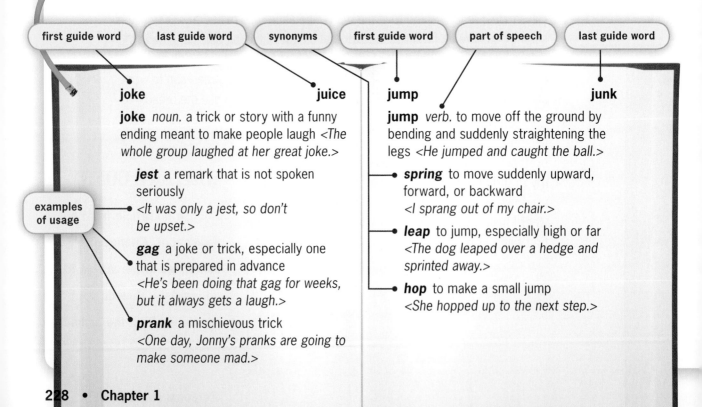

first guide word | last guide word | synonyms | first guide word | part of speech | last guide word

joke   **juice**   **jump**   **junk**

joke *noun.* a trick or story with a funny ending meant to make people laugh <*The whole group laughed at her great joke.*>

examples of usage

jest a remark that is not spoken seriously
<*It was only a jest, so don't be upset.*>

gag a joke or trick, especially one that is prepared in advance
<*He's been doing that gag for weeks, but it always gets a laugh.*>

prank a mischievous trick
<*One day, Jonny's pranks are going to make someone mad.*>

jump *verb.* to move off the ground by bending and suddenly straightening the legs <*He jumped and caught the ball.*>

- **spring** to move suddenly upward, forward, or backward
<*I sprang out of my chair.*>

- **leap** to jump, especially high or far
<*The dog leaped over a hedge and sprinted away.*>

- **hop** to make a small jump
<*She hopped up to the next step.*>

Dictionary Thesaurus

Jenna's thesaurus is a dictionary thesaurus. It is organized like a dictionary. Words are listed in alphabetical order, and each section has words that start with the same letter.

At the top of each page of a dictionary thesaurus are guide words. Guide words show you the first entry and the last entry that appear on those pages. If you were looking for the word *jump* in a thesaurus, you would know you had the right page if the guide words for that page were *joke* and *junk*. The word *jump* comes alphabetically between *joke* and *junk*.

Remember that synonyms may have slightly different meanings from one another. A hop is not exactly the same as a leap. Some dictionary thesauruses give definitions and example sentences for each synonym, but not all of them do. If you aren't sure about a synonym's exact meaning, look up the word in a dictionary.

ACTIVITY A Tell which words in Column B might be found on a page with the guide words in Column A.

	Column A	Column B
1.	pace/pale	pack, paddle, parade
2.	stall/stir	steep, sting, stock
3.	bride/broken	bronze, bristle, brilliant
4.	alike/angry	alert, alley, ancient
5.	gamble/gift	gentle, giant, gloomy
6.	ache/again	active, aid, afraid

ACTIVITY B Use a thesaurus to find the following words and write a sentence for each word. Then rewrite the sentence using a word with a similar meaning.

1.	amusing	**5.**	break
2.	clever	**6.**	happy
3.	interesting	**7.**	mad
4.	polite	**8.**	shabby

WRITER'S CORNER

Find one of the words below in a thesaurus. Write a list of the synonyms you find.

go *break* *smile* *say*

Indexed Thesaurus

A dictionary thesaurus is organized by words in alphabetical order. An indexed thesaurus is organized by ideas or categories. In an indexed thesaurus, words that express the same idea are listed together in one entry.

An indexed thesaurus is divided into two sections. To find synonyms for a word, look up the word in the index. Words in the index are listed alphabetically, and guide words show the first and last word on each page. Most entry words are followed by a list of meanings. Next to each meaning is a number that tells you where to find synonyms with that meaning. Here is an example of an entry for *jump* from the index of an indexed thesaurus.

jump

    noun: step 177.11

            advantage 249.2

            increase 251.1

            leap 366.1

    verb: be startled 131.5

            parachute 184.47

            leap 366.5

            attack 459.15

The verb *leap* is closest to the meaning Jenna needed. The entry might look like this.

366 LEAP

    5 *verbs* leap, jump, hop, spring, skip

ACTIVITY C Use the index entry for *jump* on page 230. Decide what numbers you would look under to find a synonym for *jump* in each of these sentences.

1. Petra had a jump on the competition because she had practiced her flute all summer.
2. When the monster pounced from a tree, everyone in the movie theater jumped.
3. Profits jumped when the company began to sell a new speedboat.
4. The team of soldiers jumped as their plane flew over the battlefield.
5. Anton jumped over the creek and kept on running.

ACTIVITY D Use a thesaurus to rewrite these sentences. Replace each word in italics with a synonym.

1. When Peter goes to the arcade with his friends, they *talk* for hours.
2. Jessica Montray's first film as a director was a *success*.
3. Mark's bedroom is always so *clean* you could almost eat off the floor.
4. They are using their pickup truck to *carry* pipes and lumber across town.
5. The *outlaw* escaped the hound dogs by swimming upriver.
6. We made a *trip* across the country in our beat-up car.
7. The diver looked *nervous* at the edge of the diving board.
8. A *big* lion lay behind the bush, ready to pounce on its prey.
9. The vase of flowers filled the room with a fragrant *odor*.
10. Our class *gave* the money we raised to the local food pantry.

WRITER'S CORNER

Use an indexed thesaurus to find three synonyms for the word *noise*. Write a sentence for each synonym you choose. Use a dictionary to check that you used each synonym correctly.

Tech Tip Use an online dictionary to check your synonyms.

Exact Words

Good writers choose exact words to give their readers the clearest picture with the fewest words. Often one well-chosen word can do the job of many overused words.

Exact Nouns

Read these two sentences.

A bird swooped down and knocked leaves from the tree.
A raven swooped down and knocked leaves from the oak.

When you read the first sentence, you might picture any kind of bird or tree. Exact nouns in the second sentence help you see more clearly what the writer is describing.

The writer might have changed "A bird" to "A big black bird" to create a clearer picture. But by choosing the word *raven,* the writer gave more information and painted a clearer picture in fewer words.

Exact Adjectives

Which of these two sentences creates a clearer picture by using exact adjectives?

The beautiful baton twirler wore a uniform with nice sequins.
The graceful baton twirler wore a uniform with glittering sequins.

The exact adjective *graceful* tells you that the baton twirler is beautiful because her movements are full of grace. The adjective *graceful* gives the reader more to imagine.

When someone says that something is "nice," what do you imagine? It's hard to picture what "nice" looks like. When someone says that something is "glittering," it is easier to imagine. The adjective *glittering* is exact. *Nice* is not.

When you write and revise, watch out for adjectives such as *pretty, nice, good, great, bad,* and *awful.* These adjectives do not give much information. Use exact adjectives that tell in what way something is nice, good, or awful.

ACTIVITY A Rewrite these sentences by replacing the nouns in italics with exact nouns.

1. When Maria bit into her *piece of fruit,* the juice dribbled down her chin.
2. Have you seen his furry *pet?*
3. Alfonso came running into the *room.*
4. The *picture* on the wall showed a landscape scene.
5. The passenger put his *bag* in the overhead compartment.
6. There was a colorful *bird* in a large cage.
7. The water around our boat was filled with *sea creatures.*
8. The tourists were riding *animals* up the side of the mountain.
9. A lot of *plants* were growing in the garden.
10. I need a *tool* to hang the picture.
11. Mom liked the *flowers* I gave her.

ACTIVITY B Rewrite these sentences by replacing the adjectives in italics with exact adjectives.

1. The weather yesterday was *bad.*
2. The mountains were *beautiful* at that time of day.
3. We shared a *good* meal with our new neighbors.
4. A *big* tree is growing in our yard.
5. Have you noticed the *pretty* picture hanging on the wall?
6. The *smart* student solved all the math problems.
7. There was a *strange* sound coming from the box.
8. The horror movie was so *scary* that I probably won't sleep well tonight.
9. The neighbors were *angry* because of the loud music Jon's band was playing.
10. My sister is *messy,* and her things are thrown all over her room.

WRITER'S CORNER

Imagine that you have discovered a buried treasure chest in your yard. Write five sentences describing what you might find in it. Use exact words to help readers picture what is inside.

Diary of Anne Frank

Tuesday, 20 October, 1942

We turned absolutely white. Perhaps he had heard something after all and wanted to investigate our secret den . . . The knocking, pulling, pushing, wrecking went on. I nearly fainted at the thought this utter stranger might discover our beautiful secret hiding place.

Anne Frank

Exact Verbs

Verbs such as *run, smile,* and *sing* are action words. Some verbs show an action more clearly than other verbs do. When you write and revise, use exact verbs to show readers what is happening in your writing.

I walked through the haunted house.
I strolled through the haunted house.

The second sentence tells readers that the writer walked leisurely through the haunted house. Readers get a clearer picture of how the writer walked. The second sentence also tells that the writer was not frightened in the haunted house. The word *strolled* gives more information than the word *walked.*

How does this revision change the meaning of the sentence?

I raced through the haunted house.

When you revise, look for places where you can use exact verbs. Check the adverbs you used with the verbs. When you find one or more adverbs that describe a verb, think about whether a more exact verb might do the job. A thesaurus can help.

I ran quickly and wildly through the scary forest.
I scampered through the scary forest.

What other exact verbs might you use to replace the verb and adverbs in the first sentence?

ACTIVITY C Replace each verb in italics with an exact verb. Use a thesaurus if you need help.

1. My horse *ran* across the swampy field.
2. A gray rabbit was *eating* a leaf of lettuce.
3. The campers *walked* along the crooked trail.
4. I caught the ball and *ran* toward the end zone.
5. Ned *took* the basketball from the bully and gave it back to his friend.
6. "I'm going to win!" *said* the star athlete.

ACTIVITY D Rewrite these sentences by replacing the words in italics with exact verbs.

1. The snake *went on its belly* across the basement floor.
2. A train *came loudly* into the station.
3. The bonfire *made loud noises* as we told our stories.
4. The mayor *went up* onstage and *spoke loudly* to the crowd.
5. The fox *looked for a long time* at the people *walking clumsily* through the bushes.
6. The clothes hanging on the line *moved slowly back and forth* in the wind.

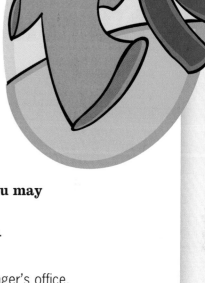

ACTIVITY E Rewrite the sentences below by replacing the words in italics with exact words. You may add words to paint a more detailed picture.

1. The main character and her family lived in an *old house*.
2. The coach *shouted* commands to the players.
3. The lost child was *crying* for 20 minutes at the park ranger's office.
4. Jackson is *sad* because his best friend is moving away.
5. The sunset was so *beautiful* that I took a photograph of it to share with my grandfather.
6. That new puppy is *cute*, but I am allergic to dogs.

ACTIVITY F Rewrite this paragraph, using exact nouns, adjectives, and verbs.

In a faraway place, a group of animals was deciding what to do next. Their homes had been ruined by a very bad storm. They came together and started talking. "I don't know what to do," said an animal. A colored snake came to the middle of the circle. "We'd better decide soon," he said. He pointed to the clouds, which were looking bad. Finally, one animal had a good idea. "Let's go into that cave for the night," he said. They were all happy with the idea, and they went into the cave.

WRITER'S CORNER

Work with a partner to list three synonyms for each of the following verbs: *talk*, *walk*, *eat*, and *take*. Then choose one set of synonyms. Write three sentences, using a different synonym from your list in each sentence.

Oral Personal Narratives

Have you ever told someone about something funny or scary that happened to you? Telling an audience about something that happened to you is sharing an oral personal narrative.

Audience and Topic

To whom are you going to tell your story? You might tell your story one way for your teacher and another way for a classmate. Knowing your audience can help you decide which experience to tell about. What kind of story will your audience enjoy? Choose a topic that you will enjoy sharing with your audience.

Introduction

Grab your listeners' attention in the introduction. You might let listeners know what kind of story you are going to tell. Will it be scary? Does it begin on a stormy night in a spooky forest?

Body

The body of your oral personal narrative tells what happened to you. Be sure to include only the most interesting details. Telling what happened in time order will help listeners follow your story. Use transition words to make your narrative clearer.

Conclusion

In the conclusion of your oral personal narrative, you might tell listeners what you learned from the experience or how you felt about it.

Tone of Voice

How you tell your personal narrative will help you connect with your audience. Use a tone of voice that shows how you feel. You might speak quickly during the exciting parts of the story. If something scary is about to happen in the story, slow down and speak quietly to keep your audience on the edge of their seats. You might also make sound effects to go with your story, such as *crash, boom,* or *whoosh.*

ACTIVITY A **Read each sentence aloud to a partner, using a tone of voice that sounds as if you are angry, scared, excited, or happy. See if your partner can guess the feeling you are showing.**

1. Finally, I saw my balloon in the branches of a tree.
2. It was the biggest toad I'd ever seen.
3. I knew my life would never be the same.
4. You'll never believe what happened next.
5. That's the last time I'll ever go there.
6. I didn't know what to say.
7. I ran to the corner as fast as I could.
8. "Where did he go?" I wondered aloud.
9. I wasn't sure what I was seeing.
10. It was the most unforgettable trip I'd ever taken.

ACTIVITY B **Retell the story on page 215 in your own words to a partner. Imagine that you are one of the people in the story. Change your tone of voice to match the emotions in the story.**

SPEAKER'S CORNER

Write a list of three ideas for an oral personal narrative. Talk with a partner about which idea would be best for an oral personal narrative you might present to your classmates. Think about which narrative your classmates would most enjoy.

Prepare and Practice

To prepare your oral personal narrative, write the important parts, or the parts you most want to remember, on note cards. You might write a few good sentences that you want to include in your introduction or conclusion. Don't put every word on your note cards. Instead, use keywords and phrases that will help you remember what to say.

Practice your personal narrative in front of a mirror a few times. As you practice, try using different tones of voice to add feeling to your story. Try adding sound effects or body movements. The more you practice, the easier your oral personal narrative will be to present to your audience.

Present

Here are some tips for presenting your personal narrative.

- Before you begin, check that your note cards are in order.
- Look at the audience as you speak. The audience wants to know that you are speaking to them, not reading from your note cards. Move your eyes from person to person to let your audience know you want to include them all.
- Talk slowly. Taking a breath at the end of each sentence can help you remember to slow down.
- Speak so everyone can hear you, but do not shout.
- Use your tone of voice, your facial expressions, and your body movements to grab your listeners' attention.

Listening Tips

Listeners make a speaker feel comfortable when they show their interest. A speaker who is comfortable is more likely to tell a story you will enjoy. Here are some tips for being a good listener.

- Look at the speaker. Pay attention to what the speaker is saying.
- Picture the story in your mind. Imagine how the people and places in the story might look. Think about how the story might end.
- If you have questions, save them until the speaker is finished.

ACTIVITY C Look at the three ideas you wrote for the Speaker's Corner on page 237. Pick one you want to present. Write a set of note cards for that idea. Use keywords and phrases in your notes.

ACTIVITY D Read each sentence several times aloud to a partner. Show a different emotion each time. Notice how the same sentence changes meaning depending on how you say it.

1. It's just around the corner.
2. I didn't expect that.
3. Is that really for me?
4. I think it's going to be here soon.
5. I don't think you should do that.
6. How did you know that?
7. When will this day end?
8. I don't believe what you're telling me.
9. My teacher told me it was true.
10. This is the worst day.

ACTIVITY E Practice your oral personal narrative with a partner. Practice using your voice to show your feelings. Try using facial expressions, body movements, and sound effects to keep your partner's interest. When you have finished, talk with your partner about ways to improve your narrative.

SPEAKER'S CORNER

Present your oral personal narrative to the class. Remember to make eye contact with your audience and to speak slowly and clearly. Use your voice to show your feelings. When your classmates present their narratives, use the Listening Tips to help you be a good listener.

Prewriting and Drafting

Writing a personal narrative is an opportunity to share an experience from your life with others. You might write about something that changed your life. You might also write about something funny, scary, or brave that you did. The choices are endless.

Prewriting

Elsa is a fifth grader who wanted to write a personal narrative to enter in the Pennsylvania "It Happened to Me" Contest. Elsa first took time to do some prewriting. During prewriting Elsa chose her topic and planned what she wanted to write.

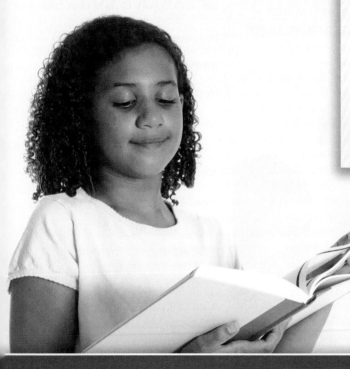

Choosing a Topic

Elsa had some ideas for what to write about, but she didn't know which one to pick. Elsa answered a list of questions from her teacher to help her narrow her possible topics. Here are some of the questions.

What is something that changed your life?

when my family moved from the Army base in Germany to Philadelphia when I was six

What is the most exciting thing that has ever happened to you?

getting to play drums on the same stage as Bricks, the hip-hop artist

What is the funniest thing that ever happened to you?

I ran into a tree while laughing at my friend for tripping.

What is the scariest thing that ever happened to you?

playing drums onstage at the Bricks concert

Elsa looked at her answers to the questions. She chose playing drums at the Bricks concert as her topic for a few reasons. She thought her amazing opportunity would interest her audience. She also thought that since the topic appeared more than once on the list of answers, she would have a lot to say about it.

Prewriting

Drafting

Content Editing

Revising

Copyediting

Proofreading

Publishing

Your Turn

Think of experiences that you have had that you would like to share with an audience. Use the following questions to help you think of ideas. Choose as your topic the idea that you would most enjoy writing about.

- What is something that changed your life?
- What is the most exciting thing that has ever happened to you?
- What is the funniest, scariest, bravest, or most embarrassing thing that you have ever done?
- What is the thing that you are most proud of doing?

Your Turn

Use a storyboard to plan your draft.

- Think about your topic. Draw the first thing that happened to you. Leave space at the top of the page to write about the picture.
- If people are speaking, write what they say in a bubble next to their mouth. If you were thinking something during that moment, write what you were thinking in a bubble next to your head.
- Draw each event of the story on a separate page. Make sure you include all the important details of the experience.
- Read the storyboard to see if it is organized in the order that your experience happened.

Using a Storyboard to Plan

Now that Elsa had her topic, she wanted to plan what she would write about in her personal

 Organization

narrative. Elsa drew on sheets

of paper simple pictures for each thing that happened to her. She left room at the top of each page to write what was going on in the picture. Then she organized the pictures in the order that the events happened. Here are a few pages from Elsa's storyboard.

We practiced the song in the empty Civic Center

I won concert tickets to see Bricks

There was a silver and black drum set

Drafting

A draft is the first chance to write ideas for your personal narrative in paragraph form. Elsa used her storyboard to help write her personal narrative. She made sure that her personal narrative was written in time order and that it had a clear introduction, body, and conclusion.

Elsa left extra space between the lines so that she would have room to make changes later. Here is Elsa's first draft.

Don't Lose the Beat

I won concert tickets to see Bricks, my favorite hip-hop artist! I also got a backstage pass to meet her two hours before the show started. I was so excited! I play drums for fun, and I loved playing the beat along with Bricks's CDs. I could hardly wait.

When the day of the concert came, I was so nervous. My stomack felt like it was doing gymnastics. My dad and I knocked on the back door of the Civic Center. The strongest-looking man I have ever seen opened the door. One of Bricks's managers took me and my dad down a dark hallway to the stage. The stage was cluttered with microphones, equipment for the DJ, and a silver and black drum set. The manager said that Bricks would be out in a minute.

I got more and more excited! I started tapping the beat to Bricks's hit song "My Street" on my leg. "My Street" was her newest song. I thought that it was her best too. Before "My Street" my favorite song by Bricks had been "Fool Me." Then I heard a voice behind me say, "You play that beat pretty well." It was Bricks! She asked if I would like to play the drums when she performed "My Street" that night. I couldn't believe it! We practiced the song in the empty Civic Center for the next hour. She told me that as long as I didn't lose the beat, I would do a good job.

The enormous crowd cheered! I started to play the beat of the song on the drum set. I concentrated hard on not losing the beat. All of a sudden, the DJ stopped scratching and Bricks stopped rapping. The song was over, but I was still playing the beat. I was so embarrassed I didn't know what to do. People in the audience saw Bricks smile and start to dance to the beat. Then Bricks starts rapping over my beat. We were making up a new part for "My Street" together. The crowd went wild. Bricks and I finally made eye contact and stopped at the same time. The crowd cheered and screamed for more!

After the show Bricks told me how well she thought I had done. She said that she might even keep the new line we made together in her song. I felt famous. I couldn't believe what an amazing night I had had with my favorite hip-hop star.

Prewriting

Drafting

Content Editing

Revising

Copyediting

Proofreading

Publishing

Your Turn

- Use your storyboard to help you write the first draft of your personal narrative. Remember to write from your point of view. Use words such as *I, me, my, our,* and *we.* Start with an introduction that catches your reader's attention.
- Write the body of your personal narrative. Make sure the events in the body are told in time order. Add all the details necessary to make it seem as real as possible to the reader.
- Finish by writing a conclusion. Try to sum up what happened in your personal narrative. You might also want to write a final line that will be remembered by the reader.

- While you write your draft, keep in mind your audience. Who are you writing for?

 Voice

How much do they need to know to understand your experience? Remember to use a voice that tells your reader how you felt about what happened. Were you excited? Were you scared? Were you happy?

Personal Narratives • 243

Editor's Workshop

Content Editing

Now that Elsa had a draft of her personal narrative, she wanted to make it better. A content editor would improve the draft by checking that all the important ideas were included. A content editor would also make sure that the story was told in time order.

Elsa wanted to ask someone she trusted to content edit her personal narrative. She decided to ask Anton, her older brother. Anton wasn't at the Bricks concert, but he had heard his little sister tell the story of meeting Bricks and playing the drums. Anton used the Content Editor's Checklist below to content edit Elsa's personal narrative.

Content Editor's Checkilst

☐ Does the writing stay on the topic?

☐ Is the personal narrative told from the writer's point of view?

☐ Are there an engaging introduction, a detailed body, and a satisfying conclusion?

☐ Are the details in the narrative necessary?

☐ Is the narrative told in correct time order?

Anton read Elsa's personal narrative. He told her that he liked how she used details to capture the excitement she felt when she met Bricks and performed onstage. He told her that although he had heard her tell the story many times, he thought that this was the best she had ever told it. Then Anton told Elsa these ideas he had for her personal narrative.

- You get off the topic in the third paragraph when you mention your favorite song before "My Street."

- The introduction doesn't catch my attention. Maybe you shouldn't say what the topic is right away. You might start with a question or an interesting fact.

- The conclusion is satisfying, but you might add a line that will stick with the reader.

- The personal narrative is in the right time order, but something seems to be missing between the third and fourth paragraphs. It jumps from practicing the song with Bricks to being called up to play the song during the concert.

Elsa thanked Anton for his help. She was happy to have ideas on how to make her personal narrative better.

Grammar in Action

Identify the nouns used as direct objects in the third paragraph of the model on page 215.

Your Turn

- Exchange your personal narrative with a partner.
- Use the Content Editor's Checklist to check your partner's paper. Pay attention to one question in the checklist at a time. Take notes on changes you would like to suggest to your partner about his or her personal narrative.
- When you have finished, take turns talking about each other's drafts with your partner. Start by saying something you like about your partner's personal narrative.

Writer's Tip Listen to your partner's comments about your personal narrative. Think about each one. Ask your partner any questions that you might have.

Prewriting
Drafting
Content Editing
Revising
Copyediting
Proofreading
Publishing

Writer's Workshop

Revising

This is how Elsa revised her draft, using the ideas from content editing.

Don't Lose the Beat

I waited on the line as the phone rang once, twice then three times. The voice that answered said that I was the winning caller!

I won concert tickets to see Bricks, my favorite hip-hop artist! I also ~~got~~ had a backstage pass to meet her two hours before the show started. I was so excited! I play drums for fun, and I loved playing the beat along with Bricks's CDs. I could hardly wait.

When the day of the concert came, I was so nervous. My stomack felt like it was doing gymnastics. My dad and I knocked on the back door of the Civic Center. The strongest-looking man I have ever seen opened the door. One of Bricks's managers took me and my dad down a dark hallway to the stage. The stage was cluttered with microphones, equipment for the DJ, and a silver and black drum set. The manager said that Bricks would be out in a minute.

I got more and more excited! I started tapping the beat to Bricks's hit song "My Street" on my leg. ~~"My Street" was her newest song. I thought that it was her best too. Before "My Street" my favorite song by Bricks had been "Fool Me."~~ Then I heard a voice behind me say, "You play that beat pretty well." It was Bricks! She asked if I would like to play the drums when she performed "My Street" that night. I couldn't believe it! We practiced the song in the empty Civic Center for the next hour. She told me that as long as I didn't lose the beat, I would do a good job.

When the time came for "My Street," Bricks invited me onstage. ✓The enormous crowd cheered! I started to play the beat of the song on the drum set. I concentrated hard on not losing the beat. All of a sudden, the DJ stopped scratching and Bricks stopped rapping. The song was over, but I was still playing the beat. I was so embarrassed I didn't know what to do. ~~People in the audience saw Bricks smile and start to dance to the beat.~~ Then Bricks starts rapping over my beat. We were making up a new part for "My Street" together. The crowd went wild. Bricks and I finally made eye contact and stopped at the same time. The crowd cheered and screamed for more!

After the show Bricks told me how well she thought I had done. She said that she might even keep the new line we made together in her song. I felt famous. I couldn't
As I left the Civic Center, Bricks yelled out, "You sure know how to follow advice, Elsa. You didn't believe what an amazing night I had had with my favorite hip-hop star. ∧ lose the beat!"

Prewriting
Drafting
Content Editing
Revising
Copyediting
Proofreading
Publishing

Elsa wanted her personal narrative to pop. She read her narrative again and made some improvements.

- Anton made some suggestions about the introduction to make it more attention-getting. What did Elsa do to fix the introduction?
- What did Elsa change in the third paragraph to keep her on the topic?
- Anton said that there was a jump between the third and fourth paragraphs. How did Elsa fix the problem?
- How did Elsa improve the ending?

Your Turn

Use your ideas and those of your content editor to revise your draft. Use only the ideas that you agree with.

When you have finished revising, look at the Content Editor's Checklist again. Make sure that you can answer yes to each question.

Copyediting and Proofreading

Copyediting

Elsa had improved the ideas in her personal narrative by revising it. Now she wanted to check whether all her sentences made sense and

 Sentence Fluency

whether her words were used correctly. Elsa decided to copyedit by using the Copyeditor's Checklist.

Elsa realized that she had used too many exclamation points. She decided to keep the exclamation points only when she was really excited or surprised. She kept the second exclamation point in the first paragraph because winning tickets to the concert was exciting. She kept the second exclamation point in the third paragraph because Bricks had startled her. What exclamation points in the final two paragraphs would you keep? Why would you choose the ones you did?

Elsa thought that she could use exact words

 Word Choice

to describe what she saw at the Civic Center. She used exact words to describe the door and the drum set.

Copyeditor's Checklist

☐ Are all the sentences complete sentences?

☐ Do the sentences follow each other in an order that makes sense?

☐ Are the sentences different lengths?

☐ Are questions and exclamations used correctly?

☐ Are exact words used?

Your Turn

Copyedit your personal narrative. Use the Copyeditor's Checklist. Check your questions and exclamations. If you overuse these, they will lose their effect. Be sure that you use exact words to describe your experience.

Proofreader's Checklist

☐ Are the paragraphs indented?

☐ Are all the words spelled correctly?

☐ Are capitalization and punctuation correct?

☐ Is the grammar correct?

☐ Were any new mistakes added while editing?

Proofreading

Elsa thought that a proofreader might catch mistakes that she had missed. Elsa's neighbor, Ms. Gabriel, often helped Elsa with her English homework. While proofreading, Ms. Gabriel would check the grammar, spelling, capitalization, and punctuation. Ms. Gabriel used the Proofreader's Checklist to help keep her organized.

 Conventions

Ms. Gabriel found a misspelled word in the second paragraph. Can you find it?

Ms. Gabriel found one punctuation mistake. In the first sentence, Elsa put a comma after the word *once*, but she forgot to put a comma after *twice*.

In the fourth paragraph, Elsa had written *Then Bricks starts rapping over my beat.* Ms. Gabriel told Elsa that she needed to use the same verb tense throughout. Ms. Gabriel suggested replacing *starts* with *started.*

Your Turn

Ask a partner to use the Proofreader's Checklist to check your draft. Make sure that the changes from your partner are correct.

Common Proofreading Marks

Symbol	Meaning	Example
¶	begin new paragraph	over.¶ Begin a new
⌒	close up space	close u͜ p space
∧	insert	students ∧think (should)
℈	delete, omit	that the the book
/	make lowercase	Mathematics
∼	reverse letters	reveɾꙅe letters
≡	capitalize	washington
⌄'' ⌄''	add quotation marks	I am, I said.
⊙	add period	Marta drank tea

Publishing

Elsa made the changes Ms. Gabriel suggested. Then she wrote the final copy of her personal narrative. She was ready to share her narrative with an audience. Her audience was her teacher, her classmates, and the judges of the Pennsylvania "It Happened to Me" Contest. Once she published her personal narrative, there would be no more chances to change her work. She knew her published copy had to be her best possible work.

Don't Lose the Beat

I waited on the line as the phone rang once, twice, then three times. The voice that answered said that I was the winning caller. I had won concert tickets to see Bricks, my favorite hip-hop artist! I also got a backstage pass to meet her two hours before the show started. I was so excited. I play drums for fun, and I loved playing the beat along with Bricks's CDs. I could hardly wait.

When the day of the concert came, I was so nervous. My stomach felt like it was doing gymnastics. My dad and I knocked on the back door of the Civic Center. The strongest-looking man I have ever seen opened the heavy red door. One of Bricks's managers took me and my dad down a dark hallway to the stage. The stage was cluttered with microphones, equipment for the DJ, and a glittering silver and black drum set. The manager said that Bricks would be out in a minute.

I got more and more excited. I started tapping the beat to Bricks's hit song "My Street" on my leg. Then I heard a voice behind me say, "You play that beat pretty well." It was Bricks! She asked if I would like to play the drums when she performed "My Street" that night. I couldn't believe it. We practiced the song in the empty Civic Center for the next hour. She told me that as long as I didn't lose the beat, I would do a good job.

When the time came for "My Street," Bricks invited me onstage. The enormous crowd cheered. I started to play the beat of the song on the drum set. I concentrated hard on not losing the beat. All of a sudden, the DJ stopped scratching and Bricks stopped rapping. The song was over, but I was still playing the beat. I was so embarrassed I didn't know what to do. Then Bricks started rapping over my beat. We were making up a new part for "My Street" together. The crowd went wild. Bricks and I finally made eye contact and stopped at the same time. The crowd cheered and screamed for more!

After the show Bricks told me how well she thought I had done. She said that she might even keep the new line we made together in her song. I felt famous. I couldn't believe what an amazing night I had had with my favorite hip-hop star. As I left the Civic Center, Bricks yelled out, "You sure know how to follow advice, Elsa. You didn't lose the beat!"

Whenever you publish your work, your goal is to share your thoughts and experiences. Whatever you do, make sure you find a special way to share your personal narrative so that others can enjoy it.

 Create a classroom book. Your classmates may have photographs, illustrations, or other souvenirs of their experience. Donate it to the school library for a limited time.

 Record your personal narrative as a podcast. Upload your podcast to the class blog for your classmates.

 Have your class book on hand for Parents' Night. You might wish to video record it to share later.

 Use a PowerPoint presentation to create a slide show of your narrative. You can use photos to illustrate your story.

Your Turn

- Make a final copy of your personal narrative. Add the changes from proofreading that you decided to use.
- Be careful making this final copy. Use your best handwriting or type it using a computer program. Be sure that your finished **Presentation** piece is as clean and polished as possible.

How-to Articles

LiNK ## Skipping Stones

from *The Dangerous Book for Boys*

This is quite a tricky skill, but it is possible to bounce a stone on water five or six times without too much trouble.

First of all you need to pick your stone, as flat as possible without being too thin. It needs some weight to carry, but if it weighs much more than an apple, you won't get the range. Most beaches will have a variety of stones to choose from, but if you find the perfect "skipper" in the park, hang on to it.

The skill is in the grip and the angle. Curl your forefinger around the stone, resting it on your middle finger. Secure it with your thumb.

The action of throwing the stone is all important—too steep and the stone will just plonk into the water. Bend your knees to keep the angle of descent around 25 degrees and try to get the flat side to hit the water when you release, to help it bounce on the surface.

The power you use to throw the stone can be increased once you get the hang of the technique. More than one bounce and you are "skipping."

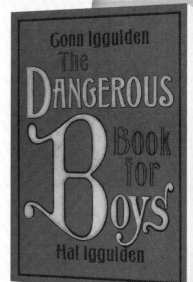

> How-to articles, like "Skipping Stones," inform a reader, using step-by-step instructions.

Erich Danaher
Room 403

Babysitting Basics: What to Do in an Emergency

In the event of an emergency while you are babysitting, it is best to be prepared, stay calm, and follow instructions. Here are a few tips on how to stay calm, cool, and collected in an emergency.

1. First, be prepared ahead of time so that you are not wasting minutes if an emergency event happens. Before the parents leave, make sure important phone numbers are available and in an easy to locate area. Keeping them next to the telephone is a smart place. For serious emergencies you should call 911. Wait for the operator to pick up. Then describe the problem clearly, give your address, and wait for further instructions. For a minor emergency, do you have the parents' cell phone to call, or is there a neighbor you can ask for immediate help?

2. Your job as babysitter is to make sure the children are safe at all times. Watch younger children carefully because they might put dangerous things in their mouth or play near unsafe devices, like electrical cords. When you arrive at the parents' house, take a tour of the house. Next, locate the first-aid kid and all fire exits in the house.

3. Last, enjoy your time babysitting, knowing that you are prepared and can handle yourself in a crisis. The best way to stay cool, calm, and collected in an emergency is to minimize potential problems. Have fun!

Emergency Telephone Numbers

Mom's Cell: 555-1234   Dad's Cell: 555-2345
Dr. Levitt: 555-6363   Mrs. Hoffstedt: 555-2626
Emergency: 911

What Makes a Good How-to Article?

Have you ever read directions for playing a new computer game? Have you followed directions to get to a party? Maybe you have used a recipe. How-to writing teaches a reader how to do something or how to make something. You can share your knowledge with others by writing a how-to article.

Topic

Write about what you know. Choose a topic that you can get excited about and can explain to others with confidence. Make sure you have a strong, clear topic. It might be hard to write a how-to article about cooking. A narrower topic, such as how to cook scrambled eggs, is much easier to explain.

Remember to stay on the topic. If you are writing about how to cook scrambled eggs, don't explain how to cook fried eggs or hard-boiled eggs. Too much information can confuse your audience.

Audience

Think about the people you are writing for. How old are they? Might they already know something about what you want to teach? What are the most important things your audience might need to know? Clear, simple steps written with your audience in mind will help readers follow your directions.

Point of View

When you write a how-to article, you are the expert and your readers are the learners. Use imperative sentences, such as "First, heat the milk," to tell your reader how to do the steps.

ACTIVITY A Tell which of the following would be good topics for how-to articles. Explain your choices.

1. the way to make a tasty sandwich
2. your day at a theme park
3. learning the rules for playing chess
4. watching a sunset at the beach
5. how to review for a math test
6. taking a good photo
7. how to use a smart phone
8. how I won the talent show
9. making a sculpture with recycled objects
10. why joining a school club is fun

ACTIVITY B The following are titles of how-to articles. Match each title in Column A to the intended audience in Column B.

Column A	Column B
1. Applying Stage Makeup	a. high school students
2. Caring For Your Baseball Card Collection	b. actors
	c. card collectors
3. Study Skills for Exams	d. fishers
4. How to Put Up a Tent	e. runners
5. Training for a Marathon	f. campers
6. A Guide to Trout Fishing	

WRITER'S CORNER

Imagine that you need to teach a first grader how to make a peanut butter and jelly sandwich. Write step-by-step directions for him or her.

Create a PowerPoint presentation of your directions.

Sometimes how-to articles are written as numbered or lettered lists. Sometimes they are written in paragraph form. When you write how-to articles in paragraph form, include an introduction, a body, and a conclusion.

Introduction

An effective introduction to a how-to article catches the readers' attention. A short description of what they will learn to make or do is often a way to get readers interested. Using exact words will help readers imagine the end result of following your directions.

Body

The body of a how-to article in paragraph form has the steps needed to complete what you will teach. Using transition words such as *first, next, then,* and *finally* will help readers keep track of the steps. Make sure that the steps are in the correct order so that your audience does not become confused. The body of your how-to article may be one paragraph, or it may be many paragraphs.

Conclusion

The conclusion of your how-to article might explain the usefulness of what your audience just learned. You might also give tips or ideas for ways to adjust the directions for other situations. For example, in a how-to article about how to make homemade wrapping paper, you might conclude with ideas for other paper crafts.

ACTIVITY C Write introductions for how-to articles on two of the following topics.

A. how to train a dog

B. directions for getting to the new basketball court

C. how to do face painting

D. Grandma's secret apple pie recipe

ACTIVITY D Read the three sentences below each how-to article topic. Tell which sentence would be a good sentence for an introduction, which would be a good conclusion, and which does not belong with the topic.

1. Topic: How to Make a Weather Vane

   a. If you are puzzled about which way the wind is blowing, build your own weather vane.

   b. Did you know that sailors used stars to guide them on long journeys?

   c. Use your weather vane to solve the puzzle of the wind's direction.

2. Topic: How to Make a Delicious Smoothie

   a. Once you've mastered this one, invent your own delicious combinations!

   b. Nothing beats the summer heat like this simple fruit and juice smoothie.

   c. Yogurt with fruit added is my friend's favorite snack.

3. Topic: How to Make a Soapbox Derby Car

   a. One time a wheel came flying off my car.

   b. Have you ever wanted to race in your own homemade car?

   c. Be sure you always wear a helmet when you are racing and always have lots of fun.

4. Topic: How to Make a Friendship Bracelet

   a. Do you want to show how pleased you are to have someone as a friend?

   b. Give the completed bracelet to your friend, who can wear it until it falls apart.

   c. Jewelry doesn't have to be expensive, although I like my mother's ruby and diamond ring.

WRITER'S CORNER

Work with a partner to write a list of snacks or crafts that can be made using popcorn. Write an introduction to begin your how-to article.

Order, Accuracy, and Completeness

The purpose of a how-to article is to teach readers how to do or make something. To help readers understand the body of your article, be sure that it is accurate, complete, and in logical order.

Logical Order

Imagine that you are reading an article about how to fix a hole in a bicycle tire. What would happen if the step for putting air in the tire came before patching the hole?

In a how-to article, the steps are presented in logical order, or the order in which the steps will be completed. Putting the steps in a numbered list before you write them in paragraph form can help you keep the steps in order.

ACTIVITY A The steps below are out of order. Write the steps in the correct order, using a numbered list.

How to Plant a Garden

1. Plant the seeds.
2. Turn over the soil with a rake.
3. Water the seeds.
4. Choose a spot for the garden.
5. Clear weeds around the young sprouts.

ACTIVITY B The directions below are for playing charades. Put them in the correct order.

a. The team with the most correct guesses wins the game.

b. Stop when your team correctly guesses or when time runs out.

c. Begin with two teams and decide on a time limit for each round.

d. Use gestures to show what is on your paper and have your team try to guess the answer.

e. Have each team write on slips of paper the names of famous people or the titles of books, TV shows, and movies. Then have each team place their slips in separate bowls.

f. Teams should take turns having players act out what the slips say.

g. When it's your turn, pick a slip from the other team's bowl. Read it to yourself.

ACTIVITY C Read the following how-to articles. Which steps are out of order? Explain what would happen if the directions were followed as written. Then identify where you would put the misplaced sentences.

Make a Puzzle

Start with a sheet of heavy paper. Cut the picture into eight irregular shapes. Then draw a colorful picture on the paper. Trade envelopes with a partner and see whether he or she can put your puzzle together. Clip the pieces together or put them in an envelope.

Make a Chinese Dragon Drawing

Design your dragon on a white sheet of watercolor paper. Wet the paper. Add colors for the background and the body of the dragon. Copy your design of the dragon lightly with a pencil on the sheet. Let the colors spread for a nice effect. Use markers to make the details of your dragon stand out to finish the drawing.

WRITER'S CORNER

Write a numbered list of directions from school to a place that your classmates know, keeping the place secret. Then use your numbered list to write the body of a how-to article. When you have finished, trade papers with a partner to guess each other's secret places.

Accuracy

Accuracy is important when you write a how-to article. Writing is accurate when it explains something exactly and without errors. For example, if you were writing a how-to article about putting a desk together, you might make sure that you told readers the right kind of screwdriver to use. If readers do not know what tools to use, or if they have been told to use the wrong tools, readers might become discouraged. Giving readers accurate information will make what you are teaching easier for readers to complete.

Completeness

Completeness, which is including all the necessary information, is important for a how-to article. When information is missing, readers can become confused. If you write about how to bake a pie, make sure that you include all the ingredients. The pie could be a disaster if you don't tell readers to use flour.

ACTIVITY D The list of ingredients below is for making blueberry muffins, but some of the information is not accurate. Identify the incorrect information. Explain your answers.

Ingredients for Blueberry Muffins

2 eggs	4 orange juice boxes
100 cups flour	1 cup raspberries
1 tbsp cinnamon	½ tsp baking soda
5 strips of bacon	1 tbsp of butter

ACTIVITY E In the following steps, some important information is missing. Write the information a reader would need to be able to complete the instructions.

How to Make Marbles

1. For regular marbles, begin with 1-inch cubes of air-dry clay. Use a piece of clay about 3 inches long to make a shooter.
2. Let the balls of clay harden overnight.
3. Allow time for the paint to dry.
4. Have fun playing marbles with your friends.

How to Make Cinnamon Toast

1. Make sure the toaster is plugged in.
2. Spread butter or margarine on the bread.
3. Pour 1 teaspoon of cinnamon into a small bowl.
4. Mix in the sugar evenly.
5. Cut the toast into two triangles.

ACTIVITY F The recipe below is missing some information. Imagine that you are making these pretzels with a grown-up. What information would you need to make your pretzels?

Soft Pretzel Shapes

loaves of frozen bread dough   water

1 egg white   coarse salt to sprinkle

Separate thawed bread dough into 1-inch balls. Roll each ball into a long rope. Use the rope to make pretzel shapes, such as letters. Place the pretzels on a greased cookie sheet and let stand for 20 minutes. Then brush the pretzels with a mixture of egg white and water and sprinkle with salt. Place a shallow pan containing 1 inch of boiling water on the bottom rack of the oven. Bake the pretzels at 350°F on the rack above the water.

Family Photo Vase   LiNK

You Will Need:
- Colorful tissue paper
- Medium-size paintbrush
- Glue wash (equal parts white glue and water)
- Clean glass vase
- Photocopies or printouts of
- family photos
- Magazines (optional)

Tear the tissue paper into several pieces. Paint glue wash on the vase in small sections, then stick on one piece of tissue paper at a time until the vase is covered. Let dry. Trim the photocopies to the size you want. Glue on one photo at a time until your collage is complete. Let dry. Paint glue wash over the entire vase for a glossy look.

WRITER'S CORNER

Choose a craft project you like to do. Make a list of the materials you need and the steps to complete the project. Check your list for accuracy and completeness.

Transition Words

You can help your readers follow the steps in a how-to article by using transition words. Transition words identify the order of the steps. These words help carry the reader from one step to the next. Read this list of common transition words.

after that	finally	one day
afterward	second	at first
last	soon	at last
later	next	then
first	now	third

Vary the transition words that you use when you write. Read the following examples and explain which is more interesting to read.

A First, fill a 2-liter bottle 2/3 full of water and add a few drops of food coloring. Second, place a washer on the lip of the bottle. Third, tape a second 2-liter bottle to the first bottle, with the washer between them. Fourth, place the bottles on a flat surface with the water-filled bottle on top. Fifth, rotate the bottles to create a vortex as the water flows from the top bottle to the bottom bottle.

In paragraph A, the steps seem more like a numbered set of directions.

B Begin by filling a 2-liter bottle 2/3 full of water and adding a few drops of food coloring. Then place a washer on the lip of the bottle. Next, tape a second 2-liter bottle to the first bottle, with the washer between them. After that, place the bottles on a flat surface with the water-filled bottle on top. Finally, rotate the bottles to create a vortex as the water flows from the top bottle to the bottom bottle.

In paragraph B, there is a connection between the steps, and the paragraph reads more smoothly.

ACTIVITY A The paragraph below comes from Louisa May Alcott's book *Little Women*. It describes Amy's daily chores. Read the paragraph and identify the transition words.

She had to wash the cups every morning, and polish up the old-fashioned spoons, the fat silver teapot, and the glasses till they shone. Then she must dust the room, and what a trying job that was. Not a speck escaped Aunt March's eye, and all the furniture had claw legs and much carving, which was never dusted to suit. Then Polly had to be fed, the lap dog combed, and a dozen trips upstairs and down to get things or deliver orders, for the old lady was very lame and seldom left her big chair. After these tiresome labors, she must do her lessons, which was a daily trial of every virtue she possessed.

ACTIVITY B Read the how-to paragraph below. Choose a transition word for each blank. You may use transition words from the list on page 262 or use other transition words that you know.

Here's how to draft a writing assignment. _____ write your name and the date in the upper right-hand corner of a sheet of paper. _____ begin to write your ideas, skipping a line after each line that you write. Don't worry about spelling right now. _____ reread your work and make your corrections. _____ ask a classmate to edit your work. _____ copy your final draft in your best handwriting.

ACTIVITY C Rewrite the paragraph below, replacing some of the *thens* with other transition words.

Would you like a delicious breakfast that is also nutritious? Follow these steps. First, pour a package of cinnamon-flavored instant oatmeal into a microwavable bowl. Then put in a half cup of applesauce. Then stir in some extra cinnamon if you want. Then put in a cup of boiling water. Then mix the ingredients. Then place the bowl in a microwave oven and cook the oatmeal for one minute. Then let the mixture stand for a minute. Then eat it!

WRITER'S CORNER

Look at the list you wrote for the Writer's Corner on page 261. Use the list to write the body of a how-to article. Remember to include transition words to help your readers move from step to step.

How to chip pass in soccer

To make a chip pass, you kick the ball with the top, flat part of your foot, where your toes end. First, get your foot under the ball. Then wing with the lower part of your kicking leg. The ball should go six to eight feet in the air.

Jane Mersky Leder

ACTIVITY D The steps below belong in a how-to article about giving a dog a bath. The steps are out of order. Number the steps in the order in which they should be done. Then write the steps in paragraph form, using a transition word for each step.

1. Fill the tub with water.
2. Bring the dog to the tub.
3. Set up a tub in the yard.
4. Bathe the dog.
5. Stand out of the way while the dog shakes off the water.

ACTIVITY E Write the steps for this decorative rice-filled candleholder in logical order. Use one of these transition words to begin each step: *first, finally, next, after that, then, now.*

Rice-Filled Candleholder

a. Place the plain rice in the container that's not your decorative jar.

b. Find and clean a good-sized jar. Make sure it is dry before you begin your work.

c. Ask an adult to help you light it.

d. Use the food coloring to tint the rice the desired color.

e. Push a candle into the middle of the jar, pushing it into the rice.

f. Fill the decorative jar about two-thirds full with the colored rice.

g. Enjoy your homemade candle holder.

h. Tie a ribbon around the top of the jar.

ACTIVITY F **Where could you put transition words to make the how-to article below flow more smoothly? Rewrite the body paragraph to include transition words.**

Are you ever bored on a rainy day? Make your own sculpting clay and make those rainy days go away.

You will need need 4 cups of all-purpose flour, 1 cup of salt, 1½ cups of water, a large heavy bowl, a wooden spoon, and a nonstick baking sheet. Combine all the ingredients, and work with the clay until it develops a doughy feel. It can be stored in airtight containers until you are ready to use it. If you want the clay to harden, ask a grown-up to bake it in a 350-degree oven for approximately one hour, depending on its size. Allow it to cool completely on a wire rack before painting or decorating.

ACTIVITY G **Write a numbered list of steps about one of the following topics.**

1. how to build a snowman
2. how to become a rock star
3. how to capture a troll
4. how to fold a paper airplane
5. how to make a friend
6. how to use the dishwasher
7. how to find a book in the library
8. how to decide on the kind of running shoes to buy
9. how to order T-shirts online
10. how to be a good brother or sister

WRITER'S CORNER

With an adult, go online to map the route between your house and school. Print out the directions and circle the transition words. Are the directions as clear and concise as they could be? Add your own sentences to fill out the directions.

Synonyms

Synonyms are words that have the same or almost the same meaning. The words *gaze, glance, observe, peek,* and *watch* are all synonyms for the word *look.* Writers use synonyms to make their writing more interesting. Can you name a synonym for each of these words?

kind	easy	funny	say	special

Words often have more than one synonym. Each synonym has a slightly different meaning. Notice how synonyms for the word *surprise* are used in the following examples. How does each synonym fit the meaning of the sentence?

> **The dolphins *astounded* the audience with their grace and playfulness.**
> **I was *startled* when I won first prize at the science fair.**

The word *astounded* means "caused wonder." It gives the idea that the audience was surprised and impressed. The word *startled* means "jumped in surprise." It describes the action of the speaker or writer when the science fair winner was announced. Choosing the best synonym helps readers get the clearest meaning of what you are trying to explain.

Use a thesaurus to find other synonyms for the word *surprise.* How might the synonyms you find change the meanings of the sentences above?

Read these two sentences. How does each synonym in red fit the meaning of the sentence? Can you think of a synonym for the two words in red?

> **We were *pleased* that we raised over $100 in the bake sale.**
> **We were *joyful* to see our old friends again.**

Both *pleased* and *joyful* mean "happy." *Pleased* suggests a sense of satisfaction. *Joyful* suggests a strong feeling of happiness.

ACTIVITY A Tell which synonym for the word in italics best fits each sentence. Use a dictionary or a thesaurus if you need help.

1. Because the detective was *alert*, he noticed the evidence at the crime scene. (wide-awake observant)

2. The audience roared with laughter after hearing the comedian's *funny* joke. (amusing hilarious)

3. Please *shut* the gate. (seal close)

4. I just finished reading a really *good* book. (nice excellent)

5. My sister was *glowing* on her wedding day. (radiant shiny)

6. Lily's skateboard is her most prized possession, so I was *puzzled* when she gave it to me. (baffled confused)

7. Gunter thinks he is a great *writer*. He even rhymes when he talks. (scribe poet)

8. The books in his bedroom were *neat*; they were in rows on shelves. (tidy orderly)

9. His *habit* is to walk the dog after school. (pattern routine)

10. We got soaked in a few minutes when we were out in the *rainstorm*. (downpour drizzle)

ACTIVITY B In each of the synonym groups below, write a sentence using each synonym.

1. scent, stink, fragrance
2. study, consider, ponder
3. worried, nervous, disturbed
4. comfortable, easy, relaxing
5. sad, unhappy, distraught

WRITER'S CORNER

Awesome, happy, and *nice* are words that are often overused in speaking and writing. List a synonym for each of these overused words. Then use each synonym in a sentence to show the different meaning.

ACTIVITY C Read the groups of words below. In each group one word is not a synonym for the other words. Find the word that does not belong in each group.

1. nice, likable, unapproachable, agreeable
2. unusual, ordinary, normal, customary
3. devious, untruthful, trustworthy, dishonest
4. crowded, filled, stuffed, empty
5. many, multiple, few, numerous
6. divided, split, separated, unified
7. assist, prevent, help, aid
8. escape, elude, vanish, capture
9. perfect, flawed, accurate, excellent
10. healthy, sick, ill, unwell
11. fabulous, superb, wonderful, grateful
12. strange, odd, silly, unusual
13. extend, halt, increase, expand
14. ascend, detach, disconnect, unfasten
15. congratulate, compliment, ignore, praise

Exposure to the cold virus can make you *sick*.

ACTIVITY D Match each word in Column A with its synonym in Column B.

Column A	Column B
1. succeed	a. pursue
2. firm	b. gloomy
3. examine	c. frisky
4. fall	d. serene
5. curious	e. achieve
6. follow	f. steady
7. playful	g. fix
8. dark	h. nosy
9. calm	i. descend
10. repair	j. inspect

Felipe learned how to *repair* his bicycle.

ACTIVITY E Replace each italicized word in the paragraph below with a synonym. Use a thesaurus or a dictionary if you need help.

The roller coaster *shook* on its creaky foundation. It climbed the first hill *slowly*. I felt *sick* because I was so *scared*. A warm *wind* blew through my hair as the car reached the top of the hill. There was a *pause*, and then suddenly the car *went* down the hill at a *fast* pace. A *scream* burst out of my mouth as we zoomed toward the ground. I *like* roller coasters!

ACTIVITY F Think of a synonym for the italicized word that will make each sentence clearer.

1. My older brother *walked* through Europe last summer.
2. The gardener had to *cut* down the sick elm tree.
3. When Marty heard the whistle, he *hurried* to the train.
4. The *noise* from my chinchilla's cage always startles people.
5. I saw a *wonderful* exhibit of Celtic art at the museum.
6. When we were hiking, we saw some *large*, mysterious tracks.
7. Maddy always gets the *correct* answer, even without a calculator.
8. There are a lot of school activities to *select* from this year.
9. Mom *said* that I could go camping if I got an A on the spelling test.
10. Andi makes *good* tandoori chicken.
11. The crowd was *shouting* when the player scored the winning touchdown.
12. The angry child *shut* the door to his bedroom.
13. Many excited fans *ran* toward the movie star.
14. The crane at the construction site was *large*.
15. We were *tired* after we had skateboarded in the park for several hours.

WRITER'S CORNER

Write a paragraph about a day when you did something special or exciting. Use the synonyms that you listed for the Writer's Corner on page 267 in your paragraph.

Grammar in Action. Identify two synonyms for the adjective in the first sentence of the page 252 excerpt.

Using the Internet

Some people call the Internet the world's biggest library. Writers use the Internet to find facts that they can use in almost any kind of writing.

Reliable Information

The main challenge for writers who conduct Internet research is to determine how reliable the information on a Web site really is. You need to be sure that the information is correct.

First, check the three-letter extension at the end of a Web site address. The following are some common extensions:

.com	commercial sites	**.mil**	military sites
.edu	sites developed by schools	**.org**	sites developed by organizations
.gov	government sites		

Of the different types of Web sites, the ones ending in .com may be the most unreliable. These are commercial Web sites, and anyone can set one up. Check who put the information on the Web site. A Web article created by students, for example, will be less reliable than one written by a professor.

Check who the author of the information is and when the site was last updated. Check the facts that you want to use in a reference book or on at least two other Web sites.

The Internet Research Checklist can help you determine whether the information on a Web site is reliable.

Internet Research Checklist

☐ Who wrote the information?

☐ Is the author an expert on the topic? How do I know?

☐ What is the purpose of this site: to sell? to entertain? to inform?

☐ When was the site last updated?

☐ Does the site include facts, such as examples or quotations, that I can check in other sources?

☐ Does the information agree with other sources?

ACTIVITY A Find the Youth Service America Web site and answer the following questions.

1. What is the purpose of the Web site?
2. Does the Web site seem reliable to you? Explain why or why not.
3. What information does the Web site give?
4. Is the information up-to-date? Explain how you know.

ACTIVITY B Choose two of the following topics. With an adult, go to a Web site that gives information on each topic. Use the Internet Research Checklist on page 270 to determine if each Web site is reliable.

1. global warming
2. volunteer programs for students
3. immunization
4. extreme sports
5. Walt Disney
6. health benefits of pomegranates
7. acupuncture
8. good pets for kids

ACTIVITY C Imagine that you are writing a how-to handbook about first aid. Which Web sites below would be reliable sources to check for information?

1. www.kidshealth.org
2. www.medicalsupplies.com
3. www.health.gov
4. www.redcross.org
5. www.adhesivebandage.com

WRITER'S CORNER

Pick a first-aid skill that you might explain in your handbook in Activity C. Research that skill, using at least two Web sites and one book. Then write a list of steps explaining how to do that skill.

Grammar in Action Identify the possessive adjectives in the model on page 253.

Search Engines

Internet research usually starts with a search engine. A search engine locates Web sites about the topic that you are researching. Many search engines were made especially for kids. These search engines are helpful because they have many links to school topics.

Keywords

When you use a search engine to research a topic, you will type keywords into the search field. The keywords will help the search engine find Web sites about your topic.

Choose keywords carefully. Use words that are important to your topic. Which of the keywords below do you think will get the best results if you were researching blue jays?

A Search the Web | birds, blue | **Go**

B Search the Web | blue jays, habitat, recognizing | **Go**

Example A would probably get results for all blue birds, such as the blue heron or the blue-winged warbler. Example B will get better results because the search engine will know to look only for Web sites about blue jays. It will also search for specific information you might need, such as where blue jays live and how to recognize them.

Internet Safety

The Internet is used daily by millions of people for millions of different things. Just as in the real world, you need to be cautious online. Here are some tips for using the Internet safely.

- Do not give out any personal information, such as your name, age, address, phone number, or information about your family. If you register a screen name, use a catchy nickname instead of your real name.
- If you read or see something that makes you uncomfortable or suspicious, alert an adult right away.
- Do not download files without asking the person who owns the computer you are using. Some downloads can cause problems for a computer.

ACTIVITY D For each topic below, choose the set of keywords that will get the best search results.

1. fifth-grade science fair projects.
   a. science, easy
   b. science projects, science fair, fifth grade

2. nurses in the Civil War
   a. Civil War, nurses, training
   b. nurses in history

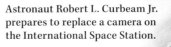

Astronaut Robert L. Curbeam Jr. prepares to replace a camera on the International Space Station.

3. space exploration
   a. explorers, outer space
   b. astronauts, NASA

4. the best computer for your needs
   a. computers, price
   b. computer, software package, special deals

5. how to grow tomatoes
   a. tomatoes, kinds of
   b. tomatoes, growing, caring for plants

ACTIVITY E Choose something that you would like to know about each topic below. List keywords that might get good results in an Internet search.

1. the Revolutionary War
2. ancient Rome
3. a famous author
4. the history of television
5. women in sports
6. a famous expedition
7. an important battle
8. a well-known artist

WRITER'S CORNER

Choose one of the topics from Activity E and use the keywords that you listed to search the Internet with an adult. Decide how well the first five Web sites fit the topic. Change your keywords if necessary to get better results.

How-to Talks

If you've ever given directions to your home or explained to a friend how to blow chewing-gum bubbles, then you have given a how-to talk. How-to talks teach an audience how to do or make something.

Topic

When you choose a topic for your how-to talk, think about what you know how to do. You could give a how-to talk about how to play your favorite sport or how to plan a birthday party. Choose a topic for your how-to article that can be done in a few steps that are easy to explain. Choose a topic you know a lot about.

Audience

Knowing who your audience is will help you think of how to give your talk. Your audience should be able to understand the steps you talk about. If you need to do so, define words or phrases that you think your audience will have trouble understanding.

Organization

Start your how-to talk with an introduction that grabs your audience's attention. You might want to start with a question such as "Have you ever wanted to learn how to . . . ?" Or you might want to begin with an exclamation such as "All right, everybody, let's learn how to . . . !" Be sure to organize your steps in the order they need to be done and to use transition words to help your audience understand the order.

Let's learn how to plant a tree!

End your talk with a sentence or two about why it's good to know how to do what you are teaching your audience. You might end your talk with some tips on the usefulness of what your audience has learned to do.

ACTIVITY A Explain why each topic would or would not be interesting for fifth graders.

1. how to tie your shoe
2. how to play tic-tac-toe
3. how to get to your home from school
4. how to run the 50-yard dash
5. how to catch butterflies
6. how to find seashells on a beach
7. how to make a telephone call
8. how to play the harmonica
9. how to paint a picture
10. how to snap your fingers
11. how to build a birdhouse
12. how to go bird-watching
13. how to play checkers
14. how to dress yourself in the morning
15. how to tie a bow tie

ACTIVITY B Identify which group would be the best audience for each topic.

volleyball team	police officers	kindergarten students
Cub scouts	fund-raising committee	

1. how to tie your shoes
2. how to clean your campsite
3. how to start a neighborhood watch
4. how to serve overhand
5. how to advertise a charity event

SPEAKER'S CORNER

Choose a topic from Activity A. Write an introduction for a how-to talk about that topic. Practice saying your introduction aloud.

Prepare Your Talk

Writing the steps of your how-to talk on note cards can help you. Write each step on one note card and number the note cards. Then look over your cards and make sure that they are in order, that the information is complete, and that you remembered to include all the steps.

You might want to prepare note cards for your introduction and conclusion too. If you think of something that will grab your audience's attention, write it on a note card. If you have ideas for other ways to do or use what you are teaching, write those on a note card. Label which card is for your introduction and which card is for your conclusion.

Prepare Your Visual Aid

Sometimes a how-to talk needs a visual aid. A poster that shows the steps of your topic can help make the steps easier for your audience to understand. Another kind of visual aid is a demonstration. For example, if you are doing a how-to talk on tying a tie, you can bring a tie to show your audience while you explain what to do for each step. If you are explaining how to make something, it might be a good idea to bring in an example of the finished product.

Practice

Practicing can help you discover and correct any problems in your presentation. As you practice, keep these questions in mind:

- Will my audience understand what I'm saying?
- Do I start my topic with an attention-grabbing introduction?
- Am I speaking loudly and clearly enough for my audience to hear and understand?
- Are all my steps in the right order?
- Have I taken out steps that the audience doesn't need?
- Does my conclusion tell the audience why knowing my topic is good for them?

When you feel comfortable with your presentation, practice with a friend or family member. Ask your listener the above questions.

Listening Tips

Listening to a how-to talk can be just as important as giving one. Keep these points in mind while you listen to how-to talks:

- As you listen, imagine doing each step yourself.
- Carefully watch what the speaker does.
- Take notes of the steps if you can.
- When the speaker has finished, ask questions about any steps you didn't understand.

ACTIVITY C Select a topic for your how-to talk. You may choose your own or choose one of the topics from Activity A on page 275. Remember to select a topic that you know about and that can be done in a few easy-to-do steps.

ACTIVITY D Use the topic you chose in Activity C and prepare and practice your how-to talk. Write your steps on note cards. Prepare a visual aid if you need one.

ACTIVITY E Practice your how-to talk with a partner. Then listen to your partner's how-to talk. Give your partner suggestions on how to make the talk better.

SPEAKER'S CORNER

Present your how-to talk to your class. Remember to speak slowly, clearly, and with enthusiasm for your topic. Make sure everyone in your audience can see and hear you. When you have finished, invite your audience to ask questions.

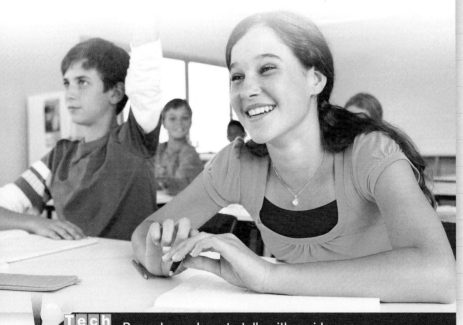

Tech Tip Record your how-to talk with a video camera.

Prewriting and Drafting

You probably know how to do and make many things. This will be your chance to write an article that teaches how to do or make something.

Prewriting

Javier's class was writing how-to articles. Javier wanted to jump right in, but he knew he should get ready before he started writing. By prewriting, Javier could choose a topic and organize his directions.

Choosing a Topic

Javier began by making this chart to help him think of topics.

Things I do well
-tell jokes
-hit home runs

Things I can make
-clay figures
-tuna surprise
-a lasso

Things I do indoors
-draw
-magic tricks
-collect comic books

Things I do outdoors
-swim
-in-line skate

Javier looked at his chart and knew he had to shorten his list. First, he crossed off the topics that were too broad, such as drawing and swimming. He could have narrowed the topic of swimming to how to do the butterfly stroke, but he wanted a different topic. Some of his topics would be too hard to

Ideas

explain in writing, such as how to hit a home run or how to tell a joke. Of the topics left, he liked magic tricks the best. Javier thought his classmates would find it fun to learn how to do a magic trick.

Your Turn

Make a chart like Javier's to help you think of topics.

- When you finish, cross off any that would be hard to write about in a how-to article. If your topics are too broad, think of narrower ones.
- Pick a topic you are excited to write about. An enthusiastic writer can get a reader to become excited too.

Organizing Directions

Javier knew his magic trick pretty well. But he thought that explaining how to do his trick might be difficult. To make sure he kept the body of his article in logical order, he decided to organize his steps. Since a flowchart shows how one step flows to the next, he thought it might be a useful tool for organizing his article. It helped him

👀 **Organization**

see how each step leads to the next. He kept his flowchart to refer to when he started writing. Here is Javier's flowchart.

```
┌─────────────────────────────────────┐
│        Count out 21 cards.          │
└─────────────────────────────────────┘
                 │
                 ▼
┌─────────────────────────────────────┐
│        Volunteer picks card.        │
└─────────────────────────────────────┘
                 │
                 ▼
┌─────────────────────────────────────┐
│     Take cards back and shuffle.    │
└─────────────────────────────────────┘
                 │
                 ▼
┌─────────────────────────────────────┐
│     Deal cards into three piles.    │◄──────┐
└─────────────────────────────────────┘       │
                 │                             │
                 ▼                             │
┌─────────────────────────────────────┐   ┌────────────┐
│  Have volunteer point to pile with  │   │ Repeat     │
│              card.                  │   │ twice.     │
└─────────────────────────────────────┘   └────────────┘
                 │                             ▲
                 ▼                             │
┌─────────────────────────────────────┐       │
│            Pick up piles.           │───────┘
│  Volunteer's pile goes in the middle.│
└─────────────────────────────────────┘
                 │
                 ▼
┌─────────────────────────────────────┐
│          Count out 10 cards.        │
└─────────────────────────────────────┘
                 │
                 ▼
┌─────────────────────────────────────┐
│          Reveal 11th card.          │
└─────────────────────────────────────┘
```

Your Turn

A flowchart can help you see whether your steps are in logical order.

- Make a list of the steps in your how-to article.
- Rewrite the steps as a flowchart. Do the steps lead from one to the next? Are any steps missing? Should you delete any steps?

Prewriting

Drafting

Content Editing

Revising

Copyediting

Proofreading

Publishing

Drafting

Javier was ready to begin. He had taken good notes, and he knew in what order to give his directions. Javier double-spaced his draft. He knew that his draft would be good, but he would want room to make changes later.

How to Do Magic

Everyone loves a magic trick. I know a magic trick that is based on math, not magic. If you follow these easy directions, you'll dazzle your friends every time! I love this trick so much that I just can't wait to tell you about it!

All you need are a deck of playing cards, a table, and a volunteer. First, count out 21 cards. Then ask the volunteer to pick a card and to look at it without showing it to you? Tell the volunteer to put it back. Then take the cards back and schuffle them.

Explain that you are going to deal out the cards faceup in three piles. Deal the cards in three piles. Deal left to right. Put one card in each pile. Do this until all the cards are in one of the three piles. Tell the volunteer to watch for his or her card without saying anything when it appears. When you finish, ask the volunteer to point to the pile that the card is in.

Now pick up the piles one at a time. The important part is to be sure that when you put the three piles together, the pile with the volunteer's card is in the middle. Then lay the cards on the table again in three piles, the same as before. Ask the volunteer to point to the pile that has the card. Then pick up the piles with that pile in the middle. Lay the cards on the table a third time. After the volunteer has pointed to the pile, pick up the cards again the same way. Be sure that the cards never get shuffled or mixed up.

To finish the truck, count out the first 10 cards, placing them facedown on the table. Then with a dramatic toss, drop the 11th card on the table faceup.

If you follow these directions exactly, the volunteer's card will always be the 11th card. Make sure you practice this trick alone a few times to get used to it. When you get used to it, you can think of ways to add dazzle to the trick.

Your Turn

Use your notes to help you organize the body of your how-to article.

- Be sure you also make notes about what you could write in your introduction and conclusion.
- As you write your first draft, keep your audience in mind. Try to get them interested in your topic and be sure that your directions are clear.

Grammar in Action

Identify the personal pronouns in the first paragraph of Javier's draft on page 280.

Writer's Tip Remember to double-space your draft so that you have room to make changes later.

Prewriting

Drafting

Content Editing

Revising

Copyediting

Proofreading

Publishing

Content Editing

Javier knew his magic trick pretty well, but writing about it had been harder than he thought it would be. Still, he felt good about his first draft. He knew that if he edited his draft for content, he could make sure that readers would understand it. To content edit, he would check that his ideas were clear and that his article was complete. Here is the checklist Javier used to content edit his draft.

Content Editor's Checklist

- ☐ Does the introduction tell readers what they will make or do?

- ☐ Are the steps in logical order?

- ☐ Are the directions accurate and complete?

- ☐ Does the conclusion give readers a sense of completeness? Does it offer further tips?

- ☐ Does the article use imperative sentences?

Javier knew that asking someone else to read his draft might be a good idea. His pen pal Talisha lived in Chicago, and she was the best writer Javier knew. Javier decided to e-mail his first draft to Talisha. He also sent a copy of his Content Editor's Checklist.

Talisha replied to Javier's e-mail with several comments. She knew that she had to be extra careful writing her comments because Javier could not hear her tone of voice and might misunderstand something.

She started by telling Javier how much she liked his draft. She thought his topic was interesting and fun. Then Talisha made suggestions for how Javier might improve his draft.

- The introduction is good, but the title confused me. The title says it is a magic trick, but the introduction says the trick is based on math, not magic. Maybe you can fix the title.

- The last sentence of the introduction doesn't seem right. It's good to know that you **👓 Voice** are excited, but that sentence sounds like something you might say to your friends. It doesn't sound like a sentence that should be in a how-to article.

- Your directions are logical and accurate. I tried the trick on my mom, and it worked. I thought it might be more logical to tell the volunteer to look for the card before you deal the cards out. If you don't, he or she might not be looking for it when you deal.

- The second-to-the-last paragraph doesn't seem complete. You tell the reader to drop the 11th card, but you don't say what the 11th card should be.
- I think you might want to add something to your conclusion. Maybe tell us how we can use this trick.

Javier was glad he'd e-mailed his how-to article to Talisha. She had some good ideas for how to make his draft better. Javier printed out Talisha's reply. He wanted to read it over later and decide which changes to make.

Your Turn

- Read your draft and answer the questions on the Content Editor's Checklist one at a time.
- After you have made notes on how to improve the content of your draft, trade drafts with a partner.
- Use the Content Editor's Checklist as you read your partner's draft. Make notes on ways your partner's draft could be improved.
- Talk to your partner about your ideas. Remember to start by telling your partner what you liked.
- Some of your partner's ideas may help you write a better article. Think about them carefully.

Writer's Tip Remember that you do not have to make all the changes your partner suggests.

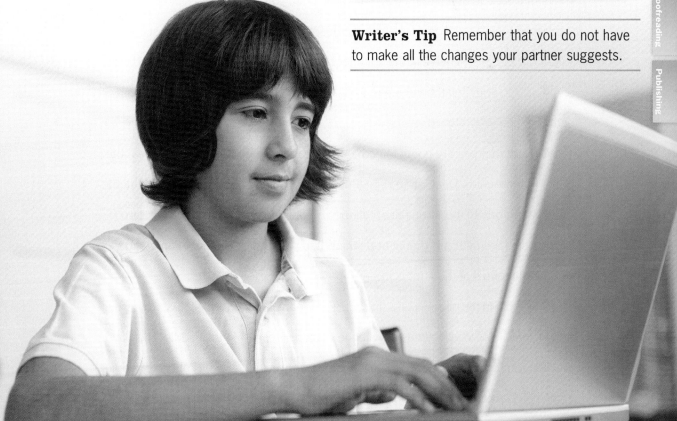

Revising

This is Javier's revised draft.

How to Do ^Mathematical^ Magic

Everyone loves a magic trick. I know a magic trick that is based on math, not magic. If you follow these easy directions, you'll dazzle your friends every time! ~~I love this trick so much that I just can't wait to tell you about it!~~

All you need are a deck of playing cards, a table, and a volunteer. First, count out 21 cards. Then ask the volunteer to pick a card and to look at it without showing it to you? Tell the volunteer to put it back. Then take the cards back and schuffle them.

Explain that you are going to deal out the cards faceup in three piles. Deal the cards in three piles. Deal left to right. Put one card in each pile. Do this until all the cards are in one of the three piles. Tell the volunteer to watch for his or her card without saying anything when it appears. When you finish, ask the volunteer to point to the pile that the card is in.

Now pick up the piles one at a time. The important part is to be sure that when you put the three piles together, the pile with the volunteer's card is in the middle. Then lay the cards on the table again in three piles, the same as before. Ask the volunteer to point to the pile that has the card. Then pick up the piles with that pile in the middle. Lay the cards on the table a third time. After the volunteer has pointed to the pile, pick up the cards again the same way. Be sure that the cards never get shuffled or mixed up.

To finish the truck, count out the first 10 cards, placing them facedown on the table. Then with a dramatic toss, drop the 11th card on the table faceup. ∧

Your volunteer will be perplexed to see that the 11th card is his or her card.

If you follow these directions exactly, the volunteer's card will always be the 11th card. Make sure you practice this trick alone a few times to get used to it.

When you get used to it, you can think of ways to add dazzle to the trick. ∧

Think about putting together a magic show for your friends. Save this trick for last it is a real showstopper.

Look at Javier's new draft and notice the changes he made.

- How did Javier change the title? Why do you think that he made the change?

- Why do you think Javier deleted the last sentence in the first paragraph?

- How did Javier change the third paragraph? Why do you think that he changed the order of the sentences?

- What word in the sentence that Javier added in the next to last paragraph means "surprised"?

  ───◉◉─── **Word Choice** Do you think his choice is better than *surprised*? Why or why not?

- What information did Javier add to the ending? Do you think it was an improvement? Why or why not?

Your Turn

Revise your how-to article. Use the ideas you and your partner had. When you have finished, go over the Content Editor's Checklist again.

Copyediting and Proofreading

Copyediting

Javier knew he could improve his draft further by copyediting it. He checked that his sentences were clear and correct and that he'd used the words in his article correctly. Below is the Copyeditor's Checklist Javier used to check his draft.

Javier had used plenty of transition words, but he checked to see if he could add more. He added *First* in the second paragraph to show that the trick was beginning. He also added *Finally* to

Copyeditor's Checklist

- [ ] Are transition words used to help readers follow the steps?

- [ ] Are other kinds of sentences beside imperative sentences used to add variety?

- [ ] Are all of the sentences complete?

- [ ] Do all the words mean what I think they mean?

the sentence that tells the reader to lay the cards out a third time. This transition word let the reader know that this is the last time to lay out the cards.

Sentence Fluency

Most of the sentences in Javier's article were imperative sentences. He had also used other kinds of sentences for variety.

As Javier read his article, he noticed that the third paragraph sounded choppy. He decided to combine sentences to make it read more smoothly. He combined three sentences into the sentence "Deal left to right, one card in each pile, until all the cards are in one of the three piles." Do you see the three sentences he combined?

He also wondered if he used the word *perplexed* correctly. He liked the sound of the word, but he wasn't sure that he knew exactly what it meant. The dictionary said it meant "to confuse or puzzle." That wasn't really what he wanted to say. He replaced *perplexed* with *amazed,* which was closer in meaning to what he wanted to say.

Your Turn

Read your revised draft carefully. See if you can answer yes to the questions on the checklist. Look for ways to make your writing read smoothly. Remember to check for one kind of mistake at a time.

Proofreading

Javier wanted to check his article one more time so that he did not publish it with any mistakes.

 Conventions Proofreading his draft meant he would look for mistakes that he might have made in spelling, punctuation, capitalization, and grammar. Javier used this checklist to proofread his work.

Proofreader's Checklist

- ☐ Are the paragraphs indented?
- ☐ Are all the words spelled correctly?
- ☐ Are capitalization and punctuation correct?
- ☐ Is the grammar correct?
- ☐ Were any new mistakes added while editing?

Javier found two spelling errors in his draft. In the fifth paragraph, he'd written *truck* when he meant to write *trick*. Do you see the other misspelled word?

Javier asked his friend Ella to proofread his draft. Javier knew that someone who hadn't already read his work would be more likely to see mistakes in it.

Ella found that the punctuation at the end of the third sentence of the second paragraph was incorrect. The sentence is not a question. What kind of punctuation should Javier use?

Ella pointed out that the last sentence should be written as two sentences. Javier saw that he had added that mistake when he was revising for content. He was especially glad that Ella had caught that mistake.

Your Turn

- Read through your draft carefully. Use the Proofreader's Checklist to look for mistakes.
- Each time you read through your draft, check for only one kind of mistake.
- When you have finished, trade drafts with a partner. Go over each other's drafts, using the Proofreader's Checklist.
- When you get your draft back from your partner, decide if the changes your partner suggested are correct before you make those changes in your draft.

Writer's Tip A dictionary can help you spell words correctly.

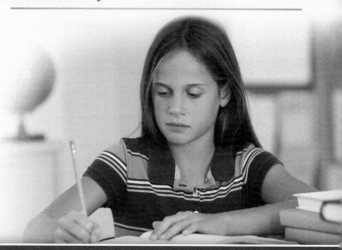

Prewriting

Drafting

Content Editing

Revising

Copyediting

Proofreading

Publishing

Publishing

Publishing happens the moment you share your finished work with your audience. Javier couldn't wait to publish his how-to article. He had worked hard, and he knew it was his best work. He was also excited because he knew his audience would enjoy reading about how to do a magic trick. He carefully typed his final copy on a computer and passed out copies of his article to his whole class.

Presentation

How to Do Mathematical Magic

Everyone loves a magic trick. I know a magic trick that is based on math, not magic. If you follow these easy directions, you'll dazzle your friends every time!

All you need are a deck of playing cards, a table, and a volunteer. First, count out 21 cards. Then ask the volunteer to pick a card and to look at it without showing it to you. Tell the volunteer to put it back. Then take the cards back and shuffle them.

Explain that you are going to deal out the cards faceup in three piles. Tell the volunteer to watch for his or her card without saying anything when it appears. Deal the cards in three piles. Deal left to right, one card in each pile, until all the cards are in one of the three piles. When you finish, ask the volunteer to point to the pile that the card is in.

Now pick up the piles one at a time. The important part is to be sure that when you put the three piles together, the pile with the volunteer's card is in the middle. Then lay the cards on the table again in three piles, the same as before. Ask the volunteer to point to the pile that has the card. Then pick up the piles with that pile in the middle. Finally, lay the cards on the table a third time. After the volunteer has pointed to the pile, pick up the cards again the same way. Be sure that the cards never get shuffled or mixed up.

To finish the trick, count out the first 10 cards, placing them facedown on the table. Then with a dramatic toss, drop the 11th card on the table faceup. Your volunteer will be amazed to see that the 11th card is his or her card

If you follow these directions exactly, the volunteer's card will always be the 11th card. Make sure you practice this trick alone a few times to get used to it. When you get used to it, you can think of ways to add dazzle to the trick. Think about putting together a magic show for your friends. Save this trick for last. It is a real showstopper.

Now that you have finished, it's time to share what you know. How will you share your how-to article?

 Host a how-to fair in your classroom. Each student can set up a station at which to share his or her information.

 Make a classroom manual. Collect all the how-to articles in a binder. Add interesting items to the articles such as photos or visual aids.

 Present your how-to article as a PowerPoint presentation. Include sound and graphics to interest your audience.

 Record your how-to article on video. Incorporate props and visual aids to help you demonstrate to your audience.

Whenever you publish your work, your goal is to share your thoughts and experiences with other people.

Your Turn

Now it is time to make one last check of your work before you share it with your audience. When you are done, follow these steps:

- Type your draft on a computer or rewrite it in neat handwriting.
- Make sure you did not leave out any words or punctuation as you made your final copy.
- Proofread one more time to make sure you caught all the mistakes.
- Add drawings or diagrams to your work. Some how-to articles can be made clearer with a visual aid.
- Choose one of the publishing methods to share your work with an audience.

Prewriting
Drafting
Content Editing
Revising
Copyediting
Proofreading
Publishing

Business Letters

LiNK

COOL KIDS DAY CAMP
67 High Street • Des Moines, Iowa • 44199

November 10, 20—

Ms. Amy Gonzalez
36 Highland Court
Des Moines, Iowa 44199

Dear Ms. Gonzalez:
Thank you for your interest in our camp. We enjoyed your interview and would like to offer you a position as counselor-in-training.

Orientation begins June 30th at 9:00 a.m. We will send you further details next week. We look forward to welcoming you to our camp community and expect to have a successful summer season.

Sincerely,

Adam Quinn

Adam Quinn
Personnel Director

834 Gutherie Lane
Rooster River, MI 49103

March 3, 20—

Ms. Gertrude Bea
Coordinator of Youth Activities
Rooster River Park District
1002 North Case Drive
Rooster River, MI 49103

Dear Ms. Bea:

My family and I would like to encourage you to offer junior golf lessons
or junior golf leagues at Quarry Greens this year. A visit to your excellent
Web site did not indicate that you are offering either of these.

I am a fifth-grade student, and I am beginning to enjoy the game of golf.
My family and I are new to the area, and as spring approaches, our
thoughts turn to our favorite family sport. I want to hone my golf skills and
would like to have that opportunity at the park district.

I have spoken about this with my school's physical education teacher and
my parents. We would all be interested in working with you to encourage
student participation. I feel that many parents will sign their children up if
you offer club rentals and lesson fees at a reduced rate.

Please consider sponsoring golf activities for fifth-grade boys and girls this
spring or summer. I look forward to your response. Thank you for your
consideration.

Sincerely yours,

Mike Hernandez

Mike Hernandez

What Makes a Good Business Letter?

Mike Hernandez's letter on page 291 is a letter of inquiry, which is a type of business letter. Business letters are written for a specific purpose to a company, an organization, or a person. Unlike a personal letter, a business letter is formal in tone and sticks closely to a single topic. Mike Hernandez does not know Ms. Bea, so he communicates his ideas to her in a formal way. Business letters all have the same parts to make the information easy to find. Look at Mike's letter below to see where the parts of the business letter are placed.

Heading
The writer's return address is in the top left corner of the letter. The date of the letter should be placed below the address. Notice the correct punctuation and capitalization of the address and date.

Inside Address
The receiver's name is first. It is followed by the receiver's job title if you know it, and the company or organization's address. Notice the correct punctuation and capitalization of the address.

Closing
This is the part of the letter in which the writer says good-bye to the receiver. Use a formal closing such as *Sincerely* or *Sincerely yours*, followed by a comma.

Salutation
This is the greeting of the letter. It begins with "Dear" followed by the person's name and a colon. If the person's name is not known, "Dear Sir or Madam:" or "To whom it may concern:" is used.

Body
The body is the main part of the letter. It is single-spaced, with a line between paragraphs and an extra line after the last paragraph. The paragraphs are not indented.

Signature
The writer's signature comes after the closing. It is followed by the writer's printed or typed name.

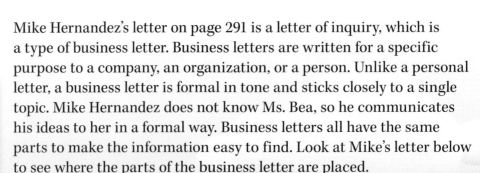

834 Gutherie Lane
Rooster River, MI 49103

March 3, 20—

Ms. Gertrude Bea
Coordinator of Youth Activities
Rooster River Park District
1002 North Case Drive
Rooster River, MI 49103

Dear Ms. Bea:

My family and I would like to encourage you to offer junior golf lessons or junior golf leagues at Quarry Greens this year. A visit to your excellent Web site did not indicate that you are offering either of these.

I am a fifth-grade student, and I am beginning to enjoy the game of golf. My family and I are new to the area, and as spring approaches, our thoughts turn to our favorite family sport. I want to hone my golf skills and would like to have that opportunity at the park district.

I have spoken about this with my school's physical education teacher and my parents. We would all be interested in working with you to encourage student participation. I feel that many parents will sign their children up if you offer club rentals and lesson fees at a reduced rate.

Please consider sponsoring golf activities for fifth-grade boys and girls this spring or summer. I look forward to your response. Thank you for your consideration.

Sincerely yours,

Mike Hernandez

1. *Maria Ranier* Maria Ranier
2. To whom it may concern:
3. I would like to know when the Goose Island Park will open.
4. Mr. Wally Schiller
   Lead Writer
   Hanover Magazine
5. December 8, 20—
6. Sincerely,

ACTIVITY B Rewrite the business letter so that all the parts are in the right order.

November 11, 20—

2434 Redwood Drive
Marin City, CA 94965

Dear Dr. Stein:

Dr. Mariel Stein
Oakland Community College
42 College Circle Drive
Oakland, CA 94606

I would like to bring my fifth-grade class to your botany lab. I feel that it would be worthwhile for them to see a botanist at work. Please let me know if you can make time for us.

Sincerely yours,
Gerald Fitzscott

Gerald Fitzscott

WRITER'S CORNER

Write all the parts of a business letter except the body. Make up a name and an address for the business or organization to which you are writing.

Grammar in Action. Identify three adjectives in the last paragraph of the page 290 excerpt.

Language

The language of a business letter is more formal than the language of a personal letter. Choose words carefully. Keep descriptions and explanations brief and to the point. Don't include unnecessary details.

Formal Language

When you write a business letter, do not use slang, such as *cool* and *bummed*. Avoid casual language, such as contractions. Here are some other ways to make your writing more formal.

- Replace long phrases of short words with single, more formal words.

  I <u>took a look</u> at the damaged shoe.
  I <u>inspected</u> the damaged shoe.

- Replace strong adjectives with more neutral adjectives.

  There was a <u>massive</u> hole in the bag.
  There was a <u>large</u> hole in the bag.

- Replace general verbs with more specific verbs.

  When I <u>got</u> the DVD, it was scratched.
  When the DVD <u>arrived</u>, it was scratched.

Thank you for your time.

Polite Tone

Have you ever been told to be polite? Do you change your behavior when you are being polite?

Being polite means showing consideration and respect for other people. Saying things such as "when you have an opportunity" and "thank you for your time" are ways to show consideration for the receiver of your letter. You can show respect when you write a business letter by using words such as *please, thank you, sincerely,* and *I look forward to.*

ACTIVITY C Read the body of the business letter below. Identify the parts of the letter that are informal.

I recently heard your cello concert at the Parkway Symphony. It was really cool! Boy, you're one great cello player. I would like to invite you to visit my fifth-grade orchestra class. Perhaps you could talk to us and play a short piece on your cello. We need to hear some good tunes from a real pro.

Our class meets every Monday, Wednesday, and alternate Fridays between 11:00 and 12:00. So whenever you want to cruise on by, then go on ahead. If you are interested, please contact me at the address above.

ACTIVITY D Change the language in each of these sentences to more formal language for a business letter.

1. The clerk was really crabby, and I got mad.

2. I want to get that game you have called *Exploring the Amazon.*

3. I'm writing a report about your state, and I need some stuff. You must have lots of information.

4. I think you're so cool! Want to speak to my English class?

5. Your Web site said delivery would take six to eight days, but it took way longer!

6. The crummy T-shirt for the Barnyard Brothers Band you sent faded the first time I washed it. How can you sell such bad stuff?

7. This is the third time I'm writing to say that I didn't get the book I ordered. What's wrong with you? Didn't you get the letters I sent?

8. You have a super job. Do you want to come and speak at our school's career day?

LiNK

I. Paint Co.,
22 Branch St.,
New York.

Dear Sirs: Your estimate for painting my dining-room, library, south bedroom, and dressing-room is satisfactory, and you may proceed with the work as soon as possible.

I find, on the other hand, that wainscoting the hall comes to more than I anticipated, and I have decided to leave it as is for the present.

Very truly yours,

C.R. Town

WRITER'S CORNER

Use one of these sentence starters in a body paragraph of a business letter. Use formal language and a polite tone.

A. Please send me . . .

B. I am enclosing . . .

C. I would like to inquire about . . .

Tech Tip Write a business letter, using a computer program.

Purpose

LiNK

Dear Mr. Wheeler,

On August 29, I purchased your Young Artists paint set. The label said that it contained three different types of paint—acrylic, water, and oil. However, when I opened the box, I was surprised to find only acrylic and water paints. I informed Sara Robinson, the manager of Elmwood Art Supply where I bought the set, and she suggested I contact you for a refund.

I have enclosed the store receipt. Please send me a refund of $21.85. I look forward to your reply.

Sincerely,
Robyn Fisher

Businesspeople have many things to do at their jobs. So when you write a business letter, it's important to state the purpose of your letter quickly and clearly. When you write a business letter, state briefly why you are writing the letter, and what action you want the person to take.

Types of Business Letters

Business letters generally fall into three groups. Here are some common types of business letters.

Ordering a Product

Imagine you want to order a hollow log for your tarantula habitat. If you were to order the log from a magazine ad, you might write a business letter. You would include information such as the product number and where to ship your order.

Inquiry or Request

What if you wanted to invite a famous author to speak to your class? You might write a letter of inquiry. You would tell the author where your school is and times that the author could give a presentation. You might also write a letter to request information from an organization. The organization might answer questions in a response letter or might send you books or pamphlets with the information you requested.

Complaint

You might write a letter of complaint if a product you ordered was broken or took longer to arrive than you expected. When you write a letter of complaint, you should first explain what the problem is. Then you might suggest ways that the problem could be fixed, such as by getting a refund or a replacement.

ACTIVITY A Read each situation below and identify the purpose of the business letter you might write about it.

1. Your parents said you could subscribe to a magazine that you like.

2. A server at a restaurant was rude to you.

3. You want information about rock formations for your report on the Carlsbad Caverns.

4. You received an order of invisible ink that turned out not to be invisible.

5. You want to know what the requirements are to become a video game designer.

6. You didn't get the play money for a board game you ordered.

7. You need information on how to return a pair of sneakers you ordered because they are too big.

8. You want to know the schedule of special programs for students at the art museum.

Stalagmites and stalactites in the Carlsbad Caverns

ACTIVITY B Match each item below to one of the following types of business letters: *ordering a product, inquiry or request, complaint*. You may use each type of letter more than once.

1. I have not yet received the tulip bulbs that I ordered a month ago.

2. Because you are Central's most accomplished graduate, we would like your permission to name a scholarship after you.

3. I want to ask my state representative if I can attend a session of the state legislature with my family.

4. The pages of the books were torn or dirty, and I am unsatisfied with the shape in which my order arrived.

5. I would like to know the requirements to become Drama Club treasurer.

6. I would like a one-year subscription to your excellent magazine, *Extreme Skateboards*.

WRITER'S CORNER

Brainstorm three reasons you might have for writing a business letter. Identify the type of letter that you would write.

Grammar in Action — Use three adjectives to describe a product you are writing about in a letter of complaint.

The Body of a Business Letter

The body of a business letter is where you tell the person or company what you want. You might ask for a product or service, make a complaint, or offer a compliment.

No matter what you write about, it is important to be clear and to the point when you write a business letter. Stay on the topic and only write detailed information directly related to your problem or request.

The body of a business letter usually has three parts.

Beginning

In the beginning of a business letter, you state the purpose of the letter. In the letter on page 291, Mike Hernandez wants to encourage the park district to offer golf activities for children. That was his purpose for writing.

Middle

The middle of a business letter includes information that explains more about the letter's purpose. In Mike's letter, he supports his request by saying that he and his family enjoy playing golf and that his physical education teacher and his parents are in favor of his idea.

Ending

In the ending of a business letter, you invite the receiver to act on or respond to whatever you are asking. The ending of Mike's letter asks Ms. Bea to consider starting a golf program for fifth graders. He also thanks her for considering his request.

ACTIVITY C Identify whether each sentence below belongs in the beginning, the middle, or the ending of a business letter.

1. Thank you for your time.
2. I would like to know whether you have any information about rock formations in the Clovis area.
3. I am hoping you will talk about some of your new paintings.
4. I look forward to a quick resolution of this problem.
5. My class has already read *River Wolf*. What else might you suggest?

ACTIVITY D Write the first two sentences of the beginning of a business letter that relates to each situation below. Be sure that the receiver of each letter can easily figure out why the letter was written.

1. The clerk at a toy store laughed at your younger sister when she tried to buy a doll with the change in her piggy bank.

2. You bought a bread maker that makes great bread. You want to tell the company how happy you are with the product.

3. You bought an MP3 player that stopped working about a week later.

4. You read in the newspaper that the city council wants to tear down your favorite historic building to build a shopping center.

5. You want to request that a local author come to your school and talk about his work.

ACTIVITY E Read the body of the business letter below. Tell which parts are not on the topic.

Dear Sir or Madam:

I really like your magazine. The articles on whales are really awesome. Please have more articles on them. I also like the games and puzzles. I eagerly wait for my copy to come in the mail every month.

My aunt gave me a subscription to the magazine, and I've been receiving copies for several months. I recently got the September issue. The article on underwater exploration was the most interesting. However, the August issue of the magazine never came. I don't know what happened to it. It may have gotten lost in the mail.

Could you please send me a copy of the August issue? Thank you for your attention to this matter.

WRITER'S CORNER

Write three sentences that go in the middle and in the ending of the letter you began in Activity D. Remember that the middle should support the purpose of the letter and that the ending should ask the receiver to act on or respond to what you are asking.

Roots

What do the words *bibliography, fortitude,* and *thermometer* have in common? All three words are formed from roots. A root is a building block for other words. Knowing the meaning of a root can often help you figure out the meaning of an unfamiliar word. The root *bibl* means "book." A bibliography is a list of books.

Often the root comes from an ancient language, such as Latin or Greek. Sometimes you add letters to the beginning (a prefix) of a root to form a new word. Sometimes you add letters to the end (a suffix) of a root to form a new word.

ROOT	MEANING	EXAMPLES
dict	to speak	pre<u>dict</u>, <u>dict</u>ionary

Another root is *cred*. It comes from the Latin word *credere,* meaning "to believe." Here are some words that share the same root. Read each word. Check the pronunciation and the meanings of unfamiliar words in a dictionary. How does each word relate to *believe*?

credence	miscreant	credibility
credit	credo	creed
discredit	incredible	incredulous

Notice that sometimes the spelling of the root changes. Which words are not spelled with *cred*? Which words have prefixes added to the root? Which words have suffixes added to the root?

ACTIVITY A The Greek root *graph* means "to write or to draw." Read the words below and answer the questions that follow.

graphic   epigraph   autograph   biography   paragraph

1. Which words have prefixes added to the root?
2. Which words have suffixes added to the root?
3. Which word has both a prefix and a suffix added to the root?
4. Which word means "an inscription, motto, or quotation"?
5. Which word means "a written or pictorial representation"?
6. Which word means "a person's own signature"?
7. Which word changes the pronunciation of *graph*?

ACTIVITY B The Latin root *finis* means "end or limit." Read the words below and answer the questions that follow.

unfinished   finish   finally   finale   infinite   finalist

1. Which word means "to bring to an end"?
2. Which word means "a contestant in the finals of a competition"?
3. Which word means "not complete"?
4. Which word means "without limits or bounds"?
5. Which word means "lastly or at last"?
6. In which words does *-is* change to *-al*?

ACTIVITY C The Latin root *spec* means "to see." Read the words below and answer the questions that follow.

spectacle   inspect   spectacular   circumspect   expect

1. Which word means "an impressive display"?
2. Which word means "to look over carefully"?
3. Which word means "cautious or careful"?
4. Which word means "to think something will happen"?
5. Which word means "making a great display"?
6. What words have prefixes added to the root?

WRITER'S CORNER

Identify the meaning of the common root in the words below. Then use the words in separate sentences that show the meaning of each word.

audible   audiovisual

audience   auditorium

Tech Tip Create a class dictionary of roots on the class Web page.

ACTIVITY D Read these roots and their meanings. Combine two of the roots to make a word that completes each sentence below. You may use a root more than once.

Root	Meaning	Root	Meaning
auto	self	scope	see
chrono	time	graph	write
tele	far	meter	measure
audio	hear	phone	sound
micro	small		

1. The nurse used an _____ to measure our ability to hear.
2. We used a _____ to see the tiny plant cells.
3. The author wrote her name in my book when I asked for her _____.
4. The _____ measured the time to the exact second.
5. My best friend lives far away, so I call him on the _____.
6. With my new _____, I can see the farthest stars clearly.

ACTIVITY E Read the following paragraph. Make a list of words that have the root *port*. Give the meaning of the root. Then write the meaning of each word. Use a dictionary if you need help. Finally, list other words that contain the root *port*.

We were up early and ready for a day at the beach. Mom watched the weather report and told us that we would have a hot, sunny day. I brought my portable radio so that we could listen to music. Dad packed sandwiches and cold drinks for us to transport to our destination. With food, blankets, towels, and everything else, we almost needed a porter to help us carry everything.

ACTIVITY F Fill in the missing roots, examples, and meanings to complete the chart below. Use a dictionary for help.

	Root	Meaning	Example	Meaning
1.	cardi	_____	cardiac	of or near the heart
2.	therm	heat	thermal	_____
3.	_____	climb	ascend	go or move upwards

Root	Meaning	Example	Meaning
4. *act*	do	_____	act in response
5. *vis*	see	vision	_____
6. _____	say	dictate	say or read aloud
7. *tract*	pull	tractor	_____
8. *clar*	_____	clarify	make or become clear
9. *scribe*	write	_____	give an account of
10. _____	sea, pool	marine	of the sea
11. *aster*	star	astronomy	_____
12. *gen*	birth	_____	study of heredity
13. *avi*	_____	aviary	bird sanctuary
14. _____	of the eye	binoculars	device to magnify what the eye sees

ACTIVITY G Identify and try to define the shared root of each of the following groups of words. Check your answers in a dictionary.

1. digress, progress, transgress
2. convert, divert, revert
3. eject, interject, project
4. depend, pendant, pendulum
5. biography, antibiotic, biology
6. local, locate, location
7. benefit, benefactor, benevolent
8. aquarium, aquatic, aquamarine
9. geology, geography, geometry
10. erupt, interrupt, rupture
11. vacant, evacuate, vacate
12. signal, signature, insignia
13. manufacture, factory, factor

WRITER'S CORNER

Expand the chart in Activity F by adding three other examples of words with the same root. Define each word you add. Use a dictionary for help.

Combining Sentences and Sentence Parts

Combining sentences and sentence parts can help your writing read more smoothly. You use conjunctions when you combine sentences. Study the chart below to know when to use the conjunctions *and, but,* or *or.*

and	connects ideas that are alike in some way
but	connects ideas that are different
or	connects ideas that give a choice

Combining Simple Sentences

Imagine that your teacher asked you to deliver a note to another class and also to pick up a book in the library. You might decide that it is easier to do both tasks in one trip instead of two. Combining sentences is like that. You write one longer sentence instead of two short ones.

A My father said I couldn't go to Brandon's house until I finished my chores. I still needed to take out the trash and rake the leaves.

B My father said I couldn't go to Brandon's house until I finished my chores, and I still needed to take out the trash and rake the leaves.

C Megan and Molly want to walk to the beach. Their mother says it is too far for them to go alone.

D Megan and Molly want to walk to the beach, but their mother says it is too far for them to go alone.

Notice that in example B the conjunction *and* joins the two sentences from example A. In example D the conjunction *but* joins the two sentences from example C. Can you give examples of sentences that use the conjunctions *and, but,* and *or*? Where would you put a comma in those sentences?

ACTIVITY A Combine each pair of sentences into one sentence. Use the conjunction in parentheses. Remember to use a comma before the conjunction.

1. Some animals have become extinct over time. Today many animals are dying out because of the actions of people. (but)

2. Many animals are already extinct. Many more are now on the list of endangered species. (and)

3. Illegal hunting and deforestation are changing our world. Few people worry about what the changes mean to wildlife. (but)

The tiger, an endangered species

4. We must take care of our wildlife. We may lose many more animals. (or)

5. A lot of animals have become endangered. Wildlife organizations were formed to help save animals. (and)

6. Human activity leads to the disappearance of many animals. Many people are also working to save animals. (but)

7. National parks are important homes for endangered animals. People can see animals in their natural environment. (and)

ACTIVITY B Add a second simple sentence to each of these sentences. Then use both sentences to make one sentence. Use the conjunctions *and, but,* or *or.*

1. I can make delicious pancakes.

2. It is a warm day today.

3. Would you like to see the new movie that just opened?

4. Talia's book report is due on Friday.

5. Should I wake Dustin now?

6. Marta likes going to the ice-skating rink.

7. Did Jerry finish the race?

8. Last winter was so cold.

WRITER'S CORNER

Imagine you recently bought a DVD from the store ShowTimes, but it was cracked when you opened it. Write three sentences explaining the problem. Use a conjunction in each sentence.

Combining Sentence Parts

Sometimes two sentences are related, and the same words are repeated in both sentences. Often you can combine parts of sentences to make a compound subject, a compound predicate, or a compound direct object. You can use the conjunctions *and, but,* or *or.*

Compound Subjects

A compound subject is made up of more than one subject. Look at the examples below. The compound subject is underlined.

> A Columbus Day is a fall holiday. Thanksgiving is a fall holiday.
> B <u>Columbus Day and Thanksgiving</u> are fall holidays.

Compound Predicates

A compound predicate has more than one predicate connected by a conjunction. Look at the examples below. The compound predicate is underlined.

> A On our camping trips, we sleep in a tent. We cook outside.
> B On our camping trips, <u>we sleep in a tent and cook outside.</u>

Compound Direct Objects

A direct object answers the question *whom* or *what* after the verb. A compound direct object has more than one answer to the question. Look at the examples below. The compound direct object is underlined.

> A We planted cherry tomatoes in our garden. We planted lettuce in our garden.
> B We planted <u>cherry tomatoes and lettuce</u> in our garden.

ACTIVITY C Combine each pair of sentences into one sentence by combining sentence parts. Identify whether each revised sentence has a compound subject or a compound predicate.

1. Hero sandwiches are large. Submarine sandwiches are large.
2. I picked the beautiful wildflowers. I put them in a large vase.
3. I ride my bike to school. I walk to school.
4. In the evening we roast marshmallows at the campfire. We sing songs at the campfire.

5. Bayani saw three movies in a row. Paul saw three movies in a row.

6. Frogs are amphibians. Newts are amphibians.

7. We walked to the top of the hill. We saw a great view of the town.

8. Cal came to my birthday party. Luke came to my birthday party.

9. I ate a peanut butter and jelly sandwich. I drank some milk.

10. Jake went to the secondhand store. Jake bought some old DVDs.

ACTIVITY D Complete each sentence with a compound direct object. Remember that direct objects answer the questions *whom* or *what* after the verb.

1. For the next assignment, we will write a _____ or a _____.

2. My Aunt Steph bakes the best _____ and _____ in the world.

3. Ignacio invited _____ and _____ to his party.

4. Alexis and her friends like to play _____ or _____ on rainy days.

5. I like to read _____ and _____.

6. The winner of the spelling bee will be _____ or _____.

7. Chris and Nick practiced _____ and _____ for the decathlon.

8. Cooper paints _____ and _____ very well.

9. For the talent show, Riley will sing _____ or _____.

10. Casey orders a _____ or a _____ whenever she goes to that restaurant with friends.

WRITER'S CORNER

Think of all the things that you have done since you got up this morning. Write a paragraph to describe the events of your day. Include each of the compound sentence parts that you practiced in this lesson. Identify the compound parts.

Business E-Mails

You probably send e-mails to friends. Have you ever sent an e-mail to a business? When you do, you should follow many of the same rules as for business letters.

Parts of a Business E-Mail

Heading and Subject Line

The heading is the e-mail address of the person who will receive your e-mail. Be careful to type it correctly, or the person will not receive your e-mail. The e-mail program automatically puts your e-mail address and the date at the top of the e-mail when you send it.

One important part of a business e-mail is the subject line. State the topic of your e-mail clearly in a few words. Businesses get many e-mails. They can use the subject line to find out quickly why you are writing. Then they can take appropriate action.

Salutation and Body

Use the same salutation as you would for a business letter. The body of a business e-mail also follows the rules for business letters. Be brief. Have a beginning, a middle, and an ending. Use formal language. Do not use abbreviations such as IMHO or emoticons such as ;), which you might include in personal e-mails.

Closing, Signature, and Address

The closing is the same as in a business letter. Your signature comes at the end of the letter. Some e-mail programs allow you to type in your name once and will automatically put it at the bottom of e-mails. In some programs you can include your handwritten signature. After the signature it is common for people to type their street address or phone number. This allows the receiver to send you a response by regular mail or to call you.

Attachments

You may want to include a document or image with your e-mail. For example, you might include a copy of a letter you had sent previously or a photo of a damaged product. People applying for a job typically send their résumé as an attachment. Mention in the body of your e-mail that you are including an attachment.

E-mail programs give instructions to show you where and how to include an attachment. They also show where you can read attachments you receive.

ACTIVITY A **Read the business e-mail below. Tell how it is similar to other business letters you have studied. Tell how it is different.**

To: MarionLeibman@cityanimalshelter.org
From: SarahColeman@computernet.com
Subject: Request for information on pet adoption

Dear Sir or Madam:

My family and I want to adopt a dog from your shelter. I'm writing to get some information on the requirements for adoption.

Can you answer these questions for me?

- What times can we visit your shelter to see animals?
- Do you make a visit to our home before we adopt?
- Do we have to provide references?
- What is the fee for adopting an animal?

I appreciate your answers to these questions before my family and I come to visit the shelter.

Very truly yours,

Sarah Coleman

WRITER'S CORNER

Imagine the reply Sarah Coleman might receive in Activity A. Write how the director of the animal shelter would respond. Pay close attention to the language the director might use.

Draft your response to Sarah Coleman in an e-mail.

Internet E-mail Safety

It is important to follow some rules when you send an e-mail. These rules apply to both business and personal e-mail.

- Keep the password for your e-mail private.

- Do not open e-mail for which you do not know the sender. Do not be fooled by subject lines, such as "Remember me?"

- Do not open attachments unless you know the sender. E-mail attachments may have viruses that can harm your computer.

- Spam e-mails are mass mailings, often from commercial businesses. They clog mailboxes and are annoying. It is best not to open them. Also, do not unsubscribe from them. The company will then know your e-mail address is correct, and you will get even more spam from other sources.

- Do not give personal information on the Internet, especially when asked for it by a site or business you do not know. Some sites try to get personal information, which they should not do.

- Do not reply to e-mails that say that you have won a prize or other such offers. These e-mails are likely scams to get your personal information.

- Do not put your e-mail address on public Web sites. You may want to set up an account with a nickname if you want to reply to Web sites that anyone can use.

- Remember that there is no guarantee that your e-mail will stay private. Always be careful what you write and send in an e-mail.

ACTIVITY B Write a clear subject line for each of the following business e-mails.

1. You want to order some extra paints for a kit that you have.
2. You lost your cord to recharge your cell phone and want to order a new one.
3. A pump you ordered for your bike arrived damaged.
4. You need to find out the date and time for the town picnic.

ACTIVITY C Fill in the missing parts of the business e-mail.

To: Edward.Porter@wqfxatv.com
From: RobynS@comphome.com
Subject:_____

Dear _____:

I'm writing to you because _____
_____.

A few days ago, we found out the news that the TV show *Skits and Songs* is being canceled. It is my favorite program, and it is for many of my friends too. My friends and I always watch in the afternoon when we get home from school.

We know that the program is continuing on other TV stations. We do not want to miss any new episodes.

I want to add my voice to those who are requesting that you put back the show in its current time slot. Thank you for considering my request.

_____,

Robyn Smyth

WRITER'S CORNER

Use one of the subject lines you wrote in Activity B to write a business e-mail. Use the correct parts. Make up an e-mail address to send the letter.

Business Telephone Calls

Have you ever made a business telephone call? Business calls are different from personal calls, just as business letters are different from personal letters.

Imagine that you wanted to call Waterbrook Art Supplies to complain about an incomplete set of paints that they sent you. You might first look for the telephone number in a phone book, on the Internet, or on the product packaging. After you have the correct telephone number, what would you do?

Speaking Professionally

It is important to speak in a professional, polite tone when you make a business call. Getting angry or forgetting what to say because you didn't plan your call wastes time and energy. Here are some tips to help you sound professional when you make a business call.

- Before you make your call, write notes about what you want to say. Use the notes to help you stay on the topic of your call. Notes can also help you leave an accurate message if you cannot reach the person you need to speak with.
- Identify yourself and explain why you are calling. If you are speaking to a receptionist or an operator, this information can help direct your call to the correct person. If you know the person you need to talk to, this information can help that person assist you.
- At the end of the call, sum up what was said during the conversation. This helps you make certain that you understand what was said and what action will be taken.

Leaving a Message

Sometimes the person that you are calling is unavailable. You might have to leave a short message on that person's voice mail. Here are some things to remember when leaving a message.

- Begin by giving your name and your telephone number. Speak slowly, especially when giving your telephone number. If you speak too fast, the person listening may not understand you or might miss important information.
- Briefly explain why you are calling. Remember to use a polite and professional tone of voice.
- End the message by giving your name and telephone number again. This will give the person a chance to check that he or she wrote the information correctly.

ACTIVITY A Read the following reasons for making a business call. Write notes about what you would say during a business call for each reason.

1. A statue that you ordered has a chip in it.
2. There is a fallen telephone line in your backyard.
3. You've been chosen to select and order your soccer team's new uniforms.
4. You want to find out about the after-school classes for young people at the art museum.
5. A magazine is sponsoring a short-story contest and you have questions about how to enter.
6. For extra credit, you want to invite the town historian to speak to your class.
7. Grandma asked you to make a reservation for a backstage tour of a theater for people who buy tickets to the play you are attending.
8. You want to call the city transit system to get information about a bus going downtown and the hours the bus runs.

SPEAKER'S CORNER

Choose one of the reasons for making a business call in Activity A. Work with a partner to role-play that business call. Take turns being the caller. Remember to use a professional and polite tone.

Listening Tips

It is important to listen actively when you make a business call. Here are some tips to help you listen actively.

- Keep a notebook and pencil nearby so that you can write important information.
- Pay attention to the speaker's name. Write the speaker's name so that you know whom to contact in the future.
- If the speaker explains anything complicated, repeat what was said to be sure that you understand completely. Ask questions about anything that you do not understand.
- Give verbal clues to let the speaker know that you are listening. Saying things such as *yes, OK,* or *I understand* will help the other person know that you are following the conversation.

Follow-up Calls

Occasionally, you might have to make a follow-up call to a person or a company. It might be to check the results of your first call, to continue a previous conversation, or to thank someone for helping you. When you make a follow-up call, remember to identify yourself. Sum up the purpose of your previous call. Then explain why you are calling again.

Call Review Checklist

Use this checklist after you make business telephone calls.

Call Review Checklist

- ☐ Did I greet the person and give my name?
- ☐ Did I write the name of the person I spoke with?
- ☐ Did I briefly explain why I called?
- ☐ Did I ask the person to take action or fix a problem?
- ☐ Did I give verbal clues that I was listening?
- ☐ Did I thank the person for taking time to talk with me?

ACTIVITY B Choose one of the situations below. Write notes about what you would say during each of the following parts of the call: *greeting the person, identifying yourself, explaining your reason for calling, requesting help or action, thanking the person.*

A. Your new handheld video game has a defective battery, and you would like a replacement. You call Monstrous Games and speak with Tia, a customer service representative.

B. Famous filmmaker John Stedman has agreed to speak at your school's film club. You call him to arrange the details.

C. You call Matteo, the manager at Gia's Italian Restaurant, to thank him for the great service at your birthday dinner.

D. You call local librarian Gayle Burke with a proposal to set up a Saturday afternoon book club for kids.

E. You are on the planning committee for the end-of-year school party. Your job is to call local businesses, such as Hoffmann's Hobbies, to see if they will donate money or prizes for the party.

ACTIVITY C Work with a partner to role-play the business call you chose in Activity B. Take turns being the person making the call and the person receiving it. Use the Listening Tips from page 314. When you have finished, use the Call Review Checklist to decide how well you made your call.

SPEAKER'S CORNER

Choose one of the business calls you practiced with a partner and present the call to the class. Use real telephones as props if you can. When you have finished, invite your audience to use the Call Review Checklist to give you feedback about your call.

Prewriting and Drafting

Writing a business letter is a great way to get the attention of a company or an organization. In a business letter, you can make sure that everything you want to say is expressed clearly and in logical order.

Prewriting

Gabriella is a fifth grader who is interested in birds and bird-watching. She wanted to find out more information about the types of birds that are in her area. She decided to write a letter of inquiry to the National Audubon Society. Gabriella first took the time to do some prewriting. She stated the purpose of her letter and then gathered and organized the information.

Stating the Purpose

Gabriella thought about the purpose of her letter, or what she wanted to accomplish. Gabriella knew that she wanted to inquire about the birds in her area. Did she just want to ask what types of birds could be found? Did she also want to ask where to look for the birds? Did she want to find out about other types of birds in other parts of Alabama? Gabriella wanted to go out and actually see the birds in her neighborhood, so she decided to ask for information on what types of birds to look for and where to look for them.

Your Turn

Think of something you would like more information about.

- Maybe you would like to know about volunteer opportunities in your community.
- Maybe you would like to learn how to start a business.
- You might ask for information about a product, a service, a place, an event, or how to do something.

Whatever you decide will be the purpose of your letter of inquiry. Write what you would specifically like to inquire about.

Gathering Information and Organizing Your Letter

After stating the purpose of her letter of inquiry, Gabriella gathered the information she needed to write the letter. She already knew that she was writing to the National Audubon Society. She looked at their Web site and found that there was a chapter of the society near her town. She wrote that address. She also found the name of someone from that chapter.

Next, Gabriella planned how to organize her letter by drawing a diagram. In each box

Organization she wrote something that would remind her what to put in that part of the draft. She also filled in the information she had already gathered. Gabriella thought that by doing this she would have an easier time remembering what she wanted to write in her draft. Here is Gabriella's diagram.

My home address

Robert Paulsen
Mobile Bay Audubon Society
P.O. Box 483
Fairhope, AL 36532

Dear Mr. Paulsen

1. Ask what types of birds in area.
2. Ask where to find them.
3. Thank for help.

closing

Prewriting
Drafting
Content Editing
Revising
Copyediting
Proofreading
Publishing

Your Turn

Gather the information you need to include in your letter of inquiry.

- Decide to whom you should send your letter.
- Find the address. You may need to look online or in a phone book, or you may need to call the company directly.
- Draw a diagram of a letter of inquiry, using Gabriella's as a model.
- In each box write something to help you remember what to include in your draft. Be sure to include the information you gathered.

Drafting

Gabriella wrote a draft of her letter of inquiry. She used her diagram from prewriting to guide her writing. Here is the first draft of Gabriella's letter.

2804 Poissonniere Road

Loyola Villa, AL 36532

July 14, 20—

Robert Paulsen

Mobile Bay Audubon Society

P.O. Box 483

Fairhope, AL 36532

Dear Mr. Paulsen:

My family and I have recently moved to the Mobile Bay area from New Orleans. I need some information before I go down to the bay with my binoculars. What types of birds should I be looking for in this area? I am used to looking for the types of birds that live in the city and on the Mississippi River, and I am not sure what will be living on and around Mobile Bay. In Louisiana my favorite birds to see were kingfishers.

Since I live so near the bay, the area I live in is swampy and wooded. Where would be a good place to start looking for birds? I would like to be able to find birds that live by the water and birds that I can see in the forest behind my house.

Could you please send me the information to get me started birdwatching? Thank you for your time.

Sincerly,

Gabriella Breton

In the body Gabriella tried to use formal language and a polite tone. The beginning of the body stated what she was inquiring about, the middle explained why she was interested in the information, and in the ending, she asked for a response to her inquiry.

Your Turn

Use your diagram from prewriting to help you write the first draft of your letter of inquiry. Be sure to include the following:

- A beginning that states the purpose of the letter
- A middle that gives more information about the purpose
- An ending that requests an action from the receiver of the letter

Remember to use formal language and a polite tone.

Writer's Tip Look for words in your letter that can be replaced by more formal ones. Use a thesaurus to find words with similar meanings.

Using Formal Language

Business letters should be written using formal language so the person you are writing to will take you seriously. Look for words in your letter that can be replaced by more formal ones. For example, *receiving* something in the mail sounds more formal then *getting* something in the mail. When making these changes, be sure to look up the words in a dictionary to make sure they mean what you think they do.

Prewriting

Drafting

Content Editing

Revising

Copyediting

Proofreading

Publishing

Content Editing

Now that Gabriella had a draft of her letter, she wanted to check the meaning, the order, and the tone.

Gabriella thought it might be a good idea to ask someone to content edit her letter. She thought that another person might catch mistakes that she hadn't noticed. Gabriella asked her twin sister, Nadia, to content edit her letter. Nadia often went out on nature adventures with her sister, so Nadia was happy to help with the letter. This is the Content Editor's Checklist that Nadia used.

Content Editor's Checklist

☐ Does the beginning clearly state the purpose of the letter?

☐ Does the middle give detailed information about the purpose of the letter?

☐ Does the ending ask for a response or some kind of action?

☐ Does the order in which the information is presented make sense?

☐ Does the letter use a polite tone and formal language?

Nadia read Gabriella's letter of inquiry. She told Gabriella that she liked that the letter had a polite tone. Nadia said that words and phrases

 Word Choice such as *please* and *thank you for your time* made the letter sound formal. Then Nadia told Gabriella these ideas she had for her letter of inquiry.

- The beginning doesn't state the purpose of the letter clearly enough. It seems as if the purpose is about what types of birds are in the area, but the next paragraph talks about where to look for birds.

- The middle seems to give information to support a different purpose. I thought the letter was about types of birds, not where to find them.

- I think the two questions you ask are out of order. You should ask where to find birds before you ask what types of birds are in the area.

Gabriella thanked Nadia for her help. She noticed that Nadia hadn't commented on the ending of her letter. In addition to asking for a response, Gabriella decided to ask for information on the society's events and meetings. She wanted the reader of her letter to know that she was serious about her requests.

Your Turn

Exchange your letter of inquiry with a partner. Use the Content Editor's Checklist to check your partner's paper.

- Pay attention to one question on the checklist at a time.
- Take notes on changes you would like to suggest to your partner about his or her letter of inquiry.

When you have finished, take turns talking with your partner about each other's draft.

- Start by saying something you like about your partner's letter. Think about each of your partner's suggestions before you use them in your letter.
- Then content edit your own letter, using the Content Editor's Checklist.

Revising

Gabriella carefully considered the content editing ideas that she and Nadia had. Here is Gabriella's revised draft.

2804 Poissonniere Road

Loyola Villa, AL 36532

July 14, 20—

Robert Paulsen

Mobile Bay Audubon Society

P.O. Box 483

Fairhope, AL 36532

Dear Mr. Paulsen:

I loved birdwatching in Louisiana, and I would like to continue here.

My family and I have recently moved to the Mobile Bay area from New Orleans. I need

some information before I go down to the bay with my binoculars. What types of birds ¶

should I be looking for in this area? I am used to looking for the types of birds that live

in the city and on the Mississippi River, and I am not sure what will be living on and

around Mobile Bay. In Louisiana my favorite birds to see were kingfishers.

Prewriting

Drafting

Content Editing

Revising

Copyediting

Proofreading

Publishing

Since I live so near the bay, the area I live in is swampy and wooded. Where would

There are not a lot of people, houses or factories.

be a good place to start looking for birds? I would like to be able to find birds that

live by the water and birds that I can see in the forest behind my house.

Could you please send me the information to get me started birdwatching? Thank

Please also send me any news about upcoming meetings and events held by the Mobile Bay Audubon Society.

you for your time.

Sincerly,

Gabriella Breton

After reviewing Nadia's comments, Gabriella revised her letter of inquiry.

- What change did Gabriella make to the introduction? How does it make clearer her purpose for writing?

- Gabriella started a new paragraph in the second line. She also added a sentence to her third paragraph. How do these changes improve her business letter?

- Nadia suggested that Gabriella ask where to find birds before asking what types of birds are native to her area. Gabriella did not make this change. Do you think that the letter is clear without the change?

- What information did Gabriella add to the end of the letter? How does this information strengthen or weaken her letter?

Your Turn

Use your ideas and those of your content editor to revise your letter of inquiry. Use only the ideas from your content editor that you think will make your draft better.

When you have finished revising, look at the Content Editor's Checklist again. Make sure that you can answer yes to each question.

Grammar in Action

Identify three adjectives in the ending of Gabriella's letter.

Copyediting and Proofreading

Copyediting

When Gabriella was finished content editing her draft, she was happy that her ideas were in order

Sentence Fluency

and that they were written clearly. She wanted to copyedit her letter to make sure that each of her words and sentences were also clear and correct. She used this Copyeditor's Checklist to help her.

Gabriella thought that she really didn't need the last sentence of the second paragraph. Although she did see many kingfishers in Louisiana, this letter was about birds she would like to see in Alabama.

Gabriella realized that two parts of her business letter were incorrect. Because this was a business letter, she would need to write her name above where she typed it.

Copyeditor's Checklist

- [ ] Have you checked that there are no awkward or confusing sentences?

- [ ] Is every sentence in the letter needed?

- [ ] Is there a variety of sentence lengths?

- [ ] Are the parts of the business letter correct and in the right order?

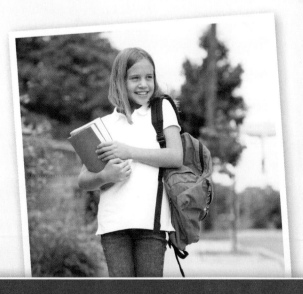

Your Turn

Use the Copyeditor's Checklist to check your letter for mistakes. Look for only one kind of mistake at a time. Make sure that all your sentences are clear and necessary. Check that you have correctly included all of the parts a business letter.

Prewriting

Drafting

Content Editing

Revising

Copyediting

Proofreading

Publishing

Proofreading

Gabriella was close to sending her letter. But first she wanted someone to proofread it. She knew that it was important that her letter did not have any spelling or grammatical mistakes.

Gabriella asked Ruby, her first new friend in town, to proofread her letter. Ruby used this Proofreader's Checklist to check Gabriella's letter for mistakes.

Proofreader's Checklist

☐ Are all the words spelled correctly?

☐ Are capitalization and punctuation correct?

☐ Is the grammar correct?

☐ Have you checked to be sure that no new mistakes were made during revising?

After she proofread the letter, Ruby shared with Gabriella the mistakes that she found. Ruby found two misspelled words. The word *birdwatching* should have been written with a hyphen. Gabriella used this word twice, so she made sure to fix it in both places. Can you find the second misspelled word?

Ruby also found a punctuation mistake. A comma was missing in the series in the second

👓 **Conventions**

sentence of the third paragraph. Gabriella thanked Ruby for her help and made this change. Gabriella then proofread her letter herself so that she would be sure that there were no mistakes.

Your Turn

- Trade your letter with a partner.
- Use the Proofreader's Checklist to check your partner's draft. Check for only one kind of mistake at a time.
- When your partner returns your letter, make sure that the changes are correct.
- Proofread your own letter.

Writer's Tip Ask someone to help you if you are not sure about any of the changes that your partner made.

Publishing

Here is the final copy of Gabriella's letter.

2804 Poissonniere Road
Loyola Villa, AL 36532

July 14, 20—

Robert Paulsen
Mobile Bay Audubon Society
P.O. Box 483
Fairhope, AL 36532

Dear Mr. Paulsen:

My family and I have recently moved to the Mobile Bay area from New Orleans. I loved bird-watching in Louisiana, and I would like to continue here. I need some information before I go down to the bay with my binoculars.

What types of birds should I be looking for in this area? I am used to looking for the types of birds that live in the city and on the Mississippi River, and I am not sure what will be living on and around Mobile Bay.

Since I live so near the bay, the area I live in is swampy and wooded. There are not a lot of people, houses, or factories. Where would be a good place to start looking for birds? I would like to be able to find birds that live by the water and birds that I can see in the forest behind my house.

Could you please send me the information to get me started bird-watching? Please also send me any news about upcoming meetings and events held by the Mobile Bay Audubon Society. Thank you for your time.

Sincerely,

Gabriella Breton

Gabriella Breton

Letters are meant to be read. Here are some ideas to publish your letter.

 Create a classroom tracker for all the letters your class sent out, using a spreadsheet computer program. When classmates receive a response, mark it in the tracker. Note how long it took the recipient to respond.

 Ask a local community action club if they need volunteers to help contact local politicians. Use your letter-writing skills to help spread a message that is important to you.

 Post your letter on the classroom blog. Ask your classmates to post comments about your letter.

 Record a podcast of you reading your letter. Discuss the responses and reactions it receives.

Remember to write neatly or use a word-processing program to type and format your letter.

Your Turn

- Make your corrections from copyediting and proofreading, type your letter, print it out, and read it over one more time.
- Make sure all the parts of the letter are included. Check to see that you didn't add any new mistakes while typing. Don't forget to add your signature.
- When you are sure that your letter is ready to be sent, fold it into thirds. Begin by folding the bottom third of the paper up. Next, **Presentation** fold the top third of the paper down. Last, press the folds firmly so that the letter is flat.
- Address a business-sized envelope to the recipient and put your return address in the upper left corner. Put your letter in the envelope with the last fold on the top.

You might share your letter with a classmate. You might also send your letter of inquiry. Before you send your letter, make sure your teacher has a chance to read it. If you do send it, share any response you receive with your teacher and classmates.

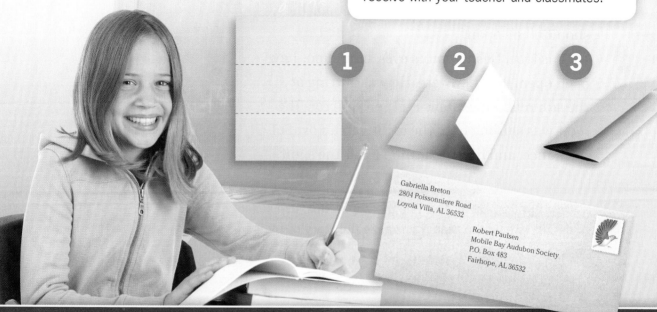

Descriptions

LiNK ## The Tale of Despereaux
by Kate DiCamillo

Her husband handed her a small shard of mirror. The mouse mother, whose name was Antoinette, looked at her reflection and gasped aloud. "Toulése," she said to one of her sons, "get for me my makeup bag. My eyes are a fright."

While Antoinette touched up her eye makeup, the mouse father put Despereaux down on a bed made of blanket scraps. The April sun, weak but determined, shone through a castle window and from there squeezed itself through a small hole in the wall and placed one golden finger on the little mouse.

The other, older mice children gathered around to stare at Despereaux.

"His ears are too big," said his sister Merlot. "Those are the biggest ears I've ever seen."

"Look," said a brother named Furlough, "his eyes are open. Pa, his eyes are open. They shouldn't be open."

It is true. Despereaux's eyes should not have been open. But they were. He was staring at the sun reflecting off his mother's mirror. The light was shining onto the ceiling in an oval of brilliance, and he was smiling up at the sight.

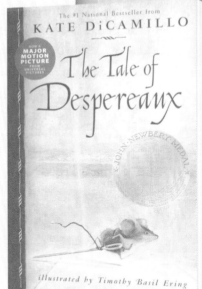

The #1 National Bestseller from
KATE DiCAMILLO

NOW A MAJOR MOTION PICTURE FROM UNIVERSAL PICTURES

The Tale of Despereaux

JOHN NEWBERY MEDAL

illustrated by Timothy Basil Ering

> Descriptions, like in *The Tale of Despereaux*, use sensory details to help the reader visualize the story or topic.

Room: 129

Name: Raven Radke

Man Leads a Dog's Life

The best way to get tips about fire prevention is to listen to Coach, the friendly mascot of the Glen Lake Fire Department. Before you question a dalmatian's ability to give advice, let me tell you that Coach is no ordinary dog.

Coach's tall six-foot body is covered from head to toe in a costume of white fur sprinkled with jet-black dots. A bright red firefighter's hat sits between his floppy ears, and he wears a brown protective coat. Shiny yellow boots complete the picture that captures the attention of his audience. When you shake his large right paw, you know this dog is your friend!

Watching Coach at a school assembly helps you understand the caring personality of the man behind the dog. His boundless energy and funny skits keep the students interested. They love his history of dalmatians, especially when he runs in crazy circles around the gym. He is trying to show how these swift runners sped alongside horse-drawn carriages and earned the name "coach dogs."

Coach's main message, however, is completely serious. He talks about the dangers of things such as matches, electricity, and fireplaces. He explains how to hold family fire drills. He shows how to check smoke detectors and change the batteries. Everyone at the assembly follows his directions to "stop, drop, and roll" and practices speaking slowly and clearly to 911 operators.

You can see that Coach is more than just a watchdog for the fire department. He is a teacher whose message students will always remember. His fire safety tips truly make this "dog" everyone's best friend.

What Makes a Good Description?

An effective description paints a picture with words. It makes the reader see and experience a particular person, place, thing, or event.

You can find descriptions in many places. A new video game might be described in an ad, or a park could be described in a travel brochure. A description can also be a part of a longer piece, such as a description of a character or of a setting in a novel.

When you write a description, choose a topic that is familiar or very important to you. The more you know about a topic, the easier it will be to remember a lot of details about it.

Here are some things to keep in mind when you write a description.

Visualizing

Before you write a description, try to visualize, or picture, the topic in your mind. Think about how the topic looks, but don't stop there. Imagine everything you hear, smell, taste, and touch. This will help you describe your topic completely and accurately.

Audience

Consider who will be reading your description. If you are writing for younger children, use words that they will understand. For adults use language they will find interesting.

Think about how much your audience already knows about your topic. A sports fan doesn't need to be told what a soccer goalie wears. Someone who doesn't know anything about soccer, however, might need to be told that the goalie's uniform is different from that of the other players on the team.

ACTIVITY A Read each of the following pairs of topics. Choose the one that is a better topic for a description. Explain your answers.

1. my sports hero   team sports
2. Grandmother's china cabinet   how to collect art
3. directions to my classroom   my school building
4. the history of airplanes   my favorite lunch
5. birds of the desert   the Gila woodpecker

ACTIVITY B Each of these sentences was written for an audience of older students and adults. Rewrite each sentence to make it suitable for young children. Use a dictionary or a thesaurus if necessary.

EXAMPLE   The sky was an intense cerulean blue.
          The sky was bright blue.

1. A dalmatian has a dense white coat randomly splashed with black spots.
2. His hands were gnarled and weatherbeaten with cracked, filthy fingernails.
3. A prairie dog is a small, burrowing rodent.
4. A serpentine path leads you past a thicket of evergreen trees and low brush.
5. Suddenly an eerie wail pierced the air around the dilapidated barn.
6. The pungent aroma of the vinegar brought tears to my eyes and made my nose burn.
7. The intense winds from the tornado horrified the inhabitants of the remote village.
8. The antics of the frisky kitten were comical.
9. As the ice-cold water whipped about my face, I felt the rip currents thrash our raft like a rag doll.
10. A snow-capped peak against the eggplant colored sky is the best way to view the sunset.

WRITER'S CORNER

Think of an object that you see or use every day, like the school bus. Write five words you could use to describe that object to a young child and five different words you could use to describe it to an adult.

Grammar in Action. Identify the verb in the first sentence on page 328. Is it an action verb or a being verb?

Sensory Details

You experience the world by using all of your five senses: sight, sound, taste, smell, and touch. When you write a description, you should use words that appeal to all the senses. Using sensory details will help your reader visualize your topic and share your experience.

Read these two sentences. They both describe the same thing. Which one helps you feel more like you are actually there?

The waves lapped against the beach.

The waves gurgled against the rocky beach and filled the air with a cool, salty spray.

The first sentence tells only what the writer saw. In the second sentence, the writer used words to appeal also to the senses of sound, touch, and taste. This helps readers visualize the experience.

ACTIVITY C In the book _Sarah, Plain and Tall_, Sarah has moved from Maine to the prairie. Sarah describes her former home to those who have never seen the coast. Name the words and phrases in each description that appeal to different senses.

1. I've touched seals. Real seals. They are cool and slippery and they slide through the water like fish. They can cry and sing. And sometimes they bark, a little like dogs.

2. In Maine, there are rock cliffs that rise up at the edge of the sea. And there are hills covered with pine and spruce trees, green with needles. But William and I found a sand dune all our own. It was soft and sparkling with bits of mica, and when we were little we would slide down the dune into the water.

3. The sea is salt. It stretches out as far as you can see. It gleams like the sun on glass.

ACTIVITY D Write a one-sentence description of each subject below. Use the sense given in parentheses.

1. an old clock (sound)
2. stale pretzels (taste)
3. a putting green (touch)
4. a popcorn shop (smell)
5. a sunset (sight)
6. a basketball game (sound)
7. an aquarium full of fish (sight)
8. a lemon slice (taste)
9. a day at the beach (smell)
10. towels out of the dryer (touch)

ACTIVITY E Write at least three sentences to describe each topic below. Use details that appeal to two or more senses for each.

1. a busy restaurant at lunchtime
2. a marching band in a parade
3. a playground at recess
4. a garden on a summer afternoon
5. a sailboat race on a lake
6. a sledding hill on a snowy day
7. an outdoor concert on the Fourth of July
8. a bicycle ride through the park

ACTIVITY F Choose a topic from Activity E. Write a paragraph describing that topic. Try to appeal to all five senses in your paragraph.

The Tale of Despereaux LiNK

The sound was King Phillip playing his guitar and singing to his daughter, the Princess Pea, every night before she fell asleep.

Hidden in a hole in the wall of the princess' bedroom, the mouse listened with all his heart. The sound of the king's music made Despereaux's soul glow large and light inside of him.

"Oh," he said, "it sounds like heaven. It smells like honey."

Kate DiCamillo

WRITER'S CORNER

Write five sentences describing a food you like. Use details that appeal to as many different senses as you can to make your readers' mouths water.

Grammar in Action. Identify the action verbs in the excerpt above.

Ordering a Description

A good description is well organized. The reader is led from detail to detail in a way that makes sense. Irrelevant details, things that do not stick to the topic, are left out. The result is a vivid snapshot of a person, a thing, a place, or an event.

Spatial Order

The most common way to organize a description is spatial order. In spatial order you might describe something from side to side, from near to far, from top to bottom, or from inside to outside. If you are describing a person, you might work from head to toe or from toe to head. Whichever order you choose, be sure to stick to that order. Lead your readers along in a clear and logical way.

ACTIVITY A The following sentences describe a market. Only the first and last sentences are in the correct spatial order. Rewrite the sentences as a paragraph that describes the market from side to side.

1. Our local farmers' market is a feast for the senses.
2. In the center of the market are baskets of plump strawberries.
3. To the left of the entrance are bins of red, ripe tomatoes.
4. Along the right side of the market are tables covered with gleaming jars of honey, jam, and pickles.
5. Next to the tomatoes are piles of crisp green lettuce, cucumbers, beans, and other delicious-looking vegetables.
6. By the strawberries are boxes of fat blueberries.
7. My mouth starts to water just thinking about it!

ACTIVITY B Read the following details that describe Paul's physical appearance. Five of the details are irrelevant and should be left out. Put the other details in spatial order, starting with detail 1 and going from head to toe.

1. narrow head with messed-up brown curls
2. always sports the latest fashion in sneakers
3. subscribes to motocross magazines
4. greets everyone with a friendly grin
5. lives on Cornelia Street
6. usually wears a Phillies T-shirt
7. belongs to the chess club
8. always wears jeans
9. big brown eyes
10. small, freckled nose
11. likes playing the drums
12. shares his bedroom with two younger brothers

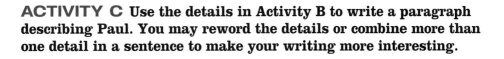

ACTIVITY C Use the details in Activity B to write a paragraph describing Paul. You may reword the details or combine more than one detail in a sentence to make your writing more interesting.

ACTIVITY D Think of someone you know well. Write a list of at least eight physical details you could use to describe that person. Check over your list. Are any of the details irrelevant? If any are, replace them with relevant ones.

WRITER'S CORNER

Look at the list you wrote for Activity D. Number the details in the order you would use them in a description organized by spatial order. Then use the details to write a paragraph describing the person.

Chronological Order

Another way to describe something is by chronological, or time, order. Chronological order tells the order in which something happens from beginning to end. It is usually used to describe an event or a process. For example, if you wanted to describe carving a jack-o'-lantern, you might start with cutting out the lid and smelling the aroma of the pumpkin. Then you might describe the feel of the seeds as you scrape them out. Next, you would describe designing and cutting out the face until the jack-o'-lantern is completed.

ACTIVITY E Tell how you would organize a description of each of these topics. Would you use spatial order or chronological order?

1. decorating a birthday cake
2. a newborn kitten
3. your family's car
4. your winning home run
5. planting a garden
6. a local skate park
7. a fishing trip
8. a king salmon
9. a motorcycle
10. a motorcycle race
11. a slide down a toboggan run
12. your uncle

ACTIVITY F Choose one of the topics in Activity E or think of a topic of your own. Write a list of five details that you would include in a description of that topic. Check to make sure that all your details are relevant. Then number the details in spatial or chronological order.

ACTIVITY G The following sentences describe a trip to the beach. Rewrite the sentences as a paragraph that describes what happened from beginning to end.

1. I came out of the dim woods into the bright sunshine.
2. My first step into the waves was a shock.
3. I sat down and put my shoes back on.
4. The first thing I noticed was the salty tang in the air.
5. I took off my shoes and started walking toward the water.
6. I jumped out and headed back toward the warmer sand.
7. I decided I might as well go home.
8. As I approached the water, I watched the waves roll in.
9. The water was as cold as ice.
10. There would be no more wading for me that day!

ACTIVITY H Think of one of your favorite places. Decide whether you will use spatial order or chronological order to describe it. Then write a list of details about the place. Number the details in the order you would use them in a description.

The Tale of Despereaux   LiNK

They moved quickly. And whenever Desperaux slowed, one of the two hoods poked him in the shoulder and told him to keep moving. They went through holes in the wall and down golden stairs. They went past rooms with doors that were closed and doors that were flung wide. The tree mice traveled across marble floors and under heavy velvet drapes. They moved through warm patches of sunlight and dark pools of shade.

Kate DiCamillo

WRITER'S CORNER

Imagine you are walking down the street where you live. Write six sentences describing what you see, hear, taste, smell, and touch along the way. Write your description in chronological order.

Tech Tip Describe a digital photo you find online.

Graphic Organizers

A graphic organizer is a chart or diagram that a writer uses to map out ideas in a visual way.

Word Webs

A word web is a type of graphic organizer that can help you organize the details related to a chosen topic. It can also keep you from introducing irrelevant details.

Mary Jane is writing a description of her new kitten to send to her grandfather. She will use spatial order. She started by making a word web. First, she wrote the kitten's name and drew a box around it. Around that box she wrote the four parts of the kitten's body that she would describe and drew ovals around them. Last, she added details about the kitten's head, body, feet, and tail.

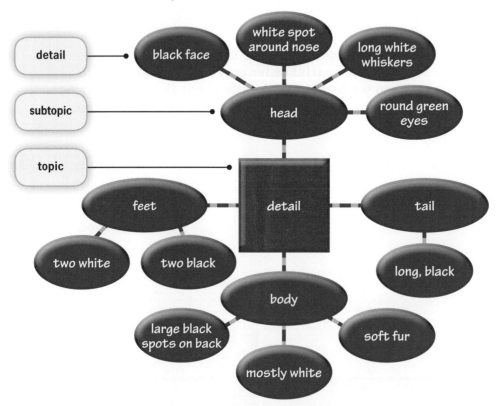

ACTIVITY A Refer to the word web on page 338 and write a short description of the kitten's head, her body, her feet, and her tail.

> EXAMPLE   Pinto Bean has a black face with a white spot around her nose.

ACTIVITY B Add to this word web to describe Carrots the Rabbit. Use your imagination to fill in sensory details.

feet

fur

Carrots the Rabbit

face

ears

ACTIVITY C Make word webs for three of the following topics.

A. your favorite childhood toy

B. an animal that lives in your part of the country

C. a storm you experienced

D. the front of your home

E. a warm spring day

F. a body of water you have visited

G. a costume you have worn

H. yourself

Tech Tip Use a computer program to build a word web.

LiNK

The Tale of Despereaux

And because Roscuro was dazzled by the light of one match and journeyed upstairs and fell into the queen's soup and the queen died, the king ordered the death of every rat in the land.

The king's men went bravely into the dungeon to kill the rats. But the thing about killing a rat is that you must first *find* a rat. And if a rat does not want to be found, reader, he will not be found.

Kate DiCamillo

WRITER'S CORNER

Use one of the word webs you made for Activity C. Write five sentences describing your topic, using the ideas in your word web. Include 10 sensory details in your description.

Venn Diagrams

Some descriptions compare and contrast two different topics. These descriptions tell how the two things are alike and how they are different. A Venn diagram is useful in organizing information for this kind of description.

Here are the steps for making a Venn diagram.

1. Draw two large overlapping ovals.
2. Write the name of one of the two topics at the top of each oval.
3. Write "Both" in the section where the ovals overlap.
4. Write things that are true of both topics in the section labeled "Both."
5. Write things that are true of only that topic under its name in the outer section of its oval.

Look at this Venn diagram that compares and contrasts frogs and toads. Can you think of a characteristic for the blank line? (Hint: To what class of animals do both belong?)

Frogs

smooth, moist skin

live mostly in water

have teeth

long hind legs

most are greenish brown

Both

no tail

sticky tongue to trap insects

go through metamorphosis

_____

Toads

rough, dry skin

live mostly on land

don't have teeth

short hind legs

most are brown or gray

ACTIVITY D People often confuse alligators and crocodiles. Here are some details about these two animals. Put the facts into a Venn diagram.

Crocodiles

reptile family

strong tail for swimming

long, pointed snout

two teeth show when mouth is closed

strong jaws to eat small animals

dark, scaly skin

Alligators

strong tail for swimming

no teeth visible with closed mouth

strong jaws to eat small animals

broad, rounded snout

reptile family

dark, scaly skin

ACTIVITY E Read this description that compares and contrasts two breeds of dogs. Then make a Venn diagram about the breeds.

At first glance, the 5-pound Chihuahua would seem to have nothing in common with the massive 200-pound St. Bernard. Less than a foot tall, the tiny Chihuahua is a snuggly dog who will curl up in your lap. Chihuahuas can live to be 20 years old. In contrast, the St. Bernard at almost 3 feet tall is not a cuddly lap dog. St. Bernards have a much shorter life span than Chihuahuas, usually around 10 years. Both breeds like lots of attention and are very loyal, affectionate pets. Both are good watchdogs. However, if you are thinking of buying one of these dogs, remember that a Chihuahua can get plenty of exercise running around in your kitchen. A St. Bernard needs a large yard in which to play.

WRITER'S CORNER

Think of two animals that you could compare and contrast. The animals should be different from each other yet share some characteristics. Make a Venn diagram. Use an encyclopedia or the Internet to find facts. Then write a descriptive paragraph about the two animals.

Tech Tip Find a digital photo of your animals online.

Suffixes

A suffix is a syllable or syllables added to the end of a base word to form a new word. Knowing the meanings of suffixes can help you increase your vocabulary.

Noun and Adjective Suffixes

Some suffixes change the part of speech of a word. The suffix -er (-or) can be added to verbs to make nouns. A *runner* is a person who runs. An *actor* is a person who acts. Other suffixes can change one noun into another. A *novelist* is a person who writes a novel.

Some suffixes change nouns to adjectives. Adding the suffix -ful to the noun *beauty* makes the adjective *beautiful*. Adding the suffix -y to the noun *star* makes the adjective *starry*.

Notice that sometimes there is a spelling change when you add a suffix to a base word. You may need to check a dictionary.

ADJECTIVE SUFFIXES

SUFFIX	MEANING	EXAMPLE
-able	capable of being	climbable
-al	relating to	parental
-ful	full of	hopeful
-ic	like a, relating to	artistic
-ish	like a, resembling	childish
-y	full of	cloudy
-er	one who	writer

ACTIVITY A Tell the meaning and part of speech of each of these words containing a suffix. Use each word in a sentence.

1. teacher
2. sorrowful
3. chewable
4. inventor
5. colorful
6. personal
7. sunny
8. readable

ACTIVITY B Copy the chart below and fill in the missing parts.

	Base Word	Suffix	New Word	Meaning
1.	snow	-y	_____	_____
2.	_____	-ful	_____	full of tears
3.	music	_____	musical	_____
4.	baby	_____	babyish	_____
5.	athlete	_____	athletic	_____
6.	_____	-ful	skillfull	_____
7.	wash	_____	washable	_____
8.	cheer	-y	_____	_____
9.	_____	_____	metallic	like a metal
10.	_____	-able	_____	able to be detected

ACTIVITY C Add an adjective suffix from the chart on page 342 to each base word in parentheses so that the new word correctly completes the sentence. Check a dictionary for spelling.

1. The chorus sang a _____ song. (joy)
2. The large suitcase has _____ wheels. (move)
3. The _____ drink was sweet and delicious. (fruit)
4. The _____ antics of the clown made me laugh. (fool)
5. The _____ sound of the train put me to sleep. (rhythm)
6. The path was lined with _____ bushes. (ornament)
7. We visited the old _____ monument. (history)
8. The water in the ocean tasted _____. (salt)
9. Her _____ smile wins the prince's heart. (cheer)
10. One of the _____ elements of grammar is spelling. (base)

WRITER'S CORNER

Brainstorm 10 words containing the suffixes listed on page 342. Then write descriptive sentences. Use at least one of your words in each sentence.

Adverb and Verb Suffixes

Some suffixes are used to form adverbs and verbs. The suffixes -ly and -ally can be added to adjectives to form adverbs. *Sadly* means "in a sad way," and *terrifically* means "in a terrific way."

Some suffixes change adjectives to verbs. Adding the suffix -ate to the adjective *active* forms the verb *activate*. Adding the suffix -fy to the adjective *simple* forms the verb *simplify*.

VERB SUFFIXES

SUFFIX	MEANING	EXAMPLE
-ate	make	activate
-en	become, make	deepen
-ize	cause to be	legalize
-fy	make	electrify
-ly	in a way	sadly
-ally	in a way	terrifically

ACTIVITY D Tell the meaning and part of speech of each of these words containing a suffix. Use each word in a sentence.

1. falsify
2. politely
3. eagerly
4. popularize
5. blacken
6. beautify
7. magically
8. realize

ACTIVITY E Add a suffix to each word in parentheses to complete the sentence. Check a dictionary for spelling. Tell whether the new word is an adverb or a verb.

1. The barbershop quartet at the carnival can _____ perfectly. (harmony)
2. The wind howled _____ through the tunnel. (fierce)
3. I _____ aimed at the middle of the target. (careful)
4. The sun will _____ the solar panels. (active)
5. His poster was very _____ done. (nice)
6. The smell of the fumes may _____ you. (sick)
7. Please _____ the directions for the children. (simple)
8. Peacocks are _____ seen in the United States. (rare)

ACTIVITY F Read each pair of words and the sentences that follow. Complete each sentence with the correct word.

1. **solidly, solidify**

   We set the fence post _____ into the concrete.

   The concrete will _____ overnight.

2. **shorten, shortly**

   Her new dress will be ready _____.

   Her mother is going to _____ it.

3. **apologize, apologetically**

   His father told him to _____.

   He spoke _____.

4. **clearly, clarify**

   Would you please _____ what you mean?

   The teacher _____ explained the facts.

5. **simplify, simply**

   I'd like to _____ this recipe.

   It should be possible to make a tart more _____.

6. **beautiful, beautify**

   Our garden looks _____ in the summer.

   A few rosebushes would _____ it even more.

7. **sweetly, sweeten**

   Honey is a natural way to _____ a slice of bread.

   She smiled _____ when the judges complimented her baked goods.

WRITER'S CORNER

Find in a newspaper an article with at least five words with suffixes. Write a new sentence for each word. Identify other suffixes that each word might use and what you think the definition might be. Look up each word in a dictionary to make sure you used and spelled each word correctly.

Dictionary

Could you find a ptarmigan in your neighborhood? In what situations is it appropriate to use the word *aloha*? To what family of animals does a gibbon belong? A dictionary can give you the answers to these questions and many others.

A dictionary is a book of words that are listed in alphabetical order. When you look up a word, you find the spelling, pronunciation, part of speech, and definition of that word. The words that are defined in the dictionary are called entry words.

Alphabetizing

The entry words in a dictionary are arranged in alphabetical order. When words begin with the same letter, they are alphabetized by the second letter. For example, the word *pat* would come before *pot* because *a* comes before *o* in the alphabet. If words have the same first and second letters, they are alphabetized by the third letters, and so on. The word *pan* would come before *pat* because *n* comes before *t*.

Guide Words

At the top of each dictionary page, you will find two words. These are called guide words. The first guide word is the first entry word on the page. The second guide word is the last entry word on the page. Check the guide words to see whether the word you are looking for can be found on that page. For example, if you want to find the word *pelican*, first look for the guide words that begin with *p*. Then look at the second and third letters of the guide words. You might see the guide words *peg* and *pen*. Since *pel* comes between *peg* and *pen*, you will know that you can find the word *pelican* on that page.

ACTIVITY A Write each set of words in alphabetical order.

1. animated	**2.** dolphin	**3.** curious	**4.** soft
appealing	diver	cat	sandy
alien	delightful	cuddle	smooth
actual	deliberate	cute	seaside
anxious	direction	creep	seclude

ACTIVITY B Look at each pair of guide words. Then look at the entry words that follow each pair. Write the word that does not come between those guide words.

1. web/week   weed, weep, wedding

2. about/absolute   absent, above, abound

3. dachshund/daisy   damage, dairy, dainty

4. sample/sandwich   sandal, sane, sand

5. magnify/maintain   magnet, mailbox, magpie

ACTIVITY C Write three words that would be on a page with each pair of guide words below. You may use a dictionary for help.

1. contain/contest

2. lean/leavening

3. parody/participate

4. tinder/tire

5. neophyte/neuralgia

6. bell/benevolent

7. trace/truth

8. hulking/hungry

9. sink/sixteen

10. whale/whirlpool

WRITER'S CORNER

Use a dictionary to find where your first name would appear if it were an entry word. Write the entry word just before and the entry word just after where your name would appear. Then write the guide words for that page of your dictionary.

A Dictionary Entry

The parts of a dictionary entry give you important information about that word. The following example shows what is included in most dictionary entries.

A   B   C   D
cack•le (kak'əl) *v.* **1.** to make the shrill noise a hen makes after laying an egg **2.** to laugh or talk in a shrill way
E
They cackled at the boy's silly behavior.

n. **1.** the act or sound of cackling **2.** shrill laughter

The witch's cackle scared the villagers. **3.** noisy chatter
                                                          F
The cackle from the cafeteria was deafening. **-ling, -led.**

A. division into syllables
B. dictionary respelling for pronunciation
C. part of speech
D. definition
E. sample phrase or sentence
F. spelling of last syllable with endings added

ACTIVITY D Use the sample dictionary entry above to answer these questions.

1. What parts of speech are listed for *cackle*?
2. How many pronunciations are given for *cackle*?
3. How many meanings does *cackle* have as a noun?
4. How many meanings does *cackle* have as a verb?

ACTIVITY E Use a dictionary to find out which of these things you would eat and which you would wear.

1. kohlrabi
2. amulet
3. oxford
4. flounder
5. hominy
6. fedora
7. papaw
8. puttee
9. tam
10. puree

ACTIVITY F List how many different meanings and parts of speech your dictionary shows for each of these words. Then choose two of the words to use in three sentences, showing three different meanings of the word.

1. strike	**3.** nose	**5.** down	**7.** ring	**9.** make
2. point	**4.** mark	**6.** run	**8.** pop	**10.** right

ACTIVITY G Two of the words in each set rhyme. Look up the words in a dictionary and use the pronunciation key to find which one does not rhyme with the others.

1. chary	ferry	weary	**6.** grain	mien	dean
2. bier	ire	pyre	**7.** zeal	creel	cruel
3. pawl	haul	loll	**8.** panache	ache	hake
4. lurk	torque	dirk	**9.** quay	queue	lieu
5. urge	gorge	merge	**10.** league	fatigue	siege

ACTIVITY H Choose five words that you found especially interesting in Activity G. Use each one in a sentence that shows what it means.

WRITER'S CORNER

Look up the meanings of these words in a dictionary. Then use each word in a sentence that tells about something you did or something that happened to you recently.

lamentable	vexatious
momentous	scrupulous
intriguing	restorative

Oral Descriptions

Have you ever described a new shirt to a friend? Have you told your parents how your fifth-grade teacher looks and acts? If you did, you were giving an oral description. An oral description is a lot like a written description. You use vivid sensory details to paint a picture in your listeners' minds. You organize your description in a way that your listeners can follow.

The descriptions you tell to your friends and family are informal. At times you may need to give a more formal description. These are some things to keep in mind as you prepare an oral description.

Audience

It is important to consider the audience as you plan your description. Choose a topic that your audience will find interesting. Plan your use of language. You will probably use different words if you are talking to five-year-olds than if you are talking to fifth graders.

Keep in mind how much your audience may already know about your topic. If you think they know very little about it, you will have to add some background information and use a lot of sensory details. If you think your audience may be completely unfamiliar with your topic, you may want to show a picture or diagram as a visual aid.

Sensory Details

To begin planning your oral description, visualize your topic. Jot down notes about how it appeals to each of the five senses: sight, sound, taste, smell, and touch. You might make a five-senses chart or a word web to help you remember these details.

Look over your notes. Did you overuse words such as *nice, pretty, big,* or *good*? Use a thesaurus to find more exact, colorful language that will help your audience visualize your topic.

Organization

Think about the best way to organize your description. You don't want your audience to become confused because you jump around in your description. If you are describing a person, a place, or a thing, you may want to use spatial order. If you are describing a process or an event, chronological order may be better.

Whichever order you choose, lead your listeners logically from one detail to the next. Write your ideas on note cards and arrange the cards in your chosen order. Check to make sure all your details are relevant and help create a clear picture in your listeners' minds.

ACTIVITY A Think of a special event you participated in recently. Perhaps it was a birthday party, a trip to the ballpark, or a family picnic. Make notes of everything you saw, heard, smelled, tasted, and touched. Decide what would be the best way to organize a description of the event and arrange your notes in that order. Check to see that your sensory details give an accurate picture of what you experienced.

ACTIVITY B Practice giving an oral description by recording your voice. Record yourself reading a passage from your description or from a story. Be sure to keep the audience in mind, as well as your sensory details, as you read aloud.

SPEAKER'S CORNER

Work in small groups and share your notes about your special event from Activity A. After each student presents, tell what three things you especially liked and three suggestions about anything that might be rearranged for clarity. Make notes of your classmates' suggestions.

Body Language and Voice

When you give an oral presentation, it is important to speak loud enough for everyone to hear and clearly enough for everyone to understand. Don't mumble. Don't use words such as *uh, um,* or *like.* Glance around at the audience so that each person feels like you are talking directly to him or her.

When you present an oral description, use your voice and body. Vary your tone to emphasize important parts of your description. Use body movements to show sensory details. You might use gestures to show size or movement. Let your enthusiasm for your topic be seen in your facial expressions.

Practice

Once you have your notes organized, you are ready to practice your presentation. First, practice by yourself in front of a mirror. This way you can see and evaluate the expressions and body movements that you will use.

When you are ready, ask a friend or family member to listen to your presentation. Ask him or her to pay close attention to your delivery and your words. When you have finished, ask for suggestions for improving your presentation.

Listening Tips

When it is your turn to be a listener, it is important to be attentive. Keep these tips in mind when you listen to a description.

- Look at the speaker so he or she knows you are paying attention. Don't fidget or stare around the room.
- Listen for sensory details that will help you know how the topic looks, sounds, feels, tastes, and smells.
- Pay attention to the speaker's facial expressions and body language as well as his or her tone. This will help you visualize the topic.
- Do not interrupt the speaker.

When the speaker has finished, give him or her some feedback. Mention parts of the description that you especially liked. Ask questions about anything you didn't understand.

ACTIVITY C Work with a partner. Take turns reading each sentence aloud. Vary your tone and expression. Use gestures to emphasize the meaning.

1. It smelled like a dirty, old tennis shoe.
2. The first bite was an explosion of delicious flavors.
3. The emerald green moss is as soft as a blanket.
4. The ferocious wind howled at the windowpanes.
5. His big brown eyes sparkle with mischief.
6. The fur on its back is rough and curly.
7. The fluffy clouds looked as tasty as cotton candy.
8. The sharp tang of the onions made my eyes water.
9. The bubbling stream splashed against the slippery rocks.
10. The soft wind in the pines creates a gentle, soothing sound.

ACTIVITY D Choose an object in your classroom. Write five sentences to describe the object. Use as many sensory details as you can, but do not name the object in your sentences. Work with a partner. Take turns reading your sentences aloud one by one. Use your voice and gestures to help emphasize the meaning. Can your partner guess your object?

SPEAKER'S CORNER

Use your notes from the Speaker's Corner on page 351. Consider your classmates' suggestions for improvements. When you are ready, practice by yourself and then with a partner. Experiment with using your voice and gestures to help get your meaning across. Present your oral description to the class.

Record a podcast of your description.

Prewriting and Drafting

Have you ever tried to explain what something is like to someone else? This is a description. Descriptions can be about anything. You can use sight, smell, taste, touch, and sound as tools to make your description come alive. The purpose of a description is to make the readers feel as if what is being described is right in front of them.

Prewriting

Noah is a fifth grader who was asked to help put together an exhibit for the Portland, Oregon, Cultural Center. The cultural center was making an exhibit about different festivals throughout the world from a student's point of view.

Some students would write descriptions, and others would paint pictures or make other displays. Noah was asked to write a description. First, he had to choose a topic and gather details about it.

Choosing a Topic

Noah thought about different festivals from around the world. He knew of many famous festivals, such as Chinese New Year. He decided to write a description about a less known festival, the International Bathtub Regatta. He also chose this topic because he had seen the race in person. He thought he would be able to write a strong description because he had seen the race up close. Since the festival was a long event to describe, he decided to focus on three of the boats in the race.

Your Turn

Choose a topic that interests you. You might describe a place, a person, a thing, or an event. Make sure that it is something you will enjoy writing about. Think about ⊙━⊙ **Ideas** your audience when you choose your topic. Your audience will be your classmates. What do you think they would like to read about?

Making a Word Web

Now that Noah had a topic, he began gathering the details he would use to make his description strong and interesting. He started by visualizing the boats as he remembered them. He closed his eyes and thought about how the boats affected his five senses. He began making word webs. He made one word web for each of the three boats he wanted to describe. Noah jotted down notes about how the boats looked and sounded. He had trouble thinking of how to use touch, smell, and taste to describe the boats. He decided that he would use only the senses that would help him describe the boats. Here is one of his word webs.

Prewriting

Drafting

Content Editing

Revising

Copyediting

Proofreading

Publishing

Your Turn

Think about all the details of your topic. Organize them in a word web. Try to think of ways of describing your topic by using all five of your senses. When you have finished, read over your word web. Add any more details that come to mind. Include only details that are relevant to the description of your topic.

Drafting

Noah wrote his draft, using his word webs. He used sensory details because he wanted his readers to feel as if they were watching the boat race. He thought of his audience as he wrote. He wanted his description to be appropriate for the people visiting the cultural center.

The Tub Boat Races of Belgium

You would think not much would be happening on a hot August day in the small town of Dinant, Belgium. But once a year the town is crowded and noisy, and the Meuse river is filled with bathtubs. People from the town wait all year to try out their wacky bathtub boats in the race called the International Bathtub Regatta.

Last year on the day of the race, the narrow river was filled with homemade boats that had bathtubs as part of their hulls. All the paddles from the bathtub boats splashing in the river sounded like giant fish jumping out of the water. The smell of the warm chocolate crepes from the outdoor cafés filled the air. The faster boat had a mast with a black pirate flag. The captain had a giant neon green toy parrot on his shoulder. He yelled out instructions in a goofy voice.

The slower boat was sinking into the water. The crew was dressed as cooks and paddled with oversized kitchen utensils. As their boat sank, the cooks threw their tall white chef's hats and giant wooden spoons and spatulas into the air. The crowd applauded and hooted, and it was as loud as a gym during a basketball game.

Another boat was built in the shape of a swan. Every few minutes a stream of water shot out of the swan's mouth. The crew of the swan boat aimed the water at the crowd. People in the crowd tried to get hit by the water so they could cool off their skin.

It's great. You've got to see it! With all the splashing water, cheering, and laughing, it sounds like a gigantic pool party. The bathtub inventions look like something out of another world. It is more of a party than a race. Sometimes in Belgium a bathtub is much more than just a bathtub.

Prewriting

Drafting

Content Editing

Revising

Copyediting

Proofreading

Publishing

Your Turn

- Write a draft of your description, using the word web you made during prewriting.
- Remember to write a title and an introduction that names the topic of your description.
- When you write the body, add as many relevant details as you can. End your description with a conclusion that brings all your details together.
- The audience you are writing for is your classmates. Make sure that the language and content of your description is understandable and appropriate for this audience.

Shaping Sensory Details

One way to make good sensory details for your description is to compare one thing to another. Instead of saying that the garbage falling out of the bag and tumbling down the stairs was loud, you might say that it was as loud as a tin

 Word Choice can in a washing machine. This

will show your audience a different way of thinking about what you are describing. Can you name some of the comparisons that use sensory details in Noah's draft?

Writer's Tip Sensory details will help your readers form a clear idea of your topic, but only if they are relevant.

Grammar in Action

Noah uses several action verbs in his draft. Identify three action verbs in the second paragraph.

Content Editing

Although Noah was happy with his draft, it could be made better through content editing. By content editing, Noah would check the structure of the description, its focus, and its tone.

Noah asked his friend Jude to content edit his description for him. Jude was familiar with the cultural center project because he was making a slide show for it about a festival he had been to in Brazil. Noah also asked Jude for help because he thought Jude might be able to catch mistakes that he hadn't noticed. Below is the Content Editor's Checklist that Jude used.

Jude read Noah's description. He saw that the introduction named the topic. Jude also liked how Noah tied his description together in the conclusion. He complimented Noah on the last line. Then Jude told Noah his ideas for making the description stronger.

- The sentence about the smell of the crepes doesn't fit the focus of the description.

- I think that you should add more details about the boats you're describing. It would make me feel more like I was there.

- You could order the body better. The description isn't in spatial or chronological order. Because of this, the description of the swan boat seems out of place.

Noah thanked Jude for his comments. Noah wasn't sure if he was going to use all the ideas, but he was going to consider each one carefully. Noah then took time to content edit his own work, using the Content Editor's Checklist. He wanted to make sure that he could answer *yes* to each question.

Content Editor's Checklist

☐ Does the description stay focused on a topic?

☐ Are sensory details used so that readers can visualize what is being described?

☐ Does the introduction name the topic?

☐ Is the body well-ordered with logical connections?

☐ Does the conclusion summarize the description?

☐ Is the tone appropriate for the audience?

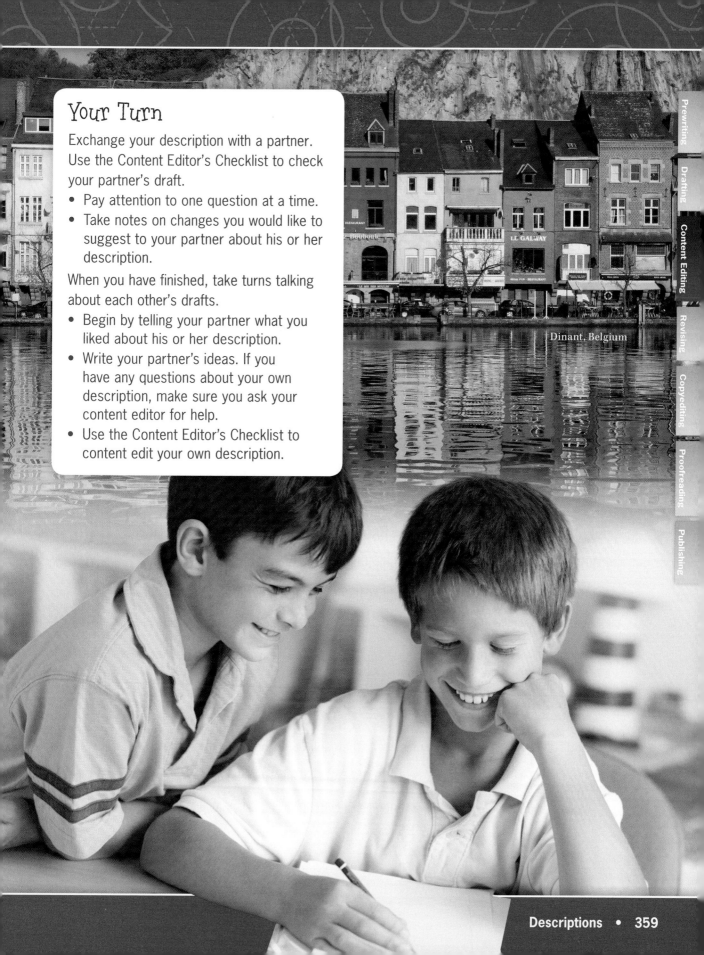

Your Turn

Exchange your description with a partner.
Use the Content Editor's Checklist to check
your partner's draft.

- Pay attention to one question at a time.
- Take notes on changes you would like to
  suggest to your partner about his or her
  description.

When you have finished, take turns talking
about each other's drafts.

- Begin by telling your partner what you
  liked about his or her description.
- Write your partner's ideas. If you
  have any questions about your own
  description, make sure you ask your
  content editor for help.
- Use the Content Editor's Checklist to
  content edit your own description.

Dinant, Belgium

Prewriting

Drafting

Content Editing

Revising

Copyediting

Proofreading

Publishing

Revising

This is how Noah used ideas from content editing to revise his draft.

The Tub Boat Races of Belgium

You would think not much would be happening on a hot August day in the small town of Dinant, Belgium. But once a year the town is crowded and noisy, and the Meuse river is filled with bathtubs. People from the town wait all year to try out their wacky bathtub boats in the race called the International Bathtub Regatta.

Last year on the day of the race, the narrow river was filled with homemade boats that had bathtubs as part of their hulls. All the paddles from the bathtub boats splashing in the river sounded like giant fish jumping out of the water. ~~The smell of the warm chocolate crepes from the outdoor cafés filled the air.~~ The faster boat had a mast with a black pirate flag. The captain had a giant neon green toy

The people rowing the boat were dressed like pirates and all had eye patches.

parrot on his shoulder. He yelled out instructions in a goofy voice.

The slower boat was sinking into the water. The crew was dressed as cooks and paddled with oversized kitchen utensils. As their boat sank, the cooks threw their tall white chef's hats and giant wooden spoons and spatulas into the air. The crowd applauded and hooted, and it was as loud as a gym during a basketball game.

switch with next paragraph

, with the bathtub as the swan's belly

Another boat was built in the shape of a swan. Every few minutes a stream of

water shot out of the swan's mouth. The crew of the swan boat aimed the water at

The weather was so humid that the air felt like a wet sponge.

the crowd. People in the crowd tried to get hit by the water so they could cool off

their skin.

The International Bathtub Regatta is a sight to see and to enjoy.

~~It's great. You've got to see it.~~ With all the splashing water, cheering, and

laughing, it sounds like a gigantic pool party. The bathtub inventions look like

something out of another world. It is more of a party than a race. Sometimes in

Belgium a bathtub is much more than just a bathtub.

Here are the changes Noah made to improve his description.

- Noah included a sensory detail about crepes, but he decided to take it out. Why? Does it make his description stronger?

- Jude suggested that Noah incorporate more details into his description, and Noah agreed. What did he do?

- Noah used a specific pattern to describe the boats. What was it? Do you think it was an effective use of order?

Noah also had an idea about something that Jude had not noticed. Noah didn't think that the tone at the start of the conclusion was appropriate for the cultural center audience. He wrote a new sentence to start his conclusion that made the tone seem more professional.

 Voice

Your Turn

Revise your draft, using your ideas and those suggested by your content editor. Be sure to look over all the possible changes before you make any of them.

Copyediting and Proofreading

Copyediting

Noah copyedited his description to make sure all his sentences made sense and were the best that they could be. Noah used the checklist below to help him with copyediting.

Noah read his description one time for each question in the checklist. He saw that all his sentences were complete and in an order that made sense.

Sentence Fluency

Copyeditor's Checklist

- [ ] Are all the sentences complete?
- [ ] Do the sentences follow each other in an order that makes sense?
- [ ] Are the sentences different lengths?
- [ ] Are exact words used?

Noah thought that he could do a better job of using exact words to express exactly what he was describing. He knew that by using exact words, he would also improve the sensory details of his description. Noah made the *hot day* into a *sizzling hot day*. He also wanted to give the reader a better sense of the sound of paddles slapping the water. To make the sound seem louder, Noah said that the sound was more like a giant fish *leaping* in and out of the water. He thought that a leaping fish would make a bigger splash noise in his readers' imaginations.

Noah added the words *barked, sparkling,* and *sun-warmed*. Can you find the places where he might have decided to use these words to make his description stronger?

Your Turn

Copyedit your description. Use the Copyeditor's Checklist. Look for only one kind of mistake at a time. Make sure that you use exact words to make your description clear. What you are describing will be easier to see, hear, smell, taste, or feel if you use sensory details.

Proofreading

Noah thought that it was a good idea to have someone proofread his description. He had read his description many times, and he wanted someone who had not read it before to read it for mistakes that he might have missed. Noah asked his classmate Archer to proofread the description. Archer used the Proofreader's Checklist below to help him.

Archer proofread Noah's description. He read for one type of mistake at a time. He found one capitalization mistake. The word *river* needed to be capitalized in one place. In the first paragraph, it is part of the proper noun *Meuse River*. This was the only place where it needed to be capitalized.

Archer also noticed two grammatical mistakes. In the second paragraph, the word *faster* should be *fastest*. Noah was describing more than two boats, so the *-est* suffix should be used. Noah found that he made the same mistake with a different word in another place in the description. Can you find it?

Proofreader's Checklist

- ☐ Are the paragraphs indented?
- ☐ Are all the words spelled correctly?
- ☐ Are capitalization and punctuation correct?
- ☐ Is the grammar correct?
- ☐ Have you checked that no new mistakes were added while editing?

Your Turn

Read your description carefully, using the Proofreader's Checklist. Look for only one kind of mistake at a time.

When you have finished, ask a partner to proofread your description. Remind your partner to check for one kind of mistake at a time. Discuss any of your partner's changes that you do not agree with or understand.

Writer's Tip When you are proofreading your work, make sure you are not adding new mistakes. Double-check your work.

Publishing

Noah took his time making changes. He knew that it would be displayed in the cultural center, so he didn't want any mistakes in his published description. Here is Noah's final version.

The Tub Boat Races of Belgium

You would think not much would be happening on a sizzling hot August day in the small town of Dinant, Belgium. But once a year the town is crowded and noisy, and the Meuse River is filled with bathtubs. People from the town wait all year to try out their wacky bathtub boats in the race called the International Bathtub Regatta.

Last year on the day of the race, the narrow river was filled with homemade boats that had bathtubs as part of their hulls. All the paddles from the bathtub boats splashing in the river sounded like giant fish leaping out of the water. The fastest boat had a mast with a black pirate flag. The people rowing the boat were dressed like pirates and all had eye patches. The captain had a giant neon green toy parrot on his shoulder. He barked out instructions in a goofy voice.

Another boat was built in the shape of a swan, with the bathtub as the swan's belly. Every few minutes a sparkling stream of water shot out of the swan's mouth. The crew of the swan boat aimed the water at the crowd. The weather was so humid that the air felt like a wet sponge. People in the crowd tried to get hit by the water so they could cool off their sun-warmed skin.

The slowest boat was sinking into the water. The crew was dressed as cooks and paddled with oversized kitchen utensils. As their boat sank, the cooks threw their tall white chef's hats and giant wooden spoons and spatulas into the air. The crowd applauded and hooted, and it was as loud as a gym during a basketball game.

The International Bathtub Regatta is a sight to see and to enjoy. With all the splashing water, cheering, and laughing, it sounds like a gigantic pool party. The bathtub inventions look like something out of another world. It is more of a party than a race. Sometimes in Belgium a bathtub is much more than just a bathtub.

After Noah finished typing his work, he made a poster on which to mount his description. On

 Presentation

his poster he put postcards from Dinant, photos of the bathtub boats, and a drawing of the cooks leaping from their sinking boat.

The best part of writing a description is sharing the experience with friends and family. They will enjoy hearing about an adventure you had and perhaps will want to share one of their own. Here are a few ways you can publish your description.

 Make a collage of your description with various photos and clippings from magazines, newspapers, or items from the experience, such as ticket stubs.

 Submit your description on a Web site for student work. Include a digital photo to go along with your work.

 Record yourself reading the description for the class blog or podcast. Use special effects to help the audience feel like they are there.

 Use a computer program to animate your description. Film your animation and show it at Parents' Night.

Whenever you publish your work, your goal is to share your thoughts and experiences with other people.

Your Turn

- Make a final copy of your description. Add the changes from proofreading that you decided to use.
- Make sure that you don't add any new mistakes while making your final copy.
- Use your best handwriting or type your description on a computer for a neat, polished look.
- You might want to make a display to go along with your description. You can make a poster to show what you described. You might bring in an audio recording to let your classmates hear what you described. Be creative with your displays!

Prewriting

Drafting

Content Editing

Revising

Copyediting

Proofreading

Publishing

Book Reports

LiNK

Holes by Louis Sachar
Reviewed by Dana Schwartz

Holes, by Wayside School books author Louis Sachar, is a hilarious, frightening and clever novel that will shock and surprise you. It received the 1999 Newbery Medal, the Boston Globe Horn Book Award, and the 1998 National Book Award for Young People's Literature, so you know it's a winner.

Protagonist Stanley Yelnats has really bad luck—after being falsely accused of stealing sneakers he is sent to a boy's juvenile detention center called Camp Green Lake. First of all, this is no camp, and second of all, there is NO lake—nothing green has ever grown there. The work is the worst—each day it is the same thing: dig a hole five feet by five feet, the length and depth of your shovel. Do not stop until you're finished. And do not even think about running away—there's nothing around for miles, so you can't possibly escape.

One last rule—do not upset the warden. She does really nasty things with snake venom when she's mad. She thinks that digging holes builds character—at least that's what she says, but Stanley and the other boys have different ideas. Something fishy is going on at Camp Green Lake, and Stanley has to find out what it is.

> Book reports, like this one about *Holes*, inform the reader about the characters, plot, and theme of a book.

Angela Bush
Room 117

<u>United Tates of America</u>: A Novel With Scrapbook Art
by Paula Danziger

<u>United Tates of America</u>, by Paula Danziger, is the story of Sarah Kate Tate, known to her friends as Skate Tate. Skate lives with her parents, her little sister, Emma, and her great uncle Mort (nicknamed GUM) in the small town of Chelsea, New Jersey. Comfortable with elementary school and the traditions of her family, she doesn't welcome the changes that begin on her first day at Biddle Middle.

Skate's cousin and best friend, Susie, quickly finds a new group of friends and has little time for Skate. The Happy Scrappys, Skate and Susie's scrapbooking club, continues to meet, but Skate senses that this group of close friends may be growing apart. Being chosen co-art director of the school paper with good-looking Garth Garrison helps Skate realize that new things can be good things.

GUM, one of Skate's favorite people in the whole world, encourages her artistic streak as he shares his travel adventures. GUM teaches Skate lessons about life. He gives her confidence to face tragedy and to deal with it in a way that would make him proud.

I enjoyed this story about growing up. I identified with Skate and her feelings, and I laughed at Ms. Danziger's puns. For example, the D.D.T., the Donald Duck Trio—Huey, Duey, and Louie—enjoy quacking until the teacher says there'll be no more "fowl behavior."

This book helps middle school readers realize that their mixed feelings about growing up are natural. GUM wanted Skate to know how to deal with whatever happens, even if it's not the most fun, and then to move on in life.

What Makes a Good Book Report?

Writing a book report gives you the opportunity to tell others about a book you have read. In a book report, you give information about a book through description, explanation, and example. Then you give your personal opinion about the book, stating the reasons you feel as you do about it.

Keep these things in mind when writing a book report.

Characters and Setting

An effective book report describes the important characters in a book and the setting of the story. Characters are the people, animals, or other beings in stories. The setting is where and when the story takes place.

How much your book report describes the characters and the setting will depend on how important each is to the story. For example, the book *United Tates of America* takes place in today's New Jersey. The setting is not unusual, so the writer of the book report on page 367 doesn't describe the setting in much detail.

Some settings are very important to a book and can play a larger role than the characters. In Jonathan Swift's *Gulliver's Travels*, the reader learns very little about Gulliver himself. But the reader learns a great deal about the strange lands he visits, such as Lilliput and Brobdingnag.

Plot Summary

Plot is what happens in the book, the major events. Much of a book report summarizes the plot of a book. A plot summary might start by describing the characters' situation at the beginning of the story. The summary might also tell what happens next, but it should never tell how the story ends.

Plot summaries tell only the important parts of the plot. Just like unnecessary details in other kinds of writing, if some parts of the story do not seem to be related to the main characters, leave these parts out.

ACTIVITY A Think about the characters and the setting from a book you have recently read. Then list 10 things you know about the characters and the setting that you might want to include in a book report.

ACTIVITY B Read the following plot summaries of the book *A Week in the Woods* by Andrew Clements. Tell which one would be better in a book report and why.

A. At first Mark remains aloof from others. Why should he take the trouble to make friends when he'll be going to an expensive boarding school next year? Mr. Maxwell thinks Mark is a know-it-all and seems to be punishing him for it. The approach of the fifth-grade environmental camping trip makes Mark realize how he's been acting. He changes his ways and makes new friends. But unexpected events follow when Mark gets caught with a knife. What will this do to the relationship between Mark and Mr. Maxwell? Read this book to find out.

B. Mark doesn't try to make friends at first because he'll be going to a boarding school next year. Mr. Maxwell doesn't give Mark a chance. When Mark realizes he's been acting stuck-up, he changes and makes friends. The fifth-grade camping trip begins well. But when Mark is discovered with his friend Jason's knife and takes the blame when it's found, things take a turn for the worse. Leaving the car instead of waiting for Mr. Maxwell to drive him home, Mark starts on a dangerous adventure. Mr. Maxwell follows and gets hurt. Mark rescues him, and Mr. Maxwell apologizes for the way he treated Mark. They return to the camp as friends.

WRITER'S CORNER

Write a list of five of your favorite books. Think about their plots and characters. Save your list.

Wild Magic (The Immortals)

by Tamora Pierce

Daine, a 13-year-old orphan, is running from her past, straight into the arms of the King's horse mistress. With a new job at the castle, Daine's ability to communicate with animals can't be kept hidden. With lessons from the wizard, she must learn to face and embrace her talents. As the kingdom is attacked, Daine is at the center of the war.

reviewed by Sandi Pedersen

LiNK

Theme

The theme is the idea that sums up the whole book. The theme might be the importance of friendship or the challenges of being in middle school. In a book report, you might state the theme as a life lesson that applies to everyone. The theme is part of the body of your book report.

Personal Opinion

In the conclusion give your personal opinion of the book. Tell whether or not you liked the book and why. Be specific. Use examples from the book that led you to your opinion. Tell whether or not you recommend the book.

ACTIVITY C Tell which of these examples might be a good statement of the theme of *A Week in the Woods*.

A. A boy and his teacher make up and realize they can be friends.

B. Mr. Maxwell was a knowledgeable and experienced science teacher.

C. Most people when given a chance will do the right thing and shouldn't be prejudged.

D. Mark felt that he was different but not better than the kids at Hardy Elementary School.

E. Mark becomes friends with Mr. Maxwell after spending a week in the woods.

ACTIVITY D These four paragraphs are from a book report about *Frindle* by Andrew Clements. Match the paragraphs with the following parts of a book report.

A. personal opinion

B. plot summary

C. title, author, characters, and setting

D. theme

1. This book helps readers understand the true nature of words, especially that they are important and are needed by everyone. The dictionary endures, as do words, and it changes and grows through the years and never goes out of date.

2. Trying one of his tricks to distract the teacher at the end of class so she won't assign homework, Nick innocently asks where words come from. Mrs. Granger's answer inspires Nick to invent a new word. He calls a pen a *frindle,* and soon everyone in the school, the town, and beyond does the same. Mrs. Granger is up to Nick's challenge. The local paper hears about it, and it becomes important news. A local businessman becomes involved. Where will it end? Nick found out, but not until 10 years later.

3. *Frindle* by Andrew Clements is a clever story about a very clever boy named Nick Allen. Nick lives with his parents in a small New Hampshire town and is known for turning classrooms upside down. Will fifth grade be different with Mrs. Granger, a language arts teacher who doesn't let anybody get away with anything?

4. I thought this was a very good book. It was really neat that a fifth grader could make up a word that became known all over the world. Nick, an ordinary kid, became wealthy because of his creativity and persistence. All kids could relate to Mrs. Granger and her X-ray vision. It was ordinary, yet extraordinary! I liked the illustrations in this book. Often books do not have many pictures, but these pencil sketches emphasized the book's humor.

WRITER'S CORNER

Look at the book list you wrote for the Writer's Corner on page 369. Think about the theme of each book. Write an explanation of the theme of one of the books.

Grammar in Action, Identify the negative word in the excerpt on page 370.

Writing a Book Report

LiNK

Fern Verdant and the Silver Rose

by Diane Leszczynski

. . . Quite out of the blue Fern discovers that she, like her mother, is able to communicate with plants. Somewhere Lily Verdant is in trouble and Fern has to do something to help her.

reviewed by Lookingglassreview.com

Once you have identified all the information that will go into a book report, the next step is to write the information in a way that makes a reader interested in the book.

Purpose

Effective book reports show a clear understanding of their purpose. When you write a book report, think about what you want the reader to know about the book. Think of how you can best organize and present your information to make it interesting and memorable.

Introduction

Book reports begin by telling what the title of the book is and the name of the author. The introduction of a book report tells who the main characters are and where the story takes place. It also gives an idea of what the book is about.

Body

The body of a book report gives more details about the plot and the theme of the book. The body of a book report tells what happens in the book, but it doesn't give away the ending. If you tell the ending, why would your audience want to read the book?

Conclusion

The conclusion of a book report tells the reader your opinion of the book. The conclusion should also give reasons and examples for your opinion.

ACTIVITY A Tell whether each piece of information below would be found in the introduction, the body, or the conclusion of a book report.

1. Reasons why readers would like the book
2. Plot details
3. Author's name
4. Description of the setting
5. Descriptions of the main characters

ACTIVITY B Tell what important information is missing in this introduction of a book report for the novel *Skylark*.

Readers who met the characters in *Sarah, Plain and Tall* will be excited to find out in this next book if they lived happily ever after. This story tells what happens when drought forces the family to leave their prairie home in the West and travel east to Maine.

ACTIVITY C Read the following conclusions from book reports for *United Tates of America*. Decide which conclusion supports the writer's opinions with strong reasons and examples.

1. I liked this book a lot. It's about kids our age and some of the struggles that they go through when they start middle school. The characters, especially Skate and GUM, seemed like real people. The scrapbook at the end made the story seem even more real.

2. I really didn't like this book. But then again, I don't like many books. This one just seemed boring. I also didn't like the characters or the plot.

3. My opinion of this book is very favorable. It's a definite must-read! The characters were good and so was the story. The author's use of humor added a lot. You should put it on your list of books to read.

WRITER'S CORNER

Choose one book that you have read. Write an introduction for a book report. Save your introduction to use later.

Tech Tip With an adult, search your local library's Web site.

Planning a Book Report

Before writing a book report, a writer should write all the important information to include. The book report should name the title and the author, and include the main events of the book in chronological order. The book report should also include the theme of the book and your opinion of the book based on examples from the plot.

A book report should include the features listed below.

Features of a Book Report

Title

Underline the title if you write it or use italics if you work on a computer.

Author

Copy the author's name exactly as it appears on the cover.

Setting

Describe the setting in as much detail as you need. If the setting is important to understand the story, describe it in as much detail as you can.

Characters

Name the main characters in the book and tell a little bit about them.

Plot Summary

The plot summary describes the main events in chronological order without giving away the ending.

Theme

The theme is the general idea or "life lesson" of the book.

Personal Opinion

Include your personal opinion, giving reasons and using examples from the book.

ACTIVITY D Reread the book report on page 367 and answer the following questions.

1. What information is included in the first paragraph of the book report?
2. What information is included in the second and third paragraphs of the book report?
3. What was the theme of *United Tates of America*?
4. What was the writer's personal opinion about this story? What were some things the writer especially liked?
5. Have you read this book? If so, do you agree with the writer's opinion? Why or why not? If you haven't read this book, do you think you would like to read it? Why or why not?

ACTIVITY E Find in the library three or four fiction books that you have not read. Write the titles and authors. For each book write a sentence that tells why you might want to read the book. For example, you might say that you have read other books by the same author or that something on the cover caught your attention.

ACTIVITY F Read a book report or book review in a magazine or newspaper. Then answer the following questions.

1. Who are the main characters?
2. What is the setting of the book?
3. What main events are included in the plot summary?
4. What is the theme of the book?
5. What is the writer's opinion of the book?

WRITER'S CORNER

Write five sentences about a favorite book. Do not reveal the title. Instead, make sure you mention the main characters and plot. Then trade your paper with a partner. Try to guess your partner's book title.

Tech Tip With an adult, find a review of your book online.

Revising Sentences

Rambling Sentences

Sentences that have too many words or too many ideas are called rambling sentences. Rambling sentences can be difficult to read and make readers lose interest. Some rambling sentences are just a string of short sentences linked together by conjunctions such as *and, but,* or *or.*

Effective writers use a variety of sentence lengths. Doing this keeps the reader interested. Read these two examples. Notice how they are alike and how they are different. Which example is easier to read?

A On Saturday my family took a trip to Independence Mall, and we saw the Liberty Bell and Constitution Hall, and then we watched a film on Benjamin Franklin at the end of the day.

B On Saturday my family took a trip to Independence Mall. There we saw the Liberty Bell and Constitution Hall. At the end of the day, we watched a film on Benjamin Franklin.

Both examples include a description of a trip to Independence Mall. Example B, however, breaks the same information into three sentences that are easier to read. When you use shorter sentences, the reader has a chance to take in each idea.

If you are using several conjunctions in one sentence, you may be writing a rambling sentence. Try beginning a new sentence each time that a conjunction appears.

Another way to find a rambling sentence is to look for sentences with many ideas. When you revise these sentences, try to write a new sentence for each idea.

ACTIVITY A Revise the following rambling sentences by breaking them up into shorter sentences. Add words such as *and* or *then* where needed.

1. Our science class had a video camera to use for a week, and we made a film showing chicks hatching, and we showed our film to the first graders.

2. The boots in the store are on sale, and my mother is going to buy them for me, or if she doesn't I will buy them myself.

3. Japan is a group of islands in the sea off the continent of Asia, and its land area is less than that of California, and it gets much of its food from other countries.

4. Doing chores at home is one common job for young people, and mowing lawns is another, but some young people have unusual jobs such as acting as clowns at children's parties.

5. My cousin's favorite activity is canoeing, and every summer he goes on canoe trips, and he has traveled thousands of miles by canoe.

6. My sister and I saw a cute puppy in the window and it kept looking at us and crying, so we asked the store owner if we could hold it and he let us play with the puppy for a while.

7. The Gateway Arch in St. Louis is the tallest national monument in the United States and over a million visitors ride the trams to the top each year, and on a clear day you can see about 30 miles in each direction from the viewing area at the top.

ACTIVITY B The following paragraph is one long, rambling sentence. Break it up into shorter sentences.

I enjoy Karen Cushman's books, and *Rodzina* is no exception, and this historical fiction story is about the orphan trains that carried children to the West to be adopted and work as farm laborers, and Rodzina herself tells the story, but the way she tells it made me feel like I was living it with her, and now I can appreciate that time in our history.

WRITER'S CORNER

Use your imagination and write a long sentence with several conjunctions. Then trade your sentence with a partner and break up the sentence you receive into several shorter sentences. Compare the finished sentences with the original sentence.

Run-on Sentences

A run-on sentence is two or more sentences put together without correct punctuation. Run-on sentences confuse readers. One way to fix a run-on sentence is by adding correct punctuation to make two or more sentences. Read the run-on sentence and the revision below.

A We went to the arboretum to see many varieties of trees most interesting to me were the gingko trees.

B We went to the arboretum to see many varieties of trees. Most interesting to me were the gingko trees.

In example A the run-on sentence had no punctuation between the two ideas. In example B a period after *trees* makes the second idea into a separate sentence.

Read the next pair of examples. The first example is a run-on sentence that has the wrong punctuation mark, a comma, after the first idea. In the revised sentence, the comma is replaced by a period.

A The study of plants is called botany, there are at least 300,000 different kinds of plants in the world.

B The study of plants is called botany. There are at least 300,000 different kinds of plants in the world.

Another way to fix a run-on sentence is to add a conjunction and turn it into a compound sentence. A comma should be added before the conjunction. Be sure that the ideas in the run-on sentence fit together before you revise the sentence with a conjunction. Here is a run-on sentence that was revised, using a conjunction.

A We didn't want to go home it was getting late.

B We didn't want to go home, but it was getting late.

ACTIVITY C Identify which sentences are run-on sentences and which are not.

1. The water slide is my favorite thing to do my mom likes the lazy river.

2. There was a detour in the road my father was very frustrated driving.

3. Jane put on sunblock before offering me some.

4. Jamal and Dev waited in line for the high dive, it was too scary for Mike.

5. Be careful of other swimmers. Make sure you look before you jump in.

ACTIVITY D Correct the following run-on sentences by separating them into more than one sentence.

1. Joan and I like to show each other our artwork sometimes we go to the art museum together Joan likes the paintings while I prefer the sculptures.

2. In the 1700s a Frenchman built a three-foot high robot, the robot could write and when it wrote, its eyes would follow the pen, it would even dot the *i*'s.

3. Uncle Owen gave me a large package for my birthday I shook it before I opened it in the package I found a new football.

4. I forgot to do my chores yesterday I also watched TV instead of doing my homework my mom was very upset with me I promised to do better.

5. Thomas walked to the store once he got there he realized he had forgotten his money he had to go all the way back home.

ACTIVITY E Correct these run-on sentences by separating them into more than one sentence or by adding a conjunction and the correct punctuation.

1. We planted beans in our garden, we had no idea how quickly they would grow.

2. In August we take a family vacation this year we will visit the Grand Canyon.

3. My little brother can be very helpful around the house sometimes he hides to avoid housework.

4. Our public library always sponsors Battle of the Books, I hope I can qualify for this year's battle.

5. I heard my mom and dad whispering about puppies I hope they're thinking of getting one for our family.

6. For my report I have to use encyclopedias, I'll have to go to the library after school.

WRITER'S CORNER

Look at your work from a previous Writer's Corner in this chapter. Check your work for rambling or run-on sentences. Revise any rambling or run-on sentences that you find.

Prefixes

A prefix is a syllable or syllables added to the beginning of a base word that changes the meaning of the word. Knowing what prefixes mean can help you figure out the meaning of new words as you read.

The prefixes *dis-, un-, im-,* and *in-* have similar meanings. These prefixes mean "not." Notice how these prefixes change the meanings of these base words.

dis- + honest = dishonest	im- + perfect = imperfect
un- + even = uneven	in- + correct = incorrect

Although these prefixes have similar meanings, each prefix fits only with certain words. If you are unsure which prefix to add to a base word, you can check a dictionary.

Here are some other common prefixes and their meanings.

PREFIX	MEANING	EXAMPLE
mis-	badly, wrongly	misunderstand
re-	again	rejoin
pre-	before	predawn

If you know that the prefix *pre-* means "before," it will help you remember that a prefix is added before the base word.

ACTIVITY A Complete these sentences by adding words that use a prefix that means "not." Use the words in italics as the base words.

1. If you are not *satisfied* with the ending of a story, you are _____.
2. If you think the smell of dirty socks is not *pleasant*, you think it is _____.
3. If you do not *continue* your subscription to a soccer magazine, you _____ it.
4. Bats are not *active* during the day; they are _____.
5. If sunny days are not *frequent*, they are _____.
6. If he is not *loyal* to his team, he is _____.

7. If someone is not *polite* to your family, the person is _____.

8. If you do not *complete* your homework, it is _____.

9. If the front door is not *locked* during the day, it is _____.

10. If a toddler does not *obey* her aunt, she _____ her.

ACTIVITY B Use the chart of prefixes on page 380 to tell what these words mean. Use a dictionary to check your answers.

1. mislead
2. reabsorb
3. misread
4. reuse
5. recharge
6. precut
7. misbehave
8. prepay
9. misspell
10. repaint

ACTIVITY C Identify the word or words with a prefix in each sentence. Tell what the word means. Use a dictionary if you need help.

1. The young couple wanted to buy an inexpensive used car.

2. Some of the antiques Georgia collects are prewar and worth a lot of money.

3. Jackie's polka dot pants were unflattering.

4. The Green Team remakes old items like tires into new things like planters.

5. My older sister calls me immature, but I think that is unfair of her.

WRITER'S CORNER

Pick one prefix from this lesson. Then brainstorm a list of as many words as you can that begin with that prefix. Write five sentences. Use one or more words from your list in each sentence.

Tech Tip Use a digital camera to illustrate your sentences.

Number and Amount Prefixes

Many prefixes have meanings that tell a number or an amount. For example, the word *bicycle* has a prefix. Can you see it? What do think the prefix means?

Here is a list of prefixes that tell a number or an amount.

PREFIX	MEANING	EXAMPLE
uni-	one	unicycle
mono-	one	monorail
bi-	two	biweekly
tri-	three	triangle
quad-	four	quadrangle
cent-	hundred	centimeter
mega-	million	megaton
poly-	many	polygon
multi-	many	multicolored

¡Hola! Bonjour! Hello!

ACTIVITY D Use the prefix chart above to answer these questions.

1. How many *centiliters* are in one liter?
2. How many events does a *biathlete* compete in?
3. How many watts are in a *megawatt*?
4. How many things can a *multitalented* person do?
5. How many colors are on a *tricolor* flag?
6. Who speaks more languages—someone who is *monolingual* or someone who is *multilingual*?
7. If a population *quadrupled*, how many times larger did it get?
8. How many tips would you find on a *bicuspid* tooth?
9. How many horns would you find on a *unicorn*?
10. On how many rails does a *monorail* balance?

ACTIVITY E Complete the chart below.

	Prefix	Base Word	New Word	Meaning
1.	_____	step	misstep	_____
2.	*dis-*	_____	_____	not organized
3.	*in-*	_____	incomplete	_____
4.	*im-*	pure	_____	_____
5.	*multi-*	stage	_____	many stages
6.	*uni-*	_____	unicycle	_____
7.	*bi-*	_____	_____	two focal lenses

ACTIVITY F Identify the word or words with a prefix in each sentence. Tell what the word means. Use a dictionary if you need help.

1. The speaker talked in a monotone voice.

2. The multimillionaire sailed to the islands on her yacht.

3. My brother competed in the triathlon.

4. Some scientists believe that the first life on earth was unicellular.

5. Democrats and Republicans formed a bipartisan committee.

6. I saw a centipede in the bathtub.

7. Emma gave her sister Janie her old bicycle for her birthday.

8. After Dario got his braces off, he couldn't hide his megawatt smile.

9. A polygraph machine tests several different pulses in the body to determine if someone is lying.

10. Aunt Sally thought she was having triplets, but then she learned she was pregnant with quadruplets.

WRITER'S CORNER

Imagine that you are writing a letter to your favorite author. Write three questions or comments you might include in your letter. Use words with prefixes from this lesson.

Fact and Opinion

Both facts and opinions are used in book reports. A fact is a statement that can be proved true. You can use the library or the Internet to find out if the fact is true. Here is an example of a fact.

Franklin D. Roosevelt was the 32nd president of the United States.

An opinion states a person's judgments or beliefs about a subject. Opinions cannot be proved true or untrue because they reflect a person's feelings. Here is an example of an opinion.

Franklin D. Roosevelt was the best president since Thomas Jefferson.

A person might believe that this statement is true, but it cannot be proved true or untrue.

When writers give their opinion, they try to support their opinion with facts. For example, a writer trying to support the opinion above might list good things that President Roosevelt did for the United States.

The introduction and body of a book report may contain many facts, such as what the characters do or where they live. Most statements in the conclusion of a book report are opinions. By using facts from the book, a writer can persuade the reader to agree with his or her opinion.

ACTIVITY A Identify the statements below as fact or opinion. Explain your answers.

1. **a.** Dinosaurs became extinct about 65 million years ago.

   b. Dinosaurs are the most interesting extinct animals.

2. **a.** The Vikings built a colony on Greenland.

   b. The Vikings were the toughest people in Europe.

3. **a.** The Irish Sea has the biggest waves you will ever see.

   b. The Irish Sea separates Ireland from Great Britain.

4. **a.** The four-string banjo is easier to play than the guitar.

   b. An open-back banjo doesn't have a resonator.

5. a. A gerbil is the easiest pet to take care of.

   b. Gerbils come out at night for food.

6. a. The astronauts from *Apollo 11* were the first men to set foot on the moon.

   b. Astronauts are braver than firefighters.

ACTIVITY B Read these facts and opinions. Tell whether the fact supports the opinion. Explain your answers.

1. Opinion: "A Haunted Attic" is a scary story.

   Fact: The main character hears a howling noise in the attic at night.

2. Opinion: No one can write like C. S. Lewis.

   Fact: He wrote *The Chronicles of Narnia*.

3. Opinion: Science fiction stories can help you see things that are wrong with the present.

   Fact: Kate Gilmore wrote a book about an alien living with a family called *The Exchange Student*.

4. Opinion: Books by Beverly Cleary feature the most popular characters in literature, including Ramona Quimby.

   Fact: Adaptations of her Ramona books have been made into movies and TV shows in several languages around the world.

5. Opinion: Isaac Asimov was a fast writer.

   Fact: He wrote or edited over 500 books.

6. Opinion: Shel Silverstein is best known for writing poems and stories for children.

   Fact: He received an Academy Award nomination for a song he wrote for a movie.

WRITER'S CORNER

Write one positive opinion about your school. Then research and write one fact that supports your opinion.

Grammar in Action. Identify the coordinating conjunctions in the second paragraph of the report on page 367.

Opinion Words

Knowing opinion words can help you decide if what you are reading is fact or opinion. Opinion words signal that the writer is telling his or her opinion on a subject. Here are some common opinion words you might find.

believe	good	bad
think	favorite	horrible
should	ugly	beautiful
feel	best	worst

ACTIVITY C Identify the words in these opinions that signal that they are opinions. Explain your answers.

1. I believe that this is the best basketball team our school has ever had.
2. I feel that the new school logo is too distracting.
3. Mysteries are my favorite kind of fiction.
4. That is the most beautiful roller coaster I've ever seen.
5. Bowling is the best sport for building your strength.
6. Ours is the mightiest wrestling team in Texas.
7. Latika thinks she will do well in the spelling bee next week.
8. Josie's old gym shoes are the smelliest thing in her locker.
9. Everyone should volunteer each week.

ACTIVITY D Tell whether each statement is a fact or an opinion. Explain your answers.

1. Baseball is the most elegant American sport.
2. Baseball players use a bat to hit the ball.
3. The pitcher stands on a mound to throw pitches.
4. All boys and girls should play baseball.
5. Baseball games have nine innings, unless the score is tied.
6. Left-handed players are the best pitchers.
7. A home run is always the most exciting part of a game.
8. The National Baseball Hall of Fame is in Cooperstown, New York.

ACTIVITY E Read each opinion. Tell whether the supporting statement is a fact or an opinion.

1. Opinion: The *Earthsea* trilogy is Ursula K. LeGuin's best work.

   Support: Each book about 200 pages.

2. Opinion: *Bud, Not Buddy* is a funny book.

   Support: Bugs is the funniest character.

3. Opinion: I think biographies are more exciting than fiction.

   Support: A biography is the story of a person's life.

4. Opinion: Tom Sawyer has exciting adventures.

   Support: In one part of the book, he goes to an island to become a pirate.

5. Opinion: King Arthur's story is inspiring and sometimes sad.

   Support: One of the best parts is when he pulls the sword from the stone.

ACTIVITY F Choose two of the following items. Use opinion words to write a four-sentence paragraph about each.

A. year-round school

B. curfews

C. skateboarding

D. horseback riding

E. dress codes

F. exercise

G. watching TV

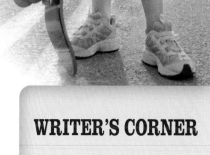

WRITER'S CORNER

Think of a book you have recently read. Write two opinions you have about the book. Then support your opinions by writing a fact for each opinion.

Oral Book Reports

Think of your favorite book. What did you do when you finished it? Did you tell your friends about it? Did you tell them that they just had to read it? An oral book report is a chance to share with an audience a book that you enjoyed.

Audience

Keep in mind the audience you will be speaking to. Will it be an audience of friends or younger children? When you choose a book to talk about for an oral book report, try to pick one that fits your audience.

You can give an oral book report about a book you liked or a book you disliked. To keep your audience interested, choose a book that you have strong feelings about.

Organization

Start by telling the title and author of your book. Then describe the setting of the book and some of the main characters. You might also say why you think the book is worth reading. That can grab the audience's attention.

Next, tell about a few things that happen in the book without giving away the ending. Use characters' names and details to keep the audience interested.

End by telling the audience your opinion of the book. Be sure to include examples from the book to support your opinion.

Delivery

You can do some things in an oral book report that you cannot do in a written one. Here are a few ideas.

- Use your voice. You can interest your audience in your book by speaking in a lively way. You can also emphasize your opinions by using your voice and gestures in the conclusion. Show how you feel about the book through the way you talk about it.

- Use visual aids. Show your audience what the cover of the book looks like. You might show illustrations of the characters, pictures of the setting, or photos of the author.
- Read aloud a paragraph or scene that you think is especially good. The audience might like to hear what the author's writing sounds like. Be sure that you keep your reading short. The audience wants to hear what you have to say.

ACTIVITY A **Make a list of books you have read. Try to think of more than one kind of book. Discuss your list with a partner. Talk about which books might be most interesting for an audience of your classmates. Then choose a book for an oral book report.**

ACTIVITY B **Think about the book you chose in Activity A. Plan a book report by listing all the important information you should include. Use the chart on page 374. Then think about a passage from the book you could read aloud. Also think of a visual aid to include in your report.**

ACTIVITY C **Read each sentence below and decide if it would be helpful to the audience listening to an oral book report.**

1. This book was good and I told my friends to read it.
2. All this stuff happened and everything worked out.
3. The characters were funny, and I could relate to them.
4. I don't know who wrote this book, but he or she should write more.
5. I would recommend this book to my friends who enjoy a good mystery and suspenseful stories.
6. It is a fact that this is the best book ever written, and if you don't read it, you'll be sorry.
7. I have read other books by this author and think that this book is the best because the characters are well-developed and funny.

SPEAKER'S CORNER

Look at the personal opinion that you listed in Activity B. Write three reasons and examples that support it. Share with a partner your reasons and examples.

Prepare

After you choose a book, prepare your oral book report. Write the information you need for the introduction on one or two note cards. You might want to include a few comments you have about the book that you think would grab the attention of the audience.

Write on note cards the major events that happen in the book. Use words to remind you of what you want to say. Describe the important parts, but don't give away the ending.

Write a few note cards for the conclusion. Include examples that support your opinion. Don't write everything you are going to say. The audience wants to hear you talk, not read from your note cards.

Practice

Practice giving your oral book report, using your note cards. If you have trouble remembering something, you may want to add new note cards. Practice in front of a mirror. As you practice, try using your note cards less and less. If you plan to use a visual aid, such as the book or a picture, practice using your visual aid.

When you are ready, practice with a friend or family member. Here are some questions you might want to ask your listener.

- Am I speaking clearly and loudly enough?
- Can you see my visual aid?
- Did I tell about the plot and characters clearly?
- Do I speak with enough or too much enthusiasm?
- Do I give examples to support my opinions?

Listening Tips

Listen closely to your classmates' book reports. You might discover a book you would like to read. Here are some tips for being a good listener.

- Pay attention to the speaker. Try to picture the characters and the setting that the speaker describes.
- Don't interrupt. If you have questions about something, write them. You might be able to ask questions at the end of the book report.

- As you listen, think about whether the book sounds like something you might like to read.
- Listen to the speaker's opinions. If you have read the book, think about whether or not you agree with the speaker. Do the examples that the speaker gives support his or her opinions?

ACTIVITY D Use this chart to help you organize your ideas. Fill in the Introduction and Body columns with the information you need for those parts of your book report. For the Conclusion column, you can use the reasons and examples you wrote for the Speaker's Corner on page 389. After you organize your ideas in the chart, use the chart to make note cards for an oral book report.

INTRODUCTION	BODY	CONCLUSION

ACTIVITY E Imagine giving your oral book report to the following audiences. How would your tone and delivery change?

1. A class of third graders
2. Teachers and parents at Parents' Night
3. A book club of your friends

SPEAKER'S CORNER

Practice giving your oral book report with a partner. When you have finished, ask your partner the questions on page 390. Then let your partner practice his or her book report.

Tech Tip Record a podcast of your oral book report.

Prewriting and Drafting

Have you ever read about a book that sounded so good that you couldn't wait to read it? Have you ever read about a book that sounded awful? You might have been reading a book report. Book reports tell others about a book and what the writer thought about it.

Prewriting

Holden's fifth-grade class was making a class magazine. Holden was going to write a book report about a book that kids his age might like to read. His book report would be printed in the magazine for the whole school to read.

Before Holden wrote his book report, he knew he would have to do prewriting. He would choose a book, freewrite details about the book, and organize his ideas.

Choosing a Book

Holden made a list of some books that he enjoyed. He asked other kids in his class what **Ideas** they liked and added those books to his list. He included a short summary of each book so that he wouldn't mix them up. Look at his list.

> <u>The Witch of Blackbird Pond</u> by Elizabeth Speare. Set in the colony of Connecticut in the late 1600s.
>
> <u>The Lion, the Witch and the Wardrobe</u> by C.S. Lewis. Four kids travel to a magic land.
>
> <u>Bud, Not Buddy</u> by Christopher Paul Curtis. An orphan looks for his father during the Great Depression.
>
> <u>From the Mixed-up Files of Mrs. Basil E. Frankweiler</u> by E.L. Konisburg. A sister and brother run away from home and live in a museum.

He had already read *The Lion, the Witch and the Wardrobe*. He chose *Bud, Not Buddy* because he had never read the book and didn't know much about the Great Depression.

Your Turn

Make a list of books and write a sentence or two about each one.

- Read your list. Is there a book you want others to know about? Is there a book that might teach you about an unfamiliar time or place?
- Consider these questions and choose your book.

Freewriting

Holden checked out *Bud, Not Buddy* from the library and read it. He knew he was going to write about it, so he wrote notes about the book as he read. He jotted down important things that happened in the story. He wrote his ideas about the theme. He also wrote notes about the things that he liked. Here are Holden's freewriting notes about the first part of the book.

Bud was 6 when his mom died. He didn't know who his dad was.

Story starts when Bud is 10. He lives in an orphanage in Flint, Michigan.

Bud's special suitcase—blanket, flyers of a jazz musician (Bud's dad?), stones with dates on them from mom, mom's picture

Bud's Rules and Things for Having a Funner Life—FUNNY!

awful foster home—Bud runs away

Before she dies, Bud's mom tells him no matter how bad things get, when one door closes, another one opens. (theme?)

Your Turn

Read your book and make freewriting notes about it.

- If you have already read the book, skim through it to help you remember the important things that happen.
- Write a lot of details.
- Don't forget to write some things that you liked.

Organizing Ideas

Holden had a lot of notes about his book. Here are some of his notes.

Title
Bud, Not Buddy

Author
Christopher Paul Curtis

Setting
Flint and Grand Rapids, Michigan; Great Depression during 1930s; On the road

Plot Summary
characters: Bud, Herman E. Calloway, Lefty Lewis, Miss Thomas, the Amoses

Bud the orphan runs away from the foster home. He travels from Flint to Grand Rapids, looking for his dad. Along the way he meets a lot of people who are poor because of the Depression. He meets some band members who help him find Herman E. Calloway.

Theme
When one door closes, another one opens.

Personal Opinion
I liked Bud's story because I could share his happiness and sadness.

Your Turn

Organize your notes the way Holden did.

👀 **Organization** Describe the events of the plot in chronological order. Remember that you can add more details as you write your draft.

Drafting

After taking detailed notes and organizing them, Holden was ready to start writing. He wanted to give people enough information to make them want to read the book, but not so much that he told the whole story. Holden looked over his notes and wrote his first draft, adding information and details as he went along.

My Review of Bud, Not Buddy

by Holden Barrow

<u>Bud, Not Buddy</u> is the name of the book and the name of the book's main character, Bud. The story is set during the 1930s. As 10-year-old Bud travels, he makes friends like Lefty Lewis, Miss Thomas, and gruff Herman E. Calloway.

Bud's mother died when he was six and ever since, he's been shuffled from the orphanage to foster homes. He takes off from an abusive foster home to find his father. The family Bud stays with locks him in a shed after he gets into a fight with their son. Bud spends a scary night thinking that vampire bats are going to bite him. Bud thinks his father is jazz musician Herman E. Calloway. He travels alone from Flint to Grand rapids in search of Mr. Calloway. He uses flyers of Mr. Calloway left by his mother as clues. Along the way Bud meets people whose lives have been changed by the Great Deppresion. He has many adventures that are funny and sad at the same time.

His courage leads him to the truth what he learns about his mom, himself, and the love of family may surprise you as much as it did Bud!

I liked this book a lot. I liked the character of Bud and his suitcase of memories, which was so special to him? I also liked Bud's Rules and Things for

Having a Funner Life because it was hilarious. His mom's picture, the flyers about Herman E. Calloway, and his precious rocks are all things that help him remember his family. I also think that the author did a great job of having Bud tell the story. I felt like I was sharing Bud's happiness and sadness.

If you like stories about brave kids and like stories set in different times in American history, I'm sure you'll like Bud's journey too.

Your Turn

Use your organized freewriting notes to write a draft of your book report. Be sure to include important information such as the characters, setting, plot, and personal opinion.

Words with Feeling

Make the characters or events come alive for

 Voice your readers. Choose words that show how you

feel. Holden wrote about Bud's *precious rocks*. He refers to Bud's foster home as *abusive*.

Using exact words will help your audience feel what you felt when you read the book. A thesaurus can help you find the exact words that you need.

Writer's Tip Tell the main events of the story in chronological order, but don't give away too much.

Grammar in Action

Holden's first draft has two subordinate conjunctions in the second paragraph. Can you find them?

Content Editing

Holden had worked hard on his book report. He was happy with his first draft. But he knew that it could be made better by content editing. A content editor could check his ideas for logic, order, and clarity. A content editor could also tell him if he gave away too much information or if he needed to add more details.

Holden asked his cousin Daisy to content edit his draft. Daisy was the editor of her high school newspaper, and she often wrote reviews of movies, plays, and music. Daisy used this Content Editor's Checklist to check Holden's draft.

Daisy read Holden's book report carefully. Then she used the Content Editor's checklist to content edit the draft. Daisy checked for one question at a time and made notes and suggestions about what she read. Then she and Holden talked about the draft.

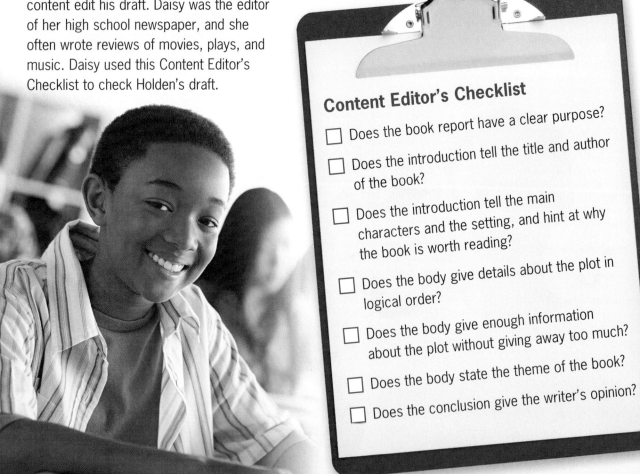

Content Editor's Checklist

☐ Does the book report have a clear purpose?

☐ Does the introduction tell the title and author of the book?

☐ Does the introduction tell the main characters and the setting, and hint at why the book is worth reading?

☐ Does the body give details about the plot in logical order?

☐ Does the body give enough information about the plot without giving away too much?

☐ Does the body state the theme of the book?

☐ Does the conclusion give the writer's opinion?

Daisy first told Holden about the things she liked. She liked how Holden wrote the conclusion with so much feeling. It was clear that Holden liked the book. Daisy also liked that the purpose of the book report was clear and that the body told the plot in logical order. Here are Daisy's other comments.

- You say what the book's title is, but you don't say who wrote it. People who read your book report might use the author's name to find the book.
- You did a great job of naming the characters in the introduction. But can you say more about the setting? You say when the book takes place, but not where.

- I think you should take out the part about Bud getting locked in the shed and being afraid of the vampire bats. It's interesting, but people might rather read about it in the book.
- I like what you say about Bud in the third paragraph. But is there a theme in the book that applies to everyone?

Holden thanked Daisy for her help. He thought that Daisy had made some really good suggestions. Holden was glad that he had asked his cousin to content edit the book report.

Your Turn

Read the draft of your book report. Then read it again, using the Content Editor's Checklist.

- Have you included the introduction, body, and conclusion?
- Try to put yourself in the place of your readers. Do you think that readers will trust your opinion about whether to read the book after reading your book report?

Ask a classmate to be your content editor. There may be a classmate who likes the same books as you do. You might content edit each other's work.

- Content edit your partner's draft.
- Meet with your content editor and discuss his or her suggestions. Think carefully about what your content editor says.
- Remember that your content editor may see things in a way that you cannot. But keep in mind that you will make the final decision about what you will change.

Revising

Look at how Holden used Daisy's suggestions and his own ideas to revise his draft.

~~My~~ Review of Bud, Not Buddy
Great, Not Good

by Holden Barrow

<u>Bud, Not Buddy</u> is the name of the book and the name of the book's main *by Christopher Paul Curtis. It is also*

character, Bud. The story is set during the 1930s. As 10-year-old Bud travels, he *in Flint and Grand rapids, Michigan*

makes friends like Lefty Lewis, Miss Thomas, and gruff Herman E. Calloway.

Bud's mother died when he was six and ever since, he's been shuffled from the

orphanage to foster homes. He takes off from an abusive foster home to find his

father. ~~The family Bud stays with locks him in a shed after he gets into a fight with~~

~~their son. Bud spends a scary night thinking that vampire bats are going to bite~~

him. Bud thinks his father is jazz musician Herman E. Calloway. He travels alone
mysterious

from Flint to Grand rapids in search of Mr. Calloway. He uses flyers of Mr. Calloway

left by his mother as clues. Along the way Bud meets people whose lives have been

changed by the Great Deppresion. He has many adventures that are funny and sad

at the same time.

Before Bud's mom died, she told him that when one door closes, another opens. Everyone should remember
His courage leads him to the truth what he learns about his mom, himself,   *that. Bud did, and*

and the love of family may surprise you as much as it did Bud!

I liked this book a lot. I liked the character of Bud and his suitcase of

memories, which was so special to him? I also liked Bud's Rules and Things for

Having a Funner Life because it was hilarious. His mom's picture, the flyers about Herman E. Calloway, and his precious rocks are all things that help him remember his family. I also think that the author did a great job of having Bud tell the story. I felt like I was sharing Bud's happiness and sadness.

If you like stories about brave kids and like stories set in different times in American history, I'm sure you'll like Bud's journey too.

Holden used proofreading marks to mark changes in his draft. Look at how he revised his book report.

- What did Holden add to the introduction?
- What did Holden add because he thought it was important to the setting?
- Holden agreed with Daisy's suggestion about providing too much information. What unnecessary information did Holden take out?
- Daisy had some notes about the theme. What should Holden's next step be to make the book report apply to every reader?

Holden changed the title. He thought that the new title was more interesting because it told how he felt about the book. His new title was also similar to the title of the book.

Holden also added the word *mysterious* to his

 Word Choice

description of Herman E. Calloway. He thought that *mysterious* described Mr. Calloway perfectly.

Your Turn

Use your ideas and the ideas from your content editor to revise your book report. When you have finished, go over the Content Editor's Checklist again. Can you answer yes to each question?

Prewriting

Drafting

Content Editing

Revising

Copyediting

Proofreading

Publishing

Copyediting and Proofreading

Copyediting

Holden knew that Daisy's suggestions and his own changes had made his book report better. He thought that now the plot summary gave just enough information to get people interested in the book. He wanted to make sure that all his sentences were correct and that his word choices were exact. He used the Copyeditor's Checklist to copyedit his book report.

Holden found a rambling sentence in the second paragraph of his draft. He decided to

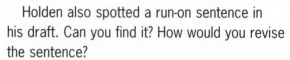 Sentence Fluency

make it into two sentences. Look at how Holden revised the rambling sentence.

Old Sentence: Bud's mother died when he was six and ever since, he's been shuffled from the orphanage to foster homes.

Revision: Bud's mother died when he was six. Ever since, he's been shuffled from the orphanage to foster homes.

Holden also spotted a run-on sentence in his draft. Can you find it? How would you revise the sentence?

Holden did not like the word *sadness* at the end of the fourth paragraph. He checked a thesaurus and found the word *disappointments*. It was the exact word he needed.

After making his copyediting changes, Holden used the Copyeditor's Checklist again to check his changes.

Copyeditor's Checklist

☐ Have I checked for any run-on or rambling sentences?

☐ Have I checked for any sentences that should be combined?

☐ Is each sentence grammatically correct?

☐ Are words with prefixes used correctly?

☐ Do all the words mean what I think they mean?

Prewriting

Drafting

Content Editing

Revising

Copyediting

Proofreading

Publishing

Your Turn

Look over your revised draft. Use the Copyeditor's Checklist to copyedit your book report.

- Make sure that every sentence is clear, logical, and correct.
- After making your changes, check your draft again. Pay special attention to the revisions you made.

Proofreading

Holden knew that he should proofread his draft before writing his final copy. Daisy had told Holden that proofreading was very important. A proofreader would check for spelling, capitalization, and punctuation mistakes in the draft.

Daisy's friend Jay was the proofreader for his high school newspaper. He offered to proofread Holden's book report. He used this Proofreader's Checklist.

Proofreader's Checklist

- ☐ Are the paragraphs indented?
- ☐ Are all the words spelled correctly?
- ☐ Are capitalization and punctuation correct?
- ☐ Is the grammar correct?
- ☐ Have I checked that no new mistakes were added while editing?

Jay found a misspelled word in the draft. Can you find the misspelled word?

Jay noticed one mistake in capitalization and one in punctuation. He thought that *Grand rapids* should be *Grand Rapids.* He checked a Michigan **Conventions** state map to be sure and saw that he was correct. Can you find the mistake in punctuation?

Holden thanked Jay for his help. Holden was so excited to have had high school newspaper editors edit his book report!

After making sure that he made all the changes, Holden proofread his draft again. He wanted to make sure that he had not made any new mistakes.

Your Turn

Read your book report carefully, using the Proofreader's Checklist.

- Check to make sure that your paragraphs are indented and that your words are correct.
- Check for misspelled words and correct grammar, capitalization, and punctuation.
- Finally, make sure that you did not make any new mistakes while revising.

After you have proofread your draft, trade book reports with a partner.

- Go through your partner's report carefully, using the Proofreader's Checklist.
- Remember to keep a dictionary nearby.

Publishing

Holden carefully typed the draft on his computer. Then he printed it out and checked it one last time, using the Proofreader's Checklist. Here is the copy of Holden's book report that was published in his class magazine.

Great, Not Good

by Holden Barrow

Bud, Not Buddy is by Christopher Paul Curtis. It is also the name of the book's main character. The story is set in Flint and Grand Rapids, Michigan, during the 1930s. As 10-year-old Bud travels, he makes friends like Lefty Lewis, Miss Thomas, and gruff Herman E. Calloway.

Bud's mother died when he was six. Ever since, he's been shuffled from the orphanage to foster homes. He takes off from an abusive foster home to find his father. Bud thinks his father is mysterious jazz musician Herman E. Calloway. He travels alone from Flint to Grand Rapids in search of Mr. Calloway. He uses flyers of Mr. Calloway left by his mother as clues. Along the way Bud meets people whose lives have been changed by the Great Depression. He has many adventures that are funny and sad at the same time.

Before Bud's mom died, she told him that when one door closes, another one opens. Everyone should remember that. Bud did, and his courage leads him to the truth. What he learns about his mom, himself, and the love of family may surprise you as much as it did Bud!

I liked this book a lot. I liked the character of Bud and his suitcase of memories, which was so special to him. I also liked Bud's Rules and Things for Having a Funner Life because it was hilarious. His mom's picture, the flyers about Herman E. Calloway, and his precious rocks are all things that help him remember his family. I also think that the author did a great job of having Bud tell the story. I felt like I was sharing Bud's happiness and disappointments.

If you like stories about brave kids and like stories set in different times in American history, I'm sure you'll like Bud's journey too.

A book report is something that can appeal to many people. Here are a few ways you can share your report.

 Post your book report on the class bulletin board. Perhaps you can include a picture of the book cover for reference.

 Use a video camera to record yourself giving an oral book report. With an adult's permission, submit your video on a video-sharing program.

 Submit your review to a magazine or Web site that accepts student submissions. Ask your teacher or librarian to help you find one.

 Start an online book club with your friends and classmates. Post your book reports online and see who agrees or disagrees.

Whenever you publish your work, your goal is to share your thoughts and experiences with other people. Book reports are fun to share. They give you a chance to share your opinion with others.

They are also a good way for you to learn about books you have not read. One way that you can publish is by sharing your book report with your classmates. You might inspire someone else to read the book!

Your Turn

Look over your book report one last time before you publish it. If you typed your book report, use your computer's spell-checker. Make sure your final report is neat and that your name is clearly marked. Print out your

 Presentation final copy and check it one

last time, using the Proofreader's Checklist.

Writer's Tip Remember, if you publish your book report online, don't use your full name. You might choose a screen name instead. Or you can use just your first name. Follow the rules for Internet safety whenever you publish your work online.

Creative Writing

LiNK **Swamp Angel**

by Anne Isaacs

On August 1, 1815, when Angelica Longrider took her first gulp of air on this earth, there was nothing about the baby to suggest that she would become the greatest woodswoman in Tennessee. The newborn was scarcely taller than her mother and couldn't climb a tree without help. . . .

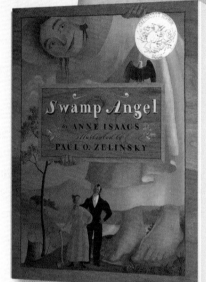

When she was twelve, a wagon train got mired in the Dejection Swamp. The settlers had abandoned their covered wagons and nearly all hope besides. Suddenly, a young woman in a homespun dress tramped toward them out of the mists. She lifted those wagons like they were twigs in a puddle and set them on high ground.

"It's an angel!" cried the gape-mouthed pioneers.

Ever since that time, Angelica Longrider has been known as Swamp Angel. To this day, stories about Swamp Angel spring up like sunflowers along the wagon trails. And every one of them is true.

> Tall tale stories, like *Swamp Angel*, use figurative language and exaggeration to show how the larger-than-life heroes solve everyday problems.

Room: 27

Name: Thi Thieu

Paul Bunyan

Long ago when our country was young, the biggest baby on record was born. His name was Paul Bunyan, and he was so big that it took a whole herd of cows to fill up his bottle. By the time he was a year old, his clothes were so large that he had to use wagon wheels for buttons.

At that time settlers on the frontier needed lumber to build houses, stores, barns, and churches. Most loggers were big and strong. Paul grew up to be the biggest, strongest, toughest logger in the country. His voice was so loud that the other loggers had to wear earmuffs all year long. Whenever he sneezed, the roof blew off his cabin. Paul could chop down six acres of trees with one mighty swing of his giant steel ax.

During the winter of the Blue Snow, Paul found a baby ox lying in a drift and carried him home to his logging camp. When the ox thawed out, his color stayed as blue as the snow. Paul named the ox Babe. Babe grew fast and soon measured more than 42 ax handles between the eyes. The tips of his horns were so far apart that it took a bird a whole day to fly from one to the other. Paul soon learned that Babe was not only big, but that he was also very strong. Babe could haul logs as fast as Paul could chop them.

Babe helped Paul in other ways too. Once Paul hooked him up to the end of a crooked road through the logging camp, and Babe pulled all the kinks out of it. In fact, when all the curves were pulled straight, there were 10 miles of road left over. Paul rolled it up and gave it to a nearby town to use as Main Street.

What Makes a Good Tall Tale?

Tall tales were the movies, TV, and video games of America in the 1800s. Pioneers of the time traveled to the West across territory in which everything seemed huge and dangerous—dark forests, vast prairies, tall mountains, arid deserts, and ferocious animals. Everything seemed bigger than life, so their stories were about people who were bigger than life.

Some of their stories were based on real people such as Johnny Appleseed and Davy Crockett. Others were about made-up characters like Paul Bunyan and Pecos Bill. The one thing the stories had in common was that everything was exaggerated.

Larger-than-Life Hero

The hero of a tall tale always has a specific job, such as cowboy, logger, railroad worker, or steelworker. He or she is always the biggest, bravest, strongest, fastest worker of them all, able to do things that no ordinary human could do. Tall tales often start by telling amazing things about the hero's childhood.

Problems, Solutions, Explanations

The hero of a tall tale often has a problem that he or she solves in an exaggerated and humorous way. For example, Sourdough Sam, Paul Bunyan's camp cook, had to make a lot of pancakes to feed all the loggers. Sam solved the problem by making a big griddle. It was so big that it had to be greased by skaters wearing slabs of bacon strapped to their feet.

Often a tall tale will explain how some familiar thing began. It is said that Babe the Blue Ox was so big and heavy that his footprints created Minnesota's 10,000 lakes.

Everyday Language

Tall tales are told using everyday language about ordinary things. Tall tales use exaggeration to create surprising and amusing pictures in the reader's mind.

Characters in tall tales speak in the everyday language of the people of their time and place. They use slang, contractions, and the vocabulary that a logger, a cowboy, or a railroad worker would use.

ACTIVITY A Answer the following questions about the tall tale on page 405.

1. What was Paul Bunyan's job?
2. What problem did Paul have, and how did he and Babe solve it?
3. What are some exaggerated details about Paul's size?
4. What are some exaggerated details about Babe's size?
5. What ordinary things does the author mention to make exaggerated points about Paul and Babe?

ACTIVITY B Use your imagination to describe what these items owned by Paul Bunyan might have looked like. Use descriptions that exaggerate the size of each object.

1. his cabin
2. his bed
3. his bathtub
4. his ax
5. his wagon
6. his toothbrush
7. his comb

WRITER'S CORNER

Reread the tall tale on page 405. Think about what else Paul might have eaten or worn. Write four sentences giving exaggerated details about Paul's food and clothing.

LiNK

Swamp Angel

Soon Swamp Angel was the
only one left who hadn't met
up with Tarnation. Until one
morning she awoke from
dozing in the shade of a creek
to find that four-legged forest
of stubble staring at her across
the stream. They faced off for
a few minutes. "Varmint," says
Angel, "I'm much obliged for
that pelt you're carryin'."

Anne Isaacs

**ACTIVITY C Read the following
adventure of tall-tale hero Pecos Bill.
Then answer the questions.**

When Pecos Bill was just a baby, his family
headed west all the way into Texas with a
caravan of covered wagons. Baby Bill was so
big that he wrestled grizzly bears for fun. One
day, unnoticed by his parents, he fell out of the
wagon and into a river.

Bill was rescued by coyotes and raised
as part of their family. His happy days as
a teenaged coyote were interrupted when
a cowboy came riding through and spotted
him. "Howdy, pardner, who are you?" asked
the cowboy. After about a week of trying, the
cowboy convinced Bill that he was a human
and not a coyote. "Wanna head for the nearest
ranch? Just follow me, fella," offered the cowboy.

Before leaving, Bill tamed himself a mountain
lion. He rode his lion instead of a horse. On the
way he encountered a huge rattlesnake and a
pack of vicious Gila monsters that an ordinary
person would have tried to avoid. Not Bill. He
grabbed the snake and whipped it around,
beating the poison out of it. He made a rope out
of the flattened snake and used it to lasso the
Gila monsters. When he got to the ranch, Bill
said, "How da ya like my herd, fellas?" Then he
showed the ranch hands how to rope cattle with
his rattlesnake lasso!

1. What are some amazing stories about Pecos Bill's childhood?

2. What is another example of exaggeration in the story?

3. What problem did Pecos Bill solve in an unusual way?

4. What unusual item did Pecos Bill invent?

5. How would you describe the way the characters speak in the story? Read
   the characters' exact words the way the characters might have said them.

ACTIVITY D Tell why each sentence is from a tall tale.

1. John Henry drove spikes into railway ties faster than a steam engine could.
2. Pecos Bill rode a tornado and carved out the Grand Canyon.
3. Davy Crockett killed a bear when he was just three years old.
4. Three hours after Paul was born, he weighed 80 pounds, and his family had to use a lumber wagon as a baby carriage.
5. Flatboat Annie was almost 10 feet tall.
6. Slue-foot Sue rode up on the Rio Grande on a catfish as big as a whale.
7. "By golly, I'm gonna tame that river or die trying!" said Paul.
8. The rattlesnake could not bite through Johnny Appleseed's skin, which was as tough as an elephant's hide.
9. "I will bend this red-hot rail of steel with my own hands," said Joe Magarac.
10. Alfred Bulltop Stormalong had a clipper ship so big it scraped the moon.

ACTIVITY E Tell whether each of the following sentences describes a larger-than-life hero.

1. The baby fussed and cried all night.
2. The boy studied six hours for his final exams.
3. The girl whooped so loud that the moon started to spin.
4. The bricklayer worked so fast that he could build a whole town in an hour.
5. The children skied to school after the big blizzard.
6. The woman was so hungry that she ate three cheese sandwiches.
7. The traveler was so thirsty he drank Lake Michigan dry.
8. The librarian read 10 books last month.
9. The man pounded his fist on the ground and caused an earthquake.
10. The farmer plowed all his fields in an hour.

WRITER'S CORNER

Choose one of the sentences in Activity E that does not describe a larger-than-life hero. Rewrite it, using exaggeration to make it fit in a tall tale.

Writing a Tall Tale

The people who told tall tales in the 1800s told stories about the things they knew best. Loggers told stories about Paul Bunyan. Railroad workers told stories about John Henry. Cowboys told stories about Pecos Bill. The storytellers took things that happened in their own lives and exaggerated them to make them funny and entertaining. If there was a lot of snow, they said that the snow was so deep that loggers had to dig down to find the trees. If it was hot, they said it was so hot that the corn popped right on the stalks in the fields. The bigger the exaggeration, the more amusing the story would be.

Tall-tale writers of today write about things they know. You might write about the world's best soccer player or the world's fastest skater. Someone who likes to travel might write about the world's greatest explorer.

Creating a Character

The first step in writing a tall tale is choosing the hero. The hero should have a job that the writer is familiar with. Then the writer needs to decide what things can be exaggerated about that hero to make the hero larger than life. A baseball player must be able to throw, hit, and run. A baseball player who is the hero of a tall tale should be able to throw harder, hit farther, and run faster than any other baseball player. This baseball player might be able to run fast enough to catch the ball that he or she hit!

ACTIVITY A Complete each of the following sentences to exaggerate something about the hero of a tall tale.

EXAMPLE **The boy was so tall that _____.**
The boy was so tall that he could wash the windows of a skyscraper without a ladder.

1. The wrestler was so strong that _____.
2. The teacher had such good vision that _____.
3. The bike rider pedaled so fast that _____.
4. The week-old baby was so big that _____.
5. The baker could make breads so good that _____.
6. The musician could hear so well that _____.
7. The figure skater jumped so high that _____.

ACTIVITY B Think of a special quality that each of these people might have. Then write a sentence that makes the person larger than life.

EXAMPLE **fifth grader**
The fifth grader was so smart that she could finish a whole math chapter in less than a minute.

1. football player
2. news reporter
3. zookeeper
4. deep-sea fisher
5. in-line skater
6. taxi driver

WRITER'S CORNER

Imagine that you are the hero of a tall tale. Write a list of three exaggerated things that you can do.

Tech Tip Find tall tales from around the world online.

Creating Problems and Solutions

The problem that the hero faces in a tall tale should be an exaggeration of something that could happen in real life. In real life it would get cold in the winter at the logging camps. One story of Paul Bunyan says it got so cold that when he spoke, his words froze in midair. Paul's companions had to thaw out the words over the fire to find out what he had said.

Solutions also involve exaggeration and humor. Once Paul's foreman sent the wrong logs all the way down the Mississippi River from Minnesota to New Orleans. Paul had Babe the Blue Ox take a huge gulp from the river to reverse its course and bring the logs back to the camp.

As the writer of a modern tall tale, you should do as the storytellers of old did and let your imagination run wild. Think of a problem your hero might have and then exaggerate it. Does he meet up with a strange dog? Then it should be the biggest, meanest dog in town. Is she caught in the rain? Then it should be the worst storm of the century.

The solution to the problem should also be exaggerated. Perhaps the hero tricks the dog by throwing a stick so far that the dog chases it all the way to South America. Perhaps the hero stays dry by running in a path so crooked that the raindrops don't touch her.

Remember that in a tall tale, everything is superlative. It's the hottest, coldest, wettest, driest, tallest, shortest, biggest, loudest, strongest, worst, or best.

Vocabulary

When you are writing a tall tale, use vocabulary that your hero would use. If you are writing about a baseball player, use words like *sinker* and *grounder.* If you are writing about a skateboarder, use words like *half-pipe* and *freestyle.* This will give a sense of reality and make the exaggerations even funnier.

ACTIVITY C Match each problem in Column A with a possible solution in Column B.

Column A

1. The logging-camp table was two miles long.

2. A drought dried up the prairie.

3. Lucy the Purple Cow was happy only when the grass was green.

4. A wagonload of rice and vegetables fell into a lake.

5. Johnny Inkslinger was running out of ink.

Column B

a. Paul gave her green-tinted glasses to wear in the wintertime.

b. Pecos Bill lassoed a thundercloud and squeezed it until it rained.

c. Boys on bicycles rode down the middle to deliver the salt and pepper.

d. He saved five barrels by not dotting his *i*'s or crossing his *t*'s.

e. The cook built bonfires on the shore and boiled the lake to make soup

ACTIVITY D Write a humorous or an exaggerated explanation to answer each of these questions.

1. Why is the sky blue?

2. Why can't dogs talk?

3. What caused the Rocky Mountains?

4. Why does it get cold in the winter?

5. Why does the moon glow?

6. Why are oceans made of salt water?

7. Why does a kangaroo have a pouch?

8. What caused the Grand Canyon?

9. Why does Saturn have rings around it?

10. Why is the sun hot?

I'm hungry!

WRITER'S CORNER

Write a problem that the hero of a tall tale would need to solve. Trade papers with a partner. Write a brief solution to your partner's problem. Use exaggeration to make your problem and solution as humorous as possible.

Grammar in Action

Use four kinds of sentences in your solution for a tall-tale hero.

Figurative Language

Good writers try to create vivid pictures in the reader's mind. One way to do this is to use sensory language—words and ideas that appeal to sight, hearing, taste, touch, and smell. Another way is to use figurative language—language that compares one thing to another in a new and revealing way. Here are some types of figurative language.

Exaggeration

Exaggeration is used to make a dramatic or humorous point by describing something in impossible terms. Real loggers did chop down trees, but no real logger could chop down six acres of trees with one swing of an ax. The teller of the tall tale used exaggeration to show that Paul Bunyan was larger than life.

Many exaggerations use expressions such as *it was so hot that, he was so tall that,* or *she was so strong that.* Exaggerations often contain superlatives such as *coldest, deepest, fastest, loudest,* and *biggest.*

Simile

A simile describes one thing by telling how it is like something else. A simile uses the word *like* or *as.* In the examples below, Flatboat Annie's height is compared to a paddle wheel, and her voice is compared to thunder. These details help create a vivid picture of Annie.

> **Flatboat Annie was as tall *as* a paddle wheel.**
> **Her voice was *like* a roll of thunder.**

Some similes have been so overused that they have become clichés. *As quiet as a mouse* and *as old as dirt* are clichés. Good writers try to think of a fresh comparison that will give readers a new idea of the thing they are describing.

ACTIVITY A Complete each of the following similes. Be creative. Try not to use clichés.

1. Danny is shy. His voice is as quiet as _____.
2. Molly is nervous. Her mouth feels as dry as _____.
3. Jacob took swimming lessons. Now he swims like _____.
4. Cara was very happy. She was smiling like _____.
5. Ryan is a fast runner. He's as fast as _____.
6. José makes a lot of noise. He's as loud as _____.
7. Linda is a good singer. Her voice is like _____.
8. Gavin lifts weights. He is as strong as _____.

ACTIVITY B Write a simile to describe each of the people below. Use exaggeration to make your similes humorous.

1. someone who is smart
2. someone who dances well
3. someone who is tall
4. someone who is friendly
5. someone who plays guitar well
6. someone who reads quickly
7. someone who is funny
8. someone who loves animals
9. someone who talks a lot
10. someone who is good at a sport

LiNK

Swamp Angel

Swamp Angel took hold of that bear and tossed him so high he was still on the way up at nightfall. Even when the first star came out, there was no sign of him. Angel began to think she had lost him in the sky.

Anne Isaacs

WRITER'S CORNER

Choose a pet or an animal in the zoo. Write four sentences to describe something about it, such as its eyes, ears, tail, or paws. Include exaggeration and similes. Example: The monkey's tail was as long as a jump rope.

Grammar in Action. Identify the direct object in the third sentence of the excerpt above.

Metaphor

A metaphor is a way of comparing two things without using *like* or *as*. A simile states that one thing is like another thing. A metaphor states that one thing is another thing.

> **The preschool classroom is a beehive of activity.**
> **The stream is a green snake slithering through the woods.**
> **The jets are enormous silver birds against the blue sky.**

These sentences say that the classroom is a beehive, the stream is a snake, and the jets are birds. Using metaphors can make writing interesting and colorful by creating a vivid picture in the reader's mind.

ACTIVITY C Tell whether the comparison in each of these sentences is a simile or a metaphor. Explain how you know.

1. The inside of the car was a blast furnace.
2. The water lilies covered the pond like a heavy blanket.
3. The sunset is a fire in the evening sky.
4. When Kelly dances she's as graceful as a swan.
5. John rushed through the door like a tornado.
6. The runners are racehorses approaching the finish line.
7. The woods were a cool umbrella on a hot, sunny day.

ACTIVITY D Explain each of these metaphors by telling what two things are being compared and how they are alike.

1. His laughter is sunshine on a gloomy day.
2. My room was a refrigerator when I got home.
3. The snow was a white blanket on the lawn.
4. Her hat was a garden of wildflowers.
5. The party was a three-ring circus.
6. The hamster was a bolt of lightning across the room.
7. Jake was a mule about making up his mind.
8. Our dog Derby is a pillow for us.

ACTIVITY E Match the metaphor parts in Column A with those in Column B to make complete sentences.

Column A

1. The aroma of breakfast cooking
2. The child's messy room
3. The astronomy book
4. The tall hedge
5. The black clouds
6. Our teacher
7. The bubbling coffeepot
8. His new computer

Column B

a. was a volcano about to erupt.
b. were the warning flags for the storm.
c. is the captain of our learning ship.
d. is my personal alarm clock.
e. was the guardian of the garden.
f. is his window on the world.
g. was her private spaceship.
h. is a wastebasket with windows.

ACTIVITY F Write a sentence using a simile or a metaphor to describe each of these things.

1. rush hour in a big city
2. a mountain road
3. a sleeping baby
4. an old car
5. a worn-out baseball glove
6. a playful kitten
7. a new skateboard
8. an old quilt
9. a skyscraper
10. a thunderstorm

WRITER'S CORNER

Think of a person you admire. It can be a person you know or a character you have read about in a book. Write four sentences describing the person, using similes and metaphors. Use exaggeration to make your description humorous or dramatic.

Homophones

Homophones are words that sound alike but have different spellings and meanings. There are many homophones in the English language. They can sometimes be confusing for writers. Here are two sentences with pairs of homophones. What is the meaning of each word in red?

> I saw the cat *peek* around the corner to watch the birds on the *peak* of the roof.
>
> Don't lose your bus *fare* or you'll have to walk home from the *fair*.

Peek and *peak* are homophones, and so are *fare* and *fair*. Because homophones have different meanings, make sure to use the correct one when you write. Check a dictionary if you are unsure of the spelling.

ACTIVITY A Choose the correct homophone for each of these definitions. Then use the word you did not choose in a sentence. Use a dictionary if necessary.

1. a material used in making paper (would wood)
2. a survey of people's opinions on an issue (poll pole)
3. a time of calm and quiet (piece peace)
4. a place to dock a boat (pier peer)
5. the head of a school (principle principal)
6. a rabbit (hair hare)
7. a street or highway (road rode)
8. a period of seven days (week weak)
9. a type of drink (tee tea)
10. a tool used to chop logs (acts ax)
11. a home for an airplane (hanger hangar)
12. a piece of string (chord cord)

ACTIVITY B Complete these sentences with the correct homophones from the list.

paws, pause	wood, would	ate, eight
break, brake	moose, mousse	scent, sent

1. The bear held the food in its huge _____ while it _____ its dinner.

2. Speeding downhill, I was afraid that the _____ on my bike _____ not work.

3. Did you see the _____ at the zoo?

4. Paul Bunyan helped the pioneers get _____ to build their towns and villages.

5. The fragrant _____ of the roses made me _____ for a few moments to smell them.

6. I was afraid the window would _____ if I tried to force it open.

7. My uncle _____ me _____ comic books for my birthday.

8. Carmen made chocolate _____.

ACTIVITY C Give definitions for each pair of homophones below. Use a dictionary if necessary.

1. guessed, guest
2. gait, gate
3. lie, lye
4. taught, taut
5. fair, fare
6. aisle, isle
7. miner, minor
8. idle, idol

WRITER'S CORNER

Work with a partner to write a homophone for each of these words: *made, seller, urn, prints, hale, hour, doe.* Then try to use each pair of homophones in one sentence. Be creative and write some fun sentences. Use a dictionary if necessary.

Tech Tip Find three homophones in an online article.

The following homophones are often confusing for writers. Do you use these words correctly when you write?

HOMOPHONE	MEANING OR USE	EXAMPLE
your	possessive adjective	Your drawing is beautiful.
you're	contraction for *you are*	You're very kind.
there	adverb that tells *where*	I put it there.
their	possessive adjective	Their books are lost.
they're	contraction for *they are*	They're late.
to	preposition meaning "toward"	Let's go to the store.
too	adverb meaning "also" or "overly"	It's too bright!
two	adjective meaning "one more than one"	I have two cats.

Did you notice that sometimes three words are homophones? Some other examples are *so, sew,* and *sow* and *rein, rain,* and *reign.* You have to be especially careful when you use one of these words.

ACTIVITY D Complete these sentences. Choose the correct homophones from the chart.

1. If you're not _____ tired, we can go _____ the movies after dinner.

2. _____ parents asked the girls to be home early, but _____ walking home now in the dark.

3. _____ going to brush _____ teeth before bed, aren't you?

4. Put these _____ books on the shelf _____.

5. _____ dogs always want to run over _____.

6. Let's go _____ the store and get _____ baseball cards for our collection.

7. _____ brother thinks _____ lucky because you won the contest.

River City ROCKETS

Alejandro Nicolini   pitcher

left field

Astoria THUNDER

Springfield PANTHERS

ACTIVITY E Tell which of the three homophones belongs in each blank. Use a dictionary if necessary.

1. When the _____ started, Katy held tight to the horse's _____. (rein reign rain)

2. The _____ was resting under the branches of the straggly _____. (yew you ewe)

3. Put your _____ into the water and row fast, _____ we won't have a chance to win the race. (or ore oar)

4. On the high _____, the pirates were about to _____ the unsuspecting ship. (sees seas seize)

5. My jacket is _____ torn that my aunt will have to _____ it. (so sow sew)

6. Mom and I will _____ each other at the _____ counter in the grocery store. (meat mete meet)

7. The twins _____ their bikes on the _____ through the forest. (rowed road rode)

ACTIVITY F Rewrite these sentences to make sense by finding and correcting the incorrect homophones. Check a dictionary if necessary. Each sentence has more than one incorrect homophone.

1. She was so vein that she looked at herself in the mirror for ours.

2. He cent an e-mail to his friend, who replied write away.

3. My sister has a knew diamond engagement wring.

4. We're going too take a sightseeing crews on Lake Erie.

5. The Straight of Gibraltar connects the Mediterranean See and the Atlantic Ocean.

WRITER'S CORNER

Write five sentences with incorrect homophones like those in Activity F. Trade papers with a partner and correct each other's sentences.

Nonsense Verse

Nonsense verse is poetry that is completely silly. It describes things that are so strange that they could never happen in the real world. Writers of nonsense verse dream up weird creatures and unbelievable situations. Poets use rhyme, choose funny-sounding words, and even make up words. Sometimes poets use couplets, which are a pair of pairing lines. The purpose for writing nonsense verse is to have fun and make readers laugh.

Poet Jack Prelutsky likes to have this kind of fun with words. Here are two examples of his nonsense verse.

A Foolish Cow

A foolish cow, declining greens,
ate jumping and vanilla beans.
Now she quivers, now she quakes,
now she gives vanilla shakes.

The Otter and the Ocelot

The otter and the ocelot,
as fortunate as they could be,
now sail the seas upon their yacht—
they won the OCELOTTERY.

Otter

Ocelot

What silly, impossible thing happens in each poem? What picture of the cow do the words *quivers* and *quakes* help form in your imagination? What words did the poet use to make up *ocelottery*? Which words in each poem rhyme?

ACTIVITY A Which of these characters do you think might appear in a nonsense verse? Tell why you think so.

1. a cow that jumps over the moon
2. a girl and boy who fall down a hill
3. a flying groundhog
4. a rooster that lives in a barn
5. an ostrich ballerina

6. a sunburned polar bear

7. a truck driver

8. a singing soccer player

9. an owl in a tree

10. a sad clown

ACTIVITY B The characters from tall tales can be good subjects for nonsense verse. Copy these couplets and fill in the blanks with rhyming words.

1. Paul Bunyan sneezed a mighty sneeze
   And felled an acre full of _____.

2. Sourdough Sam cooked eggs and ham
   And served them up with toast and _____.

3. Pecos Bill gave the snake a terrible shake
   And said, "A fine lasso you'll _____."

4. Sue rode a fish as big as a whale.
   It had flashing eyes and a lashing _____.

5. Flatboat Annie spins with style and grace,
   But sometimes she falls on her _____.

6. John Henry could lift two cows with one hand.
   He was the strongest steel driver in the _____.

Barn owl

Tech Tip Use a computer program to illustrate your nonsense verse.

WRITER'S CORNER

Choose an idea from Activity A or one of your own to use in a rhyming nonsense couplet. You might try making up an animal name combination.
Example:
When the alligatortoise comes over to play,
Will the eerie elephantom scare him away?

Creative Writing • 423

Rhyme Scheme

Rhyme is one of the features that make nonsense verses fun to read. There are many ways to make a rhyming verse. Look back at Jack Prelutsky's poems on page 422. The first one is written in rhyming couplets. Each pair of lines rhymes. In the second poem, every other line rhymes. These are examples of rhyme schemes. A poet usually uses the same rhyme scheme throughout a poem.

Meter

In a word with more than one syllable, one syllable is always stressed. It is pronounced more loudly than the other syllables. When you speak, you also stress, or emphasize, different words within a sentence. In a poem these stressed words and syllables fall in a regular pattern. This pattern is called meter.

Read the poem and notice how the syllables are marked. The checks are above the stressed syllables. Each line has four stressed syllables. There is one unstressed syllable between each pair of stressed syllables.

A foolish cow, declining greens,

ate jumping and vanilla beans.

Now she quivers, now she quakes,

now she gives vanilla shakes.

A poem can have a different number of stressed syllables in each line and a different number of unstressed syllables between the stressed ones. The beginning of this nursery rhyme has just two stressed syllables in each line and two unstressed syllables between the stressed ones.

Little Jack Horner

Sat in a corner

ACTIVITY C Read each line of poetry. Tell how many stressed syllables it has.

1. The owl and the pussycat went to sea
2. Simple Simon met a pieman
3. Peter Piper picked a peck of pickled peppers
4. Betty Botter bought some butter
5. Whether the weather be fine

ACTIVITY D This is the beginning of a nonsense verse by Laura Richards. Copy it and circle the pairs of rhyming words. Mark the stressed and unstressed syllables. Then underline the made-up words.

Eletelephony

Once there was an elephant,

Who tried to use the telephant—

No! No! I mean an elephone

Who tried to use the telephone—

(Dear me! I am not certain quite

That even now I've got it right.)

Ring! Ring!

WRITER'S CORNER

Write a nonsense verse that is at least four lines long. You can use your couplet from the Writer's Corner on page 423 or think of a new idea. Choose a rhyme scheme and use it throughout your poem. Try to keep the same number of stressed syllables in each line.

Storytellers' Contests

Imagine a group of loggers or cowboys sitting around a campfire in the 1800s. There is no radio or TV, so they are telling stories to one another. Each one tries to get the biggest laugh by making his story funnier and more exaggerated than anyone else's. These stories might even have become part of the tall tales about Paul Bunyan and Pecos Bill.

The same kind of thing happens today when storytellers enter storytelling festivals or liars' contests. The point of these contests is to win the prize by telling the funniest, most outrageous story of all the contestants.

The stories told in these festivals and contests have many of the same features as tall tales.

- There may be a main character who is larger than life.
- There is often a problem that needs to be solved or something that needs to be explained.
- The solution or explanation might involve things that cannot happen in the real world.
- Exaggerations, similes, and metaphors are used to make the story funny.

Audience

A storyteller needs to think about the ages and interests of the audience. Young children may not understand similes and metaphors that older students would. People in the country might find different things funny than people in the city. Adults might not get the exaggeration in a story about playing video games. You will be telling a story to your classmates. Keep their interests—and senses of humor—in mind.

Body Language and Voice

Storytellers in festivals and contests generally do not use props. They use their voices and body language to win over the audience and to make people laugh.

When you tell your story, speak loudly enough so everyone can hear you. If your story includes dialogue, try to change your voice for each character. Use your voice to make your exaggerations more effective. Emphasize actions by using appropriate body language. For example, use your arms to show size and movement. Smile to let everyone know that you are enjoying the humor in your story.

ACTIVITY A **Take turns reading aloud these selections from tall tales. Read the dialogue the way you think the character might have said it. Discuss the differences in the way your classmates perform.**

1. John Henry was anxious to prove that he could beat the steam drill that threatened his job. Determined, he insisted, "A man ain't nothing but a man. I'm gonna do my best and beat that machine."

2. Johnny Appleseed carried his apple seeds all across the country. When settlers tried to pay him for the seeds, he'd say, "No, no, I don't want any money. Just take and plant the seeds. Sow them and wait for the harvest."

3. Stormalong was 20 feet tall before he was 12. That year he strolled down to the wharf and said to a boat captain, "There's nothing I can't do. I want to hire on to your boat. I'm a fighter and a worker. I'll make you proud."

SPEAKER'S CORNER

Your class is going to have a storytellers' contest. The topic is "why I can't turn in my homework today," and the story cannot be longer than two minutes. Start writing ideas. Make them as wild and as imaginative as possible. Remember that this story is not supposed to be true. It's supposed to make people laugh.

Prepare Your Story

Telling a funny story requires careful preparation. Look over your ideas from the Speaker's Corner on page 427. Choose the one that you can expand with the most exaggerated details. Maybe a spaceship full of pirates landed in your backyard, and the pirates stole your homework paper to draw a treasure map. Think of the wildest ideas you can of how the pirates looked, what they wore, and how they talked.

Make notes or a graphic organizer to help you come up with details. Write any similes and metaphors that will help you describe your characters. Use the wildest exaggerations you can to make your story funny. Remember that in a story like this, anything is possible.

Practice

Before you present a funny story to an audience, practice telling it several times in front of a mirror. Experiment with different voices, facial expressions, and body language to see which ones best convey the meaning. Choose words and expressions that seem the funniest when you say them aloud.

When you are satisfied with your presentation, ask a friend or family member to be your audience. Tell your story, paying attention to the parts that make your listener laugh. Check that there are no "dead spots" where your listener does not seem at all amused. Ask your listener to give you suggestions for making your storytelling even better.

Listening Tips

Just as practice makes you a better speaker, practice can make you a better listener. Here are some things that you will want to keep in mind when you are listening to a storyteller.

- Keep your eyes on the speaker so he or she will know you are listening.
- Pay attention to the speaker's tone of voice and body language so you do not miss any clues about what happens in the story.
- Listen carefully for figurative language and use it to create pictures in your imagination.
- Show that you are enjoying the story and its humor. Laugh!

ACTIVITY B Complete the story you began in the Speaker's Corner on page 427. Write details on note cards that you can refer to as you talk. Jot down exaggerations, similes, and metaphors that you want to use. Experiment with different ways to use your voice and body to make your story as funny as you can.

ACTIVITY C Practice telling your story to a classmate. Use the practice tips from page 428. Have your listener time you to make sure your story is not longer than two minutes. Ask your listener to give you ideas for which parts of your story work and which do not. Ask the person to identify any details that he or she did not understand or did not find funny. You may want to change those details before presenting your story.

SPEAKER'S CORNER

Take turns with your classmates in telling your stories. As each person finishes, you might jot down a few notes about his or her story so that you can remember who gave what explanation for the missing homework. When everyone has finished, talk about your favorite parts of one another's stories.

Prewriting and Drafting

Tall tales are fun to read and to write. Now it is time to use what you have read about in this chapter to write your own tall tale.

Prewriting

Imogen's family was having a party to celebrate her grandfather's birthday. At the party each family member was going to perform something special. Imogen's grandfather enjoyed tall tales, so she decided to write a tall tale and read it aloud at the party.

Imogen began by choosing a hero and a setting, freewriting her ideas, and then organizing her ideas. She thought of her favorite characters and activities to brainstorm ideas.

Choosing a Hero and a Setting

Imogen liked tall tales about super-strong heroes of the frontier. But she thought that a modern hero might be fun too. She made a list of some ideas for both.

- *a cowgirl who can run faster than any person or animal*

- *a boy who has a computer for a brain*

- *a very tall boy who can jump over mountains*

Imogen's grandfather was the tallest person Imogen knew. So she decided to write about a tall boy. She even decided to name the character Jack, after her grandfather.

Imogen's family lived near Sequoia National Park in California. Imogen once went on a hike there with her grandfather. She thought it might be fun to set her tall tale in a familiar place.

Imogen thought that Jack could be a park ranger. She imagined many ways that a very tall boy could be helpful as a park ranger.

Your Turn

Choose your hero and setting. If you are having trouble, answer the following questions.

- Is my hero a boy or a girl?
- What is my hero's special ability?
- Is my hero's special ability better suited to the city or to a country setting?
- What job does my hero have? How does my hero's special ability help him or her do that job?

Choose the hero that interests you the most. Which one makes you think of a lot of ideas for your tall tale?

Freewriting

Imogen thought about her hike at Sequoia National Park. A ranger had told about a huge snowstorm a few years earlier. Imogen thought that a snowstorm might create a good problem for Jack to solve.

Imogen started writing notes about Jack's childhood, his abilities, a problem, and how Jack solves the problem. Here are Imogen's notes.

- *Jack Johnson, a big, bouncy baby, is born in a town right by the park.*

- *huge snowstorm hits and buries the whole town in snow*

- *Jack is the only one who can get anywhere because he can do stuff that real people can't do.*

- *went up to the clouds and made snowballs out of them*

- *found out that the clouds tasted like mashed potatoes*

- *He became a park ranger.*

Organizing Ideas

Imogen had to organize her notes before she started to write. Here is the plan that Imogen made.

Setting: Sequoia National Park

Hero: Jack Johnson

Jack's Life: born in town near park, popular athlete, becomes a park ranger

Problem: snowstorm that traps the townspeople in their houses

Solution: Jack gets rid of clouds by making them into scoops of mashed potatoes. He invites the town to celebrate with him by eating snow-cloud mashed potatoes.

Prewriting · Drafting · Content Editing · Revising · Copyediting · Proofreading · Publishing

Your Turn

Use your freewriting notes to organize your tall tale. Look at Imogen's plan if you **Organization** need help. Organize your notes by naming your setting, hero, hero's life, problem, and solution.

Your Turn

Freewrite your ideas about your tall tale. If you have chosen a character and setting that are based on real life, write what you know about the person or place.

Drafting

Imogen was ready to begin writing her tall tale. She used her plan and her freewriting notes to begin her draft. As she wrote she realized that she would have to exaggerate the details of her tale more to fit the style of a tall tale. She also added some dialogue so that readers could get an idea of Jack's personality. Here is Imogen's first draft.

Jumping Jack Johnson

Jack Johnson was born in a town just outside of Sequoia National Park in central California. He was a happy baby who just wasn't still in his crib for a moment. He was a bouncing ball that never stopped. By the time Jack was in his teens, his legs were as long as stilts and he spent his high school years as captain of the basketball team, high-jumping champion, and the county's undefeated pole-vaulter. He was very popular. He was never alone at the lunch table. Everyone new him as Jumping Jack.

When he applied to become a park ranger at Sequoia National Park, he was immediately accepted. "In a single jump, I'll reach people who are lost," said Jack. "I can care for the trees and the animals. My gifts can help everyone." By the time Jumping Jack was 20, he could jump higher than a sequoia tree, higher than a skyscraper, even higher than a bird could fly. The townspeople would whisper "That young Jack must have springs in his feet." But Jack was more than his jumps. He also had the nicest personality of anyone in town.

Nature didn't wait long to put Jumping Jack to the test. On a cold day in January, a sudden snowstorm blue up. Snow fell for three days straight. When the snow finally stopped, all that could be seen were the tips of chimeneys peaking out of the snow. The thick snow clouds would not let a ray of sunshine through. The townspeople were buried in a sea of white.

Only Jumping Jack had no problems getting to work. Jack waited for several hours for the head ranger, but he never came. No one came. It was then that Jack realized the townspeople couldn't leave their homes. So Jack went back to the town to come to their rescue. He jumped as straight and as high as he could. Then he grabbed a corner of one of the snow clouds. He formed a small snowball. He did this again and again. When he got hungery, he took a bite from one of these snowballs. "Yummy! Mashed potatoes," he said in surprise. Soon he had turned the snow clouds into thousands of scoops of mashed potatoes.

Jack came back down. The sun was shining. The snow melted in minutes. The townspeople flooded out of their houses, cheering. "celebrate with me!" invited Jack. "Let's all share this delicious solushun to our problem." That night everyone had mashed potatoes for dinner.

Prewriting

Drafting

Content Editing

Revising

Copyediting

Proofreading

Publishing

Your Turn

- Use your plan and freewriting notes to write your first draft.
- Remember to describe your hero's childhood. Include details about your hero's special ability.
- Make the problem or the solution exaggerated and funny.
- Tell the events in time order.
- Double-space your draft so that you will have room to make changes later.

Say Something!

Just as in other kinds of stories, dialogue can be important in a tall tale. When characters speak, they often reveal something about their feelings, personalities, or thoughts. Dialogue can help make your tall tale more interesting.

When you write dialogue for your characters, remember to use words that are appropriate to the time in which they live. Put each character's exact words within quotation marks.

Content Editing

Imogen liked what she had written so far. She was sure that her grandfather would enjoy the main character of the tall tale being named after him. But Imogen knew that the tall tale could be made better by content editing. She used the following checklist to content edit her draft.

When Imogen was finished, she asked her friend Viola to content edit her draft. Viola was in a book club at school. The club talked often about what was good and bad about stories. Imogen knew that Viola would be able to give her helpful feedback. Viola would check to make sure that the ideas were clear. She could also suggest things that Imogen might delete or ways in which Imogen might improve her tall tale.

Viola read Imogen's tall tale once to get an idea of the story. She laughed out loud when she got to the part about the mashed potatoes. Then Viola read the draft a few more times, checking for each item on the checklist. She wrote some notes and suggestions to talk with Imogen about later. When Viola was finished, she and Imogen looked at the draft together.

Content Editor's Checklist

- [ ] Does the story revolve around a larger-than-life hero?
- [ ] Is there an interesting setting?
- [ ] Are the events told in time order?
- [ ] Are the hero, main events, and details described in an exaggerated way?
- [ ] Are all the details necessary?
- [ ] Are similes and metaphors used in the descriptions?
- [ ] Is the tale told in everyday language?
- [ ] Does the hero solve the problem in a funny way?

Grammar in Action

Find one exclamatory sentence and one imperative sentence in Imogen's draft.

Viola liked Imogen's idea. She thought that it was a funny tall tale. She thought that Imogen had made Jack very likable. Viola also thought

Voice that the draft had a nice conversational tone. Here are some of Viola's suggestions.

- I like the way you describe Jack. But can you add any more details that describe him as a baby?
- Can you give more description of the town? At first I pictured a big city.
- The second paragraph is kind of confusing. Does Jack become a ranger before he is 20 or after?
- The part about Jack being popular at school seems unnecessary.
- I like the metaphor *he was a bouncing ball*. You might add a simile in the second paragraph when you describe Jack's jumps—maybe *graceful as a swan*.
- I really like the way that you exaggerated the details. But can you add more? I think they would make your tall tale even funnier.

Imogen thought that Viola had some good ideas. She really liked Viola's suggestion about the simile. Imogen always had trouble thinking of similes. She went right to work making her changes.

Your Turn

- Read your tall tale again. Do the characters come alive? Did you include enough dialogue?
- Use the Content Editor's Checklist to remind you of things to look for as you content edit your draft. Remember to read for one item on the checklist at a time.
- Work with a partner to content edit each other's drafts. Take notes as you content edit. Be positive in your comments.
- Meet with your partner and discuss each other's suggestions. Remember to compliment your partner on the things you liked in his or her draft.
- Listen carefully to the suggestions that your partner has. Consider his or her suggestions, but remember that the final decisions are yours.

Writer's Tip Use similes and metaphors to exaggerate details or show how a character is like something. It will make your story fun to read.

Prewriting

Drafting

Content Editing

Revising

Copyediting

Proofreading

Publishing

Revising

This is Imogen's revised draft.

Jack Johnson
Park Ranger

Jumping Jack Johnson

Jack Johnson was born in a ~~sleepy, little~~ town just outside of Sequoia National Park in

central California. He was a happy baby who just wasn't still in his crib for a

He jiggled and wiggled and giggled.

moment. He was a bouncing ball that never stopped. By the time Jack was in his

teens, his legs were as long as stilts and he spent his high school years as captain

of the basketball team, high-jumping champion, and the county's undefeated pole-

vaulter. ~~He was very popular. He was never alone at the lunch table.~~ Everyone new

him as Jumping Jack.

When he applied to become a park ranger at Sequoia National Park, he was

immediately accepted. "In a single jump, I'll reach people who are lost," said Jack.

"I can care for the trees and the animals. My gifts can help everyone." By the time

Jumping Jack was 20, he could jump higher than a sequoia tree, higher than a

When Jack jumped, he was as graceful as a swan.

skyscraper, even higher than a bird could fly. The townspeople would whisper

"That young Jack must have springs in his feet." But Jack was more than his jumps.

He also had the nicest personality of anyone in town.

Nature didn't wait long to put Jumping Jack to the test. On a cold day in

as thick as cotton

January, a sudden snowstorm blue up. Snow fell for three days straight. When the

snow finally stopped, all that could be seen were the tips of chimeneys peaking out of the snow. The thick snow clouds would not let a ray of sunshine through. The townspeople were buried in a sea of white.

He just jumped through the mountain of snow that covered his house and landed in the park eight miles away.

Only Jumping Jack had no problems getting to work. Jack waited for several hours for the head ranger, but he never came. No one came. It was then that Jack realized the townspeople couldn't leave their homes. So Jack ~~went~~ *jumped* back to the town to come to their rescue. He jumped as straight and as high as he could. Then he grabbed a corner of one of the snow clouds. He formed a small snowball. He did this again and again. When he got hungery, he took a bite from one of these snowballs. "Yummy! Mashed potatoes," he said in surprise. Soon he had turned the snow clouds into thousands of scoops of mashed potatoes.

Jack came back down. The sun was shining. The snow melted in minutes. The townspeople flooded out of their houses, cheering. "celebrate with me!" invited Jack. "Let's all share this delicious solushun to our problem." That night everyone had mashed potatoes for dinner.

Prewriting

Drafting

Content Editing

Revising

Copyediting

Proofreading

Publishing

Imogen looked over Viola's suggestions and decided to make a few changes to her draft.

- What words did Imogen add to describe Jack as a baby?
- How did Imogen describe the town?
- Imogen saw that the order in the second paragraph was confusing. What did she do to make the paragraph clearer?
- Why did Imogen delete the sentences about Jack being popular and never being alone at the lunch table?

As Imogen was revising, Viola suggested

 Word Choice

another simile. Do you see it? Imogen added another exaggerated detail and changed the word *went* to *jumped* in the fourth paragraph. She thought that both changes made her tall tale funnier.

Your Turn

Use your own ideas and suggestions from your content editor to improve your tall tale. When you have finished, go over the Content Editor's Checklist again. Can you answer yes to each question?

Copyediting and Proofreading

Copyediting

Imogen was glad that Viola had content edited her draft. But she knew that her tall tale would be even better after she copyedited it. She wanted to make sure that the sentences in her draft were correct and that the words she used were exact. Imogen used this Copyeditor's Checklist.

Copyeditor's Checklist

☐ Has the writing been checked for rambling or run-on sentences?

☐ Are short, choppy sentences combined?

☐ Is there a variety in sentence length?

☐ Do all the words, especially those that are homophones, mean what you think they mean?

Imogen found a run-on sentence in the first paragraph. Look at how she revised it.

Revision: By the time Jack was in his teens, his legs were as long as stilts. He spent his high school years as captain of the basketball team, high-jumping champion, and the county's undefeated pole-vaulter.

In the fourth paragraph, Imogen combined *Then he grabbed a corner of one of the snow clouds* and *He formed a small snowball* into one sentence.

👀 Sentence Fluency

Do you see another place where Imogen might combine sentences?

Imogen found three homophone mistakes. In the first paragraph, she wrote *new* when she meant to write *knew.* In the third paragraph, she wrote that the chimneys were *peaking out* instead of *peeking out.* Can you find the other homophone mistake?

Your Turn

Use the Copyeditor's Checklist to copyedit your draft. Remember to look for one kind of mistake at a time. Reading aloud your draft might help you hear rambling and run-on sentences. It also might help you hear places where sentences might be combined. Pay special attention to your word choice. Don't forget to check that homophones are spelled correctly.

Proofreading

Because Imogen would be reading her tall tale aloud, she did not want to get tripped up at the party over misspelled words or incorrect grammar. A proofreader would check for misspelled words and mistakes in capitalization, grammar, and punctuation.

Proofreader's Checklist

- ☐ Are the paragraphs indented?
- ☐ Are all the words spelled correctly?
- ☐ Are capitalization and punctuation correct?
- ☐ Is the grammar correct?
- ☐ Have you checked that no new mistakes were added while editing?

Imogen's brother Edmund was in the seventh grade. He was really good at language arts and agreed to proofread Imogen's draft. Edmund used the checklist below.

Edmund found three misspelled words. In the third paragraph, he changed *chimeneys* to *chimneys*. He also changed *hungery* to *hungry*. What was the third misspelled word that Edmund found?

Conventions

He also spotted a capitalization mistake in the fifth paragraph. Do you see Imogen's mistake?

Your Turn

Read your tall tale carefully, using the Proofreader's Checklist.

- Look for only one kind of mistake at a time. Each time you read, you have another chance to find mistakes that you missed.
- Pay special attention to the dialogue in your tall tale.
- Make sure that spoken parts follow the rules for the capitalization and punctuation of dialogue.

When you have finished proofreading your draft, trade drafts with a partner. Go through each other's drafts carefully. Be sure to have a dictionary nearby.

Prewriting
Drafting
Content Editing
Revising
Copyediting
Proofreading
Publishing

Publishing

Imogen read her draft with the revisions one last time to make sure that she had included all her corrections. Then she was ready to write the final copy. Again, she typed her tall tale on a computer.

Jumping Jack Johnson

Jack Johnson was born in a sleepy, little town just outside of Sequoia National Park in central California. He was a happy baby who just wasn't still in his crib for a moment. He jiggled and wiggled and giggled. He was a bouncing ball that never stopped. By the time Jack was in his teens, his legs were as long as stilts. He spent his high school years as captain of the basketball team, high-jumping champion, and the county's undefeated pole-vaulter. Everyone knew him as Jumping Jack.

By the time Jumping Jack was 20, he could jump higher than a sequoia tree, higher than a skyscraper, even higher than a bird could fly. When Jack jumped, he was as graceful as a swan. The townspeople would whisper "That young Jack must have springs in his feet." But Jack was more than his jumps. He also had the nicest personality of anyone in town. When he applied to become a park ranger at Sequoia National Park, he was immediately accepted. "In a single jump, I'll reach people who are lost," said Jack. "I can care for the trees and the animals. My gifts can help everyone."

Nature didn't wait long to put Jumping Jack to the test. One cold day in January, a sudden snowstorm blew up. Snow as thick as cotton fell for three days straight. When the snow finally stopped, all that could be seen were the tips of chimneys peeking out of the snow. The thick snow clouds would not let a ray of sunshine through. The townspeople were buried in a sea of white.

Only Jumping Jack had no problems getting to work. He just jumped through the mountain of snow that covered his house and landed in the park eight miles away. Jack waited for several hours for the head ranger, but he never came. No one came. It was then that Jack realized the townspeople couldn't leave their homes. So Jack jumped back to the town to come to their rescue. He jumped as straight and as high as he could. Then he grabbed a corner of one of the snow clouds and formed a small snowball. He did this again and again. When he got hungry, he took a bite from one of these snowballs. "Yummy! Mashed potatoes," he said in surprise. Soon he had turned the snow clouds into thousands of scoops of mashed potatoes.

When he came back down, the sun was shining. The snow melted in minutes. The townspeople flooded out of their houses, cheering. "Celebrate with me!" invited Jack. "Let's all share this delicious solution to our problem." That night everyone had mashed potatoes for dinner.

Imogen drew a picture of Jack. Her mom took the completed tale and picture and had them bound between two covers because she was going to give the tall tale to her grandfather as a gift. Whenever you publish your work, your goal

 Presentation

is to share your thoughts and experiences with other people. Be sure your tall tale looks as neat, clean, and clear as you can make it.

There are many ways you can publish your tall tale. Ask friends and family to tell you what they think.

 Write a song about your tall-tale character. Using poetry and verse, turn your tall tale into a funny song.

 Record yourself reading your tall tale and upload it as a podcast on the class blog. Invite classmates to listen and share their thoughts on the class blog.

 Make your tall tale come to life. Using computer programs, illustrate and then animate your tall tale. You can add music and sound effects to round out the story.

 Action! Cast your classmates as the characters in your tall tale. Use a video recorder to film the tall tale and play it on Parents' Night.

Your Turn

Before you write or print out your final copy, read your tall tale one more time.

- If you type your tall tale, use your computer's spell-checker. Then write or print out your final copy.
- You might make a drawing of your hero to include with your tale, just as Imogen did.
- Decide as a class how you will publish your tall tales.
- You might also share your tall tales with other classes, especially classes of younger kids. The tall tales could be read to a whole class, or each person could read to one or two younger kids.

Persuasive Writing

LiNK

R U Reading Online?

Elizabeth Birr Moje, TimeforKids.com

Does surfing the Internet count as reading?

Many kids spend hours online. They move from site to site, checking e-mails and chat[ting]. Are they reading? That question is at the heart of a current debate.

Yes!

Sometimes we read in short bursts and snippets. That is the way we read when we're surfing the Web. Studies show that reading on the Web is a sophisticated reading experience because readers must process information in so many different forms: photos, videos, charts, and graphs. The information that readers access is unlimited. Links may lead to related information, which might enrich the reading experience. . . .

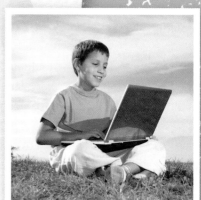

Without Internet access, these kids would not have been reading in their free time. The more people read, the more likely they are to develop stronger skills. If surfing the Web motivates kids to read—even if it is a short period of time— then that is a good thing. . . . It just depends on the type of text and how you use it.

> Persuasive writing, like this piece above, convinces
>   the reader of a point.

442

CHAPTER 7

Monday, April 18, 20— • Hillsdale Herald • Premier Publications, Inc.

Section 1 | Page 8

Letter to the Editor
Be Hardheaded About Wearing a Bike Helmet!

Spring is in the air, and many people are out riding their bikes again. One thing I am not seeing, though, are many people wearing helmets while they are riding. I believe our city should pass a helmet law for bike riders, both young and old alike.

Statistics show that wearing a helmet while bike riding can prevent a serious head injury or even death. According to the Bicycle Safety Institute in Arlington, Virginia, more than 800 lives per year are lost as a result of bike accidents in the United States. About three-fourths of them involve head injuries. Hundreds of thousands of bicyclists with injuries visit emergency rooms each year. More than half of these are children and young teens.

There are no federal laws regulating bicycle helmets. However, at least 20 states and more than 100 communities nationwide have helmet laws. While most of the current laws apply only to younger riders, police tell parents to set a good example for their children by wearing helmets themselves.

The cost of a helmet is a small price to pay for the safety it can give. Safety-approved helmets for children can be purchased for about $30.

In my opinion, adults must take a stand on the issue of wearing bike helmets. The statistics are clear, police agree, and the price is right. Let's use our heads and join the states and cities that can say, "It's the law!"

Jake West
Hoover Elementary School

Jake Wes

443

What Makes Good Persuasive Writing?

Persuasive writing tries to make readers agree with a position on a topic. Stating a position is easy, but persuading others to agree with you often requires presenting reasons that are supported by evidence. You can find examples of persuasive writing almost anywhere, such as advertisements, letters to the editor, newspaper editorials, and political speeches.

Position

Before drafting a persuasive article, a writer must choose a topic that has two sides, which are sometimes called opposing views. Then the writer chooses one side, or viewpoint, taking a clear position on the topic. The position appears in the introduction of the article and should tell exactly where the writer stands on the topic. The position is summarized again in the conclusion.

Introduction

The introduction to a persuasive article is where you state your position on a topic. The introduction is also a place to grab the reader's attention and to explain your purpose for writing.

Body

The body of your persuasive article is where you will convince your audience. This is where you present your reasons and evidence in detail. Each reason often has its own paragraph with statistics, facts, or examples that support it.

You can also use the body of your persuasive article to rebut arguments against your position. State the opposing arguments, then show why they are weak or unimportant.

ACTIVITY A Choose three questions below and write one reason for each side of a persuasive article on each topic.

EXAMPLE **Should school lunchrooms have vending machines that sell cold drinks and snacks?**

Yes—These foods and drinks taste good.

No—Most of these kinds of foods and drinks are not nutritious snacks.

A. Should our school have a "no homework on weekends" policy?

B. Should dog owners be made to keep their dogs on leashes?

C. Should students be able to use the school library after school or on Saturday?

D. Should all schools have swimming pools?

E. Should students be able to play music on the school bus?

F. Should students get a longer summer break?

G. Should students be fined if they litter?

H. Should parents pay their kids for doing chores?

I. Should kids be allowed to skip one test per school year?

ACTIVITY B **Brainstorm four topics that might be good topics for a persuasive article. Be sure that there are two sides to each topic.**

LiNK

Volunteering

You've seen news reports about people who need assistance after a natural disaster or animals in need. Maybe you've walked past people who are living on the streets. Or perhaps you've watched TV programs about how lonely and isolated older people can get. So what can you do about any of those things, you ask? The answer: You can volunteer.

Kidshealth.org

WRITER'S CORNER

Choose a topic from Activity B that you feel strongly about. Write four sentences to grab the reader's attention that might be found in the introduction to a persuasive article. Share your position with the class.

Grammar in Action What kinds of sentences are used in the last paragraph of the letter on page 443?

Conclusion

The conclusion to a persuasive article briefly summarizes the strongest reasons for your position. Avoid adding new reasons in the conclusion. Restate your position in a positive, convincing way. A persuasive conclusion should leave readers thinking about the topic. A well-written persuasive article might even cause a reader to take action in support of the writer's position.

ACTIVITY C Read the following pairs of introductions to persuasive articles. Tell which is the better introduction. Explain your answers.

1. **a.** The beauty of our national parks is unequaled in any other country. If we want that beauty to last, we must limit automobile traffic in the parks.

   b. There is a need for limiting automobile traffic in our national parks. I will present several good reasons for you to think about.

2. **a.** Even if you like to choose the outfits you wear to school each day, you ought to support the vote for uniforms in our school.

   b. Students in crisp shirts and blouses and coordinated slacks and skirts could soon describe a typical classroom in our school. Best of all, no more worrying about what to wear! Uniforms will take care of that decision.

3. **a.** If the new after-school program passes, you can visit with your friends after school. You might even work on projects together.

   b. Students should have an opportunity to stay in their own school after the day is over. This is only fair.

ACTIVITY D Write a position for each of these topics for a persuasive article.

1. the installation of traffic signals at a busy corner near school

2. a special area for skateboarding in a new park

3. a proposal to extend the school day by a half hour

4. a later curfew on weekend nights

5. limiting the amount of homework assignments to one hour a day

ACTIVITY E Rewrite each position to reflect your own feeling on the issue. Then write a reason for supporting it.

1. I believe we (should/should not) have tests in two subjects on the same day.
2. We (should/should not) be expected to clean our lunch tables before going outside.
3. I believe our city (must/must not) enact a bicycle licensing law.
4. I believe the gym (should/should not) be open for all students after school.
5. I believe there (should/should not) be a dress code for students.
6. We (should/should not) be allowed to hang out in front of the building before school.

ACTIVITY F Read this paragraph about the need for a local library. Write another paragraph that features a different reason for the library. Include explanations to support your reason.

One reason that our community must build a library is so our children and adults will have a resource for knowledge and pleasure. Statistics show that teenagers are more likely to excel in school if there is a library within three miles of their home. Besides books and magazines, public libraries offer computers with Internet access.

ACTIVITY G Choose a position that you wrote in Activity D. Then think of one reason for your position on the issue. Write a paragraph giving supporting evidence for that reason.

WRITER'S CORNER

Use the paragraph you wrote for Activity G to write a four-sentence conclusion for a persuasive article. Remember to summarize the reason and restate the position in a positive way.

Writing a Persuasive Article

Deciding what your topic is and your position on it are the first decisions you make when writing a persuasive article. Once you decide what your position is, the next step is to craft the evidence you gather into a clear and convincing article.

Persuasive Voice

A writer's voice, or tone, is one of the best tools to use in a persuasive article. The way you state your opinion and reasons affects the way your readers receive your message.

Here are some tones that writers use in persuasive writing.

uplifting	confident	enthusiastic
hopeful	concerned	warning

Effective persuasive writing shows readers that you care about your position on a topic. Your choice of words shows that you are confident and that your position and evidence are reasonable.

The writer of this paragraph about a possible permanent base on the moon used an enthusiastic tone to encourage readers to support the position.

The prospect of a permanent base on the moon is exciting. We could use the forces of the universe for an easier and cheaper mission to Mars. Just think of it! A spacecraft flying to Mars from the moon would need only one-sixth the amount of thrust to lift off from the surface of the moon compared with lifting off from Earth. Why is this? Because the moon's gravity is only one-sixth that of Earth's. The craft could be much lighter. It would not need to be aerodynamically built, because there is no atmosphere on the moon to cause drag on the spacecraft.

ACTIVITY A Tell which sentence in each pair is written in a more confident voice. Explain your answers.

1. **a.** A new Olympic-sized pool will meet the needs of our town on those hot summer days when we all want to relax in the sun and not be crowded.
   b. Our town could really use a second public pool.

2. **a.** If the curfew is passed, we can expect teens to be home earlier and to be less likely to get into trouble.
   b. Teens will be teens, but passing the new curfew might help families in our community.

3. **a.** The school district needs your vote next week to provide money for after-school activities.
   b. There is no limit to what our kids can do if we give them after-school activities, so we should pass next week's referendum.

4. **a.** Perhaps the county needs another fire station to keep up with the growth in population.
   b. Population growth in this county requires us to add a new fire station.

5. **a.** The city's water supply is in danger of drying up if we don't think about how to cut back on the amount we use.
   b. I think the city's water supply might dry up sometime, so get everyone you know to stop wasting so much water.

6. **a.** Undersea research seems like a good idea to me.
   b. Undersea research will have benefits for all forms of life.

7. **a.** It is unfair for town residents to get tickets for parking meters that are broken or defective.
   b. My mother says the parking meters are a menace to the tax-paying residents of this town.

WRITER'S CORNER

Think about writing an article on the position you wrote for the Writer's Corner on page 445. Talk with a partner about what tone is best for your topic. Write some ways you could revise your paragraph to make your tone stronger and clearer.

LiNK

Volunteering

Volunteering isn't like school: Instead of having choices made for you about where to go and what subjects to learn, you get to pick. You can choose what really interests you and who (or what) is most deserving of your time.

Kidshealth.org

Audience

Writers often write differently for different audiences. When you write a persuasive article, think about whom you are trying to convince. Think of reasons that appeal to that audience. For example, a person who is trying to persuade Congress to provide money for a new highway knows that politicians are concerned about the people they represent. The presenter might discuss how the highway would provide jobs for the representative's district.

Opinions

In Chapter 5 you discussed the difference between facts and opinions. When you write a persuasive article, your opinions should be supported by practical, logical ideas and facts. Opinion words are useful tools for expressing your position. Use words such as *should, ought, must,* and *best* to express your opinion.

ACTIVITY B Identify the words or phrases that make each sentence below an opinion. Then use your imagination to write one reason that supports each opinion.

1. The most amusing animal is the penguin.
2. Shel Silverstein is one of the funniest poets for kids.
3. Going to the beach is the best way to cool off on a hot day.
4. The trees in our neighborhood must be preserved.
5. I believe yellow, red, and blue are the prettiest colors.
6. Babe Ruth ought to be considered the best baseball player ever.

ACTIVITY C Write a position on an issue related to your school or community. Identify who would be the best audience for it.

ACTIVITY D Rewrite the following paragraph, changing the voice from uplifting to warning. Use your imagination.

An after-school reading program is needed. It would bring the students closer together and give us a sense of community. Together we can work for a common cause to improve students' reading ability. At the same time, we can greatly improve overall test scores. An after-school reading program is the perfect way to enrich the learning environment, both in and out of school.

ACTIVITY E Read the following sentences. The first sentence in each pair is an opinion. Tell whether the second sentence is a convincing reason. Explain your answers.

1. *Number the Stars* by Lois Lowry should be on our historical fiction book list.

   It won the Newbery Award and the Rebecca Caudill Award and is set in World War II.

2. *Wayside School Is Falling Down* by Louis Sachar should be on our list of humorous books.

   The paperback costs only $5.99.

3. Cantigny Park would be a good place for an educational end-of-year picnic.

   The First Division Museum there has historical information from World War I to the present.

4. The Museum of Science and Industry is a great place for an educational field trip.

   It has a really great gift shop and huge food court.

Museum of Science and Industry, Chicago, Illinois

Type your introduction with a computer program.

WRITER'S CORNER

Choose a tone for the position you wrote in Activity C. Then write four sentences as an introduction for a persuasive article on that position.

Expanding Sentences

Good writers vary the lengths of their sentences. You can make sentences longer by expanding them, using adjectives, adverbs, and prepositional phrases. Expanding sentences makes your sentences clearer and more interesting. Here are some ways to expand your sentences.

Expanding Sentences with Adjectives

You can write sentences that are colorful and interesting by adding adjectives before nouns. Colorful adjectives will expand sentences and help paint a mental picture for the reader. Look at the two sentences below.

Brian discovered a trunk in the corner of the attic.
Brian discovered a *dusty metal* trunk in a *gloomy* corner of the attic.

The writer expanded the sentence by adding the adjectives *dusty* and *metal* before the noun *trunk*. The writer also added the adjective *gloomy* before the noun *corner*.

Expanding Sentences with Adverbs

Adverbs also help expand sentences. Adverbs can tell how, when, or where. Adverbs usually come at the beginning of a sentence or after a verb. Look at the two sentences below.

The rain began to fall.
***Suddenly* the rain began to fall *furiously*.**

The writer improved the sentence by adding the adverb *Suddenly*, which tells when the rain fell, and the adverb *furiously*, which tells how it fell. Both words expand the sentence and help readers better understand when and how the rain fell.

ACTIVITY A Write two adjectives that could describe each noun in different ways.

1. ocean   **2.** car   **3.** picture   **4.** man   **5.** road

ACTIVITY B Expand these sentences by using colorful adjectives.

1. A _____ kite soared in the _____ sky.
2. The _____ iced tea was a treat on a _____ day.
3. We spotted a _____ whale not far from our _____ boat.
4. A _____ tourist wandered through the _____ streets.
5. The _____ tick of the clock echoed throughout the _____ house.
6. Chris bought a _____ pen at the _____ store.
7. Gavin used _____ paint to spruce up the _____ fence.
8. A _____ toad leaped into the _____ pond.
9. Dad's _____ tie was a gift from me.
10. Dominique and Ed bought a _____ car with _____ seats.

ACTIVITY C Expand these sentences by using adverbs.

1. The roller coaster sped _____ down the tracks.
2. Two astronauts floated _____ in space.
3. A cheetah walked _____ toward its prey.
4. _____ I picked up the crystal vase.
5. The ballerina danced _____ before the audience.
6. Ava opened her gift and smiled _____.
7. Shane answered the questions _____.
8. _____ I saw a deer cross the path.
9. As I _____ tiptoed across the room, the floor creaked _____ under my feet.
10. The wind whipped _____ across the field, making the trees bend _____.

WRITER'S CORNER

Write five descriptive sentences about your town. Trade paragraphs with a partner. Rewrite each other's paragraphs, adding adjectives and adverbs to make the paragraphs more interesting.

Grammar in Action.
Find the comma in the excerpt on page 445. Discuss how it is used.

Expanding Sentences with Prepositional Phrases

Prepositional phrases can also help expand sentences. A prepositional phrase is a group of words that begins with a preposition and ends with a noun or pronoun. *In the morning, behind the door,* and *over the fence* are prepositional phrases. Prepositional phrases can be used as adjectives or adverbs. They can begin a sentence or follow a noun or verb. Look at the two sentences below.

> **The boat floated slowly.**
> **The boat** *with the broken mast* **floated slowly** *down the river.*

The prepositional phrase *with the broken mast* describes the boat. *Down the river* tells where it floated. The prepositional phrases add descriptive details that give a clearer picture to the reader.

ACTIVITY D **Expand these sentences with prepositional phrases.**

1. Jon and Jan looked at the constellations _____.
2. I heard a loud noise _____.
3. Miguel carried his backpack _____.
4. _____ fell a shower of confetti.
5. The penguin waddled _____.
6. _____ the campers swam _____.
7. Stan cannot play baseball _____.
8. Put the package _____.
9. _____ is where you'll find the treasure chest.
10. The band played "The Star-Spangled Banner" _____.
11. _____ is where you will see the spotted owls.
12. _____ the submarine lurked.
13. Theo watched the movie _____.

ACTIVITY E Expand these sentences with adjectives, adverbs, or prepositional phrases.

1. I heard the _____ stairs creaking _____.
2. The _____ bear walked toward me _____.
3. The _____ cat crept _____.
4. _____ icicles hung _____.
5. A _____ spider skittered _____.
6. _____ I will go _____.
7. The _____ campfire blazed _____.
8. _____ drums boomed _____.

ACTIVITY F Rewrite the paragraph, expanding the sentences. You may change or add other words to make the paragraph more interesting.

Jennifer was reading. She heard a noise. She got up from her chair. She crept up the stairs to the bedroom. She pushed open the door. The noise was louder. She realized it was a tree branch scraping the window. Jennifer laughed. She sat back down in her chair.

ACTIVITY G Write sentences using the following adjectives, adverbs, and prepositional phrases.

1. delicious
2. terrific
3. tremendously
4. on time
5. thoughtfully
6. down the stairs
7. miniature
8. gratefully
9. over the road
10. useful

WRITER'S CORNER

Write four persuasive sentences to convince people to buy a product. Use adjectives, adverbs, and prepositional phrases to make your sentences more convincing. Think of TV commercials or magazine ads for ideas.

Antonyms

Antonyms are words that have opposite meanings. Here are a few antonym pairs.

familiar/unknown	genuine/fake
simple/complex	dense/sparse
calm/frantic	lost/found
permanent/temporary	beautiful/ugly
common/unique	light/heavy

Many words have more than one antonym. How many words can you think of that are the opposite of *small*?

Words that have more than one meaning might have antonyms for each different meaning. The words *dark* and *heavy* are both antonyms of the word *light*. Can you explain why?

ACTIVITY A The chart below shows one antonym each for four words. Copy the chart and add more antonyms to each column.

LITTLE	SPECIAL	RUDE	HAPPY
huge	common	pleasant	sad

ACTIVITY B Match each word in Column A with its antonym in Column B.

Column A	Column B
1. vain	**a.** firm
2. soothing	**b.** rare
3. bored	**c.** modest
4. end	**d.** refuse
5. agree	**e.** stressful
6. unsteady	**f.** whisper
7. yell	**g.** beginning
8. believe	**h.** decrease
9. abundant	**i.** excited
10. increase	**j.** doubt

ACTIVITY C Rewrite each sentence by replacing the word in italics with an antonym of that word.

1. A *harsh* wind blew across Crocodile Lake.

2. Do you think Raoul is *foolish* to play the game on crutches?

3. Sammy *remembered* that he left his friend Jake on the porch.

4. The *large* wave began to rise as it approached the shore.

5. The noise from the train whistle sounds very *distant*.

6. Just as we arrived on the scene, the monster in the lake *disappeared*.

7. We can walk on the *narrow* path to get to the cottage.

8. Your invention is so *simple*.

9. Professor Brown will *follow* our expedition.

10. Does that superhero *shrink*, or does he fly?

WRITER'S CORNER

Read a letter to the editor in a newspaper. List five words from the article that have antonyms. Then list antonyms for the five words.

Find a letter to the editor in an online newspaper.

ACTIVITY D Each word in italics is followed by three words. Tell which of the three words is not an antonym of the word in italics.

1. *alert*   sleepy, observant, inattentive
2. *sour*   tart, sugary, sweet
3. *sick*   healthy, hardy, ailing
4. *violent*   fierce, peaceful, calm
5. *funny*   serious, sad, amusing
6. *empty*   full, vacant, occupied
7. *amazing*   boring, dull, thrilling
8. *cooperate*   refuse, agree, resist

ACTIVITY E The word pairs in parentheses are antonyms. Choose the word that makes sense in each sentence.

1. Because of his (indifferent nosy) nature, Neil just had to know what was in the shed behind the old house next door.
2. His shaking hands showed how (scared fearless) he felt.
3. His (graceful clumsy) brother Xander started to follow, until he tripped on a garden hose in the grass.
4. The dark, (serene agitated) clouds rumbled with thunder overhead.
5. It felt good to be (idle active) outside after a long day reading at the library.
6. As he approached the shed, he realized there was a (strange normal) glow inside.
7. The (menacing harmless) light made him think twice about his exploration.
8. "Hey, Neil!" his brother (wailed whispered) from the back porch of the house. "Time for dinner!"
9. As he ran home, Neil felt (genuine fake) relief that it was time to eat.
10. Neil vowed (always never) to visit the shed alone again.

ACTIVITY F Tell which pairs of words are synonyms and which are antonyms.

1. bashful, timid
2. powerful, weak
3. mistaken, accurate
4. parched, drenched
5. flawless, perfect

6. appreciative, ungrateful
7. magnificent, splendid
8. cautious, careless
9. merry, jovial
10. gaudy, tacky

ACTIVITY G Rewrite the following paragraph to give an opposite description by replacing the words in italics with their antonyms.

It was a scene to *remember*. The lake was *peaceful* and *quiet*. A *smooth* beach led to a single *lovely* cottage. *Healthy* bushes surrounded the *clean* cottage. *Bright* curtains decorated the *spotless* windows. The whole family filled the *enormous* rooms with *laughter* and *cheerful* voices. What a *wonderful* place to be!

ACTIVITY H From the group of words after each sentence, select the word that is the antonym of the italicized word. Use a dictionary if necessary.

1. My mother received a *friendly* invitation to visit her cousin.
   nasty   neat   printed   colorful

2. There is an *abundant* supply of art materials for everyone.
   plentiful   meager   overflowing   free

3. The lion became *enraged* when the photographer got too close.
   sleepy   angry   sad   happy

4. Standing near the edge of the skyscraper roof, the superhero found himself in a *dangerous* situation.
   exciting   silly   safe   treacherous

WRITER'S CORNER

Write three sentences comparing something you like to do at home with something you do not like to do at home. Use at least three pairs of antonyms in your comparison.

Library

Libraries have a lot of books and research materials. Some libraries are several stories tall and packed with information. No matter what their size, all libraries use specials systems to organize their resources and to make information easy to find. Here are a few tips for finding books in a library.

Dewey Decimal System

Most libraries use a system called the Dewey Decimal System to organize books. Every book has a call number made up of numbers and letters. A call number is the book's address in the library. It tells you where the book lives on the shelves. A library assistant named Melvil Dewey came up with the idea in 1876. His call numbers represent different categories of learning.

Nonfiction

Nonfiction books are grouped by subject. If you look for a book about whales, the books around it will also be about whales and other marine life. Because nonfiction books are grouped by subject, they are arranged using call numbers according to the subject of the book.

A book's call number appears on the spine of the book. Just below the call number, you will find the first three letters of the author's last name. Use the computer catalog in your library to find the call number of a book.

Fiction

Fiction books usually have a section of their own. Books in the fiction section are arranged alphabetically by the author's last name. If several authors have the same last name, the books are usually further alphabetized by the authors' first names. If an author has written more than one book, the books will be alphabetized again by title. Some libraries label the spine of a fiction book with the letter *F* and the first three letters of the author's last name.

Reference Books

Some nonfiction books are put in a separate section called the reference section. Reference books include dictionaries, encyclopedias, almanacs, and atlases. Reference books cannot be checked out because people use them often and because they are very expensive. Books in the reference section are also arranged numerically by call number.

Other Materials

Many libraries offer videos, music, new and old issues of magazines, and computer software. Individual libraries organize these materials differently. Ask a librarian for help finding these materials.

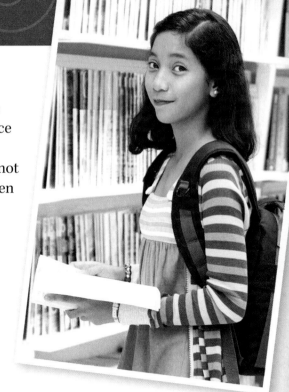

ACTIVITY A Tell in which section of the library—fiction, nonfiction, or reference—you would find these books.

1. *Huckleberry Finn* by Mark Twain
2. *The American Heritage Dictionary of the English Language*
3. *A History of American Whaling* by Fred Darling
4. *Bud, Not Buddy* by Christopher Paul Curtis
5. *Archery for Amateurs* by Neil Gaby
6. an atlas of Europe
7. *The Planets of Our Solar System* by Denise O'Malley
8. *The Encyclopedia of Flowers and Plants*
9. *The Phantom Tollbooth* by Norton Juster
10. *The Old Farmer's Almanac*
11. *The Cabin Faced West* by Jean Fritz
12. *How To Draw Manga* by Katy Coope

WRITER'S CORNER

List the titles of three books that you know are in each of the three main sections of the library. Remember that the three main sections are fiction, nonfiction, and reference.

Computer Catalogs

How quickly can you find information in the library? The first place to look is the library catalog. It tells you exactly where to find the information you need.

Today most libraries have their catalogs on computer. These electronic catalogs include entries listed by title, author, or subject.

Computer catalogs are easy to use. All you have to do is type the word into the search box and the computer will give you a choice of entries. With this list you can find the books you need.

When you type an author's name, for example, the computer will list all the books by the author that are in the library. The computer will also list any books about the author that the library has.

Here is an example of what a student found after typing the word *Thanksgiving* into the search box. When the student clicked on *Search* for subjects beginning with *Thanksgiving*, she found a list of books on that subject.

Library Catalog

Search catalog for: Thanksgiving   **SEARCH**

Search Results: Thanksgiving

DETAILS

974.4 Bruchac, Joseph
Bru   Squanto's Journey: The story of the first Thanksgiving. Illustrated by Greg Shed. Texas, Voyager Books, 2007.

975.9 Friedman, Laurie
Fri   Thanksgiving Rules. Illustrated by Teresa Murfin. Minnesota, Carolrhoda Books, 2009.

976.2 Markes, Julie
Mar   Thanks for Thanksgiving. Illustrated by Doris Barrette. New York, Harper Collins, 2008.

977.5 Pilkey, Dav
Pil   'Twas the Night Before Thanksgiving. Illustrated by Dav Pilkey. New York, Orchard Books, 2004.

When she clicked on one of the books, she saw the following screen:

Library Catalog

Catalog Record

Squanto's Journey: The Story of the First Thanksgiving

974.4 Bruchac, Joseph

Bru The first Thanksgiving feast. Illustrations by Greg Shed. Texas, Voyager Books, 2007. Retelling of the first Thanksgiving with illustrations to accompany the story.

1. Pilgrims (New Plymouth)   2. Thanksgiving Day   3. Massachusetts—History of

ACTIVITY B Imagine you are looking for a book in the library. You have only the information below. Tell whether you would use the title, author, or subject search to find the book you need.

1. pets
2. *The Rose Parade*
3. *Lava in Hawaii*
4. Beverly Cleary
5. James Howe
6. earthquakes

ACTIVITY C Visit your school library and use the computer catalog to find the following information.

1. Titles of books by
   a. Jerry Spinelli
   b. Karen Hesse
   c. Phyllis Reynolds Naylor
2. The author of the book
   a. *Catherine, Called Birdy*
   b. *What Would Joey Do?*
   c. *The Last Knight*
3. Books on the subject of
   a. automobiles
   b. Russian history
   c. Henry James
4. The titles and call numbers for books by
   a. Jack Prelutsky
   b. Jim Arnosky
   c. Seymour Simon

WRITER'S CORNER

Suppose you are doing research on each topic below. For each topic write a list of subjects you could search under in the computer catalog.

monkeys   lava   jet planes

Persuasive Speeches

Have you ever seen the president, a mayor, or a governor give a speech? Most political speeches are a form of persuasive speaking. You use persuasive speaking too. You are using persuasive speaking when you try to convince your parents to let you stay up later. Any time you try to convince someone to agree with you, you are using persuasive speaking. Here are a few things to think about when preparing a persuasive speech.

Audience and Position

Think about what your audience already knows about your topic. If they already agree with you, you might be able to make them agree more strongly and take action. If they disagree, you might be able to change their minds. Be sure to pick a topic and position that you care strongly about.

Knowing your audience can help you prepare the reasons and evidence you will use in your speech. What kinds of reasons and evidence will show your audience that your position affects their lives?

Introduction

State your position early in your speech. Try to grab the audience's attention. A personal story or an example that illustrates how your position affects people can often get an audience interested.

Body

Present your reasons and evidence in the body of your speech. Be sure to give your reasons clearly and in logical order. Speak slowly and clearly to emphasize your points. Your audience cannot go back and reread your reasons if something is not clear.

Conclusion

Use your conclusion to summarize your position and briefly restate the reasons you used in the body. Be sure to speak calmly and confidently in your conclusion. It is often a good idea to tell your audience in the conclusion what action they can take if they agree with you.

Body Language and Voice

Your voice and your body language are important in persuasive speaking. Stand up straight as you speak. It will help you breathe and will show that you are confident. Use gestures to emphasize important points. With your voice and your body language, you can make your persuasive speech even more persuasive.

ACTIVITY A Brainstorm a list of after-school activities or clubs you would like to have in your school. Think about hobbies, sports, and interests you have and could share with others. Then meet with a partner to talk about the activities on your list. Choose an activity from your list that you feel strongly about and that would be interesting to an audience of your classmates.

ACTIVITY B List a few reasons you might use in a persuasive speech about activities or clubs you would like your school to start. Think about what evidence would support your reasons.

SPEAKER'S CORNER

Write a brief introduction for a persuasive speech on the topic you chose for Activity A. If you chose a hobby or an activity you already enjoy, you might tell a story about it. Then practice your introduction with a partner.

Organize

Organize your persuasive speech in the same way you might organize a persuasive article. Once you decide on an introduction, write a few notes on a note card to remind you what your position is and how you plan to grab your audience's attention.

For the body of your speech, write each reason on the top of a separate note card. Write your evidence underneath each reason. You might number your reasons if you want to present them in a particular order.

Write on a note card a few ideas for your conclusion. You might include notes about what the audience can do if they agree with you.

Practice

Practicing is a chance to get comfortable with your speech. Being comfortable with your speech will allow you to be confident as you talk. It helps you become familiar with using note cards to deliver your speech. Practicing is also a chance for you to experiment with different gestures and tones of voice. Practice in front of a mirror and try emphasizing your points in different ways. If you find a gesture or tone of voice that you think is effective, write a reminder on one of your note cards.

When you think you are ready, practice with a friend or family member. Here are some questions you might ask your listener.

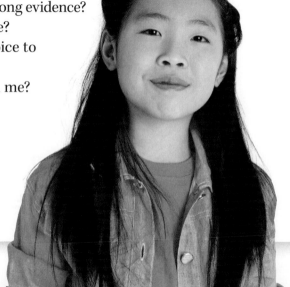

I think you'll agree with me.

- Was my position clear?
- Were my reasons in a clear, logical order?
- Do my reasons support my topic?
- Did I support my reasons with strong evidence?
- Did I appear confident as I spoke?
- Did I use gestures and tone of voice to emphasize my points?
- Did I convince you to agree with me?

Listening Tips

When you listen to a persuasive speech, be a critical listener. Listen to the speaker's reasons and think about whether they make sense. Listen to the evidence and decide if it is convincing. Here are a few more tips for listening to a persuasive speech.

- Listen to find out the speaker's position.
- Write or try to remember each of the speaker's reasons.
- Think about whether the evidence presented supports those reasons.
- You might disagree with the speaker. If so, still listen to the speaker and respect his or her position. Think about how you might argue your own side.
- Wait until the end of the speech to ask questions. Then ask your questions politely.

ACTIVITY C Organize your notes from Activity B on page 465. Write ideas for kinds of evidence you could use to support your reasons. Then gather evidence that supports your reasons. Write your reasons and evidence on note cards.

ACTIVITY D Write a conclusion that summarizes your position and your reasons. If you can, tell your audience what action they could take if they agree with you. Use what you write to make a note card for your conclusion. Then write notes on a note card for the introduction you wrote for the Speaker's Corner on page 465.

SPEAKER'S CORNER

Practice your persuasive speech with a partner. When you have finished, ask your partner the questions on page 466. Then let your partner practice his or her persuasive speech. Remember the listening tips above as you listen to your partner's speech.

Prewriting and Drafting

Persuading other people to agree with you is not always easy. But if you choose a topic that you care about, state your position clearly, give reasons to support it, and back up your reasons with evidence, you have a better chance of persuading others.

Prewriting

Cooper's dad told her about "The Best Town in Michigan" contest. Kids from all over the state would send articles to the *Lansing Gazette*, trying to persuade others that theirs was the best town. Cooper thought her town was the best town in the world. So she decided to enter the contest.

Cooper began by prewriting. She needed to 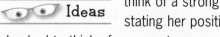 think of a strong sentence stating her position. She also had to think of reasons to support her position, back up her reasons with evidence, and organize her ideas.

Position and Reasons

Cooper's position was easy. She thought that River City was the best town in Michigan. Now she needed to think of reasons to support her position.

Cooper listed her position and reasons. Here is Cooper's list.

Position:
River city is the best town in Michigan!

Reasons:
- It is beautiful.
- It is a fun place to live.
- There are lots of cool things to do.
- Everyone loves it here.

Your Turn

- Choose a topic that you care about.
- Think about your audience.
- Think of reasons that support your position. Then write a sentence that states your position.
- List reasons why people should agree with you. The more reasons you have to support your position, the better chance you have of convincing your audience to agree with you.

Evidence

To persuade the judges of the contest, Cooper would need evidence that backed up her reasons. She made a list of her own ideas that backed up her reasons. Then she went online and found some more evidence.

Your Turn

Now it's time to back up your reasons with evidence. Remember that opinions without support are not likely to persuade your audience. Make some notes about why you think each reason is a good one. Then use the library or the Internet to find more evidence.

Organizing Ideas

Cooper saw that some of her evidence was not suitable for her main topic. She took out information that she didn't need. She organized her notes, including evidence for each reason. Here are her notes.

Introduction:
- River city is the best town in Michigan. (position)

Body:
Reason One: It is beautiful.
- parks built on the waterfront
- historic buildings from 1800s
- mansions on center Ave. built by lumber barons

Reason Two: It has a lot of festivals.
- Independence Day Fireworks Festival: three days long, fireworks each night, music groups, food
- River Roar: boat race down Saginaw River, music, food

Reason Three: There are things for families to do.
- Deer Run: pet and feed deer, amusement park, restaurant
- Sunshine Stables: trail rides, hay rides, horse shows

conclusion:
- River city is an interesting and beautiful town. (restate position)

Your Turn

- Look at your notes. Organize them with an introduction, a separate section for each reason, and a conclusion.
- Include your evidence for each reason.
- Organize your notes in a way that makes sense to you.
- If necessary, do additional research to strengthen your reasons.

Prewriting

Drafting

Content Editing

Revising

Copyediting

Proofreading

Publishing

Drafting

Cooper used her organized notes as a guide to write her article. She made sure to include opinion words to make her writing sound confident. Here is Cooper's first draft.

Why River City Is Michigan's Best Town

River City is the best town in Michigan! Other towns aren't as good as we are. Every year it gets better and better. I think that River City can win the *Lansing Gazette*'s contest for "Michigan's Best Town."

River City is one of the most beautiful towns in Michigan. River City, which is split in half by the Saginaw river, now has beautiful parks. The buildings along the river can be traced back to the earliest settlements. People can also travel down Center Avenue, which is only a short walk from the river, to see mansons and churches.

Now that people are starting to notice the beauty of River City, it has fun and interesting festivals. The most well known is the Independence Day Fireworks Festival. This festival lasts for three days. Besides the fireworks show each night, there are also music and comedy acts, rides, food, and arts and crafts shows in Waterfront Park. There is also the River Roar, an exciting boat race down the Saginaw river. The River Roar also has a lot of fun entertainment, like magicans, music, and food. There are also lots of fun things for families to do all year. One place to go is Deer Run. Deer Run has an amusement park. There is a restaurant that has good food like hot dogs and candy apples. Or families can go to Sunshine Stables. They have guided trail rides through River City State Park. They also have hay rides in the fall and sliegh rides in the winter.

We should win the *Lansing Gazette*'s contest for "Michigan's Best Town." With our beautiful rivers and parks, old buildings, and fantastic festivals, how could anyone disagree?

Your Turn

Use your notes to write your first draft. Remember to double-space your lines so that you will have room to make changes later. Keep in mind that you will probably revise your draft several times.

Grammar in Action

Identify the prepositional phrases in the second paragraph in Cooper's draft.

Establishing Tone

It is important to establish a tone that will make your readers like what you are saying. The more positive your tone is, the more effective your writing will be. You don't want your audience to think that your persuasive article has reasons based on anger or bias. Cooper made a negative comment in the first paragraph that she might want to delete. Her article is more persuasive if she says positive things about River City that she can prove, rather than saying negative things that are her personal opinion.

Content Editing

Cooper had worked hard on her persuasive article. But she knew her article could be stronger. She asked her best friend, Zosia, to content edit her draft. A content editor could check to make sure her reasons were logical and well supported. Zosia used this checklist to content edit Cooper's draft.

Content Editor's Checklist

☐ Does the introduction state the position clearly?

☐ Does the body have logical reasons that support the position?

☐ Is each reason written in a separate paragraph, and are the reasons well supported?

☐ Are all the details necessary and important to the position?

☐ Does the conclusion restate the position and give readers an action to take?

☐ Are opinion words used to express the position?

Zosia read Cooper's draft several times. She made notes about what she liked and listed her suggestions. Then Cooper and Zosia met to talk about the draft.

Zosia told Cooper that she had written good reasons to support her position. She also thought that Cooper had stated her position well. Here are Zosia's suggestions for improvement.

- In the second paragraph, you say that River City has beautiful parks. Do you mean the parks on the river or the state park? The state park isn't on the river.

- The second reason is kind of confusing. It seems like you're saying we've had festivals only since people started noticing River City.

- Maybe you should mention that the Fireworks Festival is one of the largest in the Midwest.

- You should mention the Munger Potato Fest. It's a lot of fun too.

- The third paragraph has two reasons. I think that you should make the sentence "There are also lots of fun things for families to do all year" the beginning of a new paragraph.

- You talk about the amusement park and the restaurant at Deer Run, but you don't mention the deer! People might wonder why it's called Deer Run.

- I don't see an action readers can take.

Cooper appreciated Zosia's suggestions. She hadn't realized that she forgot to mention the deer at Deer Run. Cooper thought that it was the best part about the place.

Cooper looked over Zosia's suggestions carefully. Then she checked the draft herself, using the Content Editor's Checklist. She found two things that Zosia forgot to check for. Do you see what Zosia forgot?

Your Turn

Work with a partner and content edit each other's persuasive articles.

- Use the Content Editor's Checklist to content edit your partner's draft.
- See if you are convinced by your partner's persuasive article.

When you have both finished, meet with your partner and discuss your suggestions.

- Remember to begin by telling your partner what was strong about his or her draft.
- Point out anything you really liked. Then tell your suggestions in a positive and helpful way.

It is also a good idea to use the Content Editor's Checklist to content edit your draft yourself. You might find, as Cooper did, that your content editor missed something.

Writer's Tip Take some time to make sure that you can answer *yes* to every question on the Content Editor's checklist.

Prewriting

Drafting

Content Editing

Revising

Copyediting

Proofreading

Publishing

Revising

This is Cooper's revised persuasive article.

River City Is the Place to Be!

~~Why River City Is Michigan's Best Town~~

River City is the best town in Michigan! ~~Other towns aren't as good as we are.~~
Every year it gets better and better. ~~I think~~ believe that River City ~~can~~ should win the *Lansing*

Gazette's contest for "Michigan's Best Town."

River City is one of the most beautiful towns in Michigan. River City, which is split

in half by the Saginaw river, now has beautiful waterfront parks. The buildings along the river

can be traced back to the earliest settlements. People can also travel down Center

Avenue, which is only a short walk from the river, to see mansons and churches.

Now that people are starting to notice the beauty of River City, it has started hosting some of the most fun and

interesting festivals in the state. The most well known is the Independence Day Fireworks

Festival, which is one of the largest in the Midwest. This festival lasts for three days. Besides the fireworks show each night,

there are also music and comedy acts, rides, food, and arts and crafts shows

in Waterfront Park. There is also the River Roar, an exciting boat race down the

Saginaw river. The River Roar also has a lot of fun entertainment, like magicans,

music, and food. ¶ There are also lots of fun things for families to do all year. One

place to go is Deer Run. You can actually feed and pet baby deer there! Deer Run has an amusement park. There is a restaurant

that has good food like hot dogs and candy apples. Or families can go to Sunshine

Stables. They have guided trail rides through River City State Park. They also have hay rides in the fall and sliegh rides in the winter.

River City is the most interesting and beautiful town in Michigan.

We should win the *Lansing Gazette*'s contest for "Michigan's Best Town." With our beautiful rivers and parks, old buildings, and fantastic festivals, how could anyone disagree? *Vote for River City!*

Look at how Cooper improved her persuasive article. Do you agree with her changes?

- Why do you think Cooper decided to change the title of her article?

- What did she do to strengthen her introduction?

- What word did Cooper add to clarify the park she was talking about?

- How did Cooper revise the second reason?

- What did Cooper add about the Fireworks Festival?

- Zosia suggested another festival, but Cooper decided not to add it. Why?

- Cooper agreed with Zosia about making her paragraphs clearer. What change did Cooper make?

- The part about Deer Run was confusing. What did Cooper do to fix it?

- What changes did Cooper make to her conclusion? Did her changes make her position stronger?

Your Turn

Use your content editor's suggestions and your own ideas to revise your draft. Make any other changes that you notice as you revise. Then use the Content Editor's Checklist again to make sure you can answer *yes* to all the questions.

Prewriting

Drafting

Content Editing

Revising

Copyediting

Proofreading

Publishing

Copyediting and Proofreading

Copyediting

Now that the reasons and evidence in her article were solid, Cooper wanted to copyedit it. She knew that she would have a better chance of persuading her audience if they weren't distracted by confusing sentences or by unclear word choices. Cooper used the Copyeditor's Checklist to copyedit her draft.

Cooper used adjectives to expand a sentence in the third paragraph. Look at how she revised it.

She combined two sentences in her new fourth paragraph. Do you see where Cooper might combine sentences?

Word Choice

Cooper noticed that she used the word *also* a lot in her draft. She decided to take out *also* in some places.

Cooper didn't like the word *old* in the last paragraph. She decided to replace it with the word *historic*, which means "being important to history." Cooper thought that *historic* described the buildings much better.

Copyeditor's Checklist

- ☐ Have you checked that there are sentences that could be expanded with adjectives, adverbs, or prepositional phrases?
- ☐ Have you checked that there are any rambling or run-on sentences?
- ☐ Have you checked that there are sentences that could be combined?
- ☐ Is there a variety of word choice?
- ☐ Are exact words used?

Your Turn

Use the Copyeditor's Checklist to copyedit your draft. Look for ways to make your sentences more persuasive. Try expanding sentences to make your draft come alive for your **Sentence Fluency** audience. Be sure that your feelings are clearly conveyed through your word choice. If your readers don't think that you feel strongly about your position, they won't be persuaded to agree with you.

Remember to check for one item on the checklist at a time. You might miss mistakes if you check for too many things at once. When you have finished, check your draft again, using the Content Editor's Checklist to make sure that your sentence changes did not change any of your content ideas.

Proofreading

Before she sent her article to the *Lansing Gazette*, Cooper wanted to make sure someone proofread it. She knew that a proofreader would check for mistakes in spelling, capitalization, punctuation, and grammar. A checklist like this can help when proofreading.

Proofreader's Checklist

- ☐ Are the paragraphs indented?
- ☐ Are all the words spelled correctly?
- ☐ Are capitalization and punctuation correct?
- ☐ Is the grammar correct?
- ☐ Have you checked that no new mistakes were added while editing?

Cooper had read her persuasive article so many times that she knew she was seeing what she wanted to see. So she asked her dad to proofread her draft.

Cooper's dad, Mr. Ingram, saw two words in the new fourth paragraph that should have been one compound word. Do you see the words he found?

Mr. Ingram found three misspelled words. In the second paragraph, Cooper misspelled *mansions*. She had written *mansons*. In the third paragraph, she had left out the second *i* in

 Conventions

magicians. Do you see the other misspelled word in Cooper's draft?

Mr. Ingram also found a capitalization mistake that appeared twice in Cooper's revised draft. *Saginaw river* should be *Saginaw River*, because it is a proper noun.

Your Turn

Read your draft carefully, using the Proofreader's Checklist. Check for one item at a time. This is a good way to spot mistakes and to make last-minute changes to improve your draft.

When you have finished, trade drafts with a partner. Use the Proofreader's Checklist to proofread your partner's draft. Then meet with your partner to discuss any mistakes that you each found.

Writer's Tip Remember to use a dictionary to check the spelling of words that you aren't sure of.

Prewriting
Drafting
Content Editing
Revising
Copyediting
Proofreading
Publishing

Publishing

Cooper was confident that she had written a very persuasive article. She typed her article carefully on her dad's computer. Then she checked her typed copy one last time, using the Proofreader's Checklist. She didn't find any more mistakes, so she knew her article was ready. Cooper knew that just having people at the *Lansing Gazette* read her work was a form of publishing. Even if her article didn't win the contest, Cooper was glad that she had worked so hard.

River City Is the Place to Be!

River City is the best town in Michigan! Every year it gets better and better. I believe that River City should win the *Lansing Gazette's* contest for "Michigan's Best Town."

River City is one of the most beautiful towns in Michigan. River City, which is split in half by the Saginaw River, now has beautiful waterfront parks. The buildings along the river can be traced back to the earliest settlements. People can also travel down Center Avenue, which is only a short walk from the river, to see mansions and churches.

Now that people are starting to notice the beauty of River City, it has started hosting some of the most fun and interesting festivals in the state. The most well known is the Independence Day Fireworks Festival, which is one of the largest in the Midwest. This colorful and exciting festival lasts for three days. Besides the fireworks show each night, there are music and comedy acts, rides, food, and arts and crafts shows in Waterfront Park. There is also the River Roar, an exciting boat race down the Saginaw River. The River Roar has a lot of fun entertainment, like magicians, music, and food.

There are lots of fun things for families to do all year. One place to go is Deer Run. You can actually feed and pet baby deer there! Deer Run has an amusement park and a restaurant that has good food like hot dogs and candy apples. Or families can go to Sunshine Stables. They have guided trail rides through River City State Park. They also have hayrides in the fall and sleigh rides in the winter.

River City is the most interesting and beautiful town in Michigan. We should win the *Lansing Gazette*'s contest for "Michigan's Best Town." With our beautiful rivers and parks, historic buildings, and fantastic festivals, how could anyone disagree? Vote for River City as Michigan's Best Town!

Decide with your classmates and teacher how you will publish your work. One good way is to post your persuasive article on a school bulletin board. You might convince students and teachers from all over the school to agree with you.

If your persuasive article is about an issue or a change in your school or community, talk with your teacher and parents about how you might share your viewpoint with a wider audience. Here are some ways you can publish your persuasive article.

 Send your article to the local newspaper or post it on a community Internet site.

 Create a PowerPoint presentation about your topic. Include photos and images that help make your point.

 Organize a debate with your classmates. Students with opposing topics give their speeches together. Record the debate, using a video camera.

 Songs can be compelling ways to make your point. Write a song that highlights your topic and perform it for the class.

Your goal is to share your thoughts and experiences with other people whenever you publish your work.

Your Turn

The moment that you share your work with your audience is the moment that you publish. Follow these steps to prepare your persuasive article for publishing.

- Read your article one more time to make sure that you haven't left out any facts or evidence. Remember to content edit, copyedit, and proofread any additional changes that you make.
- Use your neatest handwriting or a computer to **Presentation** produce the final copy of your draft.
- Proofread your final copy one more time to make sure that there are no misspelled words or mistakes in capitalization, punctuation, or grammar.

Prewriting

Drafting

Content Editing

Revising

Copyediting

Proofreading

Publishing

Research Reports

LiNK

Lost Temple of the Aztecs
What it was like when the Spaniards invaded Mexico
by Shelley Tanaka

Map of ancient
Mexico City known
as Tenochtitlán

Five hundred years ago, Tenochtitlán was a city of 250,000 people. It was built on an island in the middle of a sparkling blue lake....

The Great Temple stood at the heart of this remarkable city. Nine stories high, it faced a huge square surrounded by shrines and palaces. Its steep steps were stained with the blood of human sacrifices. This was where the Aztecs worshipped their gods, where their conquered enemies brought gifts and tributes, and where the Aztec ruler Moctezuma received important guests.

One fateful day in 1519, an unusual group of visitors approached Tenochtitlán. The Aztecs had never seen such people. Their skin was oddly white, their faces covered with hair, and they wore metal clothing from head to foot. They came with strange, wild-eyed beasts, and they carried heavy weapons that clanked and gleamed in the sun. Were they friends, or enemies? Should they be destroyed or treated as guests?

> Research reports use a strong introduction and factual research about a topic, like *Lost Temple of the Aztecs*.

Chris Hoffmann
Room 112

An All-American Sport

Did you know that the first basketball was a soccer ball and the first hoop was a wooden peach basket? Some things about the popular sport of basketball have changed—equipment, rules, leagues—but it is considered the invention of one man. Most sports actually develop from sports in other countries. However, basketball is truly an American game.

Dr. James Naismith, basketball's inventor, was born in Ontario, Canada, in 1861. Later he moved to the United States to study and then teach at the YMCA Training School in Springfield, Massachusetts. In 1891, while teaching physical education, Naismith created an indoor team game that students could enjoy during the winter months. The game of basketball was born.

Naismith recognized that all team games used some kind of ball. He liked the idea of using a soccer ball because it would be easy to handle. For baskets, he used two wooden peach baskets, which he attached to the railings at either end of the gym balcony. Naismith greeted his physical education class of 18 students with his 13 rules of basketball, a soccer ball, and the peach baskets. Soon the entire school and their families and friends were playing.

As teams across the country began to play, professional basketball began. The first professional league, the National Basketball League, was formed in 1898. Other leagues were founded and eventually merged to become the National Basketball Association (NBA), which we have today. Basketball has had a great influence on American athletics. For the father of basketball, the fun of playing the game was more important than the competition and the score. Maybe that's why so many of us love shooting the ball through the hoop.

Springfield
Grizzlies

Section	Row	Seat
W	26	112

Springfield
Grizzlies

	Row	Seat
on	26	113

What Makes a Good Research Report?

A research report is a kind of writing that tells readers factual information about a topic in an organized way. A research report shares ideas that a writer has read and collected from a variety of sources.

Writers of research reports first gather information about a topic, then organize the information, and finally write the report. A research report might be about almost any topic—a person, a place, or an event. It could be about T. S. Eliot, Yellowstone Park, or the Fourth of July.

Choose a Topic

Choose a topic that interests you. Your interest and enthusiasm for the topic will show through in your report. Sometimes your choice of a topic will be up to you. Other times your teacher might give you guidelines. Then you can brainstorm and choose an aspect of the topic that you want to write about.

Narrow the Topic

Once you have chosen your topic, you need to make sure it is narrow enough for an effective research report. Be specific about what you want to know. The history of England might be too broad a topic. The War of the Roses would be a more narrow topic, because it could be more easily covered in a research report.

Asking questions about your topic gives you a chance to focus your thoughts about it. Questions can guide your research and let you decide what information is important to your report and what information isn't.

Research

Research reports require research. That means you will need to spend some time gathering information from sources. The information for your report can come from a wide variety of sources, such as books, encyclopedias, or Web sites.

It's difficult to remember everything you read, so you will want to take good, organized notes as you research. Write everything that is relevant to your topic. Your notes will help you organize an effective research report.

ACTIVITY A Read these pairs of topics. Tell which topic in each pair is the narrower topic for a research report.

1. **a.** birds of North America
   b. bald eagles
2. **a.** Colonial Williamsburg
   b. Colonial America
3. **a.** exploring outer space
   b. expeditions to Mars
4. **a.** Casimir Pulaski
   b. Revolutionary War heroes
5. **a.** working dogs
   b. German shepherds
6. **a.** London
   b. cities of Europe
7. **a.** famous women athletes
   b. Jackie Joyner-Kersee

ACTIVITY B The following topics are too broad. Narrow them until each is a suitable topic for a research report.

1. insects
2. dinosaurs
3. endangered animals
4. geology
5. movie stars
6. American presidents
7. toys
8. inventors

WRITER'S CORNER

Write three questions you have about a narrow topic you identified in Activity B. Save your work.

Grammar in Action

Diagram the second sentence of the third paragraph of the excerpt on page 480.

Topic Sentence

As you do your research, you will probably find more information than you can use. To guide your research, develop a topic sentence. The topic sentence is a sentence that briefly describes or explains the topic of your research report. Read this example.

Broad topic: sports
Narrow topic: football
Topic sentence: Football is a popular sport.

By narrowing the topic to a topic sentence, this writer has a focus for the rest of the report. With a topic sentence, the writer can use the body of the report for the reasons why football is a popular sport.

LiNK

Lost Temple of the Aztecs

Long before the Europeans came to North America, a very different kind of metropolis stood on the spot where Mexico City is now. It was called Tenochtitlán, and it was the capital city of the Aztec Empire.

Shelley Tanaka

Introduction

Like other kinds of writing, an effective introduction catches the reader's attention. In a research report, a catchy introduction might start with an interesting fact about your topic. The introduction should also include the topic sentence of the report. The excerpt on this page about the Aztec Empire is a good example of an introduction. Can you spot the topic sentence?

Body

The body of a research report is the place to present what you have discovered. As in other types of writing, the body is the longest part of a research report. It can be one page or many pages long. Usually, each paragraph of the body covers one main idea that supports your topic sentence. Imagine you are writing a research report about why football is a popular sport. One paragraph might be about the increased TV ratings for football. Another paragraph might be about the rise in stadium attendance. A third paragraph might be about the growing popularity of the Super Bowl.

Conclusion

A good conclusion briefly summarizes the topic sentence of the research report. It also leaves the reader with a sense that the topic was covered well and nothing important was left out.

ACTIVITY C Tell which idea in each group does not go with the topic sentence.

1. *topic sentence:* Stars are more than just lights in the sky.
   a. what stars are made of
   b. how "The Star-Spangled Banner" was written
   c. solar radiation
   d. types of stars

2. *topic sentence:* Hurricanes are a powerful force of nature that affects millions of people every year.
   a. effects of hurricanes
   b. how earthquakes occur
   c. causes of hurricanes
   d. where hurricanes occur

3. *topic sentence:* Ferdinand Magellan lived a fascinating and accomplished life.
   a. when and where Magellan lived
   b. the kinds of expeditions Magellan made
   c. what Balboa found
   d. Magellan's discoveries

4. *topic sentence:* One of history's greatest puzzles is whether King Arthur was real or fictional.
   a. how swords are made
   b. factual accounts of King Arthur
   c. theories of who King Arthur really was
   d. fictional stories of King Arthur

WRITER'S CORNER

Use your work from the previous Writer's Corner on page 483 to write an introduction for a research report. Include a topic sentence in your introduction.

Grammar in Action Diagram the second sentence in the excerpt on page 484. What kind of sentence is it?

Gathering and Organizing Information

You will do a lot of reading as you gather information. If you have narrowed your subject and found good sources, you will be able to include many details in your report. Here are some things to keep in mind as you take notes and organize your information.

Taking Notes

When you find a source that you want to use in your report, you should read only the information that deals with your topic. If you are looking for information about your topic in a book, read the contents page in the front of the book or the index in the back of the book. Find and read the pages that relate to your topic.

To take notes on a source, read a paragraph and write in your own words what the source is saying. Write important words and phrases that will help you recall the ideas in your source. Writing in your own words helps you understand and remember what you have read.

Using Note Cards

Using note cards is a handy way to take notes. Note cards are small enough to organize easily, yet large enough for writing important information. One way to keep your notes in order is to write each note on a separate card. Once you have finished your note cards, put cards with information about the same thing into piles. Make separate piles for each idea that you researched.

To help you remember where each piece of information came from, write the name of the source, the author, and the page number on the card as well.

These two note cards were written by a student writing a research report on humpback whales.

The scientific name for humpback whales is Megaptera novaeanglia.

"Humpback Whales," Animal Encyclopedia, p. 284.

Humpback whales eat almost 1½ tons of small fish per day.

What Whales Eat, by Colleen Richardson p. 77.

ACTIVITY A Here are some ideas you might want to cover if you were doing a research report about fireflies.

> **Idea 1.** why and how fireflies light up
>
> **Idea 2.** the life of a firefly

These are notes from note cards for Ideas 1 and 2. Which notes would go in a pile for Idea 1, and which would go in a pile for Idea 2?

1. timing of flashes controlled by nerves
2. average life span = 5 to 30 days
3. lay eggs in moist places
4. chemical reaction causes light to flash
5. to attract mates or prey
6. larvae eat snails, worms, and insects

ACTIVITY B Read the passage below. Identify which sentences belong on note cards and which are unimportant.

1. Fireflies, or *Lampyridae*, are sometimes referred to as lightning bugs. 2. Fireflies are not creating lightning or fire in their bellies. 3. In fact, they get their name from a chemical in their bodies that gives off a luminescent glow to attract mates. 4. A favorite summer memory is watching the fireflies put on a spectacular light show at dusk. 5. The larvae of a firefly is sometimes called a "glowworm" because it can give off a soft light as well. 6. Sometimes we would catch them and put them in a jar. 7. Adding a leaf and a twig makes the firefly feel at home. 8. A firefly's life span is five to 30 days. 9. Living in a jar will shorten their life considerably. 10. Whatever you call them, catching fireflies is a fun way to spend a warm summer evening.

WRITER'S CORNER

Find two sources of information, such as an encyclopedia and a nonfiction book, about planets in the solar system. Make two note cards like the cards on page 486. Write on the note cards the sources of the information. Save your work.

LiNK

Lost Temple of the Aztecs

... The Aztecs ruled a great empire in what is now Mexico. Originally from a land farther north called Aztlan, they arrived ... in the fourteenth century. They created their city right in the lake, on rocky outcroppings and shallow marshes.

Shelley Tanaka

Re-creation of an Aztec temple

Works Cited Page

An important part of a research report is the Works Cited page. The Works Cited page is found at the end of the report. It lists all the sources you used in your report in alphabetical order, according to the author's last name.

Each entry of a Works Cited page is a source that you used in your report. A Works Cited page does not include sources that you read but did not use. Start each entry with the author's name, last name first. If you cannot find an author listed, use the title of the source in place of the name. The titles of books are underlined if handwritten, and italicized if typed on a computer. The titles of articles are put between quotation marks.

You will probably take notes from many different kinds of sources. As you take notes, record on separate note cards the information about each source that you will need for your Works Cited page. Here is the information you will need for different kinds of sources.

Book

For most books, you will need the name of the author, the title of the book, the publisher, the location of the publisher, and the year the book was published. You can usually find this information on the title page or the copyright page. The entry on the Works Cited page for a book would look like the one below.

Swinburne, Stephen R. The Woods Scientist. Boston: Houghton Mifflin, 2002.

Encyclopedia

Most encyclopedias do not list the names of the people who wrote each article. For these encyclopedias, you will need only the name of the article, the title of the encyclopedia, and the edition or year of the encyclopedia.

"Tigers." World Book Encyclopedia. 2010 ed.

Web Site

If a Web site gives the author's name, be sure to include it along with the name of the article, the date that you looked at the Web site, and the Web site address. Put the Web site address between angle brackets (< >).

Brody, Valerie. "Common Dolphin." 18 Apr. 2011 <www.acsonline.org/factpack/common.htm>.

Many Web sites do not tell who wrote them. If a Web site does not give the author's name, begin the entry with the name of the article.

ACTIVITY C Here are some sources for the firefly research report. Use this information to write a Works Cited page. Alphabetize the entries.

1. An article titled "A Beacon in the Night" by Lana Unger, looked up on November 20, 2011, Web site address: www.uky.edu/Agriculture/Entomology.

2. An article titled "Firefly" in World Book Encyclopedia, 2010 edition.

3. A book titled *Fireflies* by Sally M. Walker, published by Lerner Publications in Minneapolis in 2001.

ACTIVITY D Look for three sources of information about an animal or insect. For example, you might use an encyclopedia, a nonfiction book, and a Web site. Write a Works Cited page for the three sources. Remember to put the entries in alphabetical order.

WRITER'S CORNER

Use your notes from the previous Writer's Corner on page 487. Write a Works Cited page for your two sources. Use the correct form for each entry.

Outlines

After you have finished doing research and writing note cards, the next step in writing a research report is to organize your information. An effective way to organize information is to write an outline. An outline is like the skeleton of a research report. It helps you decide which information you want to use and how to present that information in an order your readers can follow.

An outline can let you know if you have more information than you need. It can also let you know if you need to look for additional information.

Parts of an Outline

An outline lays out ideas as they will appear in a research report. Main ideas are labeled with Roman numerals (I, II, III, IV, and so on). Each main idea will be explained in a paragraph in your report.

Details support the main ideas in research reports. Details are listed below the main ideas and are labeled with capital letters (A, B, C, D, and so on). If a main idea has details, there should always be two or more details.

Outline Structure

Outlines should be written neatly so that they are easy to follow. For example, the periods for the Roman numerals should line up with one another. The detail letters should line up too. Use a ruler to line up your main ideas and details if you need help keeping them straight.

Outlines list all ideas in complete sentences, in phrases, or in single words. Sentences, phrases, and words should not be mixed in an outline.

Here is an outline of a research report about the life of turtles.

I. where turtles live
   A. deserts
   B. rivers and ponds
   C. seas

II. what turtles eat
   A. plants
   B. small animals

III. turtle life span
   A. longer than people
   B. can live 100 years

IV. turtle growth
   A. small one, 3 inches
   B. long one, 8 feet
   C. most in-between

ACTIVITY A Use the following word web to create an outline. Use the outline on page 490 as a guide.

ACTIVITY B Rewrite this outline in the correct format.

Fire Safety and Prevention

1. Fire Prevention?

    plan an escape route

    make sure everyone knows what to do

    check that fire alarms work correctly

C. What to do in an emergency

    a. Call 911

    aa. Meet at a designated spot

(2). Fire Safety: 1. Do not use the stove or oven alone 2. Do not play with matches

WRITER'S CORNER

Add another main idea to the outline about firefighters. Under the main idea, write at least two details.

Tech Tip Use a computer program to create an outline.

ACTIVITY C Below are parts of two outlines. Identify the detail in each outline that doesn't support the main idea.

Outline 1

I. Olympic Games

    A. discus throw

    B. javelin throw

    C. business sponsors

    D. 100-m dash

Outline 2

II. Wonders of the Ancient World

    A. Great Pyramid of Egypt

    B. Grand Canyon

    C. Hanging Gardens of Babylon

    D. Colossus of Rhodes

ACTIVITY D Below is a list that contains two main ideas and their details. They are part of an outline for a research report about polar bears. The ideas are out of order. Write them in outline form by finding the two main ideas and putting the appropriate details under each main idea. Use Roman numerals for the main ideas and capital letters for the details.

what a polar bear looks like

body with thick white fur

five claws on each foot

northern coasts of Canada, Russia, and Greenland

islands in the Arctic Ocean

where polar bears live

long body and neck

northern coast of Alaska

ACTIVITY E These are the details for a main idea of a research report about clouds. Then write the main idea and details in outline form.

stratus clouds like blankets or sheets of fog

cumulus clouds like puffy white masses

cirrus clouds curly or wispy ice-crystal forms

ACTIVITY F Read the details that follow the main ideas below. Choose the best main idea to describe all the notes. Then write an outline using the main idea and the four details from the notes.

Main Ideas

what a gemstone is

the value of gemstones

making imitation gemstones

Details

Gemstones are treasured by many people. The value of these treasures is determined by many factors.

The brilliance and color of a stone determines its worth.

The hardness of the gem is important because the harder the gem, the longer it will last.

The way a stone is cut and polished affects its value. The rarest gemstones are the most valuable.

WRITER'S CORNER

Choose a story or book that you like. Make an outline that summarizes the plot. Choose at least three major events as main ideas. Remember to include at least two details for each main idea.

Use a spreadsheet to organize your report outline.

Compound Words

Compound words are two words joined together to form one word. In the research report on page 481, the writer wrote about the sport of basketball. *Basketball* is a compound word. What other compound words are used in games? What two words make up each of these compound words?

airport	sunflower	snowflake
farmyard	carefree	daydream
raincoat	hairbrush	lighthouse

The compound word *snowflake* is made up of *snow* and *flake*. Recognizing the two words that make up a compound word can help you figure out its meaning. A snowflake is a flake of snow.

Some compound words are written as two words. The words *firehouse* and *firefighter* are written as one word. But *fire station* and *fire engine* are not. Here are some other examples.

ONE WORD	TWO WORDS
airmail	air bag
waterbed	water bug

Compound words may also be hyphenated. For example, *half-dollar, great-grandson,* and *forget-me-not* are hyphenated compound words. Be sure to check a dictionary if you are not sure whether to write a compound word as one word, as two words, or as a hyphenated word.

ACTIVITY A Tell the two words that make up each of these compound words. Then think of two more compound words using the first part of each of these compound words.

1. newsstand
2. eyesight
3. schoolwork
4. raincoat
5. full-length
6. bedspread
7. outnumber
8. watermelon

9. all-around
10. everyone
11. sunlight
12. seacoast
13. fingernail
14. haircut
15. headquarters
16. underestimate

ACTIVITY B Make compound words by matching each word in Column A with an appropriate word in Column B.

Column A	Column B
1. head	a. mate
2. pan	b. port
3. fire	c. bolt
4. class	d. phone
5. life	e. cake
6. thunder	f. guest
7. water	g. book
8. house	h. melon
9. air	i. cracker
10. text	j. saver

WRITER'S CORNER

Write three sentences about a favorite holiday, using as many compound words as you can. Be sure to write sentences that make sense. Underline all the compound words. Use a dictionary to check your compound words.

ACTIVITY C Complete the sentences below by filling in the blanks to complete each compound word.

1. I think the baseball game will be rained out. I see thunder_____.

2. The first time Jake rode in a bumpy two-seat plane, he became air_____.

3. Our grandfathers were class_____ 60 years ago.

4. The life_____ wore sunblock to protect her from the sun.

5. Tim's mother bakes gooey home_____ cookies every Sunday.

6. My goggles are always full of water. They're not water_____.

7. My uncle loves the ocean so much that he's living in a house_____ in the San Diego Harbor.

8. It's not cold at all, but my dad is still starting a fire in the fire_____.

9. We spent all weekend building a dog_____ for our pet beagle, Toby.

10. At the carnival Donna won a gold_____ to take home.

ACTIVITY D Form compound words by answering the questions below. The first part of the compound word is provided.

1. I am at the end of a fishing line. What am I? fish_____

2. I am a mark you leave on wet sand. What am I? foot_____

3. I will protect your horse's hoof. What am I? horse_____

4. I am a helper who cares for a baby. Who am I? baby_____

5. I am a container for a plant. What am I? flower_____

6. I am also called your spine. What am I? back_____

7. I am the part of your home in which you sleep at night. What am I? bed_____

8. I am a delicious food made by cooking and crushing apples. What am I? apple_____

9. My job is to pull larger boats out to sea. What am I? tug_____

10. I am a large, wild animal that lives in North America. What am I? bob_____

ACTIVITY E Many compound words have a different meaning from that of the two words being combined. The pictures below represent two words that make up a compound word. Identify the two words that each picture represents. Then guess the compound word and look for its meaning in a dictionary.

1. _____

2. _____

3. _____

4. _____

5. _____

WRITER'S CORNER

Write a sentence for three of the compound words in Activity E. Be sure your sentences show the actual meaning of the compound word.

Library Reference Materials

Reference books give information and facts about a wide variety of topics. They are kept in the reference section of the library. Reference books cannot be checked out, so they will always be available for you. Each reference book has a special purpose. Here are some common reference materials.

Encyclopedia

An encyclopedia is usually a set of books that contains articles about people, places, things, and events. The articles are often illustrated with pictures, diagrams, and maps.

Topics in encyclopedias are organized alphabetically. Each book, or volume, of an encyclopedia has a letter or letters on the spine that show the first letter of the topics in that book. Guide words can also help you find your topic.

You might need to look for keywords for your topic, just as you do when you search for information on the Internet. If you were researching cameras, you would probably look in the *C* volume. But if you wanted to find out how film is developed, you might need to brainstorm keywords such as *film* and *darkroom* to find the articles containing that information. Some encyclopedias have an index in the last volume. You might look up your keywords there to find which articles have information about your topic.

Atlas

An atlas is a book of maps. There are many kinds of maps. Some are like maps you've probably seen before that include roads, cities, and state and country borders. There are also maps that show climate, elevation, and geographical features. Some maps show information about where people live in an area and what goods are produced there. Some maps show the mountains and trenches under the ocean. And some maps show the average income of people who live in certain areas of a city.

Historical atlases can show you all the above information as it was in the past. For example, if you looked at a historical atlas of the United States, you could see how the borders have changed over the centuries.

ACTIVITY A Read the questions below. Write the keyword or keywords under which you might look in an encyclopedia to find the answer to each question.

1. Who were the first people to settle in California?
2. How are clouds formed?
3. What were some of Julius Caesar's major accomplishments?
4. In what ways can solar energy be used?
5. What are the parts of the brain?
6. What are some important monuments in Greece?
7. What is the life cycle of a dragonfly?
8. How was the first computer invented?
9. Where were the first modern Olympic Games held?
10. How does a rhinoceros use its horn?
11. How long is the Nile River?
12. What was the route of the Oregon Trail?

WRITER'S CORNER

Choose one of the questions from Activity A. Use an encyclopedia to find the answer to the question. Write two more facts about the topic. Then write the source entry for the Works Cited page.

Almanac

An almanac is a reference book that is published every year. Much of the information in an almanac is facts and statistics that change often. In the most recent almanac, you can find up-to-date information about countries, governments, sports teams, and many other subjects. You can find out who won the last World Series and who the current ruler of Estonia is—or even if it's still called Estonia.

Specialized almanacs publish up-to-date information in a specific area. For example, a sports almanac lists historical and recent sports statistics.

Periodicals

Magazines are called periodicals because they are published periodically, such as once a month. Periodicals provide up-to-date information. Most libraries have recent issues of periodicals for you to browse. Older issues of periodicals are sometimes bound together as a large book. Another way of collecting older issues of periodicals is to put them on microfilm or microfiche. A librarian can show you how to use these materials. Sometimes an old periodical article can be useful to show you how people felt about a historical event at the time it happened.

Information in older issues of periodicals can be found by using an index or the *Readers' Guide to Periodical Literature.* A librarian can help you use these guides to find the articles you need.

ACTIVITY B Tell whether you would use an encyclopedia, atlas, or almanac to find the following information. You might use more than one reference book for each topic.

1. the names of three different types of dinosaurs
2. how coal is formed
3. how many people live in China
4. the city where the tallest building in the United States is located
5. the name of a river that runs through Pennsylvania
6. folktale heroes of Ireland
7. three islands surrounding Australia
8. how many inches of rain Germany had last year
9. the states Route 66 passed through

ACTIVITY C Tell which of these children's magazines, or periodicals, would most likely have information about the following topics. If you are unsure, look up the magazines on the Internet or in the library.

Odyssey   *Cobblestone*   *Zoobooks*

Creative Kids   *Time for Kids*   *Sports Illustrated for Kids*

1. current political election results
2. life in colonial America
3. viewing the constellations
4. short stories written by kids
5. biographies of snowboarding athletes
6. animals of the tundra

ACTIVITY D Use a current almanac to answer these questions.

1. What is the population of New Zealand?
2. Who won last year's Nobel Peace Prize?
3. Who was Major League Baseball's Rookie of the Year last year?
4. Who is the current prime minister of Great Britain?
5. Who is the current governor of Texas?
6. What is the current population of Alaska?
7. What is the average age of people living in Iceland?
8. What book won the National Book Award for fiction last year?

WRITER'S CORNER

Choose a state in the United States that you would like to know more about. Use an encyclopedia, an almanac, and an atlas to find interesting facts about that state. Record two facts from each kind of reference book.

Oral Research Reports

You will probably need to research things throughout your life for school, for work, and for your own information. You might research the history of a Caribbean island you plan to visit. You might research the diet of an iguana you want to buy as a pet. You might one day report groundbreaking research in front of a group of listeners. Here are some ideas for how to prepare and present an oral research report.

Purpose and Audience

Think about why you are sharing your information. The purpose of your talk can help you think about how you want to present your information. Are you trying to get others interested in something that interests you? Are you giving others information that will help them later?

Think about your audience. Keep in mind that your listeners have not done as much research as you have. Be sure to explain technical terms that your listeners may not know.

Organization

Organize your oral research report the way you would organize a written research report. Making notes and an outline can help you organize the information you researched. Speak slowly and let your audience know how the parts of your research report are connected. Remember that a confused listener cannot go back and reread something the way a reader can.

Visual Aids

Research reports have a lot of information. Listeners have to try hard to understand how all of that information is connected. One way you can help listeners is by providing one or more visual aids.

Visual aids can include pictures, maps, models, diagrams, posters, or drawings. Be sure that your visual aid will help readers understand, rather than get distracted from, the information. If your research report is about the Brazos River in Texas, listeners might find it helpful to see a map of where the Brazos River flows. It probably wouldn't be helpful if you showed them a glass of water from the river.

Make sure that everyone can see your visual aid. You might create a PowerPoint presentation, make a poster, or have enough copies for all your listeners.

ACTIVITY A **Read the excerpt above. What terms do you think should be explained to your audience? What visual aids would you use to highlight the topic?**

Aztec calendar

LiNK

Lost Temple of the Aztecs

...Merchants carried their goods in large sacks on their backs. Nobles paraded about in their fur cloaks, jewels, and plumes. Warrior knights wore their eagle helmets and jaguar skins. Commoners moved through the streets dressed in simple clothes and coarse cloaks. Everyone was in a hurry, like ants in a busy colony.

Shelley Tanaka

SPEAKER'S CORNER

Work with a partner to browse encyclopedias or Web sites to find an exotic location. Write four questions for an oral research report you would like to answer about your location. Write your answers on note cards.

Introduction and Conclusion

As in other kinds of writing and speaking, you will need an introduction and a conclusion. Begin with an introduction that grabs the audience's attention. You might start with an interesting question that you will answer in your report or an interesting fact that you discovered. In your conclusion briefly restate your topic sentence. Emphasize what you want the audience to remember about your topic.

Prepare

If you have taken good notes and written an outline for your research report, much of your work is already done. Your outline can help you make note cards for your speech.

Write one or two note cards for your introduction. Be sure to include your topic sentence so that your audience knows what you will be talking about.

Use your outline to make note cards for the body of your report. Write the main ideas for the body at the top of several note cards. Then write supporting information for each main idea.

Write note cards for your conclusion. Think of a brief way to restate your topic sentence. Make a note card with a statement you want your audience to remember.

Practice

As with other kinds of speaking, it is important to practice. Be sure to speak clearly and slowly. Speak loudly enough for everyone to hear. If you plan to use a visual aid, practice using it. Be sure that everyone will be able to see it.

After you have practiced your oral research report a few times, you might want to practice with a friend or family member. Be sure to get feedback from your listener. See if you can make your oral research report clearer. Ask if your delivery was loud enough and slow enough for your listener to follow the information you presented.

Listening Tips

Listening to a research report is a chance to learn something new. Here are some tips for listening to an oral research report.

- Make notes of what the speaker's topic sentence is and what each main idea is. Think about whether the details support the main ideas.
- Pay attention to the speaker's visual aids. They may help you understand more about what the speaker is saying.
- If you are confused or if you want to know more, you may be able to ask questions after the speaker has finished.

ACTIVITY B Use the notes you made for the Speaker's Corner on page 503 to write a topic sentence and an outline for a research report.

ACTIVITY C Using your topic sentence from Activity B, write an introduction and a conclusion for your research report on the exotic location. Try to grab the reader's attention with an interesting question or fact.

ACTIVITY D Use your outline and the introduction and conclusion you wrote to make note cards for an oral research report. Be sure you do not write your entire report on your note cards. Practice speaking your report, using your note cards.

SPEAKER'S CORNER

Practice your oral research report with the same partner who helped you research your topic. Talk with your partner about how your oral research reports are different, even though you started with the same information. Prepare any visual aids for your presentation.

Prewriting and Drafting

In this chapter you have practiced the skills you need to write a research report. Now is the time to apply these skills to write your draft.

Prewriting

The sixth graders at Max's school go on an overnight field trip every year. The place the sixth graders visit is chosen from the suggestions made by students when they are in fifth grade.

Max decided to submit a research report for a place to visit next year. He knew that he would have to write a report that was neither too broad nor too narrow, that included many details, and that would be well researched.

Choosing a Topic

Max had always wanted to visit Mesa Verde National Park. Max decided to write his report about the park.

Because there was so much to write about, Max's father suggested that Max narrow his topic. Since he was suggesting the park for
_____ a school trip, Max thought
👀 **Ideas** that a research report
_____ about the history of the park and some educational activities for students would be a good topic.

> ## Your Turn
>
> Choose a topic that is not too broad. Think about specific people, places, or events. Then decide what you want to know about your topic.

Researching

Max had two questions that he wanted his report to answer: "What is the history of Mesa Verde National Park?" and "What activities are there for kids to do?"

Keeping his questions in mind, Max went to the library and found some good sources. Then he did some research online. As he researched, he started thinking of other questions. He wrote a note card for each source with the information he would need for a Works Cited page.

Prewriting

Drafting

Content Editing

Revising

Copyediting

Proofreading

Publishing

Your Turn

What questions do you want your report to answer? Look for information to answer these questions. As you research, you might think of more specific questions.

- Write these questions at the tops of note cards and write the answers to the questions below.
- Write the source, author, and page number at the bottom of each note card.

Organizing Information

Max had gathered a lot of note cards with researched facts. He organized his cards into two piles. One pile was information about the history of the park. The other pile was about things to do at the park. He used the note cards to write an outline for his report. At the right is part of Max's outline.

Max included on his outline a section each for his introduction, body paragraphs, and

👀 **Organization**

conclusion. He wrote a Roman numeral before each main idea. Then he listed details under each main idea and lettered them.

Your Turn

- Organize your note cards in a way that makes sense to you.
- Sort your notes so that cards with related ideas are together.
- Use your organized note cards to write an outline. Include sections on your outline for each part of your draft.

Writer's Tip A research report is a chance for you to learn more about something that you are interested in. It can be related to anything you might want to know more about.

| III. original inhabitants |
| A. Anasazi, or ancient pueblos |
| B. from AD 550 to about 1300 |
| C. reasons for disappearance |
| IV. Anasazi homes |
| A. underground "pithouses" |
| B. above-ground adobe villages |
| C. cliff houses |

Cliff Palace, the largest cliff dwelling in North America Mesa Verde National Park

Drafting

Max typed his first draft on a computer. The following paragraphs are from the introduction, the body, and the conclusion of Max's draft.

A Gift from the Past

At the southwestern tip of Colorado is a place known as the Four Corners. It is also where you can find Mesa Verde National Park. There are a lot of unusual trees there. Mesa Verde National Park has a rich and interesting history.

The Anasazi, or the ancient pueblos, were the first people to make their home in this area. They arrived in AD 550 and stayed for about 700 years. The Anasazi spread thrughout the South west and then in about 1300, all the people disappeared and no one is sure what happened. They may have moved south along the Rio Grande and Colorado Rivers. Some people believe that droughts and dry land forced them to move on. Other people believe that the tribes had gotten too big and had used up all the area's natural resources.

Anasazi clay vessel

The next big discovery at Mesa Verde was made by Richard Wetherill and Charles Mason. Because of their discovery, they decided to explore some more. Richard Wetherill and his brothers went back many times between 1889 and 1892. Over that time they gathered eight different collections of Anasazi artfacts. They were out searching for lost cattle when they saw the Cliff Palace dwelling. Over the next two days, they found two more dwellings. Many explorers went to Mesa Verde to collect artifacts, which they would later sell. Finally, in 1906, Mesa Verde was made a national park. After that explorers could not collect and sell artfacts or destroy any part of the park.

Visiting Mesa Verde National Park is like taking a really awesome trip through time. Seeing the history of the park, and knowing just a little bit about the people who lived there, shows how even 1,000 years ago people were different from us but like us at the same time.

Prewriting

Drafting

Content Editing

Revising

Copyediting

Proofreading

Publishing

Your Turn

- Use your prewriting notes to write your first draft. Keep in mind the questions that you asked about your topic.
- As you write your draft, you may find that some of your research does not fit in your report. You may also find that you have to do additional research to support the direction your draft is taking.
- Make sure you give yourself enough time to make these changes as you work on your draft.

Anasazi ceramic ceremonial double mug

Content Editing

Max had found a lot of interesting information about Mesa Verde National Park. He was happy that he was able to use so many facts in his draft. But Max had read so much about the park that he wasn't sure if what he wrote in his draft made sense.

Max's next-door neighbor, Becky, was in his class at school. Becky was also writing a research report about a place for the sixth-grade class to visit. Max and Becky decided to content edit each other's reports. Below is the checklist they used.

Becky read Max's draft. She told Max that Mesa Verde sounded like more fun than the place she had written about.

Becky then read the draft a few more times, using the Content Editor's Checklist. As she worked, she made notes about what she wanted to tell Max when they met to discuss their reports.

First, Becky told Max that she hoped the principal chose Max's suggestion. She thought the park sounded like a lot of fun. She also told Max that she liked how his topic sentence was clearly stated in the introduction and how the main ideas of each paragraph supported the topic sentence.

Voice

Content Editor's Checklist

- ☐ Does the introduction include a topic sentence?

- ☐ Does each main idea support the topic sentence?

- ☐ Is each main idea supported with researched details?

- ☐ Does the conclusion summarize the topic sentence? Does it leave the readers with a sense that the topic was covered well?

- ☐ Does the report use formal language and a confident tone?

Then Becky gave Max her suggestions for improvements.

- You talk about the Four Corners in your introduction. Where is that?
- I don't think that the sentence about the trees in the introduction is necessary. You don't ever talk about them again in your report.
- The paragraph about Wetherill and Mason is confusing.
- In the last paragraph, the words *really awesome* stick out.

 Word Choice

I don't think they are very formal.

Max was glad that Becky had content edited his draft. She had found a lot of things that he had missed.

Max used the Content Editor's Checklist to content edit the draft himself. He found a few more things that he wanted to change.

Grammar in Action

Diagram the topic sentence in Max's research report on page 508.

Your Turn

- Work with a partner to content edit each other's work. Read the draft once to get an idea of what the report is about. Then read it again, using the Content Editor's Checklist. Take notes about your suggestions.
- Meet with your partner to discuss your drafts. Don't forget to tell your partner what you liked about the report. Remember to give your suggestions in a constructive and positive way. Listen to your partner's suggestions with an open mind, but use only the suggestions that you think will improve your report.

Remember that it is also a good idea to content edit your own work. You might find something that your content editor missed. You might see places that need further revision.

Prewriting

Drafting

Content Editing

Revising

Copyediting

Proofreading

Publishing

Anasazi home at Mesa Verde National Park

Revising

Here are the changes that Max made to his draft.

A Gift from the Past

It is the only place in America where four states touch. Utah, Colorado, Arizona, and New Mexico meet At the southwestern tip of Colorado is a place known as the Four Corners. It is *there.*

also where you can find Mesa Verde National Park. ~~There are a lot of unusual trees there.~~ Mesa Verde National Park has a rich and interesting history.

The Anasazi, or the ancient pueblos, were the first people to make their

home in this area. They arrived in AD 550 and stayed for about 700 years. The

Anasazi spread thrughout the South west and then in about 1300, all the people

disappeared and no one is sure what happened. They may have moved south

along the Rio Grande and Colorado Rivers. Some people believe that droughts and

dry land forced them to move on. Other people believe that the tribes had gotten

too big and had used up all the area's natural resources.

The next big discovery at Mesa Verde was made by Richard Wetherill and Charles Mason. Because of their discovery, they decided to explore some more. Richard Wetherill and his brothers went back many times between 1889 and 1892. Over that time they gathered eight different collections of Anasazi artfacts. They were out searching for lost cattle when they saw the Cliff Palace dwelling. Over the next two days, they found two more dwellings. Many explorers went to Mesa Verde to collect artifacts, which they would later sell. Finally, in 1906, Mesa Verde was made a national park. After that explorers could not collect and sell artfacts or destroy any part of the park.

Visiting Mesa Verde National Park is like taking a ~~really awesome~~ trip through time. ∧
You can imagine yourself there weaving baskets, making pots or climbing a ladder to your room. Seeing the history of the park, and knowing just a little bit about the people who lived there, shows how even 1,000 years ago people were different from us but like us at the same time.

Prewriting

Drafting

Content Editing

Revising

Copyediting

Proofreading

Publishing

Max read over his draft again and decided to make a few changes to improve it. Look at the changes Max made.

- What did Max do to add more information about the Four Corners?
- Why did Max take out the sentence about the trees?
- Max agreed with Becky about the language. What did he do to make it more formal?
- What did Max do with the Wetherill and Mason paragraph to make it clearer?
- How did Max make his conclusion stronger?

Your Turn

Use your partner's suggestions and your own ideas to revise your draft. When you have finished, use the Content Editor's Checklist again to check your draft.

Editor's Workshop

Copyediting and Proofreading

Copyediting

Now that the ideas of his draft were strong, Max took some time to copyedit. He used this checklist to copyedit his draft.

Copyeditor's Checklist

- ☐ Has the writing been checked for rambling and run-on sentences?
- ☐ Are compound words used correctly?
- ☐ Is there variety in sentence length?
- ☐ Are exact words used to give the writing a confident tone?
- ☐ Do all the words mean what I think they mean?

Max found a run-on sentence in the first paragraph of the part about the Anasazi. He revised the sentence

Sentence Fluency

that begins *The Anasazi spread throughout . . .* into three separate sentences.

Max found one place where he had written two separate words that should be one compound word. He changed *South west* to *Southwest* in the first paragraph of the part about the Anasazi.

Max found a place in the paragraph about Wetherill and Mason where he could combine sentences. Look at his revision below.

Revision: Because of their discovery, Richard Wetherill and his brothers came back many times between 1889 and 1892.

Max added the word *severe* to describe *droughts.* He thought that adding this descriptive word made his writing sound more confident.

Prewriting

Drafting

Content Editing

Revising

Copyediting

Proofreading

Publishing

Your Turn

Read aloud your draft to hear how the language and tone sound. Then use the Copyeditor's Checklist to copyedit your draft.

It is always a good idea to have someone else check your work. Ask someone at home to use the Copyeditor's Checklist to copyedit your work.

Proofreading

Max wanted to have someone proofread his draft to make sure that there were no mistakes in spelling, punctuation, capitalization, or grammar.

Max's neighbor across the street, Professor Danvers, taught at the state university. Max asked her to proofread his research report. Professor Danvers used this checklist to proofread Max's draft.

Proofreader's Checklist

☐ Are the paragraphs indented?

☐ Have all the words been checked for spelling?

☐ Is the grammar correct?

☐ Are the sentences and proper nouns capitalized correctly?

☐ Has the writing been checked to make sure no new mistakes have been added?

Professor Danvers found only two misspelled words. One was in the part about the Anasazi. She changed *thrughout* to *throughout*. The other misspelled word was in the part about Wetherill. What word did Max misspell?

Professor Danvers noticed *pueblos* in the first sentence of the part about the Anasazi. She

 Conventions marked the change to *Pueblos*, because she knew that it was a proper noun.

She found one punctuation mistake. In the conclusion Max had forgotten to put a comma between *pots* and *or* in the second sentence.

Your Turn

Read your draft again. Use the Proofreader's Checklist to check for misspelled words and mistakes in grammar, punctuation, and capitalization.

- Trade drafts with a partner. Use the Proofreader's Checklist to proofread your partner's draft.
- Be sure to double-check whether the misspelled words you mark are really incorrect.
- Return each other's papers and discuss the mistakes you found.

Writer's Tip Make sure to mark your corrections clearly and in a different color so they stand out.

Publishing

After a lot of work and several revisions, Max felt that his research report was ready to hand in to the teacher. He made sure to include a Works Cited page so that the principal would know where he got all his information. Now that he had learned so much about the park, he really hoped that his class would be going there next year.

A Gift from the Past

At the southwestern tip of Colorado is a place known as the Four Corners. It is the only place in America where four states touch. Utah, Colorado, Arizona, and New Mexico meet there. It is also where you can find Mesa Verde National Park. Mesa Verde National Park has a rich and interesting history.

The Anasazi, or the ancient Pueblos, were the first people to make their home in this area. They arrived in AD 550 and stayed for about 700 years. The Anasazi spread throughout the Southwest. Then, in about 1300, all the people disappeared. No one is sure what happened. They may have moved south along the Rio Grande and Colorado Rivers. Some people believe that severe droughts and dry land forced them to move on. Other people believe that the tribes had gotten too big and had used up all the area's natural resources.

The next big discovery at Mesa Verde was made by Richard Wetherill and Charles Mason. They were out searching for lost cattle when they saw the Cliff Palace dwelling. Over the next two days, they found two more dwellings. Because of their discovery, Richard Wetherill and his brothers went back many times between 1889 and 1892. Over that time they gathered eight different collections of Anasazi artifacts. Many explorers went to Mesa Verde to collect artifacts, which they would later sell. Finally, in 1906, Mesa Verde was made a national park. After that explorers could not collect and sell artifacts or destroy any part of the park.

Visiting Mesa Verde National Park is like taking a trip through time. You can imagine yourself there weaving baskets, making pots, or climbing a ladder to your room. Seeing the history of the park, and knowing just a little bit about the people who lived there, shows how even 1,000 years ago people were different from us but like us at the same time.

Works Cited

"Anasazi." World Book. 2011 ed.

Arnold, Caroline. The Ancient Cliff Dwellers of Mesa Verde. New York: Clarion Books, 1992.

Fisher, Leonard Everett. Anasazi. New York: Atheneum Books for Young Readers, 1997.

"Mesa Verde National Park." 16 Nov. 2011 <www.mesa.verde.national-park.com>.

Petersen, David. Mesa Verde National Park. Chicago: Children's Press, 1992.

Now that you have researched and written your report, why not share it with your class, friends, and family? Here are a some ways to publish your work.

 Record a podcast of yourself giving your oral research report. Post the podcast on the class blog for feedback.

 Make a PowerPoint presentation to accompany your research report. Fill it with pictures, maps, and video that illustrate your topic.

 Create a mini-encyclopedia by combining everyone's research reports within a single cover. Arrange the reports in alphabetical order and create a contents page.

 Use a video camera to create a newscast. Film each student giving an oral presentation of his or her research report.

Whenever you publish your work, your goal is to share your thoughts and experiences with other people.

Your Turn

Carefully copy your report in your neatest handwriting or type it on a computer. Don't

 Presentation

forget to include a Works Cited page. Remember to proofread your Works Cited page to make sure that you have used the correct punctuation for each entry.

Common Proofreading Marks

Use these proofreading marks to mark changes when you proofread. Remember to use a colored pencil to make your changes.

Symbol	Meaning	Example
¶	begin new paragraph	over. ¶Begin a new
⌒	close up space	close u p space
∧	insert	students ∧think *(should)*
℘	delete, omit	that the the book
/	make lowercase	/Mathematics
∽	reverse letters	reverse letters
≡	capitalize	washington
∨∨	add quotation marks	I am, I said.
⊙	add period	Marta drank tea ∧⊙

How to Do Mathematical Magic

Everyone loves a magic trick. I know a magic trick that is based on math, not magic. If you follow these easy directions, you'll dazzle your friends every t... I love this trick so much that I just can't wait to tell you about it... ...ing cards, a table, and a volunteer. First, ...k at it without

Grammar and Mechanics Handbook

Grammar

Adjectives

An adjective points out or describes a noun.

This fruit is **delicious**.

Adjectives That Compare

Most adjectives have three degrees of comparison: positive, comparative, and superlative.

The positive degree of an adjective shows a quality of a noun.

The meerkat is **cute**.   The giraffe is **tall**.

The comparative degree of an adjective is used to compare two items or two sets of items. It is often used with *than*. To form the comparative degree, *-er* is often added to an adjective.

The meerkat is **cuter** than the warthog.
The giraffe is **taller** than the okapi.

The superlative degree of an adjective is used to compare three or more items or sets of items. To form the superlative degree, *-est* is often added to an adjective.

The meerkat is the **cutest** animal in the zoo.
The giraffe is the **tallest** animal in Africa.

Some adjectives that compare have special forms.

This painting is **good**.
Her painting is **better** than mine.
Micah's is the **best** painting of all.

The baby isn't feeling **well** today.
She felt **worse** yesterday.
She felt **worst** of all on Sunday.

We had a **bad** storm yesterday.
It was a **worse** storm than the one last week.
The **worst** storm we had was in December.

More, most, less, and *least* are used with adjectives of three or more syllables and with some adjectives of two syllables.

> Carla is a **more careful** worker than Luis.
> Lindsey is **less careful** than Carla.
> Marta is the **most intelligent** student in class.
> She is also the **least gullible** student.

The comparative adjectives *fewer* and *fewest* are used with plural concrete nouns. The comparative adjectives *less* and *least* are used with abstract nouns.

> I have **fewer** pencils than Jody does.
> Mark has the **fewest** pens.

> I have **less** experience.
> Bo has the **least** curiosity.

Adjectives That Tell How Many

Some adjectives tell how many or about how many.

> Only **six** members came to the meeting.   A **few** members were sick.

Some adjectives tell numerical order.

> I finished reading the **sixth** chapter.

Articles

Articles point out nouns. *The, a,* and *an* are articles. *The* is the definite article. It points out a specific person, place, or thing. *A* and *an* are indefinite articles. They point out any one of a class of people, places, or things. Use *a* before a consonant sound and *an* before a vowel sound.

> **The** man ate **a** peach and **an** apple.

When two or more nouns joined by *and* refer to different people, places, or things, use an article before each noun. When two or more nouns joined by *and* refer to the same person, place, or thing, use an article before the first noun only.

> **The** coach and **the** players celebrated their win.
> **The** teacher and coach is Mr. Simmons.

Demonstrative Adjectives

Demonstrative adjectives point out a specific person, place, or thing. The demonstrative adjectives are *this, that, these,* and *those.*

Singular	Plural
this flower	**these** bushes
that flower	**those** bushes

This and *these* point out things or people that are near. *That* and *those* point out things or people that are farther away.

> **This** flower is red. (singular and near)
> **Those** bushes are tall. (plural and far)

Descriptive Adjectives

A descriptive adjective tells more about a noun. It can tell how something looks, tastes, sounds, feels, or smells. It can tell about size, number, color, shape, or weight.

A descriptive adjective often comes before the noun it describes.

> A **tall** tree stood near the **red** barn.

A descriptive adjective can follow a linking verb as a subject complement. It describes the subject of the sentence.

> The tree near the red barn was **tall**.

Interrogative Adjectives

An interrogative adjective is used to ask a question. The interrogative adjectives are *what, which,* and *whose.* An interrogative adjective comes before a noun.

> **What** movie did you see?   **Which** theater did you go to?
> **Whose** car did you take?

Possessive Adjectives

A possessive adjective shows who or what owns something. A possessive adjective is used before a noun. The possessive adjectives are *my, your, his, her, its, our,* and *their.*

> I have **my** camera, and Lucy has **her** cell phone.

Proper Adjectives

Proper adjectives are formed from proper nouns. A proper adjective always begins with a capital letter.

> When we went to China, I ate **Chinese** food.

Adverbs

An adverb tells more about a verb. Many adverbs end in *ly*.

An adverb of time tells when or how often something happens.

I went to the mall **yesterday**.   I **sometimes** go to the toy store.

An adverb of place tells where something happens.

I went **outside** after dinner.   I played **there** until it was dark.

An adverb of manner tells how something happens.

My new skateboard goes **fast**.   I ride it **gracefully**.

Adverbs That Compare

An adverb can compare the actions of two or more people or things. To compare the actions of two people or things, *-er* is often added to an adverb. To compare the actions of three or more people or things, *-est* is often added to an adverb.

Sam went to bed **later** than Henry.   Luke went to bed **latest** of us all.

Some adverbs that compare use *more* and *most*. Use *more* and *most* with adverbs ending in *ly* and with adverbs of three or more syllables.

Sam answered **more sleepily** than Henry.
Luke answered **most sleepily** of us all.

Negative Words

Some adverbs form negative ideas. Use *not, n't* for *not* in a contraction, or *never* to express a negative idea. Do not use more than one negative word in a sentence.

He will **not** be ready on time.   He **can't** find his sneakers.
He **never** remembers where he left them.

Antecedents

The noun to which a pronoun refers is its antecedent. A pronoun must agree with its antecedent in person and number. The pronouns *he, him,* and *his* refer to male antecedents. The pronouns *she, her,* and *hers* refer to female antecedents. The pronouns *it* and *its* refer to animals or things. See NUMBER, PERSON.

Clauses

A clause is a group of words that has a subject and a predicate.

Adverb Clauses

An adverb clause is a dependent clause used as an adverb. An adverb clause can tell when.

> **As soon as I get home**, I'll do my homework.
> I'll play video games **after we eat dinner**.

Dependent Clauses

A dependent clause cannot stand alone as a sentence.

> **While I was at the mall**, my cell phone rang.

Independent Clauses

An independent clause, or main clause, can stand alone as a sentence.

> **I put on my helmet** before I got on my bike.

Conjunctions

A conjunction is a word used to join two words or groups of words in a sentence.

Coordinating Conjunctions

A coordinating conjunction joins two words or groups of words that are similar. The words *and, but,* and *or* are coordinating conjunctions.

> My dad **and** I went to the pool.   I can swim **but** not dive.
> The pool is never too hot **or** crowded.

Subordinate Conjunctions

A subordinate conjunction connects a dependent clause to an independent clause in a sentence.

> **After** we drive to the pool, we'll change clothes.
> We'll swim **until** it is time to go home for dinner.

Contractions

A contraction is a short way to write some words. An apostrophe (') is used to show where one or more letters have been left out of the words.

Many contractions are formed with the word *not.*

do not = don't	was not = wasn't
cannot = can't	will not = won't

Many contractions are formed with personal pronouns.

I am = I'm	he is = he's
you are = you're	we have = we've

Direct Objects

The direct object in a sentence is the noun or pronoun that receives the action of the verb. The direct object tells whom or what after the verb. Two or more direct objects joined by *and* or *or* form a compound direct object.

My mom made **pasta** and **salad**.   I helped **her**.

Indirect Objects

An indirect object is the noun or pronoun that tells to whom, for whom, to what, or for what an action is done. A sentence cannot have an indirect object unless it has a direct object. The indirect object comes after the verb and before the direct object.

The reporter asked **the mayor** a question.
The mayor gave **her** a long answer.

Interjections

An interjection is a word that expresses a strong or sudden emotion. An interjection is followed by an exclamation point.

Wow! That was a great game.   You kicked the winning goal. **Great!**

Nouns

A noun is a word that names a person, a place, or a thing. See NUMBER.

Collective Nouns
A collective noun names a group of people, places, animals, or things that are considered as a unit.

The science **club** raised a **swarm** of bees.

Common Nouns

A common noun names any one member of a group of people, places, or things.

> My **cousin** saw a **dog** run down the **street**.

Nouns in Direct Address

A noun in direct address names the person spoken to. A noun used in direct address is set off from the rest of the sentence by a comma or commas.

> **Peter,** are you coming with us?
> Bring your skateboard, **Carly,** and wear your helmet.

Plural Nouns

A plural noun names more than one person, place, or thing. Most plurals are formed by adding -s or -es to the singular form. Some nouns have irregular plural forms. Some nouns have the same form in the singular and plural.

> The **children** have some **turtles** and some **fish**.

Possessive Nouns

The possessive form of a noun shows possession or ownership.

A singular possessive noun shows that one person owns something. To form the singular possessive, add an apostrophe (') and the letter s to a singular noun.

baby	baby**'s** bottle
Tess	Tess**'s** soccer ball
woman	woman**'s** purse

A plural possessive noun shows that more than one person owns something. To form the plural possessive of most nouns, add an apostrophe (') after the plural form of the noun.

babies	babies' bottles
the Smiths	the Smiths' house

To form the plural possessive of an irregular noun, add an apostrophe and s ('s) after the plural form.

women	women**'s** purses
mice	mice**'s** cheese

Proper Nouns

A proper noun begins with a capital letter and names a particular person, place, or thing.

> **Meg** saw **Shadow** run down **Pine Street**.

Singular Nouns

A singular noun names one person, place, or thing.

> The **girl** has a **kite** and a **skateboard**.

Number

The number of a noun or pronoun indicates whether it refers to one person, place, or thing (singular) or more than one person, place, or thing (plural).

Person

Personal pronouns and possessive adjectives change form according to person—whether they refer to the person speaking (first person), the person spoken to (second person), or the person, place, or thing spoken about (third person).

Phrases

A phrase is a group of words that is used as a single part of speech.

Adjective Phrases

An adjective phrase is a phrase used as an adjective.

> The woman **in the red hat** is my aunt.

Adverb Phrases

An adverb phrase is a phrase used as an adverb.

> The man sat **on the park bench**.

Prepositional Phrases

A prepositional phrase is made up of a preposition, the object of the preposition, and any modifiers of the object. See PREPOSITIONS.

Verb Phrases

A verb phrase is a group of words that does the work of a single verb. A verb phrase contains a main verb and one or more helping verbs such as *is, are, have, can,* and *do.*

They **are studying**.   They **will be studying** until dinnertime.

In some questions and statements, the parts of a verb phrase may be separated.

Did they **finish** their projects?   Dolores **has** not **finished** hers.

Predicates

The predicate of a sentence tells what the subject is or does.

Complete Predicates

The complete predicate of a sentence is the simple predicate and any words that go with it.

Tom **rode his new bike**.

Compound Predicates

Two predicates joined by *and, but,* or *or* form a compound predicate.

Karen **got a glass** and **poured some milk**.

Simple Predicates

The simple predicate of a sentence is a verb, a word or words that express an action or a state of being.

The boys **ran** noisily down the street.   They **were** happy.

Prepositions

A preposition is a word that shows a relationship between a noun or pronoun and another word in a sentence.

We put the doghouse **under** the tree.
The dog **with** the red collar is Karen's.

Object of the Preposition

The noun or pronoun that follows a preposition is the object of the preposition.

We put the doghouse under **it**.   The dog with the red **collar** is Karen's.

Prepositional Phrases

A prepositional phrase is a preposition, the object of the preposition, and any words that describe the object. A prepositional phrase can be used as an adjective or an adverb.

> We put the doghouse **under the tall green tree**.
> The dog **with the shiny**, **new red collar** is Karen's.

Pronouns

A pronoun is a word that takes the place of a noun. See ANTECEDENTS, NUMBER, PERSON.

Demonstrative Pronouns

A demonstrative pronoun is used to point out a person, place, or thing. The demonstrative pronouns are *this, that, these,* and *those.*

Singular	Plural
this	these
that	those

This and *these* point out things or people that are near. *That* and *those* point out things or people that are farther away.

> **This** is my favorite book. (singular and near)
> **Those** are my cousin's old comic books. (plural and far)

Intensive Pronouns

An intensive pronoun is used to emphasize a noun that comes before it. The intensive pronouns are *myself, yourself, himself, herself, itself, ourselves, yourselves,* and *themselves.*

> Corrine **herself** didn't know she had won.
> They created the prizes **themselves**.

Interrogative Pronouns

An interrogative pronoun is used to ask a question. The interrogative pronouns are *who, whom, what,* and *whose.*

> **Who** broke the window?   **What** happened when it started to rain?
> **Whose** is the ruined book?   **Whom** did you call about the problem?

Personal Pronouns

A personal pronoun refers to the person speaking or to the person or thing that is spoken to or about. In this sentence *I* is the person speaking, *you* is the person spoken to, and *them* are the people spoken about. See PERSON, NUMBER.

> **I** heard **you** calling **them**.

Object Pronouns

An object pronoun can be the direct or indirect object of a sentence or the object of a preposition. The object pronouns are *me, you, him, her, it, us,* and *them.* Two or more object pronouns can be joined by *and* or *or* to form a compound object.

> Karen will help **them**.
> Karen and Chris will come with **us**.
> Chris will help **her** and **me**.
> We will tell **him** the plan later.

Plural Pronouns

A plural pronoun refers to more than one person, place, or thing.

> **They** are helping **us**.

Possessive Pronouns

A possessive pronoun shows ownership or possession. A possessive pronoun takes the place of a noun. It takes the place of the owner and the thing that is owned. The possessive pronouns are *mine, yours, his, hers, its, ours,* and *theirs.*

> My cap is here, and your cap is over there.
> **Mine** is here, and **yours** is over there.

Reflexive Pronouns

A reflexive pronoun is used as the direct or indirect object of a verb or the object of a preposition. The reflexive pronouns are *myself, yourself, himself, herself, itself, ourselves, yourselves,* and *themselves.*

> Paul cut **himself** when he sliced the tomato.
> Molly made **herself** a jelly sandwich.
> The children made lunch for **themselves**.

Singular Pronouns

A singular pronoun refers to one person, place, or thing.

> *I* gave **it** to **her**.

Subject Pronouns

A subject pronoun can be used as the subject or the subject complement of a sentence. The subject pronouns are *I, you, he, she, it, we,* and *they.* Two or more subject pronouns can be joined by *and* or *or* to form a compound subject or subject complement.

She is a great tennis player.   **She** and **I** play tennis often.
The winner of our matches is usually **she**.

Sentences

A sentence is a group of words that expresses a complete thought. Every sentence has a subject and a predicate.

Complex Sentences

A complex sentence contains one independent clause and one or more dependent clauses. The clauses are joined by subordinate conjunctions. See CLAUSES, CONJUNCTIONS.

Before I go to school, I eat a good breakfast.
I watch TV while I am eating.

Compound Sentences

Two sentences, or independent clauses, joined by a comma and the coordinating conjunction *and, but,* or *or* form a compound sentence.

Ming is eating, but Lili is sleeping.

Declarative Sentences

A declarative sentence makes a statement. It tells something. A declarative sentence ends with a period (.).

Your jacket is in the closet.

Exclamatory Sentences

An exclamatory sentence expresses strong or sudden emotion. An exclamatory sentence ends with an exclamation point (!).

How cold it is today!

Imperative Sentences

An imperative sentence gives a command or makes a request. The subject of an imperative sentence is generally *you,* which is often not stated. An imperative sentence ends with a period (.).

Please wear your jacket.

Interrogative Sentences

An interrogative sentence asks a question. An interrogative sentence ends with a question mark (?).

Are you ready?   Where is your jacket?

Inverted Order

A sentence is in inverted order when the main verb or a helping verb comes before the subject.

There **are shoes** everywhere.   Piled on the desk **is** her **homework**.
Does she ever clean up her room?

Natural Order

A sentence is in natural order when the verb follows the subject.

Ophelia leaves her things everywhere.

Subject Complements

A subject complement follows a linking verb in a sentence. It is a noun or pronoun that renames the subject or an adjective that describes the subject. Two or more subject complements joined by *and, but,* or *or* form a compound subject complement.

That firefighter is a **hero**.
Her actions were **brave** and **skillful**.
The officer who received the medal was **she**.

Subjects

The subject of a sentence is who or what the sentence is about. The subject can be a noun or a pronoun.

Complete Subjects

The complete subject is the simple subject and the words that describe it or give more information about it.

The little gray kitten is playing.

Compound Subjects

Two or more subjects joined by *and* or *or* form a compound subject.

Bob, **Phil**, and **Lisa** went to the movies.
Norman or **I** will sweep the floor.

Simple Subject

The simple subject is the noun or pronoun that a sentence tells about.

His little **dog** likes to chase balls.   **It** runs very fast.

Subject-Verb Agreement

A subject and verb must agree, whether the verb is a main verb or a helping verb. If a compound subject is joined by *or*, the verb agrees with the subject closest to it.

I **like** apple turnovers.   My brother **likes** peach cobbler.
Our parents **like** cherry tarts.

I **am building** a birdhouse.   The boys or she **is going to help**.
They **are building** a garage.

A collective noun is generally considered singular even though it means more than one person or thing, and its verb must agree with the singular form.

Our **class is entering** the contest.

When a sentence starts with *there is, there are, there was,* or *there were,* the subject follows the verb. The verb must agree with the subject.

There **is** a **book** on the desk.
There **were** some **pencils** in the drawer.

Tense

The tense of a verb shows when the action takes place.

Future Tense

The future tense tells about something that will happen in the future.

One way to form the future tense is with a form of the helping verb *be* plus *going to* plus the present form of a verb.

I **am going to make** toast.   Dad **is going to butter** it.
They **are going to eat** it.

Another way to form the future tense is with the helping verb *will* and the present form of a verb.

Our class **will go** to the museum.
The guide **will explain** the exhibits.

Future Perfect Tense

The future perfect tense tells about an action that will have been completed by some time in the future. The future perfect tense is formed with *will* plus *have* plus the past participle of a verb.

> I **will have finished** my homework by dinnertime.
> I **will have made** a salad by that time too.

Future Progressive Tense

The future progressive tense tells about something that will be happening in the future. The future progressive tense is formed with *will* and the present participle or with a form of *be* plus *going to* and the present participle.

> I **will be doing** my homework this evening.
> My cousins **are going to be helping** me.

Past Perfect Tense

The past perfect tense tells about an action that was finished before another action in the past. The past perfect tense is formed with *had* and the past participle of a verb.

> She **had come** straight home after school.
> She **had finished** her homework before dinner.

Past Progressive Tense

The past progressive tense tells what was happening in the past. The past progressive tense is formed with *was* or *were* and the present participle of a verb.

> I **was feeding** the cat.   My parents **were reading**.

Present Perfect Tense

The present perfect tense tells about an action that happened at some indefinite time in the past or about an action that started in the past and continues into the present. The present perfect tense is formed with a form of *have* and the past participle of a verb.

> He **has finished** his homework.
> They **have lived** in that house for three years.

Present Progressive Tense

The present progressive tense tells what is happening now. The present progressive tense is formed with *am, is,* or *are* and the present participle of a verb.

We **are watching** TV.　　　　　I **am eating** popcorn.
My sister **is drinking** juice.

Simple Past Tense

The simple past tense tells about something that happened in the past. The simple past tense of regular verbs is formed by adding *-d* or *-ed* to the present form of a verb.

We **cooked** breakfast this morning.　　Mom **fried** the eggs.

Simple Present Tense

The simple present tense tells about something that is always true or something that happens again and again. The present part of a verb is used for the present tense. If the subject is a singular noun or *he, she,* or *it, -s* or *-es* must be added to the verb.

Prairie dogs **live** where it's dry.
A prairie dog **digs** a burrow to live in.

Verbs

A verb shows action or a state of being. See TENSE.

Action Verbs

An action verb tells what someone or something does.

The boy **is running**.　　　　　Seals **bark**.

Being Verbs

A being verb shows what someone or something is. Being verbs do not express action.

The boy **is** tired.　　　　　The seal **was** hungry.

Helping Verbs

A verb can have more than one word. A helping verb is a verb added before the main verb that helps make the meaning clear.

We **will** go to the movie.　　　　We **might** buy some popcorn.

Irregular Verbs

The past and the past participle of irregular verb are not formed by adding -*d* or -*ed.*

Present	Past	Past Participle
sing	sang	sung
send	sent	sent
write	wrote	written

Linking Verbs

A linking verb joins the subject of a sentence to a subject complement. Being verbs can be linking verbs.

My aunt **is** a professional writer.   She **has become** famous.
The winner of the writing award **was** she.

Principal Parts

A verb has four principal parts: present, present participle, past, and past participle. The present participle is formed by adding -*ing* to the present. The past and the past participle of regular verbs are formed by adding -*d* or -*ed* to the present.

Present	Present Participle	Past	Past Participle
walk	walking	walked	walked
wave	waving	waved	waved

The past and the past participle of irregular verbs are not formed by adding -*d* or -*ed* to the present.

Present	Present Participle	Past	Past Participle
do	doing	did	done
fly	flying	flew	flown
put	putting	put	put

The present participle is often used with forms of the verb *be.*

We **are walking** to school.   I **was doing** my homework.

The past participle is often used with forms of the verb *have.*

We **have walked** this way before.   He **has done** his homework.

Regular Verbs

The past and the past participle of regular verbs are formed by adding *-d* or *-ed* to the present.

Present	Past	Past Participle
jump	jumped	jumped
glue	glued	glued

Verb Phrases

A verb phrase is made up of one or more helping verbs and a main verb.

I ***should have shown*** you my drawings.

I ***am entering*** them in the art contest.

You ***can see*** them there.

In questions and some statements, the parts of a verb phrase may be separated.

Did Caroline ***bring*** the potato salad?   Marcus ***has*** not ***arrived*** yet.

Mechanics

Capital Letters

Use a capital letter to begin the first word in a sentence.

Tomorrow is my birthday.

Use a capital letter to begin the first word in a direct quotation.

Patrick Henry said, "**G**ive me liberty or give me death."

Use a capital letter to begin a proper noun. A proper noun names a particular person, place, or thing.

Jesse **O**wens competed in the **O**lympics in **B**erlin.

The **W**hite **H**ouse is on **P**ennsylvania **A**venue.

The head of the local **R**ed **C**ross is **C**ora **S**mith.

Use a capital letter to begin a proper adjective.

I love to eat **C**hinese food.

Use a capital letter to begin a title that precedes a person's name.

Mrs. Novak   **D**r. Ramirez   **G**overnor Charles Raddich

Use a capital letter for initials in a person's name.

M. **L**. King = Martin Luther King
George **W**. Bush = George Walker Bush

Use a capital letter for abbreviations when a capital letter would be used if the word was written in full.

Sun. = Sunday   **O**ct. = October

Use a capital letter to begin the directions *North*, *South*, *East*, and *West* when they refer to specific regions of the country.

On our trip to the **W**est, we saw the Painted Desert.

Use a capital letter to begin the important words in the title of a book, movie, TV show, play, poem, song, artwork, sacred book, an article, or essay. The first and last words of a title are always capitalized. Articles, prepositions, and conjunctions are usually not capitalized unless they are the first or last word of the title.

The Secret Garden   "**S**ing a **S**ong of **C**ities"
The Lion King

Use a capital letter to begin every line of most poems and songs.

My country, 'tis of thee,

Sweet land of liberty,
Of thee I sing.

The personal pronoun *I* is always a capital letter.

Punctuation

Apostrophes

Use an apostrophe to form possessive nouns.

Keisha's skateboard   the children's lunches   the horses' stalls

Use an apostrophe to replace the letters left out in a contraction.

didn't   can't   wasn't

Commas

Use a comma to separate the words in a series.

Mark, Anton, and Cara made the scenery.
They hammered, sawed, and nailed.

Use a comma or commas to separate a name in direct address.

> Carl, will you help me?
>
> Do you think, Keshawn, that we will finish today?

Use a comma before the coordinating conjunction when two short sentences are combined in a compound sentence.

> Dad will heat the soup, and I will make the salad.
>
> Dad likes noodle soup, but I like bean soup.

Use a comma to separate the names of a city and state.

> She comes from Philadelphia, Pennsylvania.

Use a comma or commas to separate a direct quotation from the rest of the sentence. When a question mark or an exclamation point ends a quotation at the beginning of a sentence, the comma is not needed.

> "Hey," called Mario, "where are you going?"
>
> "I'm going to the movies," Bo said.
>
> "Hurry up!" Juana yelled.

Use a comma after the word *yes* or *no* that introduces a sentence.

> No, I can't go to the movies tonight.

Use a comma after the closing of a letter and after the salutation of a personal letter.

Exclamation Point

Use an exclamation point after an exclamatory sentence.

> We won the game!

Use an exclamation point after an interjection.

> Wow! The dessert looks delicious.

When an exclamation point is part of a direct quotation, it is placed inside the quotation marks. When the exclamation point is not part of the quotation, it is placed outside the quotation marks.

> Tom yelled, "I quit!"   I was shocked when she said, "I'll do it"!

Periods

Use a period after a declarative or an imperative sentence.

> The cat is hungry.   Please feed it.

Use a period after most abbreviations.

Sun.	Sept.	ft.	yd.	a.m.
Ave.	St.	gal.	oz.	p.m.

Periods are not used after abbreviations for metric measures.

km   cm

Use a period after a personal title.

Mr. Frank Cummings   Dr. Hilda Doolittle   Mrs. Joanna Clark

Use a period after an initial.

John F. Kennedy   U.S.A.   J. K. Rowling

Question Marks

Use a question mark after an interrogative sentence.

Where are you going**?**

When a question mark is part of a direct quotation, it is placed inside the quotation marks. When the question mark is not part of the quotation, it is placed outside the quotation marks.

The teacher asked, "Where is Nepal**?**"
Did the teacher say, "Nepal is in Asia"**?**

Quotation Marks

Use quotation marks to show the exact words a person says in a direct quotation.

Maggie said, **"**I can't find my markers.**"**
"Where,**"** asked her mother, **"**did you leave them?**"**

Use quotation marks around the titles of poems, stories, or magazine articles. Titles of books, plays, movies, magazines, and artworks are italicized when they are typed and underlined when they are handwritten. Titles of sacred books are not italicized or underlined.

"Paul Revere's Ride**"**
"Snow White and the Seven Dwarfs**"**
Harry Potter and the Half-Blood Prince
Mona Lisa
the Koran

Index

A

A/an, as articles, 58, 521
Abbreviations
    capitalization in, 538
    periods with, 178, 540
    postal, 178
Abstract nouns, 72
Accuracy, in how-to articles, 260
Action verbs, 80, 535
Addresses, 182
    e-mail, 308
Adjective phrases, 122, 526
Adjectives, 520–22. *See also* Adjective
    phrases; Suffixes
    comparison with, 68, 70, 72, 520
    defined, 54, 520
    demonstrative, 62, 521–22
    descriptive, 54, 122, 522
    diagramming, 188–89
    exact, 232
    expanding sentences with, 452
    interrogative, 74, 522
    for numerical order, 521
    possessive, 40, 522
    prepositional phrases as, 122
    proper, 56, 522
    as subject complements, 66, 144
    telling how many, 64, 521
    words used as, 22
Adjective suffixes, 342
Adverb clauses, 114, 156, 524
    diagramming, 206
Adverb phrases, 124, 527
Adverbs, 523. *See also* Adverb phrases;
    Dependent clauses; Suffixes
    comparison with, 108
    defined, 106
    diagramming, 189
    expanding sentences with, 452
    of manner, 106
    negative words as, 110, 523
    of place, 106
    prepositional phrases as, 124
    there is/there are, 112
    of time, 106
    troublesome, 110
Adverb suffixes, 344
Agreement, subject-verb, 533
Almanacs, 500
Alphabetical order, in dictionaries, 346
Amount/number, prefixes for, 382
Anne Frank: The Diary of a Young Girl,
    (Frank), 214, 218, 222, 225, 234
Antecedents, 44, 523
Antonyms, 456
Apostrophes, 8, 40, 170, 538
    in contractions, 46, 170

    in plural possessive of irregular
      noun, 526
Articles, 521
    defined, 58, 521
    definite and indefinite, 58
    repetition of, 60
Atlases, 499
Audience
    descriptions, 330
    how-to articles, 254
    how-to talks, 274
    oral book reports, 388
    oral descriptions, 350
    oral personal narratives, 236
    oral research reports, 502
    personal narratives, 216
    persuasive speeches, 464
    persuasive writing, 448
    storytellers' contests, 426

B

Bad/worse/worst, 520
Base form, of adverb, 108
Be
    in future tense, 90
    as helping verb, 533
    as linking verb, 100
Being verbs, 80, 535
Body
    book reports, 372
    e-mail, 308
    how-to articles, 256
    letters, 182, 292, 298
    oral personal narratives, 236
    personal narratives, 220
    persuasive speeches, 464
    persuasive writing, 444
    research reports, 484
Body language, 352, 427
    persuasive speeches, 465
Book reports, 366–67
    body, 372
    characters, 368
    conclusion, 372
    content editing, 396–97
    copyediting, 400–401
    drafting, 394–95
    facts and opinions in, 384
    features of, 374
    introduction, 372
    oral, 388–91
    personal opinion, 370, 374
    planning, 374
    plot summary, 368, 374
    prewriting, 392–93
    proofreading, 401

    publishing, 402–3
    purpose of, 372
    revising, 398–99
    settings, 368, 374
    theme, 370, 374
    Writer's Workshop, 392–403
Books
    citation of, 488
    in libraries, 460–63
    titles of, 174, 538, 540
Business letters. *See* Letters, business
Business telephone calls, 312–14

C

Capitalization, 172, 537–38
    abbreviations, 178, 538
    direct quotations, 176, 180, 537
    titles of works, 174, 538
    uses of, 176
Catalogs, library, 462–63
Characters, 368
    book reports, 374
    tall tales, 410
Charts. *See* Graphic organizers
Checklists
    business telephone calls, 314
    content editor's, 244, 282, 320, 358,
      396, 434, 472, 510
    copyeditor's, 248, 286, 324, 362, 400,
      438, 476, 514
    Internet research, 270
    proofreader's, 248, 287, 324, 363, 401,
      439, 477, 515
    telephone review, 314
Chronological order, 336
Citations. *See* Works Cited page
Clauses, 524
    adverb, 114, 156, 524
    defined, 114, 524
    dependent, 114, 156, 524
    independent, 114, 154, 156, 524
Closings
    of e-mail, 308
    in letter, 182, 292
Collective nouns, 525
    defined, 10
    singular, 10, 533
Commands, imperative sentences and,
    136
Commas
    in compound sentences, 154, 166
    with conjunctions, 166
    in direct address, 168, 539
    with direct quotations, 180
    in a series, 164, 538
    uses of, 164, 538–39
    after *yes* and *no,* 539

Q

Question marks, 136, 162, 540
    in direct quotations, 180
Questions
    interrogative adjectives in, 74
    interrogative pronouns in, 48
    interrogative sentences and, 136
    verb phrases in, 82
Quotation marks
    with direct quotations, 540
    exclamation point with, 539
    with titles of poems, stories, and
      magazine articles, 174
Quotations
    capitalization in, 537
    direct, 176, 180

R

Real/very, 110
Reference books, in libraries, 461
Reference materials, 498–500
References
    almanacs, 500
    atlases, 499
    encyclopedias, 488, 498
    search engines, 272
    Web sites, 270, 489
Reflexive pronouns, 42, 530
Regular verbs, past and past participle
    of, 84, 537
Reliability of information, on Internet,
    270
Reports. *See* Book reports; Research
    reports
Request letters, 296
Researching, 482–83, 506
    on Internet, 270, 272
Research reports, 480–81
    body, 484
    conclusions, 484
    content editing, 510–11
    copyediting, 514–15
    drafting, 508–9
    information for, 486, 488–89
    introduction, 484
    note taking, 486
    oral, 502–05
    outlines for, 490–93
    presenting, 517
    prewriting, 506
    proofreading, 515
    publishing, 516–17
    revising, 512–13
    topics, 482

topic sentences, 484
Works Cited page, 488
Writer's Workshop, 506–17
Revising
    book reports, 398–99
    business letters, 322–23
    descriptions, 360–61
    how-to articles, 284–85
    personal narratives, 246–47
    persuasive writing, 474–75
    research reports, 512–13
    sentences, 376, 378
    tall tales, 436–37
Rhyme scheme, 424
Roots, 300
Run-on sentences, 378
"R U Reading Online?" (Moje), 442

S

Sachar, Louis, 366
Salutations
    of e-mail, 308
    in letter, 182, 292, 539
Search engines, 272
-self/-selves, 42
Semicolons, 154
Sensory details, 332, 350, 357
Sentences, 531–32. *See also* Clauses;
    Diagramming; Punctuation
    adverb clauses in, 114
    capitalization of, 172
    combining parts of sentences, 306
    combining sentences, 304
    complex, 156, 531
    compound, 126, 154
    declarative, 136, 531, 539
    exclamatory, 136, 531, 539
    expanding, 452, 454
    imperative, 136, 531
    interrogative, 136, 532
    in inverted order, 146, 532
    kinds of, 136
    in natural order, 146, 532
    revising, 376, 378
    run-on, 378
    topic, 484
    variety in, 224
Series, commas in, 164, 538
Settings
    in book reports, 368, 374
    in tall tales, 430
Signatures
    in e-mails, 308
    in letters, 182, 292
Similes, 414

Simple predicates, 138, 528
Simple sentences, combining, 304
Simple subjects, 138, 533
Simple tenses, 90
Singular nouns, 6, 527
    collective, 10
    defined, 4
Singular possessives, of nouns, 8, 526
Singular pronouns, 28, 530
**"Skipping Stones" (Iggulden and
    Iggulden),** 252
Songs, titles of, 538
Spatial order, 334
Speeches
    how-to talks, 274, 276–77
    oral book reports, 388–91
    oral descriptions, 350–53
    oral personal narratives, 236–38
    oral research reports, 502–5
    persuasive, 464–67
    storytellers' contests, 426–29
Storyboard, personal narratives, 241
Storytellers' contests, 426–29
Study skills. *See* Dictionaries; Libraries
Subject complements, 532
    adjectives as, 66
    compound, 148, 152, 306
    defined, 144
    diagramming, 189, 192, 202
    linking verbs and, 144, 192
    nouns as, 12
    subject pronoun and, 32
Subject pronouns, 32, 38, 531
Subjects, 532
    complete, 140, 532
    compound, 38, 148, 532
    diagramming, 188, 198
    nouns as, 12
    pronouns as, 32, 38, 531
    simple, 138, 533
Subject-verb agreement, 533
Subordinate conjunctions, 128, 156, 524
Suffixes, 342, 344
Superlative degree
    of adjectives, 68, 70, 72, 520
    of adverbs, 68, 70, 72
Swamp Angel **(Isaacs),** 404, 408, 415
Synonyms, 266

T

Taking notes. *See* Note taking
Tale of Despereaux, The **(DiCamillo),**
    328, 333, 337, 339
Talks. *See* How-to talks

Acknowledgments

Literature

Loyola Press has made every effort to locate the copyright holders for the cited works used in this publication and to make full acknowledgment for their use. In the case of any omissions, the publisher will be pleased to make suitable acknowledgments in future editions.

Excerpt and cover from *The Tale of Despereaux.* Text copyright © 2003 by Kate DiCamillo. Illustrations copyright © 2003 by Timothy Basil Ering. Reproduced by the permission of the publisher, Candlewick Press, Somerville, MA.

Excerpt from "Family Photo Vase." *National Geographic Kids.* November 2008. Copyright © National Geographic Society. Used by permission.

Review of *Fern Verdant and the Silver Rose* used by permission of Through the Looking Glass Children's Book Review. Marya Jansen-Gruber, editor. www.lookingglassreview.com

Excerpt and cover from *Anne Frank: The Diary of a Young Girl.* Copyright © 1952 by Otto H. Frank. Copyright © 1967 by Doubleday, a division of Random House Inc. Cover photo copyright © 1986 Anne Frank-Fonds Basle/Cosmopress, SA. Published by Random House, Inc. Used by permission.

Review of *Holes* used by permission of Kidsread.com. Copyright ©1998–2009 Kidsread.com All rights reserved.

Excerpt from *The Dangerous Book for Boys* by Conn Iggulden and Hal Iggulden. Copyright © 2007 by Conn Iggulden and Hal Iggulden. Reprinted by permission of HarperCollins Publishers.

Excerpt and cover from *Swamp Angel* by Anne Isaacs. Text copyright © 1994 by Anne Isaacs. Illustration copyright © 1994 by Paul Zelinsky. Published by Dutton Children's Books, a division of the Penguin Young Readers Group. Used by permission.

Excerpt from *Learning How: Soccer* by Jane Mersky Leder. Copyright © 1992 by Bancroft-Sage Publishing. All rights reserved.

Excerpt from "R U Reading Online?" by Elizabeth Birr Moje. *Time for Kids.* Copyright © Time Inc. All rights reserved. Used by permission.

Excerpt from *You Can Write a Business Letter* by Jennifer Rozines Roy and Sherri Mabry Gordon. Copyright © 2003 by Enslow Publishers, Inc. Used by permission. All rights reserved.

Excerpt from *Lost Temple of the Aztecs* by Shelley Tanaka. Text, design, and compilation copyright © 1998 The Madison Press Limited. Illustrations copyright © 1988 by Greg Ruhl. Published by Hyperion Books for Children. Used by permission.

Excerpt from "Volunteering." Kidshealth.org. Copyright 1995–2009 The Nemours Foundation. All rights reserved. Used by permission.

Review of *Wild Magic* used by permission of *Chicago Parent* magazine. Copyright © 2009 Wednesday Journal, Inc. All rights reserved.

All other excerpts come from public-domain sources, including Project Gutenberg.

Art and Photography

When there is more than one picture on a page, credits are supplied in sequence, left to right, top to bottom. Page positions are abbreviated as follows: **(t)** top, **(c)** center, **(b)** bottom, **(l)** left, **(r)** right.

Photos and illustrations not acknowledged are either owned by Loyola Press or from royalty-free sources including but not limited to Alamy, Art Resource, Big Stock, Bridgeman, Corbis/ Veer, Dreamstime, Fotosearch, Getty Images, North Wind Images, Photoedit, Smithsonian, Wikipedia. Loyola Press has made every effort to locate the copyright holders for the cited works used in this publication and to make full acknowledgment for their use. In the case of any omissions, the Publisher will be pleased to make suitable acknowledgments in future editions.

Frontmatter: vii(bl) Christopher Furlong/Staff/Getty Images News/Getty Images.

iStockphoto, Frontmatter: iii–viii **Section 1:** 2–11, 13, 14, 16, 18–22, 26 **Section 2:** 28, 30–37, 39–41, 43–49 **Section 3:** 54–57, 59–75, 78 **Section 4:** 80–98, 100, 104 **Section 5:** 106–115 **Section 6:** 121, 124–127, 129–131, 134 **Section 7:** 136, 137, 139–141, 143, 144, 146–149, 152, 154–159 **Section 8:** 162, 163, 165–170, 172–175, 177–179, 181–183, 186 **Section 9:** 188, 190–208, 210–212 **Chapter 1:** 214–224, 226–233, 237–241, 243–247, 251 **Chapter 2:** 252–254, 256–259, 261, 262, 264–269, 271–273, 275, 276, 280, 281, 284, 285, 288–289 **Chapter 3:** 290–294, 297, 298, 300, 301, 303–305, 307–310, 312, 314, 317–321, 324, 327 **Chapter 4:** 328–331, 333–336, 339–344, 346, 347, 350–353, 355, 356 **Chapter 5:** 366– 372, 374, 376, 378, 379, 382–384, 386–389, 399, 402, 403 **Chapter 6:** 404, 405, 408–415, 417, 418, 420–428, 432, 433, 436–438, 440, 441 **Chapter 7:** 442, 443, 445, 446, 448, 450–459, 463–466 **Chapter 8:** 480–481, 483–485, 487, 489–503, 506, 507, 510–512, 514, 516–517

Jupiterimages Unlimited, Frontmatter: v–viii **Section 1:** 9(b), 12(b), 13(tl), 17 **Section 2:** 52(br), **Section 3:** 62(b), **Section 4:** 85, 86, 99, 101 **Section 5:** 85 **Section 6:** 122, 129, 134 **Section 7:** 144, 147, 151, 160 **Section 8:** 165, 168, 171 **Section 9:** 196, 201, 204

Chapter 1: 214, 215, 225, 227, 230–232, 234, 235, 239, 250 **Chapter 2:** 252, 253, 255, 260, 263–265, 271, 274, 275, 277–279, 281, 283, 285, 287, 289 **Chapter 3:** 290, 291, 293–297, 299, 300, 302, 303, 306, 309, 311, 313, 315, 318, 322, 323 **Chapter 4:** 328–330, 332, 334–338, 341, 345, 348, 349, 353, 358–360, 363, 364 **Chapter 5:** 366, 367, 372, 373, 375, 377–381, 383, 385, 391–394, 398, 401 **Chapter 6:** 404, 405, 406, 407, 409, 412, 415–417, 419, 420, 430 **Chapter 7:** 442–444, 449, 450, 452, 460–462, 466–469, 473–475 **Chapter 8:** 480–482, 484, 491, 493, 497, 501, 503, 504, 508, 512–515

Section 1: 16(l) Wikimedia-Commons User Túrelio, Creative Commons BY-SA 2.0-de. **22(b)** Used with permission All-American Girls Professional Baseball League Players Association, Inc. **23** State Archives of Florida. **Section 2: 33(b)** John William Waterhouse. **Section 3: 58** Jo McCulty, Ohio State University. **59(t)** Jo McCulty, Ohio State University. **Section 4: 83(t)** Alejandro Linares Garcia. **101(t)** USDA. **Section 6: 120(t)** NASA. **123** Bettmann/Corbis. **Section 7: 142** Bettmann/Corbis. **143(t)** Wally McNamee/Corbis. **145** Bob Thomas/Bob Thomas Sports Photography/Getty Images. **153** Kevin Rushforth. **177(t)** NASA. **Section 8: 177(c)** NASA. **Chapter 1: 218(t)** Premium Archive/Getty Images. **234(t)** Getty Images. **Chapter 2: 257(b)** May Ann Licudine. **262(b)** Kathryn Seckman Kirsch. **273(t)** NASA. **Chapter 3: 327(r)** Phil Martin Photography. **Chapter 4: 356(tl)** Kathryn Seckman Kirsch. **361** Kathryn Seckman Kirsch. **Chapter 5: 402(br)** Kathryn Seckman Kirsch. **Chapter 6: 406(l)** Kathryn Seckman Kirsch. **411(tr)** Christopher Furlong/Staff/ Getty Images News/Getty Images. **436(t)** Kathryn Seckman Kirsch. **Chapter 7: 444(b)** Kathryn Seckman Kirsch. **448(br)** Kathryn Seckman Kirsch. **470(t)** Kathryn Seckman Kirsch. **471(r)** Kathryn Seckman Kirsch. **Chapter 8:** Clockwise from upper left: **480(c)** North Wind Picture Archives/Alamy. Clockwise from upper left: **481(d)** Images.com/Alamy. Clockwise from upper left: **481(f)** Kathryn Seckman Kirsch. **485(b)** Kathryn Seckman Kirsch. **488** North Wind Picture Archives/Alamy. **490(t)** Kathryn Seckman Kirsch. **508(bl)** George H.H. Huey/Alamy. **509(r)** George H.H. Huey/Alamy.

Common Proofreading Marks

Use these proofreading marks to mark changes when you proofread. Remember to use a colored pencil to make your changes.

Symbol	Meaning	Example
¶	begin new paragraph	over. ¶Begin a new
⌒	close up space	close u⌒p space
∧	insert	students ∧think *should*
୧	delete, omit	that the ~~the~~ book
/	lowercase letter	/Mathematics
∼	letters are reversed	letters are reve∼rsed
☰	capitalize	washington☰
⌄" ⌄"	quotation	⌄"I am,⌄" I said.
⊙	add period	Marta drank tea⊙